S0-AZM-274

❏ ETHICS AND PROFESSIONALISM

▢▢▢ ETHICS AND PROFESSIONALISM

▢▢ JOHN KULTGEN

upp PHILADELPHIA 1988
UNIVERSITY OF PENNSYLVANIA PRESS

16832367

Copyright © 1988 by the University of Pennsylvania Press
All rights reserved   Printed in the United States of America

Some of the material in this book appeared in an earlier form in previously published articles by the author.
"Professional Ideals and Ideology," reprinted with permission from *Ethical Problems in Engineering*, second edition, edited by Robert Baum and Albert Flores. Troy NY: Center for the Study of Human Dimensions in Science and Technology, Rensselaer Polytechnic Institute, 1980.
"The Ideological Use of Professional Codes," *Business and Professional Ethics Journal* I, 3 (Spring 1982): 53–69.
"Evaluating Codes of Professional Ethics," reprinted with permission from *Profits and Professions*, edited by Wade Robinson, Michael Pritchard, and Joseph Ellin. Clifton NJ: Humana Press, 1983.

Library of Congress Cataloging-in-Publication Data

Kultgen, John H.
  Ethics and professionalism / John Kultgen.
  p.   cm.
  Bibliography: p.
  Includes index.
  ISBN 0-8122-8094-6. ISBN 0-8122-1263-0 (pbk.)
  1. Professional ethics. I. Title.
BJ1725.K84   1988
174—dc19

Designed by Adrianne Onderdonk Dudden

CONTENTS

HOLY SPIRIT LIBRARY

89 21.95

CABRINI COLLEGE RADNOR PA

for my children, and theirs

PREFACE

In this work I take a hard look at professionalism and its effect on the moral life of our society. I examine particular practices in the professions and the rules that are proposed to govern them (for example, prohibiting professional paternalism and enjoining confidentiality); and I make suggestions about these practices and rules. My aim, however, is not to develop a detailed code of professional ethics. Rather, it is to explore the institutional and ideological context of the practices and rules and the opportunities and obstacles that context presents to moral behavior.

The question of context receives cursory attention in most philosophical discussions of professional ethics. A thorough investigation is necessary to lay a foundation for a fresh look at professionalism, a complex of attitudes and norms whose essentials are pretty well in place, though its details are hotly debated. And a fresh look at professionalism is needed because the professions contain flaws that are widely overlooked.

The conviction that institutional and ideological contexts are critical to norms determines the content, the perspective, and the form of this work. The content has to do with the structure of professions, the role of ethical norms in their institutional life, and the way the structure and norms affect individuals, both those who participate in the professions and those who have to deal with them. I will seek not only to describe the structure and the norms, but to evaluate them and proposed reforms of them.

The ethical perspective of this work is a form of institutional consequentialism or, if that label be pretentious, simply pragmatism. While I shall attempt to make the premises of this perspective clear, I shall not defend them systematically, except to the extent that their power to provide satisfactory answers to disputed questions is an indirect demonstration of their validity.

While the issues command a great deal of intrinsic interest and I found myself engaged more and more by them as I proceeded, I have tried not to let my enthusiasms and indignations intrude upon what should be a sober and balanced discussion. The form of the work is scholarly because it must take account of an extensive literature.

Before the scholarly work begins, however, I hope I may be indulged in a personal remark. I feel moved to explain how I became concerned with professional ethics and the social responsibilities of professions. Despite my personal good fortune and the serene circumstances under which I live, I share with many people a helpless despondency in the face of the new dangers and ancient evils that confront humanity in this time of its history. For a century we have lurched toward one abyss and another—exhaustion of natural resources, contamination of the biosphere, overpopulation and mass starvation, a final descent into a morass of despotism and injustice, nuclear self-annihilation. This generation may survive to allow each of us to reach his or her individual end, but what of our children and their children?

I was first attracted to the question of professional ethics by the nebulous hope that it could provide one key to meeting these threats. After all, do not the professions represent the highest level of competence in our civilization? Does not the dedication of professionals to truth and service cut across political and cultural boundaries? Is not professionalism an antidote to the infections of ideology and fanaticism? There are national wars, tribal wars, class wars, religious wars but no wars among professions. If only other institutions could be organized the way professions are . . . if only professional work could be diverted, perhaps slightly, but on a massive scale in the direction of the larger human good beyond the interests of clients, employers, patrons. . . .

Perfecting the professional ethic and extending it to other occupations would be a first step. However modest, it is a step to which philosophers can contribute in the gloom of the times. Unfortunately, as I penetrated the topic to a depth where I had ideas worth communicating, I found my optimism chastened and my hope dampened. I found that I had been bemused by yet another ideology. The facade that the professions erect conceals something in the way they are organized, perhaps essential to their existence, that causes their members to inflict harm on the public interest casually, unthinkingly, as an incidental consequence of practices that are well intentioned and conducted at a high level of expertise. Can professions be reorganized without denaturing professional practice?

Even if anyone had the power to institute basic reforms, few of us would be willing to do so. We are addicted to the fruits of professionalism and, in any case, altering the professions will not save us from our peril, since they are not its primary source. They are auxiliaries and instruments. Removing a single weapon from the reach of humanity will not prevent its suicide.

The institutional structures of this country and of every other in the industrial world that have brought professions into their present condition have proved incapable of solving the problems they generate or ensuring peace, conserving resources, preserving the environment, distributing goods with fairness, or protecting minimal liberties. And no one has a viable program for reform. The long-term prospect for our species is dismal and we cannot look to the professions for salvation. They are not geared to restrain the murderous urges that sweep through humanity. They are not mobilized to produce a plan for human survival or even implement those that come from other quarters.

Nevertheless, we can hope and we must demand that the professions take action against the evils to which professionalism contributes. Philosophers do not have the power to extort this action, but they can contribute to the moral responsiveness of professionals by calling their attention to issues and helping them understand the architecture of their obligations.

The professions are populated with people of moderate good will; they are corporately organized for limited social action; and they are effective agencies of socialization. Here is a potent force. Must it remain neutral, available to any group for any purpose, or can it acquire a unified moral purpose of its own?

The articulation of a valid ethic and its firm acceptance by professionals would be a modest first step toward the unification of human beings under common values, which in turn is a prerequisite for an organic society on a national scale, and unification of humanity across national, racial, and religious boundaries. The philosopher must admit that the hope that further steps will be taken toward a world community is a wan one, but any action is better than waiting dumbly for the end. It is the duty of philosophy to provide a vision of goals worth striving for and an interim ethic under which individuals can live with dignity during the struggle.

This then is the sense of mission that animates the present work. It is an attempt to lay foundations for evaluating and improving the way professions work under the conditions in which they have to function and in turn to make it easier for persons of good will to turn professionalism to good purposes. Improving the professions and extending professionalism to other walks of life will not forestall the larger threats to our existence, but they are well worth trying in their own right.

I wish to express gratitude to Jane Uebelhoer for interesting me in professional ethics and showing me that the subject must be addressed in institutional terms. Derek Gill reviewed the sociological portions of the argument. William Griffith and two anonymous referees made helpful suggestions about the philosophical argument. The reactions of students helped arrest the slide into pedantry, jargon and verbosity. I should also acknowledge grants provided by the Graduate Research Council of the University of Missouri—Columbia, which assisted me in the research.

Some of the materials for this study have appeared in other publications and are used here with permission of the publishers. They include "Evaluating Codes of Professional Ethics" from *Profits and Professions*, edited by Wade Robison, Michael Pritchard, and Joseph Ellin (Clifton NJ: Human Press, 1978); "Professional Ideals and Ideology" from *Ethical Problems in Engineering*, second edition, edited by Robert Baum and Albert Flores (Troy NY: Center for the Study of the Human Dimensions of Science, (1980); and "The Ideological Use of Professional Codes," *Business and Professional Ethics Journal* I (Spring 1982).

—*J.K.*

❏ ETHICS AND PROFESSIONALISM

1

Introduction:
PROFESSIONALISM
AND MORALITY

Is it a moral obligation to be as professional as possible in one's work? And is it a mark of professionalism to act morally? Or do professionalism and morality have nothing to do with one another?

On the one hand, should one always do one's work in a professional manner or does morality sometimes demand unprofessional conduct? Must one ever violate the standards of professionalism in the name of something more important?

On the other hand, must professionals remain scrupulously moral in order to adhere to the standards of professionalism? Employers and clients sometimes demand questionable actions of professionals precisely in their capacity as professionals—should they accede to such demands? What if acquiescence is necessary in order to remain on the job or in the profession?

Or, may these questions not be misconceived? Do morality and professionalism really have anything to do with one another? Perhaps they pertain to different spheres or aspects of life. Perhaps they are absolutely independent variables.

I will address the first two sets of questions and explore the ways in which morality and professionalism are connected, thus dismissing the third possibility. I shall argue that professionalism should be conceived in such a way that it is limited to moral conduct and elicits moral conduct, and that morality should be conceived in such a way as to require professionalism.

I shall also argue that some of the practices of the professions are defective from the moral point of view, despite the impression conveyed by their codes of ethics and other ideological instruments. The manifest functions of professions disguise an orientation that is inimical in some ways to the public welfare. The official reason for organizing occupations as professions would be valid if it were the overriding reason. This reason is derived from what I shall label the principle of special or role responsibilities. The general welfare in a complex society can be achieved only by assigning the responsibility for special aspects of the welfare of particular groups to specialized experts. Professionals serve clients and employers and, ostensibly, society as a whole through this service. Sometimes service to patrons does indeed redound to the public good and is justified by the principle of special responsibilities. But sometimes it does not. Patron loyalty takes priority over public interest. This pollutes the stream of professional practice at its spring.

Major deficiencies in professional morality are due to the structure of the professions rather than defects of character in professionals. A profession is an institution that confronts individuals as a reality to which they must relate without the ability to change it significantly. Most do so by conforming to its way. Few possess the thorough understanding of institutional dynamics to do otherwise. To approach such an understanding and achieve the distance necessary to evaluate what is understood, we will devote a considerable part of this study to a sociological analysis of professional structures and processes. The analysis will show that professions are interlocked with powerful institutions in such a way as to prevent more than piecemeal reforms, unless there should be a major upheaval in society. The best I can do is to propose modest changes in the existing framework, an interim ethic for the individual professional while changes are being effected, and a utopian plan to keep on the shelf in case an upheaval comes.

"Professional Ethics"

Two semantic points are in order to indicate the direction in which we will be going. They will be substantiated as the discussion unfolds.

The first pertains to the meaning of 'profession.' The term can be taken narrowly to refer to the traditional "learned" professions: medicine, law, architecture, and sometimes, the ministry. These occupations have a long history as open to gentlemen and involving intimate relationships with individual clients. 'Profession' also can be taken broadly to embrace the literally hundreds of occupations that so label themselves and fret over their professionalism. I will use the term broadly enough to include not only members of the learned professions, but scholars and teachers, engineers and scientists, accountants and business specialists, and even varieties of psychotherapists and counselors, journalists, government officials, and military officers, but not so broadly as to extend, except by analogy, to artists, athletes, or thieves. Reasons for the breadth of the concept will be explained later (Chapter 4). I will anticipate this discussion only by remarking that 'profession' and cognate terms have been used as ideological weapons in the struggle for social position. The claim of late entrants in the struggle, engineers, for example, is based on the nature of their work and their organizational structure—things with which we will be concerned in considering the moral impact of professionalism on modern society. Certainly, the traditional professions have no exclusive title morally or logically to the honorific designation and a broader base for comparison will serve us when we come to extract an ideal of professionalism from the turmoil of social conflict in which it is used and abused.

Moreover, work in large corporate units with limited direct contact with clients or customers is the occupational life of a large proportion of those who are, or intend to become, professionals, rather than the personal involvement with clients of the traditional professional. If we are to understand professionalism, we must consider it in the experience of the first kind of practitioner as well as the second.

The second semantic remark pertains to the term 'ethics.' Like 'profession,' I shall use it broadly. It will refer to ideals and aspirations as well as rules of conduct. Much of the contemporary literature in ethics is preoccupied with rule-governed behavior and we will examine the codes and practices of particular professions. However, our concern will not be with rules in their own right but with the outlook, the conception of mission, and the responsibility they reflect. When I propose content for professional ethics (Chapters 11, 12 and 13), my emphasis will be on ideals rather than rules; that is, on comprehensive norms that generate specific rules or, alternatively, concrete objectives or even modes of being for the professional, as circumstances dictate.

Who Should Be Interested?

Who should be interested in the norms professionals follow? Everyone, since almost all of us work and, I shall argue, the professional ideal is relevant to all forms of work. But even if the professional ideal were relevant only to the work of the professions, everyone would have a stake in it. Most obviously, all of us are consumers of professional services and our society functions as it does because of the role of professionals. Professionals should be accountable to society for their decisions. It is up to the rest of us to evaluate their behavior by their principles, and their principles by our own conceptions of ethics. It is up to everyone to participate in any reforms of the professions that are put on the social agenda.

More fundamentally, it is a mistake to think of professionals as the sole authors of their ethical principles. Professionals compose partnerships with their clients and with their employers in which all parties must make ethical decisions. Veatch points out that the physican, other members of the health-care team, the patient, and the patient's family all make medical decisions, some on their own and some in conjunction with the others in the partnership. Physicians cannot *unilaterally* determine the principles for the others to follow, nor even principles for their own decisions, since the others are affected by them. Medical ethics is not identical with physicians' ethics, as often assumed. It comprises principles that are valid for medical decisions whoever makes them and in the formulation of which all parties should have a share.[1] The same applies to the ethical principles of law, engineering, and other professions and for their generalization, professional ethics. In each area, everyone in society makes decisions like those of professionals, everyone makes decisions jointly with professionals, and everyone is affected by the decisions of professionals. Everyone, therefore, should have a say in the content of professional ethics.

The literature on professions is split into two parts, which have little communication with one another. One part comprises writings on professional ethics, a few dealing with professions as such and many more with the ethics of particular professions.

The authors take the structures of society and the professions as givens and debate the rules that should govern the relations between individual professionals and individual clients or employers. They ignore the impact on these micro-ethical issues of macro-ethical issues, such as the corporate responsibilities of professions and defects in their organization and practices. They describe the obligations of moral professionals in a moral society, but ignore their obligations in an immoral or at least imperfect society, where in fact they must act.

The other part of the literature discusses professions as institutions. For the most part, the authors affect the morally neutral stance of descriptive social science. After early attempts to come to grips with normative issues, there has been, as Johnson observes, "a nervous withdrawal from 'value-laden' controversy."[2] The withdrawal, however, is superficial. Below the surface, normative conceptions shape the way sociologists organize and interpret data. The professions are creatures of modern social systems and integral to their functioning. Sociologists who view professions from a functionalist perspective approve of what they see. They emphasize the beneficial features of professionalism and minimize the harmful ones. In contrast and partly in reaction to this bias, sociologists who view institutions as mechanisms for the resolution of conflict that effect the domination of some groups by others emphasize the harmful features of professionalism and minimize the beneficial ones.

The implication of this example of the subterranean influence of value-commitments on descriptive sociology is that social science should be conceived as a branch of social philosophy. The social thinker should make both factual and normative judgments explicit, acknowledge their interconnection, and defend both together. What is more relevant here is that the analysis of professional ethics, as a set of principles for individual acts, must be worked out in correlation with a social philosophy, with both descriptive and normative elements, for professions as institutions.

The present study brings the two strands in the literature together. They must be brought together for a successful resolution of the issues each turns up. On a level of personal ethics, actions involving such matters as loyalty to employer versus responsibility to the public or confidentiality versus the publication of new research appear quite different when considered solely in terms of the consequences for those directly involved and as contributing to practices that sustain an imperfect social system. Moreover, the obligations of the individual are not confined to work within the social system; they include obligations to change (or preserve) the system. To decide one's obligations, both in one's work and for the framework in which one works, one must take a critical stance toward existing institutions. A valid personal ethic must be grounded in a sound social philosophy.

In turn, the design of institutions must take into account the lives and actions of individuals who participate in them. A social program for the organization of professions must be justified not only by the benefits professional services provide the public, but by the level of moral activiy it permits and elicits from professionals. To determine this, we must have a conception of the right rules of behavior for the individual. A valid social philosophy must be grounded in a sound personal ethic.

As Aristotle teaches, ethics and politics are two volumes of the same work. Professional ethics for the individual and a social policy for the professions are integral elements of a single investigation and will be dealt with here in relation to each other.

Professional ethics is topic of concern for all members of society, but how important a topic? Let us consider its special effect on certain aspects of modern society, its role in the life of the individual professional, and its implications for ethical theory.

The Social Importance of Professional Ethics

The social impact of professional ethics is paradoxical. Moore points out the small proportion of those employed in the world that are even approximately professional. This included only 6 to 8 percent of the work force in the most professionalized countries of Western Europe, Canada, and the United States in 1950. More significant is the pattern of growth in industrial countries and in underdeveloped countries as they industrialize. The number of professionals increased from about 4 percent in 1900 to 8 percent in 1950, 12 percent in 1960, and 13 percent in 1966. Throughout the world, professionalization of occupations accompanies the application of technological knowledge to the solution of human problems. According to Moore, this connection accounts for the extraordinary prestige of professionals despite their small number.[3] Other influential students of the professions agree. Hughes observes that professionalization accompanies industrialization and affects organizational structures much the same way in different societies, regardless of their ideologies and political systems.[4] Parsons cannot imagine how a modern society could function without the smooth operation of the professions.[5]

Professionals occupy a strategic position in modern society. They provide services not available from other quarters, and the services are vital to those who receive them. Furthermore, professionals not only purport to choose the best means for the given ends of their clients and the public; they help define the ends themselves: the lawyer and accountant shape our ideas of security; the physician, of health; the priest, of salvation. The members of newer professions, such as engineering and business management, make decisions that profoundly affect large numbers of people without their consent and or knowledge. By circumscribing what is feasible and efficient through "expert" advice, they shape society's objectives.

The services of the professions are highly valued and, as a consequence, professionals enjoy status, prestige, and influence. Not the least of their influences is the model they provide for the way work should be done. Professionalism is the occupational ideal for many nonprofessionals and is likely to become the ideal for more with the advance of industrialization and proliferation of technologically based occupations.

Last, but far from least, the professions service the major economic, political, and cultural institutions of industrial society. If we believe that the social systems of developed nations work well for human good and all that is needed is more of the same, we should be pleased by the way professions operate. Professionalization is called forth by development and it propels development forward. We should intensify our efforts to push professionalization in the same channels it has followed to date.

However, we should anticipate the opposite conclusions from a study of professions if we have different beliefs about society. This discussion will be predicated on the judgment that the social systems of developed nations, in which professions figure so prominently, are structured to benefit socioeconomic elites disproportionately. The least advantaged in the developed nations are reconciled to this arrangement because they benefit at the expense of the undeveloped nations. The elites of the undeveloped nations also benefit. The great majority of humanity, the least advantaged of the undeveloped nations, are powerless to resist. Moreover, developed and undeveloped nations alike are prepared to sacrifice future generations for present benefits.

According to the model developed by Johan Galtung, many of the injustices of the world and the social problems that spring from them are due to "structural violence." Structural violence is the exploitation of one group by another through the dominant practices and institutions of a society. Galtung maintains that the modern world is characterized by extensive structural violence over and beyond overt violence and intimidation. It is inflicted by ruling elites of developed nations on their own peripheral groups and by elites and peripheries of these nations on the undeveloped nations, especially on the preripheral groups of these nations in collusion with their ruling elites. In Galtung's jargon, the center of the Center exploits the periphery of the Center and the center and periphery of the Center, with the collusion of the center of the Periphery, exploit the periphery of the Periphery. Since the periphery of the Periphery compose the large majority of humanity at this time, systematic structural violence is inflicted by the few on the many. Moreover, all groups, central and peripheral, are hell-bent for development without regard to the integrity of the ecosystem or the future of the human species.[6]

As essential agents of "development" in this destructive form, the professions cannot be absolved of responsibility. Can anything be done to change their role? A critique of the professional ethic is a first step.

The Importance of Professional Ethics to the Individual

Whether or not one approves of the present state of society, one must live with it. One needs a personal ethic pending its reform.

Work is a central part of life, so one needs a work ethic to function in an imperfect society. All men and a growing percentage of women are expected to "earn a living" by going out into the workplace. Even those who remain in the home are expected to put in a full day's work. It is no longer morally acceptable to devote one's life to amusement, even if one has the resources to do so. In the words of an anthem of the women's movement, "No more the drudge and the idler—ten that toil where one reposes, but a sharing of life's glories."[7] One of life's glories should be useful and satisfying work.

Work, besides being the most important contribution of the individual to society, shapes and expresses what that individual is. It is an important basis for our judgments of him or her as a human being. Hughes observes, "a man's work is one of the more important parts of his social identity, of his self, indeed, of his fate, in the one life he has to live, for there is something almost as irrevocable about choice of occupation as there is about choice of mate." Given the myth that men freely select their occupation (Hughes does not deign to mention women) "a man's work is one of the things by which he is judged and certainly one of the more significant things by which he judges himself."[8] This is especially true of professionals. They choose their role; they are not cast into it by birth or fate. Moreover, they devote more of their waking hours to work than members of other occupations, and they typically devote all of their working life to one occupation rather than moving from one to another. Hence, what they become and what they are seen to be are determined to an extraordinary degree by the character of their work.

The moral development of the individual does not terminate with childhood or adolescence, though this period occupies the attention of psychologists such as Piaget and Kohlberg. According to Kohlberg the highest stage of moral orientation ("to principles of choice involving appeal to logical universality and consistency, . . . to conscience as a directing agent and to mutual respect and trust") may be approximated by the normal child before maturity.[9] However, children do not *fully* attain it and they do not settle on principles for the remainder of life. Moreover, moral development continues throughout adulthood, and entry in an occupation is an important factor in adult development. Hughes observes that young people begin professional training at the time they are breaking ties with their childhood environment and questioning the orientation to life given them by their parents.[10] This is a critical time for formation of a mature moral code. The normative framework of the profession plays a profound part in shaping the individual's conceptions of right, obligation, and moral goodness. Teachers and peers are significant influences. They provide not only vocational but personal and ethical models in the process of self-definition. Venality in the ethical conceptions of the group, even where they ostensibly concern only the performance of work, nourishes venality in the individual's conceptions about all departments of life. A valid professional ethic, therefore, is critical for the moral development of the individual practitioner.

The Philosophical Importance of Professional Ethics

The scope of ethical principles would be severely limited if they were not applicable to human work. Their validity would be compromised if they were contradicted by principles that should govern work. These truisms should lead us to question a popular approach to professional ethics based on the assumption that there is an "ordinary morality" derived from intuitions of right and wrong in human relationships other than those of the workplace, for example, between friends or members of a family. If ordinary morality in this sense were ready to hand, the basic question of professional ethics would be whether ordinary morality applies to relations between professionals and their clients, colleagues, and the public. The easiest answer would be that we can derive the rules of professional ethic by simple deduction from ordinary morality.

Many professionals are impatient with the fretted questions of ethics. They feel that the members of their profession have been raised in good homes and are God-fearing, church-going men (sic). They bristle at the suggestion that moral standards change in the workplace and they take personal offense at criticisms of their professional code.

To illustrate with a personal anecdote, on one occasion I spoke on the topic of professional ethics at a national meeting of an engineering society. The past and current officers were arrayed on the dais. I congratulated myself on the opportunity to make my case before people of influence. After I had held forth for an hour or so on the ethical ambiguities and dilemmas of engineering practice and the need not only for revisions in the society's code but more sophisticated ethical training for engineering students, the meeting was thrown open to coments from the floor. The first person to his feet was a distinguished gentleman who identified himself as a past president of the organization. His remark was brief. "I could spend another hour commenting on the professor's learned paper, but it has been my experience in forty years of practice that the only rule an engineer needs is the

Golden Rule of Jesus of Nazareth." He sat down with a broad grin to a warm round of applause.

Perhaps this conception of ethics would suffice if the obligations of professionals were clear and obvious and could be met without difficulty or sacrifice, if professionals never faced ethical dilemmas and could always be counted on to do what is right as a matter of routine. Unfortunately, professionals, precisely as professionals, are confronted with serious conflicts of duty and conflicts between duty and self-interest. The stakes are high both for the integrity of the professional and the welfare of others.

Corporately, the professions do not always stand foursquare for the right and good, nor is it at all clear in many cases what their commitments should be. The issues are obscure and the options uncertain. They call for analysis in terms of clear and sound principles specific to the professional context, principles that are not satisfactorily expressed in either current ethical theory, moral customs, or the codes of the professional subculture.

Moral issues are further obscured by the arsenal of special rationalizations available to the professional, which encourage an illusion of moral neutrality and routine innocence. (I recall the bland complacency of the head of a successful engineering firm that designs equipment for nuclear power plants, who stoutly maintained, "We have no ethical problems in our business.") Such illusions can be dispelled only by a searching criticism of professional practices in terms of sound moral theory and an understanding of the dynamics of professional life.

If ordinary morality does not serve in any simple way as a foundation for professional ethics, we ought to expect professional ethics on its own foundation to make an important contribution to ethical theory. The myth of ordinary morality appears to presuppose that ethical principles are discovered and validated in a privileged area of life, perhaps relations among family or friends, and then applied to other areas. The two most extensive treatments of professional ethics currently in print, those of Goldman and Bayles, formulate their basic questions in terms of the modifications of ordinary morality required to deal with problems in the professional context.[11] This approach has heuristic value, but we must guard against the complacency it encourages about our grasp of moral principles from, in Goldman's words, "the view point of normal moral perception." There is no moral perception apart from particular contexts, and perceptions in context of family relations and friendship are no more exempt from bias than perceptions in the context of the hospital, courtroom, or industrial plant. The professional arena is an independent laboratory for testing alternative ethical principles. A study such as this one has the potential to contribute to ethical theory by tracing the implications of principles for distinctive and important circumstances of modern life.

Plan of Attack

Professionals as professionals face ethical dilemmas. The way they resolve these dilemmas determines the moral quality of their lives and the welfare of those affected by their actions. It is urgent, therefore, that the professional ethic be assessed with care.

There are flaws in the ideal of professionalism as it generally is conceived. It is sufficiently valid to merit qualified loyalty, but every effort should be made to rectify its deficiences. In addition, there is a considerable discrepancy between the ideal and the norms that professionals actually follow. We shall consider ways in which this gap may be narrowed. More fundamentally, we shall question whether work should be organized along professional lines at all and whether the social systems that rely on professionalism are worthy of support. The question of the ethical obligations of professionals thus leads into basic questions about work and society.

The book begins by laying down the ethical premises from which we will proceed (Part I). Two conflicting sociological views of professions then are juxtaposed (Part II) and possibilities for institutional reform explored (Part III). Finally, a professional ideal will be articulated in the form that seems valid given the structure of society and the place of professions in it (Part IV).

Notes

1. *A Theory of Medical Ethics*, pp. 16–18.
2. *Professions and Power*, p. 12.
3. *The Professions*, pp. 3 and 20–21. See Hughes, "Prestige," in *The Sociological Eye*; and Inkeles and Rossi, "National Comparisons of Occupational Prestige."

4. "Professions," *The Sociological Eye,* pp. 374 and 384. See "Professions in Society," *ibid.;* and Greenwood, "Attributes of a Profession," p. 45.

5. "Professions and Social Structure," *Essays in Sociological Theory,* p. 34.

6. See Galtung, *The True Worlds,* Ch. 4.

7. "Bread and Roses," music by Mimi Farina and lyrics by James Oppenheim. Permission granted by Mimi Farina, Farina Music, Mill Valley CA.

8. "Work and Self," *The Sociological Eye,* pp. 338 and 339.

9. "Stage and Sequence," p. 384.

10. Personality Types and the Division of Labor," *The Sociological Eye,* pp. 331–332.

11. *The Moral Foundations of Professional Ethics,* pp. 1–3; and *Professional Ethics,* pp. 5–7 and 16–21.

❑ PART I

NORMATIVE CONSIDERATIONS

ETHICAL PREMISES

In this chapter, concepts from current ethical theory will be utilized to evaluate professional practices, but points of theory will not be argued. The chapter will simply lay out premises for the analysis. The demonstration of their validity will be indirect, to the extent to which the analysis of professionalism is cogent.

The point of view taken here is consequentialist. 'Right' is defined in terms of the consequences of actions, including the intrinsic characteristics realized in the actions themselves and their external effects. Among the effects relevant to evaluating actions are those that flow directly from the actions in their immediate environment and those that flow from practices and social structures of which they are parts and to which they contribute. In identifying relevant consequences, elements of utilitarianism and eudaimonism will be utilized (see items 1–3), as well as a concept of justice as sharing fairly (items 7 and 8).[1] Also, the discussion borrows conceptions from idealism in conceiving the proper relation of the individual to society (see Chapter 3).

The basic principle of this position may be formulated in a preliminary way: On any occasion, one ought to perform that act which, on reasonable reflection, promises to maximize benefits for the moral community and distribute them fairly.

This formula focuses on the personal responsibility of the agent to attend to the character and consequences of his or her individual actions. This is emphasized in the statement (item 13) that the individual cannot take refuge from moral responsibility behind rules no matter how well devised. Nevertheless, we must also insist that agents in the routine of life maximize their chance of producing desirable consequences, for example, in the professional context by taking very seriously considered rules, established practices, and shared ideals. It is seldom better to try to compute the consequences of a given act in its concrete circumstances than to do certain things "as a matter of principle," that is, in conformity to and out of trust in tried and true general norms.

Reference to "reasonable reflection" in the formula reminds us that agents are responsible only for what they reasonably can be expected to know. But we also should remember that this extends to what they may reasonably be expected to find out either for themselves or by consulting authorities. This is relevant to the present discussion because in our society the knowledge necessary for important decisions is frequently in the hands of professionals. The individual can do what is best for himself or herself, and indeed what is right, only with professional advice. This imposes obligations on both the consumer of public services to seek them out and on professionals to provide them.

The formula for the rightness of actions, like any statement of basic principle, is fraught with difficulties; hence, seventeen clarifications, qualifications, specifications, and additions are presented to try to alleviate these difficulties.

The Principle of Utility

Item 1: To benefit means to provide or protect an interest of a person. 'Interest' is taken to mean not the act of being interested in (desiring, wanting, paying attention to, seeking, tending) something, but the object of interest (a thing, condition, relationship, or state of affairs in which one has an interest). "Being interested" or "having an interest" refers not to a person's actual desires but the desires he or she would have if fully rational and informed. If happiness be the secure enjoyment of objects of interest and the activities that they make possible, the criterion of the morality of an action becomes roughly the probability that it will contribute fairly to the happiness of those it affects. But we should be clear that no one can bestow happiness on another, one can only provide conditions for it. This is obviously the case with professional services, even counseling services, which may be intended as happiness therapy. In claiming that the professions should contribute to the happiness fairly distributed of all in the moral community (items 5–7), it must be taken to mean they should contribute what they can (i.e., services and products), which people may use or not, as they choose, in their pursuit of happiness.

To judge the morality of actions, as well as practices, norms, goals, virtues, social structures, and all other things that affect human life, we must estimate their utility. A thing's "utility" means its probable contribution to the happiness and reduction of the unhappiness, less its probable contribution to the unhappiness and reduction of the happiness of people. Only a few utilities can be measured; all must be at least intuitively ranked. ("Intuitively" means estimating the values of variables and their combinations and the ranking of values in an informed way that, however, may not have been entirely reduced to rules.[2])

As a general practice, one starts with a principle of indifference: If there is no reliable evidence that something affects the happiness of one individual more than another, its utility is considered equal for both. For example, in designing professional institutions it is frequently necessary to assume that access to services—medical treatment, legal representation, education, counsel, engineering—is as important to each member as to every other and hence all should be guaranteed equal access. We know that this is not true but we do not know how it is not true. Everyone's needs are not the same, but in the absence of information they should be treated as the same.

Item 2: Our inevitable ignorance of many of the differences among those affected by our actions requires us to assume that certain interests are basic for everyone. Some are essential ingredients of most people's happiness. Some are necessary means whatever their plans of life. We must design institutions to provide basic goods and services while leaving space for individual differences to operate in regard to other goods and services.

If we take seriously Mill's proposition that people are the best custodians of their own interests (see item 4), we can use their demand for goods and services as an indication of what these are. Professions flourish because there is a heavy demand for what they provide. The distribution of professions reflects society's conception of which needs are so vital as to warrant an elaborate structure and heavy investment of resources. Thus, the proliferation of engineering specialities attests to the importance of physical facilities and energy sources to carry on the business of industrial society. The health professions attest to the value we place on health, relief from pain, and longevity; the psychological professions, on adjustment to the exigencies of life, defense against stress, and mobilization of psychic resources; the academic profession, on useful knowledge and cognitive orientation to the world; the ministry, on reconciliation to the boundary conditions of existence and a satisfactory relation to the ground of being; the business professions, on the production and distribution of goods and services; journalism, on public information; the law, on order and rights; the military, on peace and security; public administration and politics, on coordination of all the rest.

Our perception of our needs is not always correct. Where an occupational group has aggressively publicized its services, demand may reflect false consciousness and false needs or an indulgence of the wants of some at the expense of the needs of others. Surely the needs to which the professions attest are genuine and important, but their form and degree may be misconceived and the ability of the professions to meet them may be misrepresented. For instance, Morison charges, "modern man has adopted physical health as his paramount value." Citing the excessive material resources devoted to health services, he observes,

> There may be . . . something magnificent about the resolve to learn God's laws and then to use them to reverse that part of the order of nature that dooms most men to less than optimal performance, if not a lifetime of physical suffering. But there is also the elimination of physical distress. It suggests that having discovered no real reason for any existence, we will devote our efforts to making that existence at least as painless as possible. For, like it or not, health is at base a negative concept.[3]

This complaint is overdrawn but it reminds us that market demand reflects many things besides basic needs and genuine benefits.

The moralist should be guided by, but not bound to, popular ideas in cataloguing the basic values that should be promoted by institutions such as professions. For example, Bayles[4] formulates norms for the professions in terms of practices that promote "values of a liberal society" (governance by law, freedom, protection from injury, equality of opportunity, privacy, and welfare); these values are widely prized, though not in just the package and conceptualization Bayles advances. A parallel move is made by nonconsequentialist authors. Goldman, for example, draws up a list of moral rights that "express interests vital to the integrity of the individual" (basic material needs, security in expectations, opportunities, freedom from unwarranted interferences, and self-respect) and that are to be respected and facilitated by professional services.[5] My own list would include physical health and vigor; reciprocal human relationships, including affection and respect; autonomy in important areas of life, which requires mental health and physical resources as well as external liberty; a sense of meaning to life and participation in a moral community; and security of person and possessions.

Lack of a minimum of any of these would ruin the happiness of most persons. Most of the values have an upper limit beyond which their marginal utility is negligible. An amount between the minimal and maximal limits is basic to most people's happiness, though in an imperfect society we must sacrifice some benefits in order to enjoy others of the same or other sorts. The sorts of benefits complement each other, so it is rational to strive to provide a level of all of them for all members of society.

The list is far from perfect. It does not pretend to be exhaustive and items overlap. In addition, important additional goods are preconditions or consequences of these, such as knowledge and self-esteem. However, incomplete though it is, the list indicates why the professions are important in modern complex society and provides a point of departure in evaluating them.

Item 3: Until we identify differences among those affected by our actions, we should treat them alike; and since we must perforce think first in terms of basic needs, we should strive to see that all receive a fair share of these. Basic goods are precisely those which everyone or almost everyone needs for happiness. But the other ingredients of happiness vary from individual to individual and the unique ingredients may be as important to an individual as those basic goods shared with others. The principle of indifference does not preclude a consideration of differences; it does not require that people should be treated identically. On the contrary, we are obligated to identify relevant differences, and we should try to contribute to the happiness of each insofar as we can determine what will make that individual happy. Professionals are obligated to make a reasonable effort to determine the service that will meet the individual needs of their client or employer, not provide routine services tailored to stereotypical needs.

As an illustration, individuals with emergency problems or standing deprivations should be given preferential treatment because they differ relevantly from ordinary members of the community. Particular services have much more utility for them. This distinction is reflected in the division of professions into those such as medicine, law, counseling, and social work, whose mission is to care for people in difficulty, and those such as education, engineering, the ministry, and business professions, whose primary mission is to give equal service to large numbers of people in the ordinary circumstances of life.

Not only do the ingredients of happiness differ, the conditions that produce them differ. Professionals should tailor their services to circumstances, rather than routinely treating everyone with similar needs the same way.

Item 4: Informed individuals are usually the best judges of what will make them happy, even though they often must resort to experts to achieve it. Professionals should defer to the wishes of competent clients after they have made a reasonable effort to help them arrive at informed judgments. When they are forced to make judgments for others because of their incapacities, they should terminate the condition of dependency as soon as possible. This principle will be emphasized in Chapter 11 as an antidote to the strong tendency toward paternalism in professions.

The Moral Community

Item 5: Utility has been discussed in terms of the effect of actions on human beings. Humans, however, are not the only beings who deserve consideration nor is it obvious that all of them deserve equal consideration. I shall define the "moral community" abstractly as all and only those individuals whose interests ought to be given moral consideration. This category does not coincide with the biological category of human beings, though human beings compose by far the most important part of the moral community.

By "moral consideration" for individuals, I mean taking their interests seriously and directing the typical mechanisms of morality, such as conscience, custom, and public opinion, in such a way as to further those interests. By the mechanisms of morality society teaches its members what it thinks is right and tries to motivate them to do it. Therefore, to give moral consideration to an individual is to attempt to assure that others in society act rightly toward him or her. Normative ethical theory attempts to determine what we *ought* to feel that we ought to do and toward whom, that is, what and who *should* be the focus of the mechanisms of morality.

An ethical theory must designate which individuals should be given at least minimal moral consideration and which need be treated only instrumentally. The decision to tie the concept of right to that of happiness determines the boundary of the moral community for the system presented here. All and only those beings who are sentient should be given moral consideration. Sentience is capacity for forms of consciousness tinged with pleasure or pain, satisfaction or dissatisfaction. These forms may be sensuous or nonsensuous in form and origin. All sentient beings are capable of happiness (albeit some at a very low level) and only sentient beings are capable of it, so all and only sentient beings fall in the range of the principles of morality.

This conception rejects the limitation of the moral community to persons, in the strict sense of those able to reason and act from reason. This concept follows Bentham in determining the "insuperable line" between those endowed with rights and the remainder of creation.

> What else is it that should trace the insuperable line? Is it the faculty of reason, or perhaps the faculty of discourse? But a full-grown horse or dog is beyond comparison a more rational, as well as a more conversable animal, than an infant of a day, or a week, or even a month old. But suppose otherwise, what would it avail? The question is not, Can they *reason?* nor, Can they *talk?* but, Can they *suffer?*[6]

I do not extend moral consideration to plants, inanimate objects, or ecosystems, as proposed by environmentalists who see "interests" wherever there are teleological processes or holistic systems.[7]

In this discussion the moral community is conceived to include as its central region, at one end, all human beings and the higher animals and, at the other, any nonhuman persons that turn up, for example, gods, angels, intelligent beings from other planets. I shall follow custom and refer to members of the moral community as persons but this should be understood to include protohumans, animals, and any suprahumans with whom we interact (e. g., those with whom the ministerial profession purports to deal).

Item 6: The principle of indifference requires us to treat persons alike when we know of no differences among them. The principle of individuality requires us to seek out differences. The paradigm group in the moral community that moralists have in mind are contemporary normal adults. Rules for the treatment of other groups are added as corollaries to rules for the paradigm. We should take care that this heuristic device does not cause us to divide the moral community into first- and second-class citizens in any absolute and wholesale way. Greater as well as lesser, and in some cases simply different, consideration is due nonparadigm groups. For myself, I acknowledge special and graver obligations to some persons (children, the physically and mentally handicapped); lesser but still serious obligations to others (higher animals, obdurate criminals, scofflaws, tyrants, unborn fetuses, future generations); and none to nonpersons (plants, rivers, "the land") and persons whose existence is questionable (gods, angels, departed spirits, extraterrestrial aliens).

Moral agents must draw boundaries around and within the moral community to determine their duties. Professionals must do so individually in discharging their role responsibilities, and professions must do so corporately to determine their social obligations. We shall see that they have failed to do so when we examine the moral codes of professional associations. We find a few provisions here and there for the treatment of animals and legally incompetent humans and stronger statements of obligation toward people with needs that bring them to the specific profession (the sick, those accused of crimes, those needing psychological counseling, etc.); but there is no careful and systematic treatment of boundaries and the differential obligations they define.

The Element of Justice

Item 7: A standard objection to the classical formulation of the principle of utility is that it sanctions the sacrifice of some persons to promote the welfare of others if the result is an increase of aggregate happiness. Whether or not the system of professionalism adds to the total happiness of society, our sense of justice is violated by the spectacle of professions serving privileged groups much more than others. To take account of the intuition of the primacy of justice over aggregate welfare, the principle at the beginning of this chapter states that actions are right that maximize benefits only if benefits are distributed fairly.

It is impossible to capture the essence of various concepts of fairness in a single definition. Therefore, I simply shall stipulate the concept that informs my vision of the ideal state of affairs for the moral community. It is that each of its members should enjoy equal opportunity for the maximum happiness of which he or she is capable and the natural environment permits.

What this implies for action in concrete circumstances is extremely difficult to determine. As an approximation, I shall adopt Frankena's concept of distributive justice. After arguing that people's needs must be considered in distributing benefits and their abilities must be considered in imposing burdens, Frankena raises the question, does justice

> always ask us, at least prima facie, to *proportion* our help to their needs and our demands to their abilities? Are we always prima facie unjust if we help A in proportion to his needs but not B, or if we make demands on C in proportion to his abilities but not of D?

He answers,

> It seems to me that the basic question is whether or not in so doing we are showing an equal concern for the goodness of the lives of A and B or of C and D. Whether we should treat them in proportion to their needs and abilities depends, as far as *justice* is concerned, on whether doing so helps or hinders them equally in the achievement of the good life.[8]

This concept salvages the idea that persons are due *equal* moral consideration though they should not all be treated *alike*.[9] Unfortunately, it does not eliminate all conflicts between utility and justice. We sacrifice justice when we send young draftees into battle to defend the republic. We sacrifice utility when we protect innocent blacks accused of rape at the cost of a race riot. In the professions, we honor justice by abstaining from research that promises important results rather than harm unwitting subjects. We honor utility when we sacrifice the comfort of patients to instruct medical students.

My way of resolving such conflicts is to opt for either utility or equality depending on which advances society toward the ideal condition in which both are fully realized. Generally, if the injustice inflicted is great and the increment in utility is small, choose justice. If the utility is great and the injustice is small, choose utility.

Item 8: Two considerations make conflicts between justice and utility rare. The first is that benefits distributed evenly usually have more marginal utility than the same benefits concentrated on a privileged few. For example, the few extra hours my lawyer might devote to my case would benefit me less than the same hours divided among new clients.

Second is the principle of special responsibilities, which is the basis for the role responsibilities of professionals. While all members of the moral community deserve moral consideration, we usually have an opportunity to affect only persons in our vicinity. Furthermore, we are in a position to benefit only some of these because of the match between their needs and our abilities and resources. A well-ordered social system, therefore, assigns special responsibility for specific groups to specific agents. Each agent contributes to the whole and in the long run to all members by contributing in a special way to some members. All are benefited by each serving some and each being served by some.

This means that no one is obligated by justice to contribute equally to the goodness of the lives of all members of society, a task that would be incalculable and physically impossible. We must concern ourselves with the people at hand, and we need not concern ourselves with all of their needs. In a well-ordered society, complementary roles filled by others would serve needs not served by our role. We would be permitted and indeed obligated to discharge special responsibilities by sticking to our role and letting others perform theirs. One qualification should be added for a less than perfect society: The people we are obligated to serve are not just those who seek us out or chance into our orbit. We are obligated to find as many persons as possible who need us or some will fall between the cracks and be neglected.

Under the principle of role responsibilities, professionals primarily serve clients, employers, and special sectors of the public who come to them for aid. A profession is part of the larger social system. It is complemented by other action-systems, professional and nonprofessional. We must demand the total system be geared to provide benefits to everyone equivalent to those provided by particular professions to their particular clientele. Is the net effect something like and equal contribution to the happiness of all members of society? If not, what changes can be made in particular professions or in complementary institutions?

Item 9: A stratified moral community has been depicted, with the strata divided into local units assigned to the care of special groups. The principles of indifference and individuality still apply. Those who are our special responsibility should be treated alike, unless there are strata or individual differences among them; and relevant differences should be sought out. Relevance here is a function of the subject's needs in relation to his or her form of happiness and the agent's ability to serve those needs.

These principles suffice to condemn the more obvious types of injustice. It is wrong for a dentist to deny treatment to one whose race or ethnic identity he dislikes. It is wrong for an administrator to deny a woman entry into an engineering school or an employer, advancement in a firm, because of her gender. The professions have been guilty of these types of discrimination but have made progress toward eliminating them in recent years. We have to look deeper below the surface to find major injustices.

Rules, Ideals, and Discretion

Item 10: Almost always, fewer mistakes in computing utilities and equities are made if actions are judged in terms of their membership in classes of action with known tendencies to produce happiness or unhappiness, rather than in trying to ascertain the consequences of the individual action in its unique circumstances.[10] Furthermore, there is utility in adhering to rules on occasions where adherence sets a precedent, strengthens a practice, or reinforces a habit that
s the benefits of diverging in the particular case.

This means that there is a limit to the obligation to tailor actions to the individuals affected by them. Rules are general. They dictate types of actions for types of persons in types of circumstances. Sensitivity to the individuality of people still requires different rules for different categories of subjects, though not ones that are so specific as to apply to single individuals.

The personal norms of agents with specific roles in society, such as professionals, should be tailored to the kinds of individuals with whom they deal. Social utility requires that such codes also be consonant with—ideally, incorporate or apply deductively—the provisions of group codes, such as those of the profession to which the individual belongs, and these in turn be consonant with the mores of society. This would be true without qualification if group codes and mores were entirely valid according to principles of rational morality. To the degree that they are not, the individual must weigh the utility of supporting a fragile structure that fosters group life of the profession and society, against the harms inflicted by imperfections in the structure.

Item 11: Rules are treated instrumentally here; they are justified as means to promote shared happiness. If other means work better, rules should be disregarded. Even rules that would be ideal were they to gain currency do not define right action. The purpose of rules is to elicit such action.

To be useful, rules have to meet certain formal requirements. The utility of a subset within a larger system, such as the rules of a professional ethic within the framework of the moral system of society, cannot be judged in isolation from other rules in the system. The ideal code for a particular institution in society is that which would maximize utility and justice within the framework of the comprehensive system ideal for existing society. The ideal comprehensive system is the one, among viable alternatives, that, were it to gain currency, would maximize utility and justice in the society with appropriate institutional rules.

The first step toward an ideal professional ethic is to formulate norms that could function effectively within present moral traditions. At the same time, it should promote improvements in those traditions. Institutional codes can serve as models for the comprehensive system; for example, a professional ethic can suggest modifications in ordinary morality and improve the conception of what an ideal morality would contain.

The whole business of adjusting specialized codes and the moral system to one another is a continuing process. Once practices are reformed and institutions altered—for example, professions come to be practiced in new ways—the comprehensive moral system has to be reformed to fit the new institutional structures. Further improvements in specialized codes then become possible.

Item 12: The references here to codes should not be taken to endorse rigid rules and casuistry. The purpose of codes is to promote practices. In some contexts, they work. In others, tacit customs work better.

Overemphasis on rules in professional codes sometimes lead the practitioner to assume that no actions not prescribed are obligatory and all actions that are not prohibited or permitted. To counteract this, codes and the traditions of the professional subculture should incorporate ideals that challenge the individual to transcend the requirements of the rules.

Our constructive approach to professional ethics, in fact, will center on ideals rather than rules, though the rules typical of professional codes will be examined at length. Given a coherent set of ideals, rules can be derived to meet actual conditions, can be modified as conditions change, and allow for a stable basis for their violation in unforeseen circumstances.

Professional ethics for the most part have been concerned with the norms that should govern roles under the organization of occupations capable of operating in the present social system and, at the same time, have the most salubrious influence on the system. Professional ethics also should be concerned with reforms in the social system that would allow a better organization. Thus, it would seek norms ideal for the existing society and modifications ideal for improved versions of it. "Existing society" included the practices that already are accepted. The social reformer should be interested in modifying mores to accommodate ideal practices for professions.

Connected with these points is the principle that no set of rules, even the best that people can devise, is absolute. To treat rules as absolute is code-fanaticism, regolatry, or nomomania. Any rule should be broken when obvious and grave disutilities would flow from its observance in extraordinary circumstances and those disutilities would outweigh the disutility of weakening the rule for ordinary circumstances. Disutilities of this character justify violation of the rule regardless of the probability or magnitude of the benefits following from actions according to the rule in other situations.

Item 13: Closely related to the foregoing is the principle that society should regulate behavior only to the degree necessary to provide essential goods, prevent major harms, and sustain a system of mutual expectations and dependable obligations in the moral community. Otherwise, the details of life should be left to individual judgment and negotiation, immune from the pressure of the state and public opinion. Principles of liberty and toleration should be central.

The escape from the iron grip of formal rules provided by the last two principles does not render rules vacuous. It is important that rules be formulated and conscientiously followed in many circumstances; but, the moral agent should be alert to occasions when ordinary rules should be disregarded and the moral community should be tolerant of conscientious dissenters.

Other principles in the theory require the moralist to build justified exceptions into general rules and devise further rules to cover the exceptions. This will minimize occasions for conscientious violations and make it safe to habituate people to follow the rules and to erect strong barriers of custom to violations. This will ensure that conscientious violations will be rare and, in most instances, justified.

Similar remarks apply to the way in which currency is gained for special codes such as those of the professions. As long as morality must contend with self-regarding motives, it needs sanctions. Egoistic persons must be motivated to do what persons of good will do from conscience. Society induces its members to follow its code by rewards and punishments imposed in a formal way by the state, the professional association, etc.; by informal praise and censure from other members of the moral community, including one's professional colleagues; and by the voice of conscience shaped by aculturation into society and its subgroups, such as professions. The best sort of sanction for particular principles and codes is a question of utility.

The Moral Point of View

Item 14: The present discussion deals with two topics, the actions of professionals (and correlatively those who interact with them) and the mechanisms that affect those actions. It examines both from what will be called the "moral point of view" (following Baier's terminology but not his concepts).[11] This is contrasted with the point of view of self-interest or the prudential point of view. Both the moral and prudential points of view evaluate decisions in terms of relations, conditions, principles, consequences, practices—that is, in terms of an intelligent estimate of their material and intellectual context—in contrast to reflexive, impulsive, passionate, ignorant, and habit-bound reactions to stimuli. The two points of view are conceived as polar opposites and, together with hybrid perspectives in between, are so conceived as to cover all that is relevant for the evaluation of deliberate behavior.

Moral persons recognize the intrinsic value of each member of the moral community; merely prudent persons recognize only their own value and treat others as instrumentalities. Since the quality of experience we call happiness gives existence its value, the moral person cherishes the happiness of everyone[12] the prudent person is interested only in his or her own. Though few people are exclusively moral or exclusively self-interested, they have the ability in their imagination to explore life from both points of view before making the existential commitment to one or the other or some mixture of the two.

Professional practices will be examined here from the moral point of view, asking how they contribute to or detract from the aggregate happiness and fair distribution of goods in the moral community. Most of the time attention will not be directed to the final end, rather the ramifications of intermediate principles in limited contexts will be considered. But the ultimate reason for intermediate principles, the end beyond other ends, is general happiness fairly distributed. To this we must always return.

Item 15: The moral point of view offers a possibility of consensus that is lacking for the prudential point of view. *A* and *B*, though occupying different positions in the community, can agree from the moral point of view about how each should behave, since they would both want both to contribute to a single end, their aggregate happiness. Prudentially, *A* might want *B* to do things harmful to *B* in order to benefit *A*, and *B* would make parallel demands on *A*. Their different ends (each his own welfare) would dictate different means.

Consensus from the moral point of view is possible in principle, but fails in practice due to limitations in knowledge. *A* and *B* are not likely to agree completely about which actions of *A* and which of *B* would really further the common end. Moreover, the moral objectivity of actual people always is skewed by self-interest in real life. Nevertheless, it is useful to reason with others from the moral point of view and set aside considerations of self-interest as much as possible. And, it is easier to do this in an abstract discussion where immediate interests are not involved, before plunging into the hurly burly decisions of life.

Some philosophers see the moral point of view as a way to resolve disputes among actual people.[13] It would be guaranteed to do so, however, only in the ideal society where everyone would take the moral point of view; no one would be biased by self-interest; and all would be equipped with perfect knowledge. In the actual world, people who view things from the perspective of morality find themselves at odds with others whose views are distorted by imperfect intentions and false beliefs. Morality then becomes a source of conflict and righteous indignation at the status quo. One who undertakes to decide what actions are best and what institutions to develop from the moral point of view cannot await consensus. Consensus is desirable but only the right kind of consensus and as an instrumental goal not as a sine qua non or mark of the moral.

Item 16: Moral reformers hope to persuade those who can be persuaded, but they cannot reach everyone whose behavior they would like to influence. They must seek other ways besides argument to elevate the level of morality, for example, in the professions.

In designing a social order for persons who are less than ideal, it is necessary to make virtue pay. Rewards are needed to ensure that prudent people prosper by contributing to the welfare of others. Punishments must ensure that they will not profit by harming others. Given the dearth of perfectly moral persons, a prudential system must be devised to approximate the behavior and consequences of genuine morality.

Furthermore, the rules of behavior that are to become standard must be pitched to what Brandt calls "persons of ordinary conscientiousness"[14] and Baier "persons of limited good will."[15] Persons of ordinary conscientiousness do what they think is right if the cost is not great. Codes that are practicable for this sort of person cannot demand heroic virtue. If the provisions of a code are to be exacting, there must be institutions that make it possible to observe them without martyrdom.

Persons of limited good will are "those who acknowledge the legitimacy of moral rules and are prepared to obey them, even in the absence of deterring sanction, but who are prepared to do so only on condition that others are doing likewise." Codes must be enforced by sanctions that discourage malfeasance if this sort of person is to be persuaded to follow them voluntarily.

By rewarding service, punishing malfeasance, and instituting rules that most people can be induced to follow out of prudence or limited good will, we can create conditions under which the moral impulses of people of limited conscientiousness can take effect. Nevertheless, we should recognize the cross-purposes of the dual attempt to exploit prudence and foster morality. The extraordinary rewards by which society induces professionals to do their work and its formal punishments for malefactors encourage a self-interested outlook: People enter their professions for money and prestige and they practice them defensively to avoid malpractice suits and decertification. The conscientious disposition to do a job well for its own sake or the well being of others languishes. One can without contradiction promote actions necessary for the common good both on the basis of the moral point of view in some and by appealing to self-interest in others. This does not put one's own moral convictions on the wrong footing. But, something is paradoxical and counterproductive in adopting this as a general program. I do not pretend to have resolved this problem, but my proposals are made with a view to weaning professionals from prudence to genuine morality while exploiting their prudence in the meanwhile. The measures are designed not only to motivate people of limited good will and ordinary conscientiousness to do what is right, which may be done by making right behavior pay, but to cultivate in them the motivation to do it *because* it is right, rather than because it pays.

Item 17: Preemption of the moral by the prudential point of view occurs in the self-serving provisions in professional codes of ethics that define "fair" business practices. The professional is encouraged to aggrandize his or her profession or employer in the name of morality. Self-deception is involved here. It is made possible by the obscurity of the meaning of 'the self.' Persons identify with a group or a cause in such a way as to experience its prosperity as their own. They sacrifice interests of their narrow selves to serve the corporate whole with an appearance of altruism and a strong sense of self-righteousness. However, if they disregard the public interest in the process, that sacrifice is a form of corporate egoism more allied with prudence than genuine morality.

I do not want to imply that there is a moral equivalence between one who pursues narrow self-interest and one who sacrifices for a group or cause. Those professionals seriously concerned with ethics and the health of their profession usually are serious and moral individuals. Many devote long hours to the business or the profession at considerable cost to their own. They are among those to whom the present discussion is addressed. However, they may so identify with their profession that they take questions about its practices as personal attacks. My plea is that they keep their eye on what their profession is for—how it can serve humanity—rather than treating it as an end in itself. They should take pride in its accomplishments, but they should remember that the needs of humanity are so great that no institution is immune to criticism.

Summary

These are the premises for the following analysis: Actions are right that promise to maximize happiness and distribute it fairly. To do what is right, we must (1) calculate utilities employing the principle of indifference and (2) a schedule of basic values common to everyone. We should treat all alike, unless we (3) identify differences in the ingredients and conditions of happiness for particular persons (4) as they themselves view their happiness. The moral community is (5) composed of all sentient beings and (6) stratified by characteristics relevant to happiness. Justice enters morality as (7) the obligation to make an equal contribution to the lives of all members of the moral community by (8) participating in systems assigning special responsibility for particular needs to particular groups and (9) adhering to the principles of indifference and difference in dealing with those for whom the agent is responsible. We (10) usually should follow tested rules rather than compute utilities in concrete situations, but (11) we must evaluate every set of rules pragmatically within the framework of the total social system and (12) avoid rule-fanaticism by giving priority to ends and ideals that (13) authorize the moral person to break rules when circumstances dictate. These ethical principles (14) determine the moral point of view, which requires us to consider all persons as intrinsically valuable and (15) seek consensus on rules of action, while both (16) exploiting prudence to approximate the effect of morality on conduct and (17) striving to transmute prudence and corporate egoism into genuine morality; that is, the pursuit of the ideal of maximum happiness fairly distributed for its own sake.

Notes

1. The position is one that balances total utility against the principle of equal distribution, according to Rawls's typology *(A Theory of Justice*, p. 124).

2. Rawls observes that every procedure for an ethical decision is forced to leave some matters to intuitive judgment *(idid.,* pp. 40, 41, and 44) We can only strive to reduce intuition to a minimum and maneuver it to situations where rational considerations can enter as fully as possible. At least, utilitarian calculations are based on objective data. The arbitrary elements that enter are surely no greater than in systems that require us to balance duties or rights against one another.

3. "A Further Note on Visions," pp. 60 and 61.

4. *Professional Ethics*, pp. 5–7 and 11.

5. *The Moral Foundations of Professional Ethics*, pp. 25 and 27.

6. *Principles of Moral and Legislation*, p. 311, n. 1.

7. See Kenneth Goodpaster, "On Being Morally Considerable" and J. Baird Callicott, "Animal Liberation."

8. *Ethics*, pp. 40–41.

9. Rawls' second principle, which stipulates that social inequalities are permissible when they benefit the least advantaged *(Theory of Justice*, p. 302), is justified, to the extent it is, by utility rather than justice.

10. Some of the principles in item 10 are adapted from Richard Brandt, "Toward a Credible Form of Utilitarianism" and "Some Merits of One Form of Rule-Utilitarianism," but the position is substantially different from Brandt's. His central propositions are: (1) An act is right if and only if it would not be prohibited by the moral code ideal for the society; (2) a moral code is ideal if its currency in a particular society would produce at least as much good per person (the total divided by the number of persons) as the currency of any other moral code; (3) for a moral code to have currency in a society, a high proportion of the adults in the society must subscribe to the moral principles, or have moral opinions, constitutive of the code, and principles belong to the code only if they are recognized as such by a large proportion of adults. "Some Merits of One Form of Rule-Utilitarianism," p. 48.

11. *The Moral Point of View.*

12. The missing links here are supplied by ideas adapted from Whitehead, that action originates in the present occasion of experience, that occasions of experience are self-transcending by nature in that even selfish persons act for the sake of future experiences, and that it is possible to value something besides one's own future experiences, but that it must be enough like one's own experience for one to imagine. It is not impossible to aim at a nonconscious reality, (e.g., a state of nature after all sentient creatures are gone), but this is only by surreptitiously imagining it observed and appreciated by a conscious being (i.e., as a component of imaginary experiences).

11. See, for example, Toulmin, *An Examination of the Place of Reason in Ethics*, Sections, 10.2 and 11.1

12. "Toward a Credible Form of Utilitarianism."

13. "Responsibility and Action."

☐ 3

UTOPIAN VISION AND PIECEMEAL REFORM

The considerations of the previous chapter were advanced from the standpoint of the agent facing moral choices. The question was, what facts and norms should an individual take into consideration in deciding what to do on a specific occasion under specific circumstances?

Our analysis also must approach the issues from another direction. Parameters for individual choices and the consequences of individual actions are determined by their institutional context. The institutions within which professionals practice empower them to act and provide them with considerable autonomy in action, while setting limits to those actions. Practicable ideals for professionalism must take account of the institutions in which they are to function. This means, for the present analysis, investigating the dynamics of the professions and the institutions with which they interact; for example, agencies of government employing organizations, the marketplace, the educational establishment. This chapter discusses the way the inquiry will proceed and then Part II undertakes it.

Professions as Institutions

Here, professions themselves are treated as institutions, that is, as sets of interrelated roles sanctioned and perpetuated by society. "Roles" are defined as patterns of activity governed by generally shared expectations and performed by replaceable individuals.[1] Because the individuals who participate in institutions may be replaced without altering expectations for their successors, institutions endure beyond the tenure of particular sets of role occupants and display enduring structural properties different in kind from the characteristics of those occupants. They, then, are objective facts that confront the individual as factors in the social environment, which are as real as the climate and terrain of the physical environment. The individual must come to terms with both environments. But, just as one can take measures to transcend the climate and modify the terrain, one has important choices in how to relate to institutions.

In discussing normative issues of professionalism, we will return to three areas of choice: (1) Individuals in modern society must choose whether to enter a profession and what profession to enter; (2) they must decide where to place themselves in their chosen profession and associated institutions and organizations and how to play their roles there; and, (3) they must decide whether and how to try to effect changes in the profession, its structure and practices. In all of these choices, social structure is a given, but it is not so tight and obdurate as to preclude discretion and hence moral responsibility on the part of the individual.

To put this in personal terms, when confronted by a complex and professionalized society at the outset of my work life, I must ask myself: What is my true vocation? Whom do I want to serve and how? What stance should I take toward the practices of the occupation charged with this kind of work? Should I follow the code of the group or my own lights? Should I be active in the formal organizations of the occupation or ignore them? Should I pursue the causes of the group? Should I devote any considerable portion of my life to influencing its practices or the policies of its organizations?

Ethics committees of professional associations and ethical theorists have devoted attention to the micro-ethical issue of the norms for the dealings of individual practitioners with clients and employers and (in a less thorough way) with third parties and the public. They generally have neglected issues connected with the individual's choice of the occupation and subsequent obligation to reform it. These issues are macro-ethical because they require one to evaluate occupations as wholes in relation to society. Nevertheless, they must be faced by the individual in his or her personal decisions. How am I to decide whether an occupation is worthy of lifelong dedication unless I estimate its impact on human welfare? How can I know the truly moral way to play my role in it unless I know the impact? And how am I to know what reforms to seek without a conception of the impact? Thus, all three choices of the individual, to enter an occupation, to play a specific role in it, and to work for its improvement require an understanding of the dynamics of the occupation as an institution and an evaluation of it from the perspective of a social philosophy.

This chapter will sketch a concept of the ideal profession and the way to derive practical proposals for actual occupations from the ideal. After a sociological analysis of actual professions in Part II, specific practical proposals for institutional change will be considered in Part III and norms for individual choice in Part IV.

Utopian and Practicable Proposals

It is one thing to determine norms for an ideal society; it is another to determine ideal norms for an actual society. The latter must be practicable, that is, norms for which it is possible to gain acceptance and, given acceptance, will approximate as nearly as possible the results of ideal norms in ideal society.

The precipitous attempt to implement the ideal norms of ideal society in actual society may produce undesirable results. In an ideal society, for example, professionals would be absolutely candid with their clients and never treat them paternalistically or encroach upon their privacy or autonomy. In the actual world, due to the imperfection of the institutions in which professions are embedded and the consequent limitations on people's ability to pursue their own welfare, these absolutes would inflict harm and deny benefits that certain restrictions and exceptions take care of. Furthermore, there are obstacles to ideal behavior for the practitioner in the structure of the professions themselves. Difficulties spring from the very features from which benefits flow, such as the esoteric character of professional knowledge and the insulation of professional practice from public scrutiny. These features expose the moral professionals to abuses of immoral ones. As a consequence, the social and ethical problems created by professionalism are found alike in capitalist and socialist economies, democratic and authoritarian political systems, entrepreneurial and bureaucratic organizational modes.

These facts suggest that improvements in the professions

would not follow automatically from wholesale changes in society according to a utopian vision. It calls for a step-by-step attack on limited aspects of the problems we will survey. Such an attack would resemble Popper's "piecemeal engineering," which he contrasts to "holistic" or utopian engineering:

> The characteristic approach of the piecemeal engineer is this. Even though he may perhaps cherish some ideals concerning society "as a whole"—its general welfare, perhaps—he does not believe in the method of re-designing it as a whole. Whatever his ends, he tries to achieve them by small adjustments and re-adjustment which can be continually improved upon.[2]

Popper believes that the holistic ambition inexorably impels the reformer to seek control of the state and transform it into a totalitarian agency. The program fails because it dispenses with experimental tests for reforms. Reforms can be evaluated only by checking their consequences within the context of a stable institutional structure, that is, one by one in a piecemeal way.

Popper's term 'engineering' has unfortunate connotations. Here, the attempt to improve institutions will not be viewed as an invention of mechanisms to program responses among people but rather the design of procedures to enable and encourage people to act as responsible moral agents using their ingenuity for the common good. A better metaphor might be moral husbandry or horticulture. Its aim is to establish a hospitable environment in which morality will develop from its natural roots in the individual.

Furthermore, 'engineering' suggests an elitism not intended here. Those appealed to in this work to form and reform professional institutions are not a small specialized group, either politicians, institutional elites, nor professional ethicists arrogating to themselves the right to decide how others should behave. Our appeal is to everyone willing to reason about norms, including most certainly those who will be asked to live by the norms but also the rest who will be affected by those who live by them. One of the problems of moral engineering or husbandry is to involve professionals in the dialogue about professional ethics. Another is to engage the attention of the enlightened public.

In the passage quoted earlier, Popper concedes that the piecemeal engineer may cherish ideals that concern society as a whole, but implies that it is not necessary for him to do so, since engineering can be applied to any end. Ends fall no more under the expertise of the social engineer than they do that of the physical engineer. But this means that it is possible to utilize piecemeal engineering to tighten the oppressive mechanisms of an exploitive society as easily as to create liberating institutions of a humane society. Hence, contrary to Popper, social engineers not only *may* have ideals, they *must* have valid and rationally grounded ideals to do their job properly.

Popper attacks Plato as an enemy of an open society, but Platonism is needed as much as Popperism for a program of reform. In *The Republic* Socrates replies to Glaucon's "gravest and heaviest assault" on his concept of the ideal state (the criticism that it would be impossible to implement) in these terms:

> We are inquiring into the nature of absolute justice and into the character of the perfectly just, and into injustice and the perfectly unjust, that we might have an ideal. We were to look at these in order that we might judge of our own happiness and unhappiness according to the standard which they exhibited and the degree in which we resembled them, but not with any view of showing that they could exist in fact.[3]

Since the ideal at best only can be approximated in practice, Socrates proposes to use it "to show what is that fault in States which is the cause of their present maladministration, and what is the least change which will enable a State to pass into the truer form . . ." Socrates' proposal, of course, is to find or develop wise rulers with a vision of the Good, who would impose the form of society (Justice) that the Good entails. This aim, however, the Athenian Stranger suggests in Plato's *Laws*, is too high for humanity in their actual condition. The best society would require a god as a ruler and perhaps gods ("beings who are more than men") to populate it.[4] The Athenian Stranger concludes that any commission designing a constitution for actual human beings in an actual historical and geographical situation should aim at the "second best" state, one ruled by laws rather than men.

While our proposals for occupational reform will be pragmatic and piecemeal, they will be informed by a vision of the ideal society. The aim is to provide norms practicable within the institutional framework of society. To determine these norms, one must conceive ideal norms for an ideal society and derive from them ideal norms for actual society, or rather for the best form of society actualizable by piecemeal reform from potentialities in the present society. One must discover norms that have a prospect for gaining acceptance under present conditions as a means of actualizing the best practicable society. It is in this light that we shall investigate norms for professionalism.

Utopian Conceptions of Professionalism

Professions share certain distinctive structural features. The professionalization of occupations, therefore, has a direction, a *telos*. By tracing the process to its ideal conclusion and imagining other institutions that would be necessary to sustain ideal professions, one can form an image of a model society and explore whether it should be used to evaluate actual institutions.

This leap into the ideal is taken by the two men who inaugurated modern thinking about professions, Durkheim and Whitehead. Perhaps their reputations explain why their remarks have been treated so uncritically. Both seem to have been under the illusion that they were describing reality in imagining the ideal. This makes them overly sanguine about the direction that actual professions were taking and inattentive to the difficulties in achieving their ideal.

Durkheim's views were expressed in three lectures prepared and revised between 1890 and 1912 and published in the *Revue de Metaphysique et de Morale* in 1939.[5] His intentions are obscure, since he lumps professions as presently conceived with ancient and medieval craft guilds and the corporations he proposes for particular industries. He believes that the role he projects for all of these is already being performed by the professions proper, but the effect is limited because there is a dearth of what he calls "business professions." "There are professional ethics for the priest, the soldier, the lawyer, the magistrate, and so on. Why should there not be one for trade and industry?"[6]

First of all, why *should* there be? The background of Durkheim's concern is the weakening of traditional moral institutions such as the family, church, and local community in industrial society due to the division of labor, economic competition, class conflict, and social and geographical mobility. He thinks that professions function in place of the family and local community because they are organized to require a detailed code of ethics of their members. He appears to think that ethical discipline is an inevitable consequence of organization, and the stronger the professional organization and more detailed its code, the more effectively it nurtures moral habits.[7] These habits include not only dedication to the profession and the work, but to the larger interests of society.

To see how this works, consider its opposite, those occupations that are not organized (he also refers to them as professions):

> Clearly, the individuals who follow the same callings are on terms with one another by the very fact of sharing a like occupation. Their very competition brings them in touch. But there is nothing steady about these connexions: they depend on chance meetings and concern only the individuals . . . There is no corporate body set above all the members of a profession to maintain some sort of unity, to serve as the repository of traditions and common practices and see that they are observed at need. . . .
>
> Now, this lack of organization in the business professions has one consequence of the greatest moment: that is, that in this whole sphere of social life, no professional ethics exists. Or at least, if they do they are so rudimentary that at the very most one can see in them maybe a pattern and a foreshadowing for the future. Since by the force of circumstance there is some contact between the individuals, some ideas in common do indeed emerge and thus some precepts of conduct, but how vaguely and with how little authority.[8]

> Consider the moral effect on individuals in such occupations: If we follow no rule except that of clear self-interest, in the occupations that take up nearly the whole of our time, how should we acquire a taste for any disinterestedness, or unselfishness or sacrifice? . . . It is therefore extremely important that economic life should be regulated, should have its moral standards raised, so that the conflicts that disturb it have an end, and further, that individuals should cease to live thus within a moral vacuum where the life-blood drains away even from individual morality.[9]

Durkheim calls for the organization of *all* occupations along the lines of the professions in the strict sense. They would become the primary political units of society, each with its particular ethic and serving as so many *milieux* for the inculcation of a common "civic morals" in their members.[10]

Later chapters will document the fact that professional organizations are neither as influential nor as morally elevating as Durkheim thought. Furthermore, there are natural limits to the professionalization of any occupation. We will explore the problems connected with Durkheim's vision of society as an organic combination of corporations for all the departments of economic life and the futility of relying on these to ensure widespread civic morality devoted to the common good. There are fundamental difficulties with organizing mass society in this way and such an organization, even if it could be achieved, would not be as salubrious as Durkheim imagined.

Yet, we should not lose sight of the valid kernel in Durkheim's thought. Professions can serve in at least a limited way as moral *milieux*. With the right ideals they can improve the way people do their work, encourage them to consider the social consequences of that work, and cultivate a heightened and more enlightened commitment to the common good. This does not happen consistently or automatically in professions in their present form; however, the moral is not to despair of these objectives but to reform the professions and their supporting institutions to achieve them more effectively.

There are interesting parallels between Durkheim's views and some remarks made by Whitehead about the same time (*Adventures of Ideas*, originally published 1933), which are frequently cited by American students of the professions.[11] The context of Whitehead's thoughts about professionalism is a discussion of the minimal social order required for freedom to flourish. Whitehead observes that order is achieved by either custom, rational persuasion, or compulsion. Civilization is proportionate to reliance on the first two: "Human society in the absence of any compulsion is trusting to the happy coordination of individual emotions, purposes, affections, and actions. Civilization can only exist amid a population in which the mass does exhibit this fortunate mutual adaptation."

The deviance of a few requires compulsion in every society and every society must work out an adjustment between compulsion and liberty. Whitehead makes the bold claim that the adjustment in Western civilization "presupposes a wide distribution of institutions founded upon professional qualifications and exacting such qualifications." He maintains. "Modern life ever to a greater extent is grouping itself into professions. Thus ancient society was a coordination of crafts for the instinctive purposes of communal life, whereas modern society is a coordination of professions."

Whitehead defines a profession as "an avocation whose activities are subjected to the theoretical analysis, and are modified by theoretical conclusions derived from that analysis." This function requires self-governing institutions that are guaranteed liberties by society in the form of "a special license to a particular group to organize itself within a special field of action." The institution exercises liberty and controls its members. It imposes discipline on professionals in their special field of action and removes control of that field from external agencies, even the state: "where the state ceases to exercise any legitimate authority is when it presumes to decide upon questions within the purview of sciences of professions." The reason is that only professionals have the knowledge to make rational judgments within the field: "moral authority is limited by competence to attain those ends whose immediate dominance is evident to enlightened wisdom. Political loyalty ceases at the frontiers of radical incapacity."

Furthermore, as seen from the perspective of Whitehead's process philosophy, social stasis is impossible. Civilized society requires progress inspired by valid ideals; otherwise, it degenerates into barbarism. Hence, to preserve civilization, its members must actively pursue freedom, truth, and beauty. Since progress requires the destruction of old forms of life in the hope of constructing higher ones, it entails risk. Hence, civilization requires adventure, the adventure of ideas. Whitehead conceived of professionalism as part of a great adventure of humanity in pursuit of truth and beauty.

Implicit in these remarks is the view that professions cultivate that "happy coordination of individual emotions, purposes, affections, and actions" in which rational persuasion on the basis of common values can operate and minimize the need for compulsion. Whitehead believes that professions supply a foundation of common values across national boundaries to the extent that they are based on science. The transformation of professions through science and the professionalization of a great many occupations in the contemporary world promote a unified world social order based on rational persuasion and common values.

This notion retains its appeal today. Toulmin traces the threat of nuclear destruction to nationalism and argues that it can be combatted only by loyalties that cut across national boundaries:

we need to find foci of loyalty that are as powerful as those of nationalism, but also less abstract, more familiar, and associated with values that are less easily corrupted. One such focus is the loyalties and values we encounter in professional life. Commonly, these loyalties have a transnational, or even international scope and institutional expression. . . . If any alternative focus of loyalty can serve today as an immediate check on the unqualified claims of the idolatrous "sovereign" nation, it is the duties that are well known to all professionals: duties toward clients, patients, and fellow-humans in general, whose scope carries across boundaries between different nations and states.[12]

A close look at professions will expose the naivete of these eloquent statements if they are taken as a factual description, but as with Durkheim, they deserve to be evaluated as a vision of an ideal built upon potentialities latent in professionalism. The professions are formally dedicated to noble goals, however, they stray from the path to those goals. They inculcate common values in their practitioners and to an extent in the public, whatever the imperfections of those values. They have a limited power to mobilize people for the common good, however they lend themselves to use by special interests. The potentialities revealed here should not be ignored though we should be realistic about the degree to which they have been actualized.

The evaluation of professionalism is not the simple matter it appeared to Durkheim and Whitehead. However, we should not lose sight of the possibilities they glimpsed, and we dare not ignore the problems of civilization they hoped to solve. The world community and the nations themselves threaten to fly apart in the absence of civic morals and shared adventures. Fulfilling the *telos* of professionalism may not be a solution at all, and it certainly is not the whole solution, but the problems are still there.

The Moral Organism

It would be helpful now to outline the ideal structure for society that we will use to chart reforms in the professions. This is the structure that the theories of Durkheim and Whitehead foreshadow.

The discussion of the preceding chapter assumed that human beings are so constituted that under favorable conditions they will take the moral point of view and support the institutions its demands. Furthermore, it maintained that an essential ingredient of happiness is the consciousness of participating in a morally sound system of social interaction. At the same time, it took into account the obvious fact of life that self-interest is an important part of human nature. Imperfect institutions pit people against one another and all institutions are imperfect. People find that they often must obstruct the enjoyment of benefits by others to enjoy them themselves or forego benefits if they are to allow others to enjoy them. Morality competes with prudence in the actual world.

The institutions of an ideal society would maximize happiness and distribute it fairly in a way that would eliminate the conflict between morality and prudence. Doing one's duty for its own sake would be rewarded incidentally. Pursuing one's interests in an enlightened way would benefit others incidentally. Everyone would find in the perfection of the system and its smooth operation a fulfillment of their individual desires, whether these were self-regarding or other-regarding, and the satisfactions of each person would be welcomed as an achievement by all.

It was from thoughts such as these, borrowed in his case from Hegel, that Bradley developed the notion of the ideal self, which he contrasted to the empirical or actual self we find in ourselves. In the essay "Why Should I Be Moral?" he maintains that the ultimate motive for morality is the desire, inchoate and unconscious at the outset, to actualize the ideal self. The empirical self struggles against the ideal self. It is from the perspective of the ideal self that we criticize and discipline the empirical self. Ethical reflection brings the perspective of the ideal self to full analytical consciousness. Ethical culture strives to promote the victory of the ideal self over the empirical self or, more precisely, to bring the empirical self into conformity with the ideal self.

Bradley expresses the ideal self's categorical imperative as "Realize yourself as an infinite whole." The empirical self is finite in the sense that as a matter of empirical fact I find myself related externally to other people, in conflict with them, prevented by them from doing as I choose, and not able to cooperate with them, approve their actions, or endorse their interests. How can these external relations be overcome so that my relations to the other can become part of my self and something I can wholeheartedly will about myself? Bradley introduces the notion of the "moral organism." While his metaphor utilizes a dated holistic conception of biological organisms, it illuminates a critical feature of moral communities:

> in the moral organism the members are aware of themselves, and aware of themselves as members. I do not know myself as mere this, against something else which is not myself. The relations of the others to me are not mere external relations. I know myself as a member; that means that I am aware of the whole as specifying itself in me; the will of the whole is the will of the members, and so, in willing my own function, I do know that the others will themselves in me.[13]

To overcome external relations to other persons and the internal opposition between my empirical and ideal selves, I must achieve self-realization; that is, my empirical self must become ideal. For this to happen, I must belong to a society in which others have achieved self-realization. The processes are correlative: I become an ideal person along with others as society becomes ideal, and it becomes ideal as its members do.

It is important to realize that one does not become moral by acting in isolation in the way a fit member of the ideal society would, as Kant seems to assert. One must act within a real community and adjust to its imperfections. Acting as one would act in a utopia is a sure way to bring injury to others, not to mention unhappiness to oneself.

Bradley's formula for morality in the real world is "my station and its duties." To be moral and achieve self-realization, I must find a station in actual society and perform the duties assigned to it by common moral opinion. While Bradley recognizes that actual societies fall short of the ideal and hence cannot develop to the fullest the ideal self in their members or entirely eliminate oppositions among them, he believes that the mores are the highest practicable standards available in one's actual society: "if you could be as good as your world, you would be better than most likely you are, and . . . to wish to be better than the world is to be already on the threshold of immorality."[14]

Bradley's view contains an important truth but sells rational morality short. It is true that we can be effective from the moral point of view only by acting through institutions as we find them. No other vehicle is available through which we can affect the lives of others in a significant way. To act through institutions, we must conform to most of their norms and indeed respect them as the only foundation for order and freedom. We must allow ourselves to be socialized into the sorts of persons who make those particular institutions work, and in the process, we become (imperfectly) moral beings. But it is possible to transcend roles, not to reject but to go beyond them, to establish a psychic distance from them that enables us to criticize them by ideal standards, to become better than the usual role-player and improve the role by the way we play it. The obligation to do so, in fact, is one of the norms for any social role according to the moral point of view.

Professional Obligations as Duties of Station

In Bradley's idealist model, society is an organism composed of lesser organisms, whose organic interactions constitute the concrete social relations among individual people. Durkheim imagines that professions are the most important of these lesser organisms. We will utilize the notion of the moral organism in the following theses. The moral organism and its subsidiary organisms actually exist to the extent that (1) expectations are generally shared among members of society that define the stations (roles) and duties (role obligations) in institutions, and (2) those duties are dictated by the moral point of view for the concrete circumstances of society at its particular stage of development. To the extent that the moral organism is actualized, if members of the society viewed matters strictly from the moral point of view and were fully cognizant of the circumstances under which each did his or her duty, each would approve of what each other did as a matter of duty and each would be aware of the approval of the others. In Bradley's terms, to the extent that the institutions in which we act are both *organic* and *moral*, we will that other participants do what they do and we see our will expressed in their actions; we see our self realized in them and in the moral organism as a whole. They likewise see themselves realized in our actions. This permits Bradley to speak of the "will of the whole" and the "whole willing itself" in us.

Universality sometimes is stipulated as a mark of moral rules. A rule for particular circumstances is said to be moral only if we would want anyone to follow it under the same circumstances.

Under the present view, however, the moral person would not want all behavior to be governed in this way except under the most extreme contrary-to-fact circumstances. If we imagine an ideal society in which everyone is omniscient as well as completely moral, behavior might be reducible to rules acceptable to all. However, perfectly moral persons in an ideal society with less than omniscience and, hence, facing the uncertainties about the world with which actual people have to contend would assign to social roles a wide latitude for applying principles and ideals to unforeseen circumstances. They would approve post facto one another's actions, but they would value originality and creativity. This clearly is the better model for people of limited vision and good will in actual society. It would be unwise for them to try to reduce all behavior to codified rules, as we emphasized in Chapter 2. They should rather establish institutions in which people can practice roles creatively, with an eye to the ultimate good, maximum happiness fairly distributed.

The objective for social reform proposed here is the creation of a genuinely moral community, that is, as nearly an approximation of the moral organism as possible. If we are thinking about our nation-state, our aim will be the creation of an organic society along Durkheim's lines. But what about the need for world order both for survival, as Toulmin suggests, and the advance of civilization, as Whitehead suggests? Clearly, something like a world community or a community embracing all of humanity would be necessary. As remote as this prospect is, the critical character of the times demands that we take it seriously. Let me sketch where our reflections have led us in this connection.

We have depicted moral communities as founded on a blend of consensus on general norms for important roles and tolerance for how people play the roles, as well as for their styles of life. Something like this blend is realized in good families and approximated in some friendship circles, small organizations, and local communities. It remains an unrealized ideal for entire societies but still a viable target for aspiration. However, it is likely that no nation can achieve the ideal as long as every nation's existence is dependent on interactions with other nations that are not even trying to achieve it. True community may not be possible in any society until it is achieved throughout the world.

The converse is certainly true. A world community will not

be possible until individual nations, or whatever replaces nations, develop parallel conceptions of norms of conduct for their own members and toleration of cultural differences between themselves and other nations. No system of supranational power can create community, nor even maintain peace and order, without the foundation of a common morality and mutual respect among societies and lesser groups across the world.

Here Whitehead's vision comes into play. Professions properly structured could provide links among groups with similar positions in different societies, independent of the political links among the governments of the societies. Those cultural links could strengthen and help moralize the political ones. The possibilities of social good latent in professionalism, then, include a contribution to world community. Why the realities of professionalism have fallen so abysmally short of this contribution is a question to be answered by our subsequent analysis.

Prudence and the Moral Organism

It is all well and good to imagine what an ideal society composed of persons of perfect good will would be like. But once that image is in mind, we must inquire what compromises must be made, still in the interest of the ultimate goal of maximum happiness fairly distributed, because most people have limited good will and must contend with many who lack even that. In acting within institutions and attempting to improve them, we must always remember that not all individuals will do their duty for duty's sake and the structure of society is too imperfect even to induce them to do exactly what duty requires out of self-interest.

The limited knowledge of most moral persons and the admixture of self-interest with morality in almost everyone call for a two-tiered morality, if anything like the moral organism is to be nurtured in society. The first tier would consist of rules to which all would be held and all could be brought to obey from either morality or prudence. These rules would be universalizable in the strict sense: We could not only wish them to be universal, we reasonably could undertake to *make* them so by enforcement and rational persuasion. The second tier would consist of ideals by which we would hope to inspire the more moral members of society to use their intelligence and creativity to do more than the rules require and by effect and example gradually raise the level of the first tier.

Something of the notion of a two-tier morality is at work in the American Bar Association's Model Code of Professional Responsibility. The Disciplinary Rules "state the minimum level of conduct below which no lawyer can fall without being subject to disciplinary action." The Ethical Considerations "are aspirational in character and represent the objectives toward which every member of the profession should strive." The ABA intends the Disciplinary Rules to be enacted into laws by the states but they resemble the rules in our first tier of morality in their specificity and universality. The Ethical Considerations, in contrast, have the openness for voluntary and innovative action in pursuit of remote goals (the ultimate goal for the lawyer, according to ABA, is "justice grounded in law based in respect for the dignity of the individual and his capacity through reason for enlightened self-government") which we would incorporate in our second tier of moral ideals.

A few other professions have moved in this direction. The National Council of Engineering Examiners provides Model Rules of Professional Conduct, which have been enacted into law by most states and are enforced by state registration boards under the police power vested in them. The rules are adapted from ethical codes of major engineering associations, but they are simpler and less demanding.

In similar vein, a recent committee of the American Institute of Certified Public Accountants has proposed a restructuring of the Institute's Code of Professional Ethics into two sections, Standards of Professional Conduct and Rules of Performance and Behavior. The Standards would propose basic responsibilities and broad objectives for voluntary adherence by members of the profession. The rules would be enforced in order to ensure a minimal level of conduct in the profession, however strong or weak the conscience of its members.[15]

The need to enforce some norms as laws or quasilaws within the framework of more comprehensive and demanding norms addressed to conscience parallels the practice of society at large and reflects the same imperfections in society and perhaps in human nature. Even if we could assume that human beings were perfectible, no society is a perfect moral organism and none shapes the beliefs and motives of its members in an ideal way.

Our own society is not a perfect moral organism nor are professions perfect organs in it—far from it—but they approach the ideal sufficiently for moral persons to utilize them as vehicles for action. There is no way to act apart from society. The moral life can be achieved only by working through and beyond the roles provided by imperfect institutions in an imperfect society, not by standing aside in wait of perfection. Morality dictates that we utilize the institutions that are available.

Transition to Part II

These initial chapters have laid a foundation for assessing practices of professions from the moral point of view. We have formulated principles to guide the individual in seeking norms for professional decisions and we have sketched the ideal social structure, the moral organism, that is the goal of piecemeal reforms in the framework within which the individual has to act. Next, we turn to the social dynamics of the framework as it now exists, how professions actually work, since the individual practitioner, not to mention reformer, can act effectively only with some knowledge of these matters.

Notes

1. Moore, in *The Professions: Roles and Rules*, is the sociologist who uses roles as an analytic concept most extensively in dealing with professions. See also Hughes, "Education for a Profession," in *The Sociological Eye*, pp. 392 393.
2. *The Poverty of Historicism*, p. 67.
3. *The Dialogues of Plato*, 472c and 473b, Vol. I, pp. 735 and 736.
4. *Ibid.*, 739c, Vol. II, p. 506.
5. Indicated by Huseyn B. Nail Kuball, in the Preface of Durkheim's *Professional Ethics and Civic Morals*, p. ix. The lectures appear as the initial chapter of this work.
6. *Ibid.*, pp. 29–30. See pp. 20–23 and 37.
7. *Ibid.*, pp. 8, 14, 25, and 29.
8. *Ibid.*, p. 9.
9. *Ibid.*, p. 12.
10. *Ibid.*, pp. 29 and 39.
11. All of this material, including the quotations, is found in *Adventures of Ideas*, pp. 71–79.
12. "The Limits of Allegiance in a Nuclear Age," p. 371.
13. *Ethical Studies*, pp. 79–80.
14. *Ibid.*, p. 179.
15. Special Committee on Standards of Professional Conduct for Certified Public Accountants, *Restructuring Professional Standards*, pp. 1–2.

❑ PART II

MODELS OF PROFESSIONS

☐ 4

SOCIOLOGICAL THEORIES

My barber displays a plaque awarded to him by Redken Laboratories for training in the use and merchandising of its products. It bears the motto "Professionalism through Science and Education." He is proud to be identified as a professional and Redken assures him that he is one. Clearly, however, his idea of professions is not what sociologists have in mind. They consider high status to be a mark of professions and barbering hardly enjoys that.

Superficial agreement about the characteristics of professions among sociologists masks fundamental disagreements, as I shall show in succeeding chapters. These disagreements are reflected in the variable meanings of words in what I shall label "the professional terminology," such as 'profession,' 'professional,' 'professionalism,' 'professionalization,' and words used to define these.[1] This produces "semantic confusion," which Millerson sees as a serious obstacle to scientific inquiry.[2] The confusion is itself a social phenomenon that needs to be explained, but first it must be dispelled if we are to talk clearly about professions.

Families and Family Terms

Clapp lists 170 occupations that describe themselves as professions and affect trappings such as special insignia, codes of ethics, and associations organized on the professional model. Self-designated professionals range all of the way from accountants, electrical engineers, ophthalmologists, and zoologists to automotive service technicians, fire chiefs, football coaches, hypnotists, midwives, purchasing agents, and technical writers.[3] Obviously, not everyone in the public accepts these designations or the same denotations for the terms.

Variations in technical as well as popular usage has not made the terms of the professional terminology simply equivocal. There are affinities among the several meanings of each. They are, consequently, what are called analogical terms in classical semantics and family terms in contemporary semantics. The meanings of a given term are not independent of one another: They are related because of the way they have been developed by successive users.

Something like the following must have happened and appears to be continuing. Consider the term 'profession,' for example. It was first used as a label for the traditional professions—law, medicine, architecture—and connoted their more prominent features. As new occupations struggled to be recognized, their advocates modified its meaning in order to extend the term to them, while striving to retain enough of the old connotations to warrant its continued use. Their efforts were met with resistance by other members of the speech community who were protective of the reputation of the original professions or just traditionally minded and who continued to use the term in its earlier sense. As a result 'profession' comes to designate a large family of occupations with criss-crossing similarities and differences. 'Professionalism' comes to designate a family of attitudes and skills with criss-crossing similarities and differences, and likewise 'professional' and 'professionalization.'[4]

The short way out of the confusion for the sociologist would be to treat the words as technical terms (or substitute new terms for them) and stipulate definitions in the classical mode of genus and differentia, hoping to persuade other sociologists to adopt the usage by the empirical generalizations to which they might lead. Ideally, some sociological pioneer would establish a set of laws of professionalism that would be arranged in axiomatic form, which, after the manner of physical mechanics, would generate a vast number of theorems confirmed by measurements of phenomena.

Unfortunately, the theory of professions has not worked out this way. Sociologists have not found a scheme of classification that results in generalizations with any significant predictive power. Instead statements in the various theories take the form of deductions from ideal-typical models that match real occupations only approximately, on the one hand, and statistical generalizations and tendency statements taken haphazardly from the data, on the other. Neither form of description is satisfactory for explaining the phenomena with which we are concerned.

"Ideal-typifications" are advanced as models that represent actual professions in a complex way and give stable and precise meanings to the professional terminology. These models seem to have been constructed in the following manner (their authors are not always explicit): Prominent features of occupations widely recognized as professions are catalogued, A, B, C, . . . No single occupation displays all of them. Rather the properties cluster for different occupations, AB, BC, AC, . . . More precisely, none or few of the properties are possessed in the maximum degree by any occupation, but some are displayed in a high degree by each. Also, most or all are possessed in some degree by all occupations, though in very low degree by nonprofessions.

This suggests a diagram with multiple axes representing the dimensions of professionalization arranged as spokes of a wheel. The point at the center represents the maximum degree of each dimension and those on the rim, the minimum degree. The degree to which a given occupation displays a property can be marked as a point on its axis. Connecting the points would circumscribe an area in the logical space of professionalism between the point at the center, where the ideal-typical profession is located, and the circle formed by the rim, where the ideal-typical nonprofession is located. The size of the area circumscribed for an actual profession will be inversely proportional to its degree of professionalization. The professions converge on the center; the nonprofessions approach the perimeter. A circle then can be drawn objectively, if arbitrarily, between the center and the perimeter to divide professions and nonprofessions. Better, a band can be drawn to separate the two groups and contain quasi- and protoprofessions.

The wheel is my fantasy, but otherwise the procedure has been followed by most sociologists. The characteristics of professions that various sociologists have collected (from twenty-one sources) are summarized by Millerson.[5] According to this tabulation thirteen characteristics are incorporated in more than one definition. The number of definitions incorporating a characteristic is indicated after the statement of the characteristic.

1. A profession involves a skill based on theoretical knowledge. (12)

2. The skill requires extensive and intensive training and education. (9)

3. The professional must demonstrate competence by passing a test. (8)

4. The profession is organized and it is represented by associations of distinctive character. (13)

5. Integrity is maintained by adherence to a code of conduct. (13)

6. Professional service is altruistic. (8)

7. The professional assumes responsibility for the affairs of others. (5)

8. Professional service is indispensable for the public good. (2)

9. Professionals are licensed, so their work is sanctioned by the community. (2)

10. Professionals are independent practitioners, serving individual clients. (2)

11. They have a fiduciary relationship toward their clients. (2)

12. They do their best to serve their clients impartially without regard to any special relationship. (2)

13. They are compensated by fee or fixed charge. (2)

The characteristics not included in a given definition usually are attributed by its author to professions in the form empirical generalizations.[6]

In addition to the thirteen core characteristics, individual authors mention the following:

14. Professionals are highly loyal to their colleagues.

15. They regularly contribute to professional development.

16. Their prestige is based on guaranteed service.

17. They use individual judgment in applying principles to concrete problems.

18. The work is not manual.

19. Profits do not depend on capital.

20. Professional status is widely recognized.

This is a loose assemblage. Some professions lack some of the characteristics altogether; for example, journalists and ministers are not licensed to practice their occupation by the state on the basis of standardized tests or credentials, nor are they represented by the typical kinds of professional associations. Other professions possess characteristics minimally; for example, most electrical engineers are employed by corporate organizations for salaries rather than by clients for fees, and most of the "theories" on which lawyers base their skills (e.g., interpretations of precedent) are at a low level of abstraction. All of the characteristics are matters of degree and all are displayed in some degree by non-professions. Hence, they are continua on which both professions and nonprofessions fall.

By specifying that professions possess clusters of the characteristics to a high degree, sociologists are led to classify occupations in such a way as to place the professions at or near the top of the hierarchy of importance, which they take to correspond a hierarchy of prestige. Thus, Centers lists occupational categories in descending order as business executives, professionals, small businessmen, white collar workers, skilled manual workers, semi-skilled manual workers, and unskilled manual workers.[7] Greenwood's influential definition of professions (in terms of systematic theory, autonomy, community sanction, ethical code, and distinctive subculture) produce a ranking grouped as follows:

1. Well-recognized and undisputed professions, such as medicine, the law, college teaching, and science, which are bunched at the top of the continuum and possess the attributes to a maximum.

2. Less developed professions, including social work, which possess them to a lesser degree.

3. The mid-region, with the less skilled and less prestigeful clerical, sales, and craft occupations.

4. The least skilled and least attractive occupations, bunched at the lower end, such as those of the watchman, truck-loader, farm laborer, scrub woman, and busboy.[8]

Once authors have selected core characteristics, they conceive of the ideal-typical profession in terms of the maximum degree or fullest form of the characteristics and formulate theorems about further properties. Their model, they imply, in some way or other represents actual professions, though all fall short of the ideal.

Functionalist and Conflict Models

Unfortunately, sociologists have come up with competing models reflecting opposing conceptual frameworks for understanding social phenomena. I shall reduce the models to two—two typifications of the typifications—and play them off against each other to project a realistic and critical picture of the institutional system within which professionals must function.

In reviewing the literature, Johnson finds that influential thinkers who reflect on the role of professions in society are aligned on two sides. One group sees the professions "as a positive force in social development, standing against the excesses of both laissez-faire individualism and state collectivism, and [the other] as harmful monopolistic oligarchies whose rational control of technology would lead to some form of meritocracy."[9] Among the former are Durkheim, Tawney, Marshall, Parsons, Halmos, and Carr-Saunders and Wilson. As we noted, in *Professional Ethics and Civic Morals*, Durkheim thinks that the professions are or could become communities that would cultivate order, discipline, and duty at a time when moral institutions were being dissolved by the fragmentation of labor. Tawney in *The Acquisitive Society*, Marshall in "The Recent History of Professionalism in Relation to Social Structure and Social Policy" and Parsons in "The Professions and Social Structure" in *Essays in Sociological Theory* see in the service ideal a counterforce to the self-interested individualism flourishing in other parts of society. Halmos in *The Personal Service Society* optimistically believes that this ideal is spreading from the professions to other occupations, including business. Carr-Saunders and Wilson in *The Professions* see in the continuity and tradition of professions a force for stability in society and a counterforce to the concentration of power in the state. They see professionalism to be, in Johnson's words, "the major social force freeing men from a slavish dependence upon the state behemoth."[10]

Among those who see professionalism as a negative force, Johnson lists Lees in *The Economic Consequences of the Professions* and Kuznets and Friedman in *Income from Independent Practice*. These authors think that professional associations, far from inhibiting bureaucratization, increasingly use the mechanisms of bureaucracy to promote harmful monopolistic practices. Mills in *White Collar*, Young in *The Rise of the Meritocracy*, and Veblen in *Engineers and the Price System* view with alarm the bureaucratization of professional work. The attitudes of bureaucratic professionals are scarcely those of independent experts with an enlightened vision of democratic society and resistence to concentration of power in the state and the corporation. These negative views are found in Johnson's own analysis and those of Larson in *The Rise of Professionalism* and Collins in *The Credential Society*, on which we will rely.

The authorities thus are arrayed against one another. The situation seems to be this: The professions have accomplished a great deal for humanity and we cannot abandon the ideal of professionalism in work. Those who see the professions as a force for the good are impressed by their accomplishments and protestation of high ideals. The critics are impressed by how far short they fall in realizing their potentialities and see in the pretension to high ideals an apology for the status quo.

The two models of professions in this literature have been named after the theoretical orientations from which they emerge. The functionalist orientation postulates that social systems are stable and progressive because their institutions fulfill important functions in relation to human needs. All basic needs are met by one or more institutions and each institution meets one or more needs. Institutions are coordinated so that actual societies approximate the ideal organic society depicted in the previous chapter.

Exactly how an institution serves human needs often is not evident on the surface, because structures designed for one purpose incidentally serve another. Ostensible functions, those recognized by the individuals involved in the institution, are not its only ones nor always its true ones. They mask important latent functions. The sociologist who singles out an institution for investigation looks for latent functions to explain its structure, expects to find them, and stands ready to reinterpret its ostensible functions once its latent functions are laid bare.

Functionalists recognize that institutions have dysfunctions and individuals and events disrupt their functions; but this does not shake their confidence in the social system. Apparent dysfunctions mask latent functions, and some may not be true dysfunctions at all. Real dysfunctions are tolerable aberrations or temporary disequilibriums that homeostatic mechanisms of the system rectify. Even deviance and conflict have a place. They push society to better particular structures while general stability is maintained.

According to the conflict view, institutions develop to resolve conflicts arising from competition for scarce goods and services. They involve compromises in which the needs of many are partially met, whereas often a few profit more than others and institutions perpetuate dominance and exploitation.

Conflict theorists admit that institutions have functions, which they distinguish as either social or human. What benefits the system may not benefit its members. The conflict theorist expects to find human dysfunctions behind both the ostensible human functions and the social functions of institutions. Since the oppressed eventually come to be aware of their oppression, social systems ultimately are unstable and destined to be supplanted.

Both orientations utilize evolutionary concepts; they do not depend on myths of social contract or conspiracy. Institutions begin (in analogy to random variation in biological evolution) with practices that spring up by accident in the form of uncoordinated choices of small groups for limited objectives. Practices are selected for development and perpetuation because they incidentally serve some larger purpose, the good of society (according to the functionalists) or dominant groups (according to the conflict theorists).

Both orientations take account of the rational element in human affairs. Reflection on institutions, once they have evolved, reveals their functions and dysfunctions and enables those with power to promote the one and try to eliminate the other. It may arouse those who lack power to seek it in order to change institutions.

The insights of the two schools, however, tend to motivate different practical programs. Functionalists approve the institutions that they study. They are inclined to serve and strengthen them and justify their ways to critics. Functionalists are distrustful of wholesale changes lest, in trying to reform institutions, the reformer, like a well meaning missionary condemning heathen practices, may destroy them without being able to replace them.

Conflict theorists, on the other hand, are aghast at the havoc wrought by exploitive institutions. An oppressive society need only keep the oppressed alive or replenish their ranks when it decimates them. New institutions always can be established that will function at this minimum level, so radical change poses no great risk and conflict theorists hope for much more. They aspire to create something like the organic society, the ideal that stands in mute condemnation of actual societies. Conflict theorists are as contemputous of the efforts of functionalists to patch up existing institutions as they are of reactionaries' efforts to freeze them as they are.

Reasons for the Split

Social scientists bemoan the lack of a single paradigm in their field. The existence of competing schools is a scandal for pretensions to scientific and professional status. It is not obvious, however, that society can afford a single dominant paradigm so long as social thought is an adjunct of social action: Society is better served by competing points of view. Still, it is an embarrassment not to have a single set of experts to whom to appeal when a conceptual framework is needed to address specific questions—in this case, a sociological framework to view the institutions for which we wish to design ethical norms.

To decide what to do under this condition, we must reflect on the reasons for the division among authorities. The reasons turn on the role played by conceptual frameworks in the observation of social phenomena and the peculiarities of the specific data available for understanding professions.

It is a truism among contemporary philosophers that the classical positivist model of science as a hierarchy of generalizations erected upon an accumulating body of protocols reporting theory-neutral observations[11] is simplistic. Observation is theory-laden. In order to pass from the encounter with an object (seeing an x) to observing it (seeing x as P and Q) and reporting what has been observed (saying that this P is Q), the scientist must antecedently have concepts (P and Q) and a language in which to express them ('P' and 'Q' and '—— is ——'). Two investigators viewing the same situation but utilizing different sets of basic categories and postulates will consequently observe different things. It is very difficult, though not impossible, for them to find a common ground of data to adjudicate their disputes.

In the social sciences, the problem is compounded by the fact that scientists are studying the kind of beings that they themselves are. They want to know the meaning that actions and events have for the subjects they are observing. What feelings, beliefs, and intentions do the subjects' actions express, and how are these affected by external actions and events? For example, what does a patient's illness and the reaction of the physician mean to the former? What are the physician's real aims and how does his or her ideology mediate them? Scientists must neutralize the tendency to impute their own beliefs and feelings to their subjects. Equally, they must be careful not to accept the subjects' self-understanding at face value, a danger compounded by the fact that many of the observer's categories, such as 'professional,' are used by agents in social life to make sense of and, indeed, to create social reality. Scientists must not assume uncritically that these persons think and feel what theories say they ought to think and feel under particular circumstances. Human phenomena are notoriously ambiguous in the absence of exhaustive knowledge of their contexts, which we never possess. The social scientist, consequently, deals in speculative hypotheses that interpret fragmentary data. It is no wonder that diametrically opposed models should develop for phenomena so complex as those relating to professions.[12]

As a brief example of contrary observations of the same bit of social reality, consider the following scene.

Interlude: The Doctor's Office

An aging man, John Swenson, appears at the office of James Saunders, M.D., Urologist, about 8:50 A.M. The waiting room is already crowded with patients. Swenson approaches the receptionist's window. A matronly woman in a white uniform busies herself with clerical work but finally looks up.

"Yes?"

"I had a nine o'clock appointment with Doctor Saunders. I've been having trouble with . . ."

"Please sign in and take a seat."

Swenson occupies himself by thumbing through old copies of *Time, Field and Stream,* and *Medical Economics.* He carries on a desultory conversation with other patients, exchanging symptoms. About 10:15, he returns to the window.

"When do you think the doctor can see me? I had to take off work to come in and I'm due back after lunch. And I have this pain . . ."

(A little impatiently) "Doctor is very busy this morning. He'll see you just as soon as he can."

At 11:00, a young woman, also in uniform, enters the waiting room and calls out, "John?"

"Here."

"This way, please." She ushers him into a examining room. "Please strip to your shorts, John, and put on this gown. Doctor will be with you in a minute. We would like to get a urine sample. Put a little bit in this jar—about up to here—and the rest in this."

About twenty minutes later, Dr. Saunders, wearing a white coat, briskly enters the room. He quickly examines Swenson, scrawling out an illegible prescription. "Here, take this, get plenty of rest, and come back to see me next week." He cuts short Swenson's attempt to inquire into his condition. "Don't worry. This'll take care of it."

If the functionalist Talcott Parsons were to observe this scene, he would see an expert professional with a well-organized staff efficiently processing the maximum number of persons with medical needs. These persons have delegated the care of their health to the professional and he discharges his responsibility expeditiously. He determines what is wrong with Swenson and how to cure it. He instills trust by his confident manner, his title of Doctor, the diplomas and elegantly framed Hippocratic Oath on his wall, the handsome furnishings of his office, the deference of his staff, his costume and theirs. Swenson will be only too happy to pay the rather large bill for the office visit and laboratory services and the high cost of the medication. After all, his condition is not as serious as he feared (though he is not clear about what it is) and it will be cured quickly. If he reflects, he may congratulate himself on living in a country with the best health care in the world.

Magali Larson, the conflict theorist, would observe a different scene. She would see a member of the professional elite taking advantage of people's troubles to gather a disproportionate share of society's wealth. Everyone is schooled to think that the doctor's time is important while that of the patients he "serves" is not. The physician has assembled an organization to process patients as problematic objects rather than persons whose autonomy is to be respected. The setting is calculated to maintain a social distance between Dr. Saunders and people like Swenson and intensify Swenson's psychological insecurity and dependence. The doctor carefully cultivates the aura of mystery about what he does. The deference of his aides—all women—makes it obvious who's in charge, who's important, what's important. The office is the shop where Doctor works. Patients are materials to work on. Swenson's experience in the office reinforces his resignation to life in the social system. This is how working people are treated.

The Evidence and the Criteria

The evidence to which the different sociological schools of thought appeal for their models of professions, and on which we must rely to evaluate those models, is limited and problematic. First of all, there are the technical investigations of the sociologists themselves, which turn up data that hold up under the replication of the investigation and reexamination of its results from the same perspective. Such studies have established hard facts about particular occupations but few generalizations that hold across the board for professions as such and none sufficient to decide between the models. Rather, sociologists of the two schools (e.g., Hughes and Moore in one camp and Collins and Larson in the other) marshall equally impressive arrays of statistics and generalities to defend their respective models. The functionalist and conflict perspectives are underdetermined by empirical data, which allows and forces them to utilize operationally a priori frameworks to interpret the data in opposite ways.

A second source of data are the personal experiences of the sociologists themselves. They consider themselves professionals. They have a stake in professionalism. The major theorists in the two schools appeal to their own interaction with other professionals in defending their models.

Third, the sociologists take seriously the self-presentations of and popular ideas about the professions—the functionalists, as relatively accurate portrayals of obvious realities; the conflict theorists, as an ideological code that discloses a hidden reality once one grasps its key.

The inadequacy of the first type of evidence (relatively hard data) and the consequent importance of the second and third (the investigator's personal experience and the self-presentations of the professions) are connected with the central role of normative intuitions in the selection of conceptual schemes in social thought. By 'intuition,' I mean a preanalytic grasp of specific facts and possibilities and an affective-conative reaction to them. In ordinary life, we confront concrete situations and see possibilities for action. We respond emotionally to the situations and are attracted and repelled by alternative possibilities. Situations thus are experienced as clothed with values.

It appears characteristic of sociological theories in general, and it is obviously true of the two models of professions, that each is adopted not because the author hopes it will precipitate empirically confirmed generalizations that eventually can be organized into an axiomatic system à la mechanics, but because it provides a framework to articulate the author's normative intuitions and those of others around him or her. This claim will be documented in later chapters.

The thesis advanced here is the contrapositive of a thesis of Taylor, who argues that any framework for understanding political processes "secretes" a value position.

> In general we can see this arising in the following way: the framework gives us as it were the geography of the range of phenomena in question, it tells us how they can vary, what are the major dimensions of variation. But since we are dealing with matters which are of great importance to human beings, a given map will have, as it were, its own built-in value slope. That is to say, a given dimension of variation will usually determine for itself how we are to judge of good and bad, because of its relation to obvious human wants and needs.[13]

Taylor's argument is that if one adopts certain frameworks, one undermines certain value judgments. I would like to point out that if one trusts certain value judgments, one must reject certain conceptual frameworks.

It is apparent that neither functionalists nor conflict theorists are uninfluenced by value judgments about professions. If either group could appeal to value-neutral scientific criteria to justify its conceptual framework, one might believe that its value judgments follow upon a neutral determination of the facts. Since neither can show this, one is forced to use the value judgment that each effectuates as a measure of its validity. Whether or not value judgments always must determine theories in social thought, it is clear that they have done so in theories about professions. It is not a question of whether values affect the theories, but only whether they are articulated, organized, and rationally defended.

Notes

1. Cogan remarks in reference to his extensive research of popular and sociological sources, "This analysis was undertaken with the purpose of attempting to identify some patterns implicit in generally accepted definitions of profession. No broad acceptance of any 'authoritative' definition has been observed." ("Toward a Definition of Profession," p. 47) Johnson concludes from efforts such as Cogan's that "definition-mongering" is sterile and the attempt to identify core elements of professions as such is a positive obstacle to understanding power relationships, the process of professionalization, and other important social phenomena. (*Professions and Power*, Chapter 2) In contrast, Pavalko claims, "there has developed an extensive body of literature dealing with the characteristics of 'professions'. . . . Work on this topic has become so voluminous that substantial consensus has emerged on these dimensions and it is possible to identify a few features of work groups that appear to occur in combinations and clusters that function to differentiate 'occupations' from 'professions' ". (*Sociology of Occupations and Professions*, pp. 15–16). He then proposes a list of eight features differentiating professions from other occupations and claims that these are generally accepted. Other accessible summaries of widely accepted characteristics may be found in Hughes, "Professions in *The Sociological Eye*"; Cogan, "Toward a Definition of Profession"; Greenwood, "Attributes of a Profession"; Barber, "Some Problems in the Sociology of the Professions".

2. *The Qualifying Associations*, p. 1.

3. *Professional Ethics and Insignia.*

4. Wittgenstein's Concept, *Philosophical Investigations*, paragraphs 65–67.

5. *Qualifying Associations*, p. 5. The sources are Bowen, Carr-Saunders and Wilson *(The Professions)*, Christie, Cogan ("Toward a Definition of a Profession"), Crew, Drinker, Flexner, Greenwood, Howitt, Kaye, Leigh, Lewis and Maude, Marshall, Milne, Parsons *(Essays in Sociological Theory)*, Ross, Simon, Tawney, Sidney and Beatrice Webb, Whitehead, and Wickendon. These works are cited in the Bibliography.

6. A dictionary definition illustrates both types of statements: "In the strictest sense of the term, [a profession] is a high-status occupation composed of highly trained experts performing a very specialized role in society. A profession has exclusive possession of competence in certain types of knowledge and skills crucial to society and its individual clients. . . . It tends to feel that it is by itself capable of formulating its ethics and judging the quality of its work. Thus professional groups tend to reject the control of the public or clients they serve." (Theodorson and Theodorson, *A Modern Dictionary of Sociology*)

7. Listed by Theodorson and Theodorson under "Occupations."

8. "Attributes of a Profession."

9. *Professions and Power*, p. 12.

10. *Ibid.*, p. 14.

11. As presented, for example, by Brodbeck in "Explanation, Prediction, and 'Imperfect Knowledge.' "

12. This account of the theory-ladenness of observation in science and in *verstehende* social science is taken from Hanson's *Patterns of Discovery* and Schutz's *The Phenomenology of the Social World.*

13. "Neutrality in Political Science," pp. 153–54.

☐ 5

THE FUNCTIONALIST MODEL

The functionalist model will be presented uncritically before probing its weaknesses from the conflict perspective.

The last chapter listed some twenty statements by a wide range of authors stating central characteristics of professions. To bring this material into order, the characteristics will be sorted into three categories: substantive, pertaining to the nature of professional work; structural, pertaining to the organization of professional groups; and personal, pertaining to the kind of people the professions attract and develop.

The functionalist framework provides internal coherence for the idea of profession. The work of the professions is seen to have the character it does because it enables them to perform their functions. The professions are thought to be structured and to attract and develop particular kinds of persons as the optimal way to get the work done.

The teleological relation between functions of professions and the character of their work, and between their work and their structure and personnel, binds these elements into a coherent whole. The teleological form of the model also explains its attractiveness as an ideal: Members of an occupation see in professionalism a coherent pattern for implementing the aspiration to serve society in an effective, efficient way.

The ideal character of the model suggests in turn an explanation for the way actual professions have evolved. Professions approximate the ideal because, in a few cases, their leaders have consciously shaped them after the ideal and, in every case, society has rewarded professions for developing this form. Given this dynamic, professions are the way they are because of the functions they perform for society. What is more, this functionalist *explanation* is also a *justification*. Professions deserve their status because they perform important functions.

The Goal of Service

The central features of professional practice are the application of some branch of science or systematic knowledge to the solution of important human problems.[1] We will consider the second aspect first.

The importance of the professions turns on the relevance of their work to basic biological needs—food, shelter, health, disposal of the dead, etc.—and basic instrumental needs generated by modern society—education, transportation, sanity, order, legal counsel, energy, disposal of wastes, etc. The importance of the needs they meet distinguishes professional work from other highly skilled activities. Moore notes, "the welfare of the professional's clients is vitally affected by the competence and quality of the service performed; this is certainly not true in the same sense or same degree of esthetic and expressive activities. A poor performance may distress the beholder, but it scarcely threatens his vital interests."[2] (Professional musician, professional artist, professional athlete, etc., thus are misnomers. We do not condemn the poor fingering of a violinist as we do that of a surgeon nor the poor design of a landscape by a painter as that of an orphanage by an architect.)

Professionals confine themselves to providing means to their clients' ends and proposing solutions to their self-defined problems. Parsons calls this "specificity of function."[3] The authority of the professional is based on technical competence, rather than status, wisdom, or moral character. He or she is an authority in a special field of knowledge and skill not in other matters.

In acting with authority and exercising skill, only some data relating to the lives of clients are relevant. The professional is not concerned with their full personality and indeed is obligated *not* to probe into areas that are not relevant. Furthermore, the professional relationship is determined by the problem the client brings to the professional not by who the client is.

A heart specialist, for instance, may have to decide whether a given person who comes to his office is eligible for a relatively permanent relation to him as his patient. So far as the decision is taken on technical professional grounds the relevant questions do not relate to *who* the patient is but to *what* is the matter with him. The basis of the decision will be "universalistic," the consideration of whether he has symptoms which indicate a pathological condition of the heart. Whose son, husband, friend he is, is in this context irrelevant.[4]

To put this in general terms, the professional renders disinterested and impartial service to whomever fortune puts in his hands. The client's needs concern him, not his or her class, race, sex, age, nationality, social role, or position of power.

For structural reasons, professions enjoy a monopoly of expertise in their domain of authority. The public not only *can* come to them for competent service, it *must*. While specificity of function limits professionals' authority to special areas in the lives of clients, monopoly of the function gives them sovereignty over these areas. The importance of their work, therefore, resides not only in the importance of the values but the degree to which it affects them.

The work of the professions is critical for human welfare, since they have been put in charge of so many vital areas of life in modern society. As a consequence their primary orientation is to public welfare. Any doubts of the skeptic are overwhelmed by protestations to this effect in the ethical codes of professional associations. The following is a sample (the codes mentioned here and elsewhere are listed in the Appendix):

The principal objective of the medical profession is to render service to humanity will full respect for the dignity of man. (American Medical Association)

The practice of dentistry first achieved the stature of a profession in the United States, when, through the heritage bestowed by the efforts of many generations of dentists, it acquired the three unfailing characteristics of a profession: the primary duty of service to the public, education beyond the usual level, and the responsibility for self-government. (American Dental Association)

The continued existence of a free and democratic society depends upon recognition of the concept that justice is based upon the rule of law grounded in respect for the dignity of the individual and his capacity through reason for enlightened self-government. . . . Lawyers, as guardians of the law, play a vital role in the preservation of society. (American Bar Association)

The duty of journalists is to serve the truth. . . . The public's right to know of events of public importance and interest is the overriding mission of the mass media. The purpose of distributing news and enlightened opinion is to serve the general welfare. (Sigma Delta Chi)

Engineers uphold and advance the integrity, honor and dignity of the engineering profession by using their knowledge and skill for the enhancement of human welfare. . . . Engineers shall hold paramount the safety, health and welfare of the public in the performance of their professional duties. (Engineers' Council for Professional Development)

Psychologists respect the dignity and worth of the individual and strive for the preservation and protection of fundamental human rights. They are committed to increasing knowledge of human behavior and of people's understanding of themselves and others and to the utilization of such knowledge for the promotion of human welfare. (American Psychological Association)

The American Personnel and Guidance Association is an .educational, scientific, and professional organization dedicated to service to society. This service is committed to profound faith in the worth, dignity, and great potentiality of the individual human being. . . . A profession exalts service to the individual and society above personal gain. (American Personnel and Guidance Association)

The distinguishing character of a profession is that its members are dedicated to rendering service to humanity. Financial gain or personal reward must be of secondary consideration. . . . The reputation of the football coaching profession and the fine influence which the game of football can exert upon the people of America, is dependent in large measure upon the manner in which the coaches of the nation live up to both the letter and the spirit which this code represents. (American Football Coaches Association)

The true professional man places the public's welfare above his own. Such concern for the patient or client is characteristic of a professional calling. The objective of the C. L. U. program is not only to help a life underwriter gain the subject knowledge that is needed to serve his clients well, but to instill in him the attitude of placing their interests above his own. . . . I shall place the welfare and interests of my clients above my own interests. (American Society of Certified Life Underwriters)

Under all is the land. Upon its wise utilization and widely allocated ownership depend the survival and growth of free institutions and our civilization. The Realtor is the instrumentality through which the land resource of the nation reaches its highest use and through which land ownership attains its widest distribution. He is a creator of homes, a builder of cities, a developer of industries and productive farms. Such functions impose obligations beyond those of ordinary commerce. They impose grave social responsibility and a patriotic duty to which the Realtor should dedicate himself. . . . In the interpretation of his obligations, he can take no safer guide than that which has been handed down through twenty centuries, embodied in the Golden Rule: "Whatsoever ye would that men should do to you, do ye even so to them." (National Association of Realtors)

The claim in all of these is that the profession's "collectivity orientation" (as Goode labels it[5]) is service to humanity rather than profit. Some codes emphasize generalized service (vaguely, the welfare of "humanity," "society," "the people," "the public;" more specifically, the rule of law, truth, safety, quality of life, human rights, understanding of human behavior, wide ownership of land). Other codes emphasize service to individual clients or patients (their health, development, security). The body of rules in both types are devoted to behavior of the individual professional toward clients or employers and customers, fellow professionals, and "the profession," and in rare instances specific outsiders or third parties. The implication is that the profession serves humanity *by* serving these groups (cf. the principle of special or role responsibilities) and, also by implication, that all members of society have access to the services. More strongly, it is implied that practitioners and the leaders who control the structure of the profession *aim* at such service.

Such claims about individual motivation are too strong for plausibility and unnecessary to sustain the thesis of service orientation. The most sophisticated and influential sociological analysis of the orientation is provided by Parsons. He first comments that the claim is easily misunderstood. If it is taken to mean that individual professionals are more altruistic than other workers, it is possibly false and certainly unproven.

Nevertheless, reminiscent of Durkheim's thoughts about professions and civic morals, Parsons declares, "encouragement of the professions is one of the most effective ways of promoting disinterestedness in contemporary society."[6] What does the service orientation of the professions come down to, if it does not depend on altruism? In what sense are professions, apart from the professional, "disinterested"? Parsons claims that the institutional pattern of the professions, in contrast to business, rewards service.[7]

Success in business is defined in terms of profit for the firm and personal advancement; success in the professions is defined in terms of service to clients. The successful merchant is one who sells his goods; he is not judged by the benefit they incidentally bring to those who buy them. The successful doctor is one who cures his patients; he is not judged by the fees his efforts incidentally bring him. In turn, the definitions of success determine the particular activities that are essential to the work of each occupation. Business is doing what is necessary to sell the product. Medicine is doing what is necessary to cure the patient. The institutional definition of successful performance determines the nature of the work. The motivation of the individual is irrelevant as long as he strives to succeed.

The same point can be made in terms of the kinds of rewards that are emphasized in business and the professions respectively. Barber sees a connection between the orientation of the professions and the prevalence of symbolic gratifications in them.

> Money income, general prestige and specific honors or symbols of achievement are among the different forms of social reward for occupational achievement. Since money income is a more appropriate reward for individual self-interest, and since prestige and honors are more appropriate for community interests, these latter types of reward are relatively more important in professional than in nonprofessional behavior. The actual reward system in the profession tends to consist, therefore, in a combination of prestige and titles, medals, prizes, offices in professional societies, and so forth, together with sufficient monetary income for the style of life appropriate to the honor bestowed.[8]

On this premise, Ritzer proposes an instrument to measure the degree of professionalization of practitioners. He suggests, "We might ask the individual to rank the following series of rewards in order of importance to him: (1) money; (2) respect of colleagues; (3) respect of client/customers; (4) helping others; (5) occupational honors (e.g., election to officership in union or professional association, promotions); (6) community-recognition."[9] The implication is that, while individual doctors and taxi-drivers may vary among themselves on this scale, doctors as a group would emphasize symbolic rewards and taxi-drivers monetary rewards because doctors are more professional than taxi-drivers and medicine is more of a profession than hacking.

The greater interest professionals take in their work also is assumed to be connected with the service orientation. The most beneficial work usually is the most intrinsically interesting. Occupations devoted to interesting work contribute more to humanity both because of the benefits of the work and the energy with which it is pursued.

All of these desires—for income, honors, community service, interesting work—are found in most human beings. We need not claim that people who enter the professions are unusually endowed with the more noble ones. The framework of professionalism focuses the gamut of human desire on work that serves the interests of clients and the community rather than, as in the case of business, work that maximizes profit for the agent or the organization that employs him or her.

Alliance with Science

The professions are able to contribute so efficiently and thoroughly to the central values of society because their work is grounded in scientific or quasiscientific theory. The true professional bases his decisions on rationally grounded principles. Parsons points out the variety as well as similarity among the theoretical bases of different professions. The competence of a profession, he says, is based on a form of knowledge that

> transcends the immediate practical exigencies of the particular professional function; it has been knowledge of a generalized character, not only of certain applications of a group of sciences, but of the sciences themselves, their theoretical structures and principles; not only of the particular legal rules in question, but of the law as a great tradition; not only of the liturgy, the creed, and duties to parishoners, but of theology and church history.[10]

Rationality as opposed to traditionalism is an institutional pattern of professions due to their affiliation with science. In respect to pure science, Parsons notes that "it is quite clear that the mere fact that a proposition that has been held true in the past is not an argument either for or against it before a scientific forum." He maintains that the same holds good for the professions, whose business it is to apply science.[11]

The Primacy of Practice

Professions are nourished by the sciences, but their concern is the solution of practical problems. We refer to "practitioners," to being "in practice," to "the practice" of medicine or law, to the "practices" of the profession, and to ideas that are usable as confirmed "for all practical purposes."

To be useful, theories must be cast into a specific form. They must have a degree of precision so that work based on them will be reliable and the professionals will merit the trust placed in them. Precision is obtained by formulating theoretical principles in a special technical language and deriving theorems by a special logical calculus, the languages and calculi frequently being mathematical. Professionals must master these tools in order to utilize the theories. They come to speak a different language and reason in a different pattern than their clients, thus widening their social distance.

Professionals often must master several bodies of theory to be effective. The heterogeneous problems dealt with by some professions—for example, civil engineering, psychiatry, corporate law—are best handled eclectically. Professionals must master disparate theories to a degree not required of pure scientists. This is true also because of the gamut of problems which typical professionals encounter in the course of a career.

The scientific grounding and practical orientation of the professions, then, entail a number of distinctive features for professional expertise. In addition, special forms of skill and judgment are required. The skills are essentially intellectual. Professionals may need manual skills as in the case of surgeons, dentists, and electrical engineers, but these implement intellectual operations of great subtlety.[12] Professionals also may need theoretical knowledge to understand complicated instruments used in their work.

Skillful performance involves judgment, both in the selection of relevant principles and in their application to unique and fluctuating conditions. Thus, the professions are arts rather than sciences despite their reliance on science.

The professions feed on the basic sciences, but they also

generate research programs themselves. In doing so, they invert the relation between theory and practice in pure science. Practical application becomes the goal of theorizing, rather than a byproduct or incidental confirmation of it. Basic research is pushed forward for the sake of potential applications.

The reliance of the professions on theory and research endows them with the dynamic of science. The sciences, whether considered as habits of thought or institutionalized activities, are systematically progressive. It is the profession of the scientist to extend the reach of his theories and ramify and refine them internally. As a result, the professions based on the sciences constantly are reshaped. Individual professionals must not only master and retain the knowledge and skills of their predecessors; they must continue to learn and grow throughout their careers. They must keep in touch with new developments in order to maintain competence. They must run fast to stay even.

Beyond this, they are expected to be something of scientists themselves and contribute to the field in which they practice. Of course, not all practitioners do systematic, publishable research; but all are expected to be theoretically minded and innovative. This is the basis, for example, for the distinction drawn by the primary accreditation agency for engineering education between engineering proper and engineering technology: "The engineer must be a conceptualizer, a designer, a developer, a formulator of new techniques, a producer of standards—all to help meet societal needs."

In contrast, the technologist, using established knowledge, must only be able to "produce practical, workable results quickly; install and operate technical systems; devise hardware from proven concepts; develop and produce products; service machines and systems; manage construction and production processes; and provide sales support for technical products and systems."

And the technician need only "conduct routine tests, present data in a reasonable format, and be able to carry out operational tasks following well-defined procedures, methods, and standards."

The hierarchy of the engineering team is clear: The technologists "must be able to achieve conceptual goals established by the engineer." Although able to utilize proven techniques and methods with a minimum of direction from an engineer or engineering technologist," the technician "shall not be expected to make judgments which deviate significantly from proven procedures."[13]

To generalize, the true professional is responsible for the conceptual and innovative aspects of the work, while its routine aspects are delegated to auxiliary occupations. For this the professional must be in charge. The professional is the natural ruler of the professional-technical team.

Occupation, Career, and Vocation

The functionalist model incorporates ideas prevalent among professionals themselves and their various publics. Language is a mirror that reflects and shapes popular views. Etymology confirms that the essence of professional work is the application of science to the practical solution of human needs.

Professional work is, first of all, exacting. It requires long, intensive preparation to qualify for practice and full-time dedication through the remainder of life to practice well. One's profession is thus his or her "occupation" or the activity that occupies most of his or her waking life. "Occupation" is derived from *occupare*, to seize. In English, "to occupy" first meant to take or seize; then, to hold; to use up (time); and finally, to busy oneself with. An occupation seizes one and uses up one's time.

A profession is one's "livelihood" or the way of making a living, but it is more exacting than other occupations. Professionals not only spend more hours at the work itself, they spend leisure hours keeping up with developments. Their occupation thus is not only their livelihoods but pretty much their lives or what they live for.

A profession more than other occupations is a "career," that is, a course with successive stages through which one is expected to advance throughout one's working life.[14] "Career" is derived from *carrus*, wagon, and *carraria*, road for vehicles. The English word originally meant a race-course and a short gallop at full speed; it came to mean a person's course through life: "career, in the most generic sense, refers to the fate of a man running his life-cycle in a particular society at a particular time."[15] Given the importance of work to one's fate, it means the occupation to which one's life is devoted. In other lines of work a person may move from one occupation to another, but someone can have only one career and is expected to advance through it according to established stages.

A person not only *makes* a living in the professions, he or she *earns* it in the sense of deserving that pay through hard work in the service of others. Making demands upon a person, a profession is a "vocation," a calling. 'Vocation' is derived from *vocatio*, a bidding, and *vocare*, to call. In English, 'vocation' meant first a call or summons to the religious life; then, the work to which one is called; finally, regular employment. This dilution in meaning is reversed when the word is applied to the professions. One's vocation is the work to which one is called—if not by God, then by nature as voiced in the native endowments that equip one to serve others. Thus, the "Faith of the Engineer" proclaims, "When needed, my skill and knowledge shall be given without reservation for the public good. From special capacity springs the obligation to use it well in the service of humanity; and I accept the challenge that this implies." It repeats, "our special expertness carries with it the obligation to serve humanity with complete sincerity."[16]

The call of vocation is one to which one must respond of his or her own free will. It, therefore, requires a "profession" or statement of commitment to its standards and objectives. The word "profession" is derived from *profiteri*, which comes from *pro* + *fassfateri*, to confess, to own to. In English, 'to profess' was, first, to take the vows of a religious order; then, to declare openly; then, to lay claim to some quality or feeling; finally, to declare oneself proficient or expert (thus, a *professor*).[17]

Hughes remarks on the attitude of professional schools toward those who have been admitted to their sacred halls:

> Old and new alike, the professions cherish their recruits, once they get them. Having picked their candidates with great care, medical schools, for instance, gnash their teeth and tear their hair over a sheep lost from the fold. They wonder what they have done wrong to make the lamb stray. They make it clear to the professional recruit that he owes it to himself, the profession and the school to stick with his choice. Has it not been discovered by all the tests that this is the one right outlet for his talents? Is it not his duty to use his talents for his country in the best possible way? Have not the profession and the professional school made a great investment in him? Has he the right not to give full return on it?[18]

A similar attitude is found among professionals toward colleagues who drop out in later life.

What Hughes describes is the quasireligious overtones of the ideas of career, vocation, and profession: Professionals are called to serve in their professions; in answering the call, they profess belief in its dogmas, faith in its disciplines, and lifelong fidelity to its aims. By leaving the profession, they become apostates and deserters. They say ruefully and ashamedly, "I was once a doctor (lawyer, teacher, priest, engineer)."

The semantic background for the popular acceptations of such terms as 'profession,' 'vocation,' and 'career' incorporates elements of the sociological model of the true profession. These words "in the strict sense" (as used by the sociologist) refer a demanding course of theoretically based action, to which few are called and fewer chosen, requiring lifelong dedication and the profession of high ideals, and rewarded with the opportunity of special service to one's fellow man. When we use these terms less rigorously, they are resonant with honorific connotations derived from the model. On the one hand, respect for professions as paradigms of expertise is reflected in the use of 'professional' as the contrary of 'amateur' to refer to anyone who performs an activity seriously for a living (a professional singer, ballplayer, thief, philosopher). A professional action must be performed expertly for one to obtain his livelihood from it (e.g., a professional job of barbering, house painting, car washing). The modest hyperbole reflects the respect with which the true professions are held. In an ironic twist, this respect is mirrored in the negative connotation of such descriptions as "professional liar" and "professional Texan."

The Roots of Autonomy

The structural aspects of professions as institutions that will be singled out for discussion are autonomy, collegiality, and meritocracy. Since structure is determined by function, we must ask how autonomy, collegiality, and meritocracy contribute to the social functions of professions. According to the functionalist model, the connecting link between structure and function is to be found in the nature of professional work. How then do the three structural features facilitate professional work and thus contribute to society, so that society in fostering this contribution supports the structural features?

Professional work involves the application of complex, theoretical, and specialized knowledge to problems of clients, employers, or customers. Long training is required and professionals learn to speak a new language and reason by a different logic. They solve problems for others on the basis of knowledge that the clients do not have and cannot acquire or often even appreciate.

The wide gap in knowledge between the lay person and the professional is maintained by the profession's effective monopoly over a stock of theory and skill. Professionals, of course, master the intellectual bases of their profession. In addition, they see that no one else does by controlling the channels of education and research. As a result *only* professionals are equipped to judge the work of professionals.

The monopoly of competence is the foundation for the professional autonomy. Barber stresses the connection between the character of professional work and insulation from external control. He notes that this necessitates self-control.

> Social control depends in part, obviously, upon substantive understanding of the behavior to be controlled. In the case of behavior characterized by a high degree of knowledge, the requisite understanding is available in full measure only to those who have themselves been trained in and apply that knowledge. It follows that same kind of self-control, by means of internalized codes of ethics and voluntary in-groups, is necessary.[19]

"Self-control" covers two kinds of autonomy, collective and individual. A profession enjoys collective autonomy in that it largely is exempt from control by society and left free to regulate the behavior of its members. Individual professionals are autonomous in that the profession's reins of control are slack and most of their decisions are left to their own sense of morality and prudence.

The mechanisms of collective autonomy protect the profession's monopoly of expertise by ensuring that those in the profession practice it in a uniform manner and by inhibiting competition from outsiders who might offer rival services. Some competitors, such as "jail-house lawyers" and on-the-job trained "engineers," try to utilize the same cognitive base as the profession. Others, such as chiropractors, naturopaths, and faith-healers in competition with medical doctors, and fortune-tellers, palmists, and astrologers in competition with counseling psychologists, utilize different bases.

Professions combat competition in various ways. They lobby for a system of licensure administered according to their own standards by boards staffed with their own members. They denigrate alternative methodologies. They discourage their members from collaborating with the enemy. Thus, the American Bar Association in its Model Code declares, "A lawyer shall not aid a non-lawyer in the unauthorized practice of law." It restricts the kind of partnership into which a lawyer may enter with a nonlawyer. The principle is that "A lawyer should assist in preventing the unauthorized practice of the law." The ABA defends the principle by the argument, "The nonlawyer may have lower standards of competence, integrity, and ethics than the regulated lawyer. Hence the latter is better equipped to serve the public interest." Perhaps on similar grounds, the American Medical Association states in its Principles, "A physician should practice a method of healing founded on a scientific basis; and he should not voluntarily associate professionally with anyone who violates this principle."

Monopoly over a skill is defended by a profession as a means of assuring predictable high-quality service. Measures that suppress competition are the first step, but the profession also must monitor the performance of its own members. It defines standards, motivates practitioners to adhere to them, and provides them facilities for doing so. Two types of norms are enforced, standards of technical competence to ensure that the work is done the proper way and ethical principles to ensure that the work is directed to the proper ends. (Technical standards will be of no special concern except insofar as competence itself is a moral obligation.)

The professional is motivated (and equipped) to follow the technical and moral norms of his profession by the unique relations maintained with its major institutions. We noted that professional skills cannot be mastered once and for all; the professional must continue to learn and relearn to maintain competence. This requires sustaining ongoing relationships with the profession in a way that those in other occupations do not. At the same time, *doing* the work is an essential part of *learning how* to do it, since professional work is skillful practice. Learning and doing can be distinguished analytically, but neither is confined to a single phase of one's career. The institutions designed to shape each have an important role in shaping the other. The professional school, association, accrediting board, and disciplinary committee work syncretistically to promote competent and ethical service for the public.

Mechanisms to Influence Practitioners

Let us trace the procedures by which the profession influences its members in major phases of their careers. First, entry into the profession is tightly controlled. Qualification requires technical training, and the profession controls admission to educational programs. Faculties and administrators are drawn from the profession. They control curricula, admission, and graduation and they monitor the progress of students. The profession thus selects the kinds of persons that will replenish its ranks and shapes them according to its pattern. It provides not only the knowledge and skills it declares to be necessary for competence but the values and attitudes demanded by its service orientation. The professional school is the primary socializing agency that initiates novices into the profession's subculture.

The complexity of professional knowledge requires postsecondary and in some instances postbaccalaureate education in colleges, institutes, and universities. Ideally, the professional school is located in a university. Barber thinks this to be so important that he includes it in his definition of profession, and he remarks,

> Nearly all the well-established professions are located in some measure in the university; the more professional ones, according to our definition, having the more university-connected schools. Within a given profession, the "better" professional schools are more likely to be in a university, and the very best ones are typically in the very best universities . . . the emerging or marginal professions, when they are trying to raise standards for themselves, seek to locate themselves in universities. If they already have a marginal connection there, they seek to improve their position in the university.[20]

Why should this be? Hughes ties it to validation of the change of status that an occupation seeks through professionalization.

Changes sought are more independence, more recognition, a higher place, a cleaner distinction between those in the profession and those outside, and a larger measure of autonomy in choosing colleagues and successors. One necessary validation of such changes of status in our society is introduction of study for the profession in question in to the universities.[21]

A university degree signals that its possessor is a *true* professional, sharply distinguished from workers who lack one. It is an unambiguous insignia.

In addition to legitimating professions and professionals, universities meet the substantive educational needs of new professions. Existing departments of natural and social science are available to teach and enlarge the theoretical basis of the new profession as well as teach the basics to the preprofessional student.

Professional work requires university education in other ways. It involves discretionary decisions in shifting circumstances, which call for humane values and cultivated judgment. To sustain these qualities, the professional must live the life of the mind throughout his or her career, not just during the period of formal training. Parsons sees an intrinsic connection between professionalism and the liberal spirit:

to master this intellectual content of the professional tradition the liberal spirit is essential. The man who is dominated only by the more sordid motives of gain or even the immediate success of his practical task alone is incapable of it. The valuation of knowledge for its own sake is an integral part of the professional spirit.[22]

He maintains both that the professional must be liberally educated to understand the tradition of the profession and that mastery of a professional tradition contributes to liberal education. This is his case for incorporation of professional schools in universities.

Professional educationists fancy the notion that the professions bring the whole tradition of liberal learning to bear on the practical problems in their jurisdiction. Cogan quotes Ulich to the effect, "Every profession roots deeply in the basic experiences of mankind, and it withers when these roots are not kept alive," and adds,

The practices of professions take their orientation from accumulated knowledge and wisdom. It is the wisdom that acts as a corrective to the blunders that may otherwise by inevitable to mere specialism . . . Professional practices are refined by science and corrected by wisdom.[23]

The development of professional conscience among new entrants into a profession is as important for the public welfare as technical competence. Liberally educated themselves and building on the prior liberal and moral training of the student, the faculty of the professional school takes the lead in this task. Barber says.

So far as normative standards of community orientation (or "ethics") are concerned, again the university professional school has certain essential functions. The university professional school sees to the ethical training of its students as well as their other learning. Some of this ethical training is explicit, in the form of teaching professional codes; some of it is intermixed with what is ostensibly only the learning of substantive knowledge; and some of it is implicit in the behavior of the staff. University professional-school staff members often come to serve as ethical role models for their students and even as guides to conscience after the students have themselves become mature practicing professionals.[24]

The location of professional schools in universities, finally, provides a vehicle to communicate new findings to practitioners in the field through programs of continuing education.

After formal education, the next step in professional life is entry into practice. The professional degree is a prerequisite for certification and prepares one for certification tests. In addition, the individual's academic record affects his place in the profession after graduation. Placement is a function of the prestige of his school and the "old-boy" network of personal relations between educators and prominent graduates. Such ties are strengthened by the fact that many educators are involved in practice themselves or with their own clients. They thereby maintain contact with those who devote themselves exclusively to practice.

At their most aggressive, professions seek legal status for their members by licensure, which prevents anyone who has not met their criteria from practicing, and certification, which restricts the use of the profession's titles (Medical Doctor, Attorney at Law, Psychologist, Engineer, CPA, etc.). The professional association takes the lead in formulating legislation. Thus, in 1969, the American Bar Association replaced its Canons of Professional Ethics with a Model Code of Professional Responsibility containing the Disciplinary Rules specifically designed to be enforced by law. The National Council of Engineering Examiners provides a Model Law as a guide to the states to "provide greater uniformity of qualifications for registration, to raise these qualifications to a higher level of accomplishment and to simplify the interstate registration of engineers and land surveyors." Prominent members of the professional associations staff registration boards, and the key members of regulatory agencies are drawn from the professions they regulate, sharing both its expertise and values. In these ways the profession controls its controllers and insures that only those who conform to its standards are allowed to practice.

The third and central phase of the professional's career, actual practice, continues to be shaped by the profession. The primary control is self-control, but this reflects the profession's understanding of itself. The individual typically follows the technical and ethical standards acquired through professional socialization. He or she typically fraternizes socially as well as vocationally with colleagues. Social contact reinforces shared conceptions of the work and its role in society, of the profession as a corporate body, and of economics, politcs, and even religion and morality, insofar as these bear on the profession.

Further control over the individual is exerted by a system of referral by which colleagues provide clients or business and the penetration of colleagues into the administrative posts of industry, government, health-care units, schools, etc., which are the principal places of employment. The professional's opportunities to practice thereby are screened by judgments of colleagues as to his or her competence and ethical character. The profession provides strong incentives to fit its mold.

Lastly, the professional association plays an important role in all the processes described. It serves as a vehicle for continuing education. It shapes beginning education by accrediting educational programs. It influences legislative and administrative processes by which government establishes parameters for practice. It considers complaints of malpractice and judges and punishes malfeasance, protecting the ethical professional who strives to practice within the accepted guidelines and assuring the public that it is safe in the profession's hands.

According to this ideal-typification of the mechanisms of self-rule, there is a symbiotic relationship among the major institutions with which the professional traffics. These include professional schools, associations, regulatory agencies, and employers. Since the institutions of society are integrated, there are no role conflicts for the ideal-typical professional. The professional's roles are harmonious and they afford the opportunity to work according to his or her own standards, which are those of the profession. This ensures that the professional's talents will be utilized fully and contribute maximally to the well-being of others. The integration of institutions assures society predictable service of the highest quality. The structure of the professions thus is ideal both for the professional and for society.

Meritocracy and Collegiality

The structural perfection of professions depends on two additional features that, though distinct from autonomy, are organically connected with it. These are meritocracy in leadership and collegiality among practitioners. These additional features are necessary to sustain the trust of clients. Marshall notes two features of the situation that necessitate client trust. One is the client's ignorance.

> He often hardly knows what to ask for, let alone how it can be provided. He must surrender all initiative and put himself in his lawyer's hands or under his doctor's orders. That is the great difference between the services of professional and the services of wage-earners or salaried employees. Authority passes from buyer to seller.

The second is the unstandardized and personal character of the work.

> The professional man is distinguished by the further fact that he does not give only his skill. He gives himself. His whole personality enters into his work. It is hardly possible to be satisfied with a doctor or a lawyer unless one likes and respects him as a man. He is called upon to show judgment and an understanding of human nature, as well as a knowledge of medicine or law.[25]

These are strong demands indeed—to be entrusted with vital interests and to be immune from judgment. They can be justified only if institutions ensure that professionals do not abuse their powers. Society is forced to rely on the conscience of the individual and such lax controls as the profession exercises to ensure that he will be trustworthy. It also must trust the profession to have its house in order. As a reflection of this, Marshall tells us, the qualities that make the professional trustworthy "cannot be specified in a contract, they cannot be bought. They can only be given. The clients trust to professional traditions and professional ethics to develop and train those qualities and make them available to the public."[26]

The mechanisms of self-regulation guarantee competent and conscientious service only if the levers are pulled by the best individuals the profession has to offer—best not only in professional skill, but in dedication to public service and sound ethical principles. Rule by the best is guaranteed by a training-testing-certifying-monitoring process that not only screens practitioners but selects the leading educators, officers of professional associations, role models in the professional subculture, managers of employing organizations, etc. Leaders are constantly on trial and judged by professional standards. The true profession therefore is ruled by the best. It is a meritocracy.

This, however, takes care of only half of the problem of trustworthiness. Leaders that set policy and determine standards are far removed from the day-to-day work of practitioners. The educational system, political strategy of professional associations, their ethical codes, and other measures mold the fundamental form of professional life and through them the leadership establishes parameters within which the individual works. They do not relieve the individual of the responsibility to follow his or her own judgment in applying technical rules according to ethical norms in unique circumstances, case by case, in daily practice. Despite the complex institutions of professions, the individual enjoys great autonomy in the activity that actually matters, the work itself.

Only professionals are equipped to judge the quality of professional work. The leaders of the profession and the mechanisms of collective control are too far removed to monitor it except in a few cases of egregious malfeasance. The only persons both *equipped* and *in a position* to evaluate the professional's ordinary performance are colleagues in the immediate community and worked with on a daily basis. Many of these are colleagues in the strict sense, that is, neither superiors or inferiors. Others are subordinates or superordinates in organizational hierarchies, but who enjoy the right of professional judgment. In technical matters—and to a degree on moral issues—their relationship is still one of collegiality. In an important sense, then, the structure of a profession is collegial. It is a voluntary community of equals with rights of independent judgment and obligations of mutual assistance and criticism.

To summarize, the typical pattern of professional action is one of voluntary choice of procedures to serve a client on the basis of professional skills and professional conscience, constantly submitted to peer review, and judged by both the practitioner and colleagues according to accepted standards of the profession. The institutional structure of autonomy based on meritocracy and collegiality guarantees that professional services will be of the highest quality and collectively serve the interests of humanity in the most efficient possible way.

Communities within the Community

Goode maintains that the structural features typified here make professions genuine communities with distinctive relationships with the larger community within which they operate. He implies that professions become the *milieus* for civic morals and public order Durkheim and Whitehead envisioned. They are true moral organisms.

Goode ascribes to a profession the following communal characteristics:

> (1) Its members are bound by a sense of identity. (2) Once in it, few leave, so that it is a terminal or continuing status for the most part. (3) Its members share values in common. (4) Its role definitions *vis-à-vis* both members and non-members are agreed upon and are the same for all members. (5) Within the areas of communal action there is a common language, which is understood only partially by outsiders. (6) The Community has power over its members. (7) Its limits are reasonably clear, though they are not physical or geographical, but social. (8) Although it does not produce the next generation biologically, it does so socially through its control over the selection

of professional trainees, and through its training processes it sends these recruits through an adult socialization process.[27]

Professionalizing occupations consciously foster these character-istics and society supports their efforts as it increasingly becomes dependent on professional skills.

Goode asserts that many of the traits that make the profes-sions sociologically interesting "grow from" the dimension of community. I presume that he has a causal relation in mind; that is, that there is functional connection between the communal and further traits. The professional community requires more education and a higher standard of behavior of its members than demanded by the containing community. It wins higher income and disproportionate power. This enables it to attract better talent and impose more thorough socialization, enabling greater control according to a demanding ethic and guaranteeing that its mem-bers will not take advantage of their power to exploit clients or others.

> [T]o the extent that community of profession is strong, its members face real temptations, and its behavioral demands are different from the demands of the lay world—to that extent it must put its recruits through a set of adult socialization processes and maintain proce-dures for continuing social controls over the practicing professional.
>
> Thus, in exchange for protection against the larger lay society, the professional accepts the social control of the professional com-munity. As a consequence, the larger society has obtained an *indirect* social control by yielding *direct* social control to the professional community which thus can make judgments according to its own norms.[28]

Goode concludes that it is necessary to screen the process of collegial control from interference by the containing community. The professional community has quasi-independent status and its members have role responsibilities that override obligations as defined by other institutions.

While Goode admits here and there that not all professions function this way and some professionals stray from the straight path, his criticisms are mild. It is evident that he approves of what he sees: Professions are communities with common values and these elicit from their members a high level of conduct for the public welfare. The professions, therefore, deserve their rights and privileges.

The Persons

The service orientation is a holistic characteristic of professions according to the functionalist model; it does not presuppose altruism on the part of professionals. Success is defined in terms of service to the client. Rewards take the form of either money, honor, and other things that satisfy self-regarding interests, or the consciousness of doing what is right and contributing to others, which satisfy other-regarding interests. In theory, a professional might spend his or her entire life in a profession for selfish reasons and nevertheless serve others effectively.

However, the character of professional work and the structures of professions attract a special sort of person. There is a natural selection of characteristics that equip people for the work. In particular, theoretically grounded and service-oriented occupations attract more than the average number of the intellectuals and altruists. If this consequence were not observed, we would have to question our understanding the nature of the work.

Some personal qualities are specific to each profession. One expects a different sort of person to be attracted to the person-oriented activities of the attorney, teacher, or social worker, than to the project-oriented activities of the engineer, architect, or accountant, and to activities that combine the two such as those of the physician, military officer, or business manager.

On a higher plane of abstraction, some qualities are shared by professionals of all sorts by virtue of common characteristics of their work. We will only consider a few examples of these to establish that the typical professional is a superior type of person worthy of the respect and status that are his or her reward.

The professional must possess special intellectual abilities such as the power of abstract thought, to grasp the theoretical foundations of the discipline; intuitive perception to see problems and possible solutions in concrete situations; and practical reason and the skillful manipulation of materials characteristic of the artist, to apply that knowledge and insight to the actual solution of problems. We expect professionals to take a greater interest in their work than blue- and white-collar workers because of the mesh between them and its characteristics.

Some basic moral qualities are essential to the professional. In a very useful analysis, Bayles refers to these as standards of virtue and vice.[29] He argues that the primary bond between professional and client is fiduciary, hence, the standards define "a good and trustworthy professional." While Bayles proposes the standards as norms rather than as a description of actual professionals, the mildness of his criticisms indicated that he thinks they are generally observed.

Bayles's selection of virtues is determined by his use of them to justify principles of professional conduct as he follows clues provided by provisions of professional codes—the codes reflect and hence reveal the kind of persons professionals think themselves to be. The virtues that Bayles discusses are honesty, candor, competence, diligence, loyalty, and discretion. A professional needs tenacity and self-discipline to meet the arduous technical and practical demands of the work and a firm set of values and humane spirit to discharge the duties in practice. While altruism is not a necessary condition for expert work, we are able to trust the occasional selfish professional because he or she works within a social network of ethical persons. We expect most professionals to be idealistic, dedicated to human welfare, and ready to defer private gratification to serve others, in contrast to business people and skilled laborers.

Professionals by and large are well compensated, though the wages of some, such as teachers, social workers, and librarians, lag because of a disadvantaged bargaining position, and others, such as engineers and attorneys, because of an oversupply of practitioners. The generalization holds, nevertheless, that professionals are compensated handsomely. This is especially true when we include not only money and perquisites, but autonomy, influence over others, prestige, symbolic gratification, and interesting work.

High compensation is justified on several grounds. It is simple justice to reward exceptional ability, effort, and service. Professionals need special resources to do their work, both equipment and trappings that nourish the respect of their clienteles. Handsome rewards are necessary to attract able recruits to arduous disciplines.

Professionals are paid a lot and deserve what they are paid. Nevertheless, they do not practice their profession *for* the pay. They are fascinated with the work and desire fervently to help others. The professions are structured to attract such people and utilize them for the public good. They base their claim to status on this structure. Handsome compensation, high status, and power are merely a means to an end. Hughes attributes to Marshall the definition of professions as "Those occupations in which *caveat emptor* cannot be allowed to prevail and which, while they are not pursued for gain, must bring their practitioners income of such a level that they will be respected and such a manner of living that they may pursue the life of the mind."[30]

Marshall does not say that he believes this, but he reports it as a view that is widely held: "The professional man, it has been said, does not work in order to be paid: he is paid in order that he may work. Every decision he takes in the course of his career is based on his sense of what is right, not on his estimate of what is profitable."[31]

Cogan reports that this view receives the sanction of court opinion. A judge declares, "A profession is not a money getting business. It has no element of commercialism in it. True, the professional man seeks to live by what he earns, but his main purpose and desire is to be of service to those who seek his aid and to the community of which he is a necessary part."[32]

Professions are structured to attract trustworthy people dedicated to public service and the life of the mind and they provide a hospitable environment for those qualities. They exploit them with maximum efficiency to enhance human welfare.

Cogan's definition of profession will serve to tie up the threads pulled loose in exploring the functionalist idea of profession.

> A profession is a vocation whose practice is founded upon an understanding of the theoretical structure of some department of learning or science, and upon the abilities accompanying such understanding. This understanding and these abilities are applied to the vital practical affairs of man. The practices of the profession are modified by knowledge of a generalized nature and by the accumulated wisdom and experience of mankind, which serve to correct the errors of specialism. The profession, in service to the vital needs of man, considers its first ethical imperative to be altruistic service to the client. [33]

Bravo!

Notes

1. These are singled out by Rueschemeyer in "Doctors and Lawyers," p. 17. He ascribes this view to a number of prominent authors such as Carr-Saunders and Wilson, Hughes, Parsons, Marshall, Goode, and Merton. He argues that further features attributed to professions by functionalists are dependent on this one.

2. *The Professions*, p. 3.

3. "The Professions and Social Structure," *Essays in Sociological Theory*, p. 38.

4. *Ibid.*, p. 38.

5. "Encroachment, Charlatanism, and the Emerging Professions," p. 903.

6. "Remarks on Education and the Professions," p. 365. See also p. 369.

7. "The Professions and Social Structure," *Essays in Sociological Theory*, pp. 45–46.

8. "Some Problems in Sociology of the Professions," p. 19.

9. "Professionalism and the Individual," pp. 62–63 and 65.

10. "Remarks on Education and the Professions," pp. 365–366. This idea is taken up and emphasized by Greenwood in his influential paper, "Attributes of a Profession," p. 46.

11. "The Professions and Social Structure," *Essays in Sociological Theory*, p. 37. In this paper, Parson maintains that the norm of rationality is observed in occupations other than professions, and he recognizes that some professions are not particularly scientific. Nonetheless, he identifies rationality as a prominent feature of professionalism and implies that the model of science is an important influence on the way rationality is conceived.

12. See Hughes, "Professions," *The Sociological Eye*, p. 374.

13. *Engineers Council for Professional Development 47th Annual Report*, p. 56.

14. See Hughes, "The Making of a Physician," *The Sociological Eye*, p. 405.

15. Hughes, "The Study of Occupations," *ibid.* p. 295.

16. Promulgated by the Engineers Council for Professional Development. See Clapp, *Professional Ethics and Insignia*, pp. 249 and 250.

17. "Professions," *The Sociological Eye*," p. 375.

18. *Ibid.*, p. 381.

19. "Some Problems in The Sociology of the Professions," *The Professions in America*, pp. 19–20.

20. *Ibid.*, p. 20.

21. "Professions," *The Sociological Eye*, pp. 379–380.

22. "Remarks on Education and the Professions," p. 366.

23. Ulich, *Crisis and Hope in American Education*, quoted by Cogan, "Toward a Definition of Profession," p. 46.

24. "Some Problems in the Sociology of the Professions," p. 21. See Parsons, "Remarks on Education and the Professions," pp. 366–367. Barber notes that the faculties of the professional schools, acting through professional associations, often take the lead in the profession's self-criticism and moral reflection. They are in a special position both in that they have occasion in their work to reflect more often on standards and they are removed from the commitment to external organizations and interests typical of the practicing professional.

25. "The Recent History of Professionalism," pp. 328 and 329.

26. *Ibid.*

27. "Community within a Community" p. 194.

28. *Ibid.*, pp. 196 and 198.

29. *Professional Ethics*. Bayles introduces the idea of standards of virtue to

justify principles of conduct on pp. 21–23, the fiduciary bond on pp. 68–70, and the six virtues on pp. 70–85.

30. "The Professions in Society," *The Sociological Eye*, p. 364. Marshall in "The Recent History of Professionalism" is in fact making an opposite point, that this is an image that professionals have been hard pressed to sustain in the modern world and they have had to seek other ways to justify their claim to status and compensation. See also McIver, "The Social Significance of Professional Ethics," p. 7.

31. "The Recent History of Professionalism." He remarks, "That, at least, is the impression [the professional] would like to create when defending his claims to superior status."

32. "Toward a Definition of Profession", quoting from State Ex. Rel. Steiner v. *Yelle*, 25, p. 2d. 91, 174 Wash. 402 (1933).

33. "Toward a Definition of Profession."

☐ 6

THE CLOAK OF IDEOLOGY

The reader will have sensed the reek of apology, the miasma of
moral complacency, hovering over the functionalist model. In
explicating the model, we have not allowed ourselves to be tram-
melled by critical scruples. We have taken the professions of the
professions at face value and constructed the most sympathetic
picture we could of their processes and practices. The aim was to
set forth the typification that is most pleasing to the professions
and persuasive to their patrons, dressed in the most impressive
accoutrements of social science.

The keystone of the functionalist model is the claim that
professions are oriented to public service. Viewed from the conflict perspective, they are seen instead to be organized interest
groups seeking scarce social goods such as wealth, prestige,
power, and autonomy. They do so by making their expertise
available to those able to provide the goods rather than to humanity at large. Professionalism reinforces the social system whatever
it may be. If it is hierarchical, the professions abet the exploitation of the lower strata, providing only minimal service to replenish their ranks and quiet social unrest. The main service is to the
upper strata, to help them achieve their aims whatever the cost.

If there is truth to this picture, conflict theory must explain
how professions acquired this role and how they play it. It must
also explain the plausibility of the functionalist picture despite
its distortions. Some of the facts alleged in the functionalist
picture are false, but all cannot be. Conflict theory must show
how true facts can be used to convey a false picture.

The conflict account of the rise of the professions will be

reviewed briefly, especially the role of what it calls the professional ideology. Then we will consider its criticisms of the
ideology. The conflict thesis is that the functionalist sociologists
borrow heavily from the popular form of the professional ideology
and return their own model to interest groups for ideological use.
We shall evaluate the charge and attempt to form a balanced view
of ideology and reality.

History of Professionalization

Conflict theorists argue that we must examine how professions
evolve in order to understand their role in society. We must focus
on the longitudinal process of professionalization rather than a
latitudinal cross-section of properties at a given moment. Johnson
goes so far as to decry "the sterility of definition mongering" of
the authors considered in the prior chapter,[1] but we should
recognize the need to pin down the professional terminology and,
in any event, conflict theorists produce typifications of their own.
It is not the use of definitions but the neglect of history that is to
be decried.

The historical account here is a capsulation of Larson's very
complex one in *The Rise of Professionalism*.[2] Professionalization
is the organization of an occupation into the form assumed by
paradigm professions, such as medicine, the law, and architecture, in pursuit of what Larson labels "the professional project."
The professional project is the effort by an occupational group to
organize itself to gain a monopoly over a service and control of
the market so as to develop a demand for the service in the form
it provides. The aim is collective conquest of status.[3]

In the professional project, an occupational group has two
"resource elements" available, organizational and ideological.[4] It
must adopt forms of organization that will work and ideas that
will be persuasive in the society of the day. To understand how
both organization and ideas have evolved, we must recognize two
phases in the history of professionalism. In the first, a few
occupations gained a monopoly in a largely entrepreneurial market. Most practitioners were self-employed and served individual
patrons on a fee basis. Professional organizations were independent of economic and political institutions. In the second phase, a
large number of occupations tried to follow the lead of the
established professions. Since a corporate society was evolving,

most of the new professionals were employed on a salaried basis by large organizations and professional institutions became interlocked with others in society.

In the eighteenth and nineteenth centuries, a few occupations developed the features which we now associate with full-blown professions. These notably included the "learned" professions of law, medicine, the ministry, and architecture. In struggling to attain recognition and drive rivals from the market place, they (excepting the ministry) organized associations that set standards, controlled entry into the group, sponsored schools and standardized training, regulated practice, and sought to improve their image before their patrons and the public.

It was impossible and undesirable for professions to view themselves in a way different from that in which they represented themselves to the public. Functional and moral considerations coalesced with public relations to reinforce an idealized presentation of the professional self not only to society but to the professionals themselves. In the course of time, the professions measured up to some of the ideals that they professed. They settled for less in respect to other ideals and a chronic discrepancy between ideal and actual practices settled in. This discrepancy accounts for the recurrent disillusionment generation after generation of people who enter professions and find out what they are really like.

The establishment of the first professions brought them an elevated socioeconomic status, which aroused the envy of other occupations. Status and privilege were coveted. Mobilization to conquer markets was emulated. The drive to professionalize engulfed a widening circle of occupations (nursing, engineering, penology, business management, etc.). New occupations were generated by mitosis from prior ones (anesthesiology, nuclear engineering, tax law) or created *ab ovo* in accord with the professional model (psychoanalysis, data processing, ecological engineering).

Professionalization is connected with the progress of knowledge.[5] With the scientific, technological, and industrial revolutions, the process accelerated exponentially. It is reinforced by and reinforces social mobility for individuals, occupations, and for individuals through their occupations. People find that they can move to higher socioeconomic positions than their parents by entering prestigious occupations, and occupations find that they can enhance the status of their members by moving to higher positions in the occupational hierarchy. Huge numbers of individuals in modern times, therefore, have acquired a stake in professionalization. Self-interest and loyalty to the group conspire to generate a strong pressure for professionalization and push the professional project forward pell-mell.

To gain some sense of the difficulty that claimants for the title of profession face, consider Barber's description of the initial efforts taken by elites of "marginal" professions. These individuals themselves may be clearly professional by current standards while the heterogeneous group with which they are affiliated remains marginally professional. Such elites typically (1) excuse inadequacies of their group by pointing to the early stages of the established professions; (2) publish vague codes of ethics, unenforced by effective machinery; (3) attempt to develop professional associations similar to those of established professions; (4) invent titles such as "fellow" to dignify their work and promote public licensure to promote professional behavior; (5) fight for a place in university curricula and the legitimation that this brings; (6) undertake a campaign of public relations through whatever quasiprofessional organizations are available; and (7) stigmatize rival groups offering competitive services as "quacks" or "charlatans."[6]

Naturally, such efforts are resisted. Established professionals are jealous of their title and a skeptical public is restive at being asked to defer to so many "professional" judgments. They are prone to measure newcomers by standards of an idealized image of professions that is unrealistic in many respects. When conformity to these standards proves impossible, as it must, two routes are open. The aspiring occupation may simulate properties that it does not possess, for example, drawing up a code of ethics that is operationally ineffectual, winning a place in the university, inventing a jargon to embellish commonsense concepts and dignify claptrap that passes as research. These obfuscations have not received much attention in social science, but at least one sociologist shares the impression that they are common.

> Since symbols may hide the absence of reality, and the manipulation of symbols is often easier than the changing of actual organizations and behavior patterns, it is scarcely surprising that a considerable part of the observed behavior of organized technical occupations consists in the conscientious manipulation of symbols. One can

almost envision the process of self-authentication by an occupation group: Service orientation? Provided in our adopted code. High admissions standards? We have achieved a university curriculum. Autonomy? Well, in our salaried position we do the best we can.[7]

The second way for an occupational group to legitimate itself is to modify the concept of professionalism in subtle ways, exaggerating the importance of the properties it does possess and minimizing those it does not. Engineering claims to be a true profession by emphasizing the utilization of highly theoretical knowledge. Social work emphasizes its intimate involvement in the personal lives of clients; and librarianship, its tight organization and credentialing.

Ideology

Before examining the content of the ideology that has arisen with professionalization, let us look at the concept of professional ideology. The term is used freely by occupational sociologists, but none provides an adequate definition. The term presumably is borrowed from the political sphere. We will consider how the political concept is adapted to the present use.

A political ideology is a body of ideas to which a group appeals in its effort to gain or retain control of institutions of the state in order to change or preserve a certain social order. The fundamental nature of the aim, to shape an entire society, explains why political activists are prone to propagate comprehensive world views or what Plamenatz calls "total ideologies"[8] to justify their program of action.

Some conceptions of ideology include or logically entail the notion that its ideas are false, wicked, or misleading. This seems to be taken for granted by critics of professionalism such as Larson, Johnson, and Collins. We must guard against the assumption that an idea is false because it is ideological or that ideologies are false in toto. Indeed they cannot be. They must contain moral norms, some factual truth, and a degree of rational coherence to be effective.[9] Nevertheless, misrepresentations of reality inevitably creep in because of the role of ideologies in the struggle for power of large and diverse groups of people. What makes ideas ideological is their orientation to action. Truth is pushed into an instrumental role. It is sometimes useful, so some ideology is true. Falsity is sometimes useful, so some ideology is false.

Plamenatz makes these points with considerable force. In discussing the social uses of claims about reality, he explained,

> They serve to describe and to explain, and they serve also to justify and encourage behavior, or to condemn and discourage it, or to express hopes and other feelings, or to allay fears. The first function is often called *descriptive* and the second *persuasive*. Clearly, the same beliefs or theories can serve both functions—which makes it only the more important to distinguish between them. Beliefs and theories that are against the evidence or are unverifiable or are not examined critically do come to be accepted, often widely and ardently, because they are persuasive.[10]

His point is that persuasion on a mass scale is not always served by the rational virtues of clarity, precision, accuracy, candor, objectivity, and coherence. On the other hand, neither is it always served by the corresponding vices. Truth is often useful. Plamenatz insists that for beliefs to be ideological,

> they must be shared by a group of people, they must concern matters important to the group, and must in some way be functional in relation to it; they must serve to hold it together or to justify activities and attitudes characteristic of its members.[11]

The distinctions between description and persuasion, and truth and function, are valuable. Hence, we will not define ideology in terms of falsity or deception. Under our concept, it will be a matter of contingent fact whether a given ideological claim is true or false, and the burden of demonstration will be on those who claim that it is false.

The tension between demands of rationality and persuasiveness typically generates multiple versions of any ideology, notably, unsophisticated and sophisticated versions (Plamenatz) and operative and argumentative versions (Seliger). The versions that are operative in group praxis tend to be unsophisticated, certainly at the outset and to some extent even after long use. Sophisticated versions systematize theses from unsophisticated ideologies. The debates of intellectual ideologues not only make explicit presuppositions of unsophisticated ideologies; they add to and modify them. They feed new ideas into the operative ideology of the group and make it more complex and sophisticated. They contribute intellectual authority to a diffuse family of ideas.

The last point to be made is that there is a limit to the rational coherence that can be imposed on operative ideologies no matter how well developed and sophisticated their argumentative counterparts become. Ideologies are and can be only partially designed. Ideologists must make the best of available popular prejudices and traditions, since their ultimate aim is persuasion. In turn, no matter how close they come to presenting a true picture of reality they cannot control the way their ideas are taken by those who act on them. Hence, no matter how well designed argumentative ideologies may be, operative ideologies are subject to all sorts of adventitious influences and internal incoherences. We shall find that the historical origins and destinies of professional ideologies condemn them to remain loose assemblages of inconsistent ideas, despite the efforts of sympathetic social scientists to purify and systematize them.

Plamenatz suggests that ideology holds a group together and justifies the activities and attitudes characteristic of its members. Parsons makes the same point.

> An ideology . . . is a system of beliefs, held in common by the members of a collectivity, i.e., a society, or a sub-collectivity of one—including a movement deviant from the main culture of the society—a system of ideas which is oriented to the evaluative integration of the collectivity and of the situation in which it is placed, the processes by which it has developed to its given state, the goals to which its members are collectively oriented, and their relation to the future course of events.[12]

This makes clear that an ideology must be shared, it must contain factual and normative beliefs (typically about the nature, situation, origins, and destiny of the group) and these must bind the group together for group action. I should add that the beliefs must be proposed to outsiders to justify the claims of the group and recruit new members. These functions shape the content of the ideology.

Professional Ideology

Elliott observes that the term 'professional ideology' has been used for three different things.[13] The first is to represent ideas used by the profession to justify itself in "a situation of possible conflict with outsiders." Second, the term "has also been used in the study of professions to refer to belief systems developed within the profession through which the practitioners make sense of their work experiences." These may be the same ideas as in the first use. Jamous and Peloille point out that professionals must develop a self-conception that is not so discordant with their public image as to prevent them from projecting the latter sincerely and defending their way of practice against external or internal pressures to change.[14] The occupational group usually believes what it preaches. It uses the same ideas to guide its own activities and justify them to outsiders.

Elliott observes that some authors refer to the paradigm (in Kuhn's sense) under which a profession operates at a given time as its "ideology." This third use refers to the concepts in terms of which the group understands its subject matter, as distinguished from those in terms of which it understands and represents its activities in dealing with the subject matter, and hence is a distinct set of ideas. Those who maintain that ideologies always distort truth for pragmatic ends could well investigate whether this is the case for the third sense. Do doctors, for example, conceive of disease in a way that maximizes their role in dealing with it? Do lawyers analogously conceive justice, engineers efficiency, and psychiatrists neurosis? This possibility is appealing intuitively, but it leads into uncertain thickets of speculation.

Concentrating on ideology proper, we shall conceive of a professional ideology as a set of beliefs and claims, both normative and factual, employed by an occupational group to win or preserve its status as profession by interpreting and justifying its practices to its own members and others in society. The historical context determines the content of these beliefs.

In Plamenatz's terms, professional ideologies are partial in contrast to political ideologies.[15] Not even total ideologies extend to all of the activities of life; they dictate what should be done only in some, albeit important and recurrent, situations. They are total in the sense that they justify efforts to affect the entire social system. Partial ideologies likewise dictate what should be done in special situations, and they are directed toward a more limited goal—in the case of professional ideologies toward winning a position for a fraction of society in the existing social order. Professional ideologies seek to shape the social system only to the extent of making space for the particular profession.

It generally is in the interest of the profession, in fact, to preserve the remainder of the system as it is.

Professional ideologies typically propound beliefs that pertain directly to the nature and circumstances of the work. They are vague or silent about economics and politics, not to mention religion and other philosophical matters. They are designed not to run afoul of the total ideologies that divide members of the occupation from each other or from their patrons. This is not to say that physicians or lawyers, for example, are not attracted to a particular total ideology or that they practice their profession in a way that does not reflect a total ideology or that their personal conceptions of their profession are not developed under the influence of total ideology. However, the connections between professional and total ideology are indirect and concealed. The efficacy of professional ideology is enhanced by remaining silent on broader questions. This incidentally allows a profession to flourish in different social systems and accommodate itself to changes in a given system without cutting its ideological roots.

Though I have contrasted professional and political ideologies, I do not mean to suggest that professional ideologies have no political dimension in a broad sense of "politics." Hughes notes that this dimension comes to the fore when external critics demand a change in activities for which a profession has a mandate, for example, in public attempts to reform the distribution of health care.[16]

A fiction of political neutrality is nourished by the silence of professional ideologies on matters of social philosophy, but silence is not inertia. Cogan lists the sorts of political functions that typically devolve on professional associations:

> Once a profession has become an organization united by common purposes, there seems almost inevitably to accrue to it some political power. Professional associations have assumed at least three political roles: (1) they act as a bloc of persons possessing the power of the vote; (2) or they may attract to themselves political power in those areas where governmental agencies have not actually assumed it or have allowed it to lapse—a kind of associational absorption of some residual governmental powers; (3) or they may achieve statutory recognition as agencies to which regulatory powers have been delegated.[17]

The professional association exercises quasigovernmental functions and exerts pressure as a political action group to get its way with legislatures and governmental agencies. The government turns to the association for advice in drawing up and administering legislation. Individual professionals serve as full-time employees and sometime consultants of government, representing the point of view of their profession.

The political activities of a profession tend to be conservative. Their primary aim is to win a place for their group in the hierarchy of the given social order not to change the order in a fundamental way. The rationale for political action to promote the group's interests within the system presupposes an acquiescence to the system. Criticisms of the social system in the interest of more effective service to human welfare are muted.

Professional Ideologies and Subjective Illusions

We perceive objects in meaningful patterns. What we see or take that we see is determined by the pattern in which we see it. The pattern in turn is a function not only of the objects in the surroundings, but of the conceptual framework we apply to the particular experience, as was suggested in Chapter 4. This feature of perception has been described as the "theory-ladenness of observation," the "impregnation of perception by concepts," and "the structuring of experience by presuppositions." The term 'presuppositions' is apt in that conceptual frameworks contain not only categories by which we classify objects, but cognitive and normative judgments in terms of which we deal with them. Calling interpretive concepts presuppositions rather than theories acknowledges the fact that their role in perception usually is unconscious and inarticulate. Their efficacy depends on this if they are prejudices and biases. However, they can be articulated, criticized, and reconstructed. They then become rational assumptions.

Conceptual frameworks are shaped by culture and reinforced by their acceptance by others. Through a shared framework, a group of people inhabits a common life-world and act as a community. Frameworks may be accepted unquestioningly, but they change under the impact of historical accident, cultural exchange, critical reflection, and other influences. They normally evolve over time and this mutability opens the way for groups in a society to shape parts of them pursuant to their own purposes.

The influence of conceptual frameworks on human life are especially dramatic in the social sphere. Culture equips people with taken-for-granted concepts in terms of which they understand themselves and others and decide now to interact with each other. These concepts constitute what has been called their "construction of social reality." It is their picture of social reality and controls their implementation of the picture in action: The construction controls the social reality people create through action. Because people absorb most of their construct from their group, we may speak of the *social* construction of social reality, though the construction is accomplished subjectively by the individuals involved.

An important function of the social construct is the legitimation of institutions. Institutions are objective realities with which individuals must come to terms. The perpetuation of institutions requires an understanding and acceptance of them by new role occupants.

> The transmission of the meaning of an institution is based on the social recognition of that institution as a "permanent" solution to a "permanent" problem of the given collectivity. Therefore, potential actors of institutionalized actions must be *systematically* acquainted with these meanings. This necessitates some kind of "educational" process. The institutional meanings must be impressed powerfully and unforgettably upon the consciousness of the individual.[18]

This process includes a cognitive and normative element: Individuals are taught what the institution is and why it exists. "Legitimation is this process of 'explaining' and justifying."[19]

Needless to say, legitimations may be false. Individuals may be misled about the nature of an institution and the values it produces. Deception may be functional. Mystification may induce individuals to play specific roles in an institution.

What is proposed here is the thesis that professional ideology is a part of the social construction of reality, specifically, a part promoted by occupational groups to legitimate their work as socially sanctioned institutions. The ideology is purveyed to members of the profession and to outsiders and becomes a significant part of the conceptual framework of all who buy into it.

Tying the concept of ideology to that of conceptual frameworks calls attention to the fact that to work an ideology must permeate the subjectivity of individuals. By definition, an ideology is efficacious in group action, and to be efficacious, it must determine the way individuals view reality. Falsehoods in ideologies must become illusions of individuals.

Sources of Content for Professional Ideology

Larson provides the only extensive account of the professional ideology and her account is scattered in fragments throughout her work. What follows is my reconstruction of that account.

A group's aim in the professional project is to win a place in the hierarchy of occupations, not to alter the economic system, "although professionalization may be seen as 'a power struggle, on a societal level,' it is a struggle waged within the same class, against rival occupations, rather than across class lines."[20] The utility of particular ideas in this project consequently depends on their harmony with widely accepted beliefs and values. Now, the ideology of the dominant class is the dominant ideology of a society because it is foisted on all members, including those disadvantaged by it. It becomes their construction of social reality and, to the extent that it is false, their shared illusion. "The ideology of the rising or ruling class is dominant precisely because it is *shared* by the dominated. Working through the 'subjective illusion,' it finds *material* existence in the institutions, relations, and symbols of social practice."[21]

The professional ideology thus is parasitic on the prevailing ideology of society. This is part and parcel of the determination of all aspects of professionalism by existing and emerging social structures. The elements emphasized by Larson are the market economy, first in the competitive and then in the corporate form of capitalism; urbanization; the organizational revolution and "rationalization" of production; a new social stratification with new warrants of status; and a new system of education. All of these elements are characterized by "bourgeois hegemony" led by the "industrial bourgeoisie."[22] Larson states, in her inimitable argot,

> As it rises, an occupation must form "organic ties" with significant fractions of the ruling class (or of a rising class); persuasion and

justification depends on ideological resources, the import and legitimacy of which are ultimately defined by the context of hegemonic power in a class society; special bodies of experts are entrusted with the task of defining a segment of social reality, but this trust is also to be understood within the broad confines of the dominant ideology.[23]

This explains why the postulates of bourgeois ideology are "necessarily at the center of the ideology of profession."[24]

Reference to "organic ties" with the ruling class implies that the relations between the bourgeois and professional ideologies is a reciprocal one. The latter contributes to the former—and professionalism contributes to bourgeois hegemony—as much as the reverse. The way in which it does is somewhat complex. When they adapt the bourgeois ideology, the professions specify and add to its content. Furthermore, since professions are life-long careers requiring adherence to a life-plan in the framework of stable institutions, professionals have a strong incentive to support existing institutions. "The expectation of career is . . . a powerful factor of conformity with the existing social order and a source of basic conservatism."[25]

The bourgeois ideology is an important instrument for perpetuating the bourgeois social order by legitimating that order and shaping the construction of social reality by the members of society. It is to the interest of professionals, therefore, to promulgate the general bourgeois ideology and the particularized form of it expressed in their own ideology. In so doing, they reinforce bourgeois hegemony.

This is not primarily by preachment or propaganda. Professionals propagate the bourgeois ideology by their visible example and the attitudes they communicate to clients, employers, and the public.

What is particularly significant in their role is that the superior badges of ability which they carry do not remain hidden within ruling-class circles or small intellectual coteries; they do not even remain circumscribed to the "magic circle" of elite universities: the professions carry the symbols of the new meritocratic ideology to the hospitals, to the public schools, to the factories, to the government agencies, to the everyday life of a majority of men, women, and children. Professionals do the helping, the judging, the advising. They have the jobs that seem useful, that could be helpful, that allow an expression of the self.[26]

The Bourgeois Ideology

What are the "postulates of bourgeois ideology?" To simplify Larson's simplified account, they are (with her labels):[27]

1. Individuals are proprietors of their own persons and abilities, for which they owe nothing to society (atomistic individualism).

2. All have the natural right to property, which they acquire through their own efforts, and to utilize their abilities and property as they see fit (egalitarianism).

3. Civil society is a rational contrivance of free individuals to protect their natural rights (the doctrine of the impartial state); therefore, it is democratic (democratic liberalism).

4. The major institution to be protected by the state is the free market, in which exchange relations obtain for all areas of human activity and what is exchanged is equivalent in value (*laissez-faire* capitalism).

5. Individuals are the best judge of their own interests if they are educated; hence, all enjoy educational opportunity (utilitarianism).

6. Classes in the strict sense do not exist, but inequalities of wealth and competence develop; these are legitimate, since people differ in natural ability and effort and, as a consequence, in education and success in the market ("the old liberal ideology of individual effort and rewarded hard work").

7. Those who excel not only enjoy greater privileges, but are entitled to make decisions for society in their areas of competence (the ideology of expertise, the technocratic ideology), decisions that others should accept (democratic elitism—in the words of Bachrach, democracy is "dependent upon the ability of the gifted to command the deference of the many for the well-being of all"[28]).

8. Expert decisions rationalize social processes, extending the efficiency and disinterestness of science to human affairs (the ideology of efficiency and objectivity).

One major internal shift in the bourgeois ideology should be noted. In the passage from competitive to corporate capitalism, articles (7) and (8) of the creed come to the fore and the doctrines of equal opportunity and individual achievement are construed in terms of advancement in bureaucratic organizations rather than entrepreneurial success in the open market.

The bourgeois ideology is presented by adherents as a description of the essential nature of capitalist society, though when faced with grossly contradictory facts, they retreat to the claim that the postulates are ideals. Ideologues still defend their validity as ideals and maintain that they are in the course of being realized. The flourishing of professionalism contributes to the illusion that this is so.

Occupations engaged in the professional project had to adapt the postulates of the bourgeois ideology to a somewhat different market situation than faced those created the ideology, that is, those who control capital and produce commodities. In conquering a market, professionals did not have the means at the disposal of the capitalists.

> The industrial bourgeoisie had relied, in its rise, on state protectionism and on direct coercion by the state against the proletariat and other categories of the poor. Only after its triumph did the bourgeoisie mobilize for the ideological conquest of the proletariat and the establishment of hegemony. But direct coercion does not make any sense in the conquest of a market that is essentially constituted by ideological definitions. Nor, on the other hand, could professions, as a minor sector of the rising class, mobilize the necessary coercive powers. In other words, their rise depended most crucially on ideological persuasion.[29]

Their primary problem was to effect an "ideological definition" of their product; that is, to persuade consumers they needed services in the form that the profession was equipped to provide them. Since the professions claimed that the nature of their work make professionals the only qualified judges of competence, they had to win the trust of consumers (clients and, later, employers) in both their skill and their good intentions, in the face of a natural suspicion toward their monopolistic aims.[30]

Larson believes that the resources in bourgeois ideology were not sufficient for this purpose. The professions were forced to utilize ideas from the ideology of the old order that was being subverted and that tried to defend itself by antimarket ideas that retained a hold on public consciousness. The major antimarket principles that Larson identifies as precapitalist "residues" in professional ideology are as follows (again with her labels):[31]

1. Work has an intrinsic value apart from the capital that it accumulates and other external rewards (the ideal of craftsmanship).

2. The primary objective of work is service to the entire community not to special classes or individuals (the notion of gentlemanly disinterestedness).

3. A true community is organic and establishes indissoluble moral ties among its members.

4. High rank imposes special duties as well as special rights (noblesse oblige).

Thus, according to Larson, the professional ideology fuses market and antimarket principles.

The Content of Professional Ideology

Larson's analysis of the content of professional ideology is scattered through an extensive and detailed historical study and not always is explicit. The following presentation is my interpretation of her interpretation. I have organized the elements of the ideology as she construes it around three themes of the functionalist model. The themes are that the aim of professions is service; that the superior quality of the work warrants a high social, economic, and political position; and that a professional group comprise autonomous, morally responsible communities of free agents.[32]

1. The Service Orientation: The ideology maintains that professionals adhere to the ideal of service to all of humanity. They are not affiliated with any social class or elite, but they retain the gentlemanly disinterestedness of the old nobility. They have a distaste for commerce. They serve anyone in need regardless of monetary reward or the status of the client. In a market society, they have to earn their living, but it is for humanitarian motives that they offer their services. They provide for those less able to pay by the graduated-fee system, pro bono publico activities, and the public-welfare measures of the state.

Larson referred to the organization of professions to standardize services and exchange them for a price as the "objectification of skill" through quantification (treating services as created exchange-values) and universalization (making them available to everyone).

The ideology of service adapts the antimarket principles of disinterestedness and noblesse oblige to the bourgeois ideology of the free market and classless society and the more recent ideology of expertise, technology, and rationalization of human processes.

2. *Superior Quality of the Work:* The concept of noblesse oblige incorporates not only the "oblige" of service, but a self-judgment of "noblesse." Professionals are united in a sense of the nobility of their work as compared to manual labor. The work is superior both in its value to the consumer and in the level of skill it involves. Professional skills require superior intelligence and resolve.

The use-value of professional services is reflected in their price or exchange-value, which in turn is a function of the amount and quality of professional education and the labor-time required during education to produce professional skills. (The equation, use-value = exchange-value = length of education = labor-time required to produce professional skills is used to justify the high cost of professional services.)

The idea of superior quality of professional work adapts the antimarket principles of noblesse oblige and the intrinsic value of work to the bourgeois ideology of atomistic individuals deploying their natural abilities to earn a social position in which they control the destiny of others.

3. *The Ideal of Community:* The ideology maintains that the professional is autonomous in his or her work. The opportunity for professional education is open to all who have the ability and dedication to take advantage of it. Hence, the choice of occupation is free, as reflected in the idea of vocation or calling. Professionals also are the final authorities on how their occupation should be practiced, since the character and pace of creative activity cannot be determined by rule or command. The public is guaranteed that the professionals will use their freedom responsibly by the solidarity of professional communities with their corporate definitions of competence and exacting ethical standards. In sum, professions are autonomous communities of autonomous individuals serving human welfare through the conscientious exercise of superior skill and knowledge.

In this last element of the professional ideology, the antimarket principle of the organic community is welded to bourgeois individualism.

Ideology and Social Science

'Ideology' connotes to the conflict theorist a set of distortions used to promote the cause of a group in competition for social goods. Why should functionalist ideas about professions be stigmatized as ideology? Let us break down the indictment to see what has to be proved to make it stick.

The indictment is based on three theses: that elites deliberately create ideologies as a tool in the professional project, that they utilize ideas from the functionalist model, and that the ideas are incorporated in the model because they advance the interests of the occupations.

The first thesis is formulated by Larson in terms of a theory of internal stratification of professions. She sees in each profession an elite and a body of practitioners. The interests of ordinary practitioners will not always be identical with those of the elite or "the profession;" nevertheless, the leaders speak for their members:

> a profession is always defined by its elites: the elites that wield internal power may not be the same that are visible to the outside, especially when the media become the main agents of visibility; but it is always an elite that speaks to relevant outsiders for the "whole profession," maintaining the image of a unified and solidary community, or projecting the achievements and identity of a specialty.[33]

The elites also shape the consciousness of ordinary practitioners. Consequently, practitioners project the same image of professions in interactions with their clients.

Data about who creates the professional ideology and why they do so are hard to come by; but functionalist as well as conflict sociologists testify, as noted earlier, to the self-conscious use of the professional ideology by leaders of contemporary professionalizing occupations. Larson's hermeneutic demonstration of the way professional self-presentations incorporate elements of bourgeois and antimarket ideologies to justify the claims of professions confirms the thesis of ideological intent.

The second thesis, that professional ideology incorporates ideas from the functionalist model, is confirmed quickly by comparing the model with ideas about professions in the public media and the publications, speeches, and personal opinions of members of professions. The explanation of this concordance is to be found in the need of modern ideologies to assume scientistic trappings.

The example of total ideologies is instructive. Plamenatz remarks,

> As classes have grown less exclusive (or, as some may prefer to put it, as estates or castes have made way for classes), class ideologies have become less theological and more social and political. They have also, in general, become more theoretical, that is, more often deliberately produced by professional thinkers or more influenced by such productions.[34]

The aim of an ideology is persuasion and the aim of professional ideologies is to persuade the public of an industrial society that a group should be recognized as a profession to apply a newly developed body of concepts, a science or a theory masquerading as science. To be effective, ideologies must appeal to accepted facts and norms to cast an aura of plausibility over more dubious elements in its claims. The authority of social science provides this aura in a scientistic age.

The third thesis, that the functionalist model is designed to promote the interests of professions, is more serious and more difficult to prove. Sociologists do not benefit directly from the prosperity of the professions, except to the extent that they have established their own group as a profession. If their models are distortions, the distortions are inadvertent and unconscious, because the authors have been bemused by ideology and have accepted the pretensions of the professions uncritically. A number of sociologists recognize this possibility. Hughes, for instance, notes,

> Sociologists, social psychologists, anthropologists, and economists in great number have been invited into the sacred precincts to study changes in the relations of occupations to each other in the great complexes of institutions which have grown up about the major professional services. . . . One danger is that the social scientists will become pundits when dealing with newer professions of less prestige than their own, and that they will over-identify themselves with professions of greater prestige than theirs when such deign to ask them in.[35]

Hughes thinks that fraternization with professions is worth the risk for social scientists, since it gives them access to research data.

From the conflict perspective, fraternization is fatal to claims of truth. Larson charges, "Much of contemporary sociological work on the professions participates in and accepts their ideology." Indeed, she thinks that profession itself is an ideological category, designed to promote the interests of disparate occupations and one of many "natural concepts, fraught with ideology, that social science abstracts from everyday life."[36]

Larson divides intellectual products into two sorts: They "either break with the dominant ideology (by a self-conscious effort of their authors), or remain within its bounds." The former is the exception; the latter, the rule: "the social function of intellectuals is normally that of sub-consciously articulating, propagating, and organizing culture and ideology, giving them internal coherence and realistic flexibility."[37] The functionalist model is a product of the normal function; Larson's critique breaks with the dominant ideology, presumably through a self-conscious effort on the part of its author.

This dichotomy is overly simply. We should not merely assume that any model of professions that is not highly critical of the status quo is designed to defend it or, even if it is, necessarily is false. The best we can do is to evaluate the model itself. The functionalist model serves the interests of the professions, but is it true or is it false?

Notes

1. *Professions and Power*, p. 31.
2. The history of the professions in Britain is described by Carr-Saunders and Wilson in *The Professions* and later by Reader in *Professional Men*. Larson provides the most detailed history for America.
3. *The Rise of Professionalism*, pp. 8, 66, and 105.
4. *Ibid.*, pp. 6, 47, 103, and 208. The concept of ideas and organizational forms as resources illustrates Larson's tendency to think in categories of economics, in keeping with her tendency toward economic determinism.
5. Barber, "Some Problems in the Sociology of the Professions," p. 22.
6. *Ibid.*, pp. 22–24. See Hughes, "Psychology: Science and/or Profession," *The Sociological Eye*, pp. 362–363. Marshall takes the more benign view that subprofessions can improve themselves by such efforts, "The Recent History of Professionalism," p. 338.
7. Moore, *The Professions*, p. 51.

8. *Ideology*, p. 17.

9. Seliger, *Ideology and Politics*, p. 120.

10. *Ideology*, pp. 70–71.

11. *Ibid.*, p. 31.

12. *The Social System*, p. 349.

13. *The Sociology of the Professions*, p. 132.

14. "Professions or Self-Perpetuating Systems?"

15. *Ideology*, pp. 18 and 72.

16. "The Study of Occupations." *The Sociological Eye*, p. 291.

17. "Toward a Definition of Profession," p. 44.

18. Berger and Luckmann, *The Social Construction of Reality*, pp. 69–70.

19. *Ibid.*, p. 93.

20. *The Rise of Professionalism*, p. 157. Larson cites Haug and Sussman, "Professionalism and Unionism," p. 527. See also their "Professional Autonomy and the Revolt of the Client."

21. *The Rise of Professionalism*, p. 239. See pp. 224–225 and 241.

22. *Ibid.*, pp. 9, 10, 50, 104, 127, 134, 147, and 163, where dependence on the larger social structure is emphasized; and pp. 10, 83, and 91, for reference to bourgeois hegemony.

23. *Ibid.*, p. xv, utilizing Gramsci's thoughts with apparent approval.

24. *Ibid.*, p. 221.

25. *Ibid.*, p. 229. Larson utilizes Wilensky's argument in "Work, Careers and Social Integration," p. 555.

26. *Ibid.*, p. 241. See pp. 52, 225, 238, and 243.

27. This list is assembled primarily from *ibid.*, pp. 221–224, where Larson relies heavily on Halevy, *The Growth of Philosophical Radicalism*, and McPherson, *The Political Theory of Progressive Individualism*. She deals with the individual elements of the ideology throughout: individualism (p. 225), egalitarianism (pp. 116, 134), the impartial state (p. 240), laissez-faire market and exchange relations (pp. 117, 209), utilitarian education (p. 119), success through achievement (p. 80, 240), expertise (pp. 140, 142–143, 243), and rationalization of processes (p. 143) via the rationality, objectivity, and efficiency of science (pp. 137, 140–145).

28. *The Theory of Democratic Elitism*, p. 2.

29. *The Rise of Professionalism*, p. 54.

30. *Ibid.*, pp. 6, 20, 22, 48–49, 118, and 149.

31. Summary statement, *ibid.*, p. 220. See also pp. 2, 54, 56–57, 62–63, 66, 81, and 150, and the general discussions in Chapters 5 and 7. I confess that I cannot see clearly the distinction between (2) and (4), so I have redrawn it somewhat.

32. These are discussed briefly at several points in Larson's historical review; e.g., (a) the service orientation: *ibid.*, pp. 9, 49, 56–57, 213, 214, 219, 220–331; (b) quality of the work: pp. xi, 40, 55, 60, 157, 211, 212, 214, 228, 236–237; (c) community: pp. xii, 28, 49, 51–52, 55, 61, 223, 226, 227, 236–237. They are discussed in a summary but not very organized way in Chapter 12 as a whole.

33. *Ibid.*, p. 227.

34. *Ideology*, pp. 106–107.

35. "The Professions in Society," *The Sociological Eye*, p. 369.

36. *The Rise of Professionalism*, pp. 244 and xi. See pp. 49, 80, and 219.

37. *Ibid.*, p. xiv.

☐ 7

THE SUBSCAPULAR REALITY

Typifications are avowed simplifications and idealizations. The functionalist model is proposed as an approximation of actual occupations and an ideal toward which they strive. The criticism of the model is that professions do not approximate it closely enough nor strive hard enough to achieve it for it to be a typification. Instead, it encourages the uncritical spectator to exaggerate the merits of particular occupations by imagining characteristics they do not possess and debasing ideals to fit the characteristics they do have.

This chapter argues that the functionalist model is a justificatory myth. I use 'myth' in its dictionary sense of an ostensibly historical narrative of obscure origin that explains practices, beliefs, and institutions. The term carries over from its theological use[1] the notion that a myth supports mores of a group and reinforces communal life. The pioneers of professionalizing occupations, thus, are mythmakers attempting to build a community, and sociologists are their mythologists.[2]

The Myth of Collectivity Orientation

The *Urmythos* from which all of the myths in the professional mythology spring is that professions are oriented to the service of humanity. Professions avow in their official pronouncements and the functionalist typification endorses the view that professions are oriented to service rather than to profit or the interest of any patron group. Handsome rewards are required to entice recruits, compensate for the cost of education, and provide equipment and trappings for effective practice. It is simple justice that those who serve well should be paid well. But they serve to serve, not to be paid.

In such bald form, protestations of service are easy to ridicule. Parsons and others, however, advance the claim that professions are institutionally directed toward the public good by a reward system that defines success in terms of the welfare of the client. An invisible hand assures that even the most self-seeking professional will take care of his or her clients. This claim is more difficult to refute.

We also have seen that sociologists cite the prominence of symbolic rather than material rewards as evidence of the structural orientation to service on the premise that, to quote Barber, "money income is a more appropriate reward for individual self-interest, and . . . prestige and honors are more appropriate for community interest." The intrinsic intellectual quality of professional work is taken to be further evidence of its contribution to the public good.

The functionalist offers no argument to show that desire for honors motivates one to serve others any more than desire for money or power. The significance of honor depends on what one is honored for, just as the significance of money depends on what one is paid to do and the significance of power depends on what one uses power for. Perhaps desire for honor in preference to money or pleasure reveals an elevated soul but, as Aristotle observes, only if one desires honor as a confirmation of virtue.[3] To say that a desire for professional honors betokens a service orientation begs the question of whether professionals are honored for service. They, like business persons, also may be honored because they are successful; that is, because clients or employers are satisfied with their work. As professionals themselves insist, these are poor judges of the quality of professional work and they also may be indifferent to the professional's service to humanity.

The observer may be more impressed by the honors bestowed by professional associations. Service to a profession transcends self-interest as narrowly defined, like the business person's participation in the Chamber of Commerce, United Fund, and civic boosterism. It is not to denigrate either to point out that selfless service to a group is not service to humanity unless the prosperity of the group benefits humanity. That the group possesses a system of honors does not contribute one whit to proving that it does.

Similar remarks may be made about the putative superior intellectual character and intrinsic interest of professional work. Theory and technique have their fascination. For that very reason they can become ends in themselves. Engineers may be attracted by the challenge of a complex space or weapons program to the neglect of mundane human needs. Physicians may be honored for breakthroughs with complex instrument- and expertise-intensive therapies for esoteric ailments at the expense of attention to more ordinary and widespread hazards to health. The most prestigious and intellectually demanding posts in higher education may bring no significant benefit to any by a small circle of cogniscenti. It is easy to slide from the premise that the more knowledge is brought to bear on a professional task the better it will be performed to the conclusion that the more knowledge a task requires the worthier it is.

Furthermore, the hyperintellectual character of professional work is an illusion. Larson argues that the diversity in the grounds of professional skills reduces their claim to superiority to the purely negative characteristic of being nonproletarian. The commonality among diverse professions lies not in the character of the work but in the structure they have created to achieve a market monopoly and elevated status. Morally speaking, they have seized their position rather than earned it. This is the basis for Larson's claim that 'profession' is an ideological rather than a descriptive category.

The appearance of higher quality is due to credentials of education, power, and income. The impression that these are awarded because of the quality of the work rather than service to powerful patrons reflects a fundamental ideological illusion: "As the masses unconsciously absorb technocratic visions of polity and society, those in power are progressively freer from having to prove special expertise and ability. The ideological relation is then reversed: power and privilege tend to become automatic warrants of superior competence."[4]

The reality is that professions are loose collections of individuals, most of whose responsibilities are little more complex or extensive than those of skilled labor and who are subordinate in their work to nonprofessionals. According to Larson, they are alienated from their work by the disparity between "ideological expectations and work conditions" but pacified by symbols of status. One of these is "mastery over their time" in a condition of "powerless discretion;" that is, they are allowed to decide according to their own schedule the details of technology without determining its goals.[5] The ideology of superior work promotes the interests of elite professionals and deceives ordinary professionals by exaggerating the difference between their work and that of other occupations. It deters them from organizing to promote their own interests in the way of the industrial proletariat *or* to promote human welfare in the way that the myth of community pretends.

Mechanisms of Control

If the professions were to reward service effectively, they first would have to identify and measure it. We shall see later that there is little evidence that peer review and self-evaluation do this effectively. On the other hand, mechanisms of control work with behavior that aggrandizes the group. Traditional self-employed, fee-for-service professions have developed elaborate devices for maintaining income at a high level. These include state licensure and aggressive attack on unauthorized practice, minimum fee schedules and other price-fixing devices, and strictures against contingency fees, competitive bidding, advertising, etc.[6] The involvement of professional associations with these measures is diminishing due to actions of the courts against restraints of trade. But the National Society of Professional Engineers Code of Ethics articulates the attitude of most professionals when it declares that rate-busting is immoral: "Engineers shall uphold the principle of appropriate and adequate compensation for those engaged in engineering work."

Bayles notes that the only significant complaint of professionals against one another before the disciplinary bodies pertains to price-cutting and other forms of "unfair" competition.[7] An indication of the seriousness with which professional associations view this is the attention devoted to them in ethical codes, opinions of ethical review committees, and the like. About 20 percent of the American Bar Association's code deals with economic matters, 40 percent of the Current Opinions of the Judicial Council of the American Medical Association, 40 percent of the American Institute of Certified Public Accountants' code, 50 percent of the Engineers Council for Professional Development's code, and almost all of the Opinions of the Board of Ethical Review of the National Society of Professional Engineers. In fairness, it should be noted that there are provisions in these documents to protect clients and employers and that economic provisions are negligible in codes of groups such as the American Psychological Association, American Nurses Association, and National Association of Social Workers. These latter professions are substantively or ideologically client-oriented, are late on the scene of professions, have not yet fully succeeded in the professional project, and perhaps are responding to the recent court decisions that cause even the ensconced professions to downplay economic strictures in formal codes.

If the primary aim of the professions were service, professionals would be anxious to provide it to everyone regardless of social status or ability to pay. The functionalist model would have us believe that they are. The reader will recall Parsons's concept of specificity of function, which maintains that professionals not only restrict their efforts to areas of the client's life on which they are authorities, but deal with those areas without consideration of the client's personal characteristics. Parsons's claims about the heart specialist, the paradigmatic professional, "the relevant questions do not relate to *who* the patient is but *what* is the matter with him." Specificity of function thus is connected with the alleged disinterestedness of the professional's service to humanity.

Are professionals really indifferent to the ability to pay and characteristics of potential clients such as race or ethnic identity? The question answers itself. The answer is confirmed by the way codes of ethics handle the question—or ignore it. The American Medical Association asserts that while "A physician shall be dedicated to providing competent medical service with compassion and respect for human dignity," he "shall, in the provision of appropriate patient care, except in emergencies, be free to choose whom to serve, with whom to associate, and the environment in which to provide medical services." The AMA condemns excessive fees but it says, "A fee is excessive when after a review of the facts a person knowledgeable as to current charges made by physicians would be left with a definite and firm conviction that the fee is in excess of a reasonable fee." Thus, the patient's ability to pay is not among the facts it considers relevant. Fees charged by other physicians are, implying that no fee is excessive if it is customary.

It is difficult to tell what the American Psychological Association has in mind when it states, "Psychologists make advance financial arrangements that safeguard the best interests of and are clearly understood by their clients." It does state, "They contribute a portion of their services to work for which they receive little or no financial return."

Most codes ignore the matter of the needs of the indigent. They take the position that practice-for-pay is ethically permissable and the size of fee or salary is a contractual matter between professional and client or employer as long as it is appropriate and adequate; that is, high enough to maintain the prosperity of the profession.

The American Bar Association comes closest to attacking the issue of the ability to pay head on. Its discussion is worth quoting at length, since it expresses the *most* that professions are willing to commit themselves to:

> Historically, the need for legal services of those unable to pay reasonable fees has been met in part by lawyers who donated their services or accepted court appointments on behalf of such individuals. The basic responsibility for providing legal services for those unable to pay ultimately rests upon the individual lawyer, and personal involvement in the problems of the disadvantaged can be one of the most rewarding experiences in the life of a lawyer. Every lawyer, regardless of professional prominence or professional workload, should find time to participate in serving the disadvantaged.

The ABA concedes that this obligation imposed on individuals has not been sufficient to solve the problem and cites its supplementary efforts on the corporate level such as legal aid offices and lawyer referral services as further measures to meet the responsibility. Thus, it acknowledges that not everyone is financially able to utilize the services of attorneys, that this is an undesirable state of affairs, and that the profession has an obligation to do something about it. However, the measures it endorses, especially the nonspecific and nonenforceable obligation of pro bono publico work, are not effective.

The ABA's concern is unusual among professions. The National Association of Social Workers is about the only other one that recognizes a responsibility to work for equal distribution of services.

The Archetypal Case

Ethical codes are declarations of intent—suspect in the case of public service, clearly serious in respect to the economic welfare of the profession. Professional associations routinely use the powers at their disposal to advance economic interests. The archetypal example is the opposition of the American Medical Association to health service plans based on prepaid capitation fees, as opposed to cash indemnity plans such as Blue Cross that maintain the principle of fee-for-service set by the physician. Kessel describes these efforts in the course of an examination of the practice of adjusting charges on the basis of patients' ability to pay. This practice is defended as a privately managed charity in which the physician collects involuntary contributions from the rich to provide low-cost services to the poor. The alternative interpretation is that this is a case of an enlightened monopoly charging according to what the traffic will bear. Physicians charge the poor less, since otherwise they would lose their business altogether.[8]

Kessel shows how a wide variety of devices create an in-group of doctors that discourages competition and external evaluation of medical practice at the expense of both competence and economy.[9] These are listed in his summary of the mechanisms of control in the hands of medical associations:

> Available evidence suggests that the primary control instrument of organized medicine is the ability to cut off potential price cutters from the use of resources complementary to doctors' services for producing many classes of medical care. However, techniques other than the withdrawal of staff privileges in hospitals are also employed to maintain discipline in the medical profession. These include *no-criticism rules*, professional courtesy or the free treatment by doctors of other doctors and their families, prohibition of advertising that might reallocate market shares among producers, preventing doctors from testifying against one another in malpractice suits, and the selection of candidates for medical schools and post graduate training in the surgical specialties that have a low probability of being price cutters.[10]

The connection of many of these practices with price discrimination according to ability to pay, minimum fee schedules, discouragement of price competition, etc. is indirect and requires intricate arguments to demonstrate. This is sufficient to ensure that the connection will be concealed not only from the public but from physicians, who slip into the self-serving point of view of their in-group. Indeed, the practices originally may have had a benign purpose, but their continuation amid loud avowals of dedication to human welfare can be explained only by their economic value to the profession and their rationalization through ideological mystification.

The economic practices of other professions approximate those of medicine in proportion to controls available to the professional association. The implication of Kessel's argument is that a profession acts like any monopoly that is shielded from external review. That some professions have not acted as blatantly in self-interest as the American Medical Association reflects limitation of power rather than an effulgence of good will toward humanity.

In summary, professions generally do not recognize an urgent obligation to serve those unable to pay substantial fees. Even when putting their best foot forward ideologically, their pronouncements are evasive and pliable. They are ineffectual in restraining the profit motive in their members. Professions vary in this respect—few rival the rapacity of physicians—but dedication to human welfare sufficient to cause them to make financial sacrifices is not evident.

This is not a wholesale indictment of professionals. They may be less venal on average than nonprofessionals. What we are denying is that professions are *corporately* dedicated to serving humanity at a significant sacrifice to material interests. What evidence there is indicates a disposition to promote their interests by rendering less service than they might. However, this evidence is weak.

A more cautious conclusion is that professions have no collectivity orientation at all. The unity of professions is exaggerated. They are scattered objects in the sense of clusters of individuals with similar characteristics rather than integral wholes whose parts effectively interact with one another. It enhances the prestige of the parts to convey the illusion that they function as a whole. The existence of associations with formal codes that claim to represent "the profession" reinforces the illusion. A true collectivity orientation would require a genuine community with effective mechanisms of control over its members, and this does not exist.

The Myth of Disinterest

In the absence of central control, members of professions fall under the influence of patrons. The structures of the professions give the lie to the idea that professionals are classless and disinterested. The membership of most professions, especially the more prestigious, is dominated by higher socioeconomic groups. Exceptions seek to be accepted by such groups. This is true especially of the elites who speak for the professions.

> The power of the organizational client, the connections with the state, and the prestige of universities are external forces translated into dimensions of centrality and marginality *among* professions and *within* them. Insofar as a profession is itself an organization, however loose, its elites are, precisely, the connecting links with other elites in powerful organizations. . . . Therefore, the general measures of success and power *within* a profession tend to flow, ultimately, from outside, from the central power structure of society.
>
> Hierarchies of success measured by general societal criteria such as income, influence, and power tend to merge *within* a given profession with hierarchies of prestige measured by "peer esteem."[11]

Since the attitudes of the leaders of a profession permeate the consciousness of its members, the entire profession tends to identify with high status groups, adopt their viewpoint, and affirm their position in society. This is reflected in strenuous efforts of professions to establish a social distance from other kinds of work. Indeed, the choice of professionalism rather than unionism as an organizational form reflects this aspiration.[12]

By origin, self-interest, and indoctrination, then, professionals identify themselves and largely are identified by the public with the upper strata of the social hierarchy. It should not be surprising that these are the strata that professionals primarily serve. Contrary to pretense, the professional product is not available equally to all on the open market. Higher quality services are enjoyed by those able to pay for them, and the status of the individual professionals and the entire profession is tied to the status of those whom they serve. This is mitigated, but not eliminated in the welfare state.

> In fact, the use of professional services (including those most "universal" in kind, such as medical services or elementary education) was not extended to the mass public by extension of the market; these services were generalized, rather, by the extension of social-welfare functions. However, even after the development of the welfare state, professional services of a personal kind either continue to be reserved to those who are rich enough to pay, or they tend to be qualitatively different according to the clientele's capacity to pay. The socioeconomic status of the client not only influences the quality of the service, or the nature of the use-value, that a professional provides; it also influences the professional's own status and ranking, most especially in the personal professions.[13]

Service to the higher socioeconomic elements of society is direct and obvious where professionals charge high fees. According to Larson, even social welfare professionals help to perpetuate the class system by contributing to the "reproduction of the work force."[14]

For the traditional professions, the problem of securing an affiliation with the socioeconomic elite was to control self-employed practitioners in their transactions with clients. Newer professions must deal with members who are employed by large organizations. Their efforts at acceptance are directed toward making their members faithful employees who protect trade secrets, refuse bribes, avoid conflicts of interest, and promote the professional development of their fellow employees. References to duties to humanity against the employer are notably vague in their codes. One must suspect that they are mentioned only for ideological effect.

Myths of Work

According to the functionalist model, the substantive, structural, and personal characteristics of a profession enable it to discharge its essential service to humanity with maximum efficiency. If the primary postulate of service is a myth, so are other parts of the model.

1. *Professions meet vital human needs in the most effective practicable way:* The ideological potency of the professional

mythology depends on the kernel of truth in the proposition. Professions provide services related to human needs. Doubtful cases are occupations whose professional status is debatable. What vital human needs are met by professional athletics that could not be met some other way? But then is athletics really a profession?

What may be questioned is the claim to *maximum* practicable effectiveness. Monopolies of expertise and barriers to unauthorized practice are defended in the name of competence, and professional associations, schools, and licensing boards strive to maintain a high level of competence. However, the result falls short of maximum effectiveness in important ways if we conceive effectiveness in terms of human welfare.

A. Professionals have a strong territorial sense. They resist encroachment of other occupations on the turf they have marked off for themselves: Medical doctors combat incursions of nurses, midwives, nutritionists; lawyers, of tax accountants, realtors; engineers, of architects, technicians; etc. This makes for inflexible opposition to organizational innovations that might expand service or lower costs.

B. Professionals have an immoderate estimate of the importance of the particular needs they serve. Little in their ideology or culture tempers it with an appreciation of other needs or the importance of sharing the purchasing power of the public with providers of other services. Professions typically strive to raise the public's estimation of the needs they serve and cultivate its belief that only they can meet those needs adequately.

C. Professions that harm the environment by pollution and use of nonrenewable resources, notably, technological and managerial professions, systematically are geared to serve particular employers with little regard for the public that bears the external costs of production. As long as nature's vast resources and restorative powers allow the human species to abuse the environment without visible or lasting harm, an ideology of service to humanity through service to employer is easy to maintain. The relation of the species to nature in the postindustrial world demands a radical new philosophy to protect human interests against special interests. The professions have not accepted responsibility for reform, and the mechanisms of control through government regulation, consumer resistance, and the like are overloaded.

D. Traditional practices and attitudes, such as fee-for-service, pursuit of the highest available salary, and psychological identification with upper strata of society, guarantee a maldistribution of services. The result of any social audit of the professions would show that the poor and nonelite ethnic groups and, in the case of some professions, women, the young and very old, the handicapped, and residents of rural and inner city areas receive far less medical and psychological care, legal representation, communication services, fiscal and business advice, and (in less direct and obvious ways) benefits of engineering and technology, than do favored groups. The distribution of professional services is unjust as measured by any plausible standard of justice.

The ideal of maximum effectiveness requires a way to identify genuine human needs underlying the flux of desires and preferences, to measure them against one another, and to meet them to the extent that each deserves while leaving room for the remainder. Whether there is any way to approximate this in a market economy and the limits of practicability for doing so in a highly professionalized social system are impossible to determine. The fact stands that the maldistribution of professional services offends the sense of justice and overturns the claim that the professions are organized optimally for human good.

2. *Professional work is disinterested:* The professional solution to the problem of a client or employer is often a matter of objective knowledge. It also is possible for those with the professional attitude to overcome bias to attack problems in a standard way regardless of the identity of the person served. Professionals, once they have accepted responsibility for individuals or groups, may strive to meet objective norms of competence.[15]

However, this sort of disinterestedness is not sufficient to overcome other attitudes and, more important, professionals certainly are not disinterested in the prior acts of choosing clients or employers and deciding the amount of time and effort to devote to their needs.

3. *Professionals confine themselves to determining means to clients' ends:* According to the myth, the authority of professionals is derived from mastery of the portion of science relevant to the problems that bring clients to them. Science teaches means to various ends, but not the ends to pursue. Hence, the professional's function is restricted not only to a certain area of clients' lives, but to the ends that clients already have. Since science is a

body of propositions objectively verified so as to be indisputable to any informed person, it is in the rational interest of clients to put themselves in the professional's hands. The professional pursues the interests of clients as they would if they possessed the same knowledge. Hence, as the myth has it, clients do not relinquish autonomy to the professional. The professional is only an agent or a tool.

The myth of disinterestedness rationalizes injuries to outsiders in interest of client or employer. The present myth pertains to the latter interests. *Are* they served by the system of professionalism? The myth leads us onto new ground. We must assess the rights and privileges that professions claim in the name of science as well as those claimed in the name of service.

Do professionals typically confine themselves to technical means to given ends? Consider the way senses of 'authority' get confused. "An authority" is one who possesses either knowledge, legally authorized power, or power because of a reputation for knowledge. The authority of professionals in the sense of legally or socially sanctioned power over clients is defended on the basis of their presumed knowledge, but it is often used beyond the limits that this implies. The authority provided by special knowledge mistakenly is thought, not the least by professionals themselves, to extend beyond these limits. It leads to paternalistic or, worse, exploitive behavior.

The tampering with ends as well as means occurs at both the individual and corporate level. Typically, professionals shape the objectives of individual clients and employers by the way they present alternatives. While people obviously have goals and a conception of their problem when they seek professional help, their understanding may be very general. The client knows that he is sick, emotionally disturbed, cannot grasp the details of a contract, is responsible for providing a community with a utility, or faces shortfalls in a business—otherwise he would not consult a physician, psychiatrist, attorney, engineer, or auditor. The professional typically helps the client define his problem in specific and operational terms. The professional shapes the client's ends by the way she presents the available means and their costs and consequences. She may deliberately define options in a way that persuades the client to make particular choices. At other times, the client simply puts himself in the professional's hands to choose what she thinks best.

Hughes points out that prior to intervening in the life-plans of individuals, professions define human goals at the corporate level. They dominate their clientele's conception of corporate needs and problems. They claim a mandate to determine the values of society within their domain of concern.[16]

The professions also inculcate philosophies of medicine, justice, social welfare, etc. in their members and influence the way these members exercise the authority ceded by clients and society. Professionals and professions assume a fiduciary responsibility for their clienteles and society at large. They seize, earn, or inherit power to decide matters of vital concern for other human beings and they are not held accountable to anyone but themselves. They claim the right to this power on the basis a specific function for society, a function that depends on the monopoly they hold over an area of technical competence. The specificity of their function, while restricting their authority to a limited area in the lives of clients, gives them sovereignty over this area. They sometimes use their power to exploit. More often they try to promote the interests of clients and employers paternalistically, which is equally harmful in the long run.

4. Professional practice is grounded in scientific theory: Is it really? Yes and no. The accordian character of 'science' and 'grounded' allow the ideologist to enlist the prestige of science as convenient either to laud a favored profession or denigrate a competitor. Engineering utilizes science in the sense of highly confirmed systematically interrelated quantitative hypotheses about basic physical processes; medicine and nursing, the looser but still empirically corroborated principles of physiology as well as some biology, physics, and chemistry; counseling, social welfare, educational, and managerial professions, theories from competing schools of the psychological and social sciences; the ministry, social and psychological principles melded with metaphysical abstractions; the law, detailed codified knowledge of human rules and the logic of judges; the military, a mixture of all these. As one moves down this list, the theoretical principles used by the profession become more eclectic and more mixed with "know-how" learned by doing rather than by academic study of abstract theory. The theoretical principles become either empirical and rule-of-thumb or not empirical at all, and in both cases less precise and hence less susceptible to algorithmic application.

Rueschemeyer hints at the havoc that the cognitive heterogeneity of the professions inflicted on the tight logical structure of the functionalist model.[17] In his version, the basic element of the model is application of a systematic body of knowledge to problems relevant to central values of society. Other elements such as advanced training, high pay and status, and collective autonomy are dependent variables. He argues that the less scientific base for the work of lawyers as compared to physicians reduces their quotient of the remaining characteristics. For example, there is a greater dissensus about the nature of the central value pursued by the law (justice) compared to that pursued by medicine (health) and this, together with greater tension between the central value and interests of clients, militates against cohesion in the legal profession. This in turn, together with the lesser difference between the skills of lawyers and their role partners (clients), makes them more dependent on the favor of patrons and less immune from their criticism. This weakens the profession's ability to exercise control over its members. The fact that affluent and powerful clients have the more complex legal problems makes lawyers even more the servants of the socioeconomic elite than physicians.

Rueschemeyer's point can be generalized. Divergences from the ideal-typical form of profession are the rule rather than the exception. What then is the point of obscuring the differences among professions by playing on variations in the meaning of such terms as 'scientific'? The aim simply is to put a distance between professions and blue-collar occupations.

5. *Professional judgements are guided by wisdom:* Wisdom here means a rational appreciation of all the values relevant to a problematic situation, both the values immediately at issue and those that would be affected incidentally by various measures. Professionals are trained to be sensitive to values committed to their care, but wise decisions require a sensitivity to other values as well. They require appreciation of the values of bystanders and the public as well as those of clients and employers. Technical expertise does not guarantee breadth of vision. It militates against it when fascination with technical feats leads the professional to prefer complex options and when the charism of skill persuades clients or the public to tolerate the professionals stepping over the boundaries of competence.

Myths of Structure

There is a circle in the ideological defense of professional privileges. The scientific and humanitarian character of the work are cited to justify the structure that the professions have developed. The structure is cited as a guarantee that the work has this character. Fractures in either arc of the circle weaken both. If professional work is not as disinterested and scientific as claimed, the structure must have another function than to guarantee these. If the structure is not as it is depicted ideologically, doubts about the character of the work are reinforced.

The functionalist model maintains that the professions develop a typical structure of institutions and attract particular kinds of persons *in order to* ensure that work to meet the needs of society will be performed efficiently. This teleological pattern is a myth. Many features of professions are historical accidents. Such elements as are planned, are done so by a multiplicity of agents with diverse purposes. Furthering the status and prosperity of the profession are dominant motives as frequently as service to humanity. And the planning is not always successful.

There is thus no a priori ground for assuming that the elements of any profession are well designed to discharge putative functions. To insist that this is true in general in the face of obvious contrary facts is mythologizing in its purest form. To maintain the myth of service through science, the ideologue has had to devise additional myths to screen the way structural and personal elements of the professions are viewed.

6. *Professions govern themselves for the common good:* Professions lay claim to collective autonomy and a large measure of individual autonomy for their members on the ground that the technical character of the work precludes intelligent lay control. They maintain that they must be trusted to govern themselves if they are to provide service and their structure insures trustworthiness.

At a minimum, 'autonomy' means freedom from external control. Some professions enjoy a measure of this, but negative freedom is compatible both with ends inimical to society and with anarchy. The functionalist, however, claims a positive and beneficial form of autonomy for the professions. They are represented as governing themselves by clearly formulated rules. The rules are legitimate since they are devised by the profession for the good of society and followed voluntarily by its members. Since professional autonomy is exercised within the larger social system, its rules are consonant with the law and morality and the power of self-legislation is sanctioned by society as a whole. The ethical code of the professional association is the primary statement of the rules of the profession. The implication of these rules are spelled out authoritatively in opinions of ethical review committees, pronouncements of association leaders, and the association's official publications.

Self-rule for the common good would be characteristic of functional groups in an organic society. It has been an aspiration of many occupations. Whether it is valid as an ideal for ideal conditions, professions fall short of it and the pretense that they measure up to it has harmful consequences.

7. Professional associations effectively monitor practice: To begin, we should note the limitations of the mechanisms at the disposal of professional associations for directly controlling practice. For the most tightly organized occupations, they include accreditation standards for professional schools and educational requirements and qualification examinations for licensure. Control over practice depends on the association's ability to expel members from its ranks and, through influence on accreditation boards, to suspend or revoke the license to practice.

By and large, the mechanisms are not sufficient to enforce a high level of either competence or morality. In the first place, the mechanisms do not reach most practitioners. Only a minority of professionals belong to professional associations. The one exception is the American Medical Association, which ensures membership in local medical associations by tying it to hospital privileges and the opportunity to take specialty boards. Participation in professional associations is time-consuming and dues are substantial, so active membership is an act of supererogation. Membership is not a condition of practice, so termination of membership is not a severe loss. Expulsion is a threat only to those least likely to suffer it, those who already identify strongly with the profession.

Revocation of the license to practice is a more serious matter. Its rarity could be due to the rarity of unethical conduct. A more plausible explanation is the difficulty of detecting, prosecuting and convicting malefactors. The difficulty begins with professional codes. Most are mixtures of a few specific prescriptions and prohibitions with vague principles, nonspecific ideals, and hopes. Since a large part of the code is unenforcable, including typically that pertaining to the most important ethical issues, there is little reason to enforce the part that is enforcable.

A few professions attempt to isolate enforceable provisions and focus their mechanisms of control on these, as was noted in Chapter 3. Thus, the ABA seeks the force of law only for the Disciplinary Rules of its Model Code not for the more expansive Ethical Considerations. The Disciplinary Rules are minimalist: A lawyer can obey them to the letter and still engage in all manner of unscrupulous practices. Similarly, the National Council of Engineering Examiners' Model Law specifies penalties for violation of a state's Rules of Professional Conduct, for which NCEE provides a Model Code. The latter is a sharply curtailed version of major engineering codes of ethics. It covers but a small portion of the ethically significant decisions of the engineer. Thus, even in professions taking the lead in monitoring their members, enforcement of what is currently enforcable does not go very far toward ensuring a high level of practice.

In addition to the limited scope of their enforcement efforts, disciplinary bodies typically lack resources for an effective investigatory and prosecutional staff. They rely on complaints by clients or colleagues to identify culprits; but clients understandably seek remedy in the courts or tolerate malfeasance in view of the ineffectiveness of self-policing in the professions, and professionals are dissuaded from reporting colleagues by their acculturation. Thus, equipped with meager authority, limited resources, a passive public, and a defensive profession, disciplinary bodies are powerless to penalize any but the grossest malefactors. The system is geared to punish a few culprits to reassure the public that it is governing itself but not so many as to reveal that abuses are prevalent.

One suspects that it is the public character of misdeeds that offends professions rather than the misdeeds themselves. A number of the professions declare it an ethical obligation for the individual to protect the reputation of the group. One of the fundamental canons of the Engineers Council for Professional Development reads, "Engineers shall act in such a manner as to uphold and enhance the honor, integrity and dignity of the profession." One of the canons of the ABA Model Code states, "A lawyer should avoid even the appearance of professional impropriety." In fairness, these provisions are combined with provisions pertaining to the substance of ethical conduct, but the professions clearly are very concerned with appearances. Their position in society is defined ideologically, and it is vital that their ideology be accepted by other sectors of society. This creates a strong temptation to cover up transgressions for the sake of appearances, to protect the "honor and dignity" of the profession and, not incidentally, the material interests of professionals.

9. *There is peer review of the individual's work:* Advocates of the professions might admit that the formal mechanisms of control are weak; but, they would argue, professions are collegial institutions in which the esteem of colleagues is cherished as a symbolic reward and as a condition for cooperation and referral of clients. Referrals are particularly important given the dampers on advertising and soliciting. Collegial control may be effective in the absence of corporate control by the formal organizations.

Collegiality may mean only interchange of technical information, sharing a common culture and social network, and mutual defense against outsiders. To contribute to collective autonomy in the sense of positive rules of conduct, it must serve to reinforce competent and ethical practice. The professional ideology claims that it does.

At a minimum, this would mean that colleagues are alert to expose incompetence and breaches of ethics. Almost all professional codes announce that they are. The prevalence of such provisions evinces a consensus that professionals *should* actively combat misconduct. The vagueness of the provisions reveals uncertainty about the extent to which vigilance should be carried; for example, how serious need an infraction be before action is in order, whether one who observes misconduct should take the initiative in exposing it or only stand ready to assist official tribunals, what avenues of complaint are appropriate, what sacrifices a watchdog should be willing to make to carry out this duty, what kind of support the profession should give, etc.

Even without uncertainty about rules, peer control would be hard to implement in practice. It runs counter to popular taste to squeal on fellow members of an inside group. The literature on professional ethics tries to make the practice palatable by labeling it "whistle blowing," which calls to mind the honest policeman, vigilant watchman, or alert referee. Critics stigmatize it as "singing" or "ratting," which reminds us that informants are often not disinterested. Whistle blowers or canaries, informants receive few thanks and no support from the public, outright hostility from their work organization, and ostracism by their profession. Westin remarks about his cases of whistle blowing,

> Only one of these ten individuals is back at his job, and then only because several grievance-system awards forced this management to reinstate the employee. All the others are the walking wounded of conscience; many of them are blacklisted from working in the major corporate community and all are now trying to reshape their careers along new paths.[18]

Even when whistle blowers' charges are valid, their acts destroy harmony and trust among people who must work together. The professions have no devices to distinguish among objective critics, malcontents, and hypercritical misanthropes. Most organizations and work groups are willing to do without the former in order not to encourage the latter.

Moreover, the injunction to blow the whistle is in tension with other elements of the professional ethic. The professions counsel their members against public criticism of colleagues. The American Dental Association advises, "Patients should be informed of their present oral health status without disparaging comment about prior services." The National Association of Social Workers urges their members to protect the reputation of colleagues whom they replace or are replaced by. The Engineers Council for Professional Development gives its advice in such a qualified way as to become almost tautologous (that one ought not to engage in unethical criticism): "Engineers shall not maliciously or falsely, directly or indirectly, injure the professional reputation, prospects, practice or employment of another engineer, nor shall they indiscriminately criticize another's work." Some professions leave this unsaid because the reluctance to criticize fellow professions is so ingrained that it is superfluous to mention. Criticism is bad form, unprofessional, too petty to be discussed in formal ethics.

One exception to the rule of deference to peers is the conduct of trial lawyers in adversary situations, if Seymour is to be believed. He deplores the "deterioration in the spirit of goodwill and camaraderie, as lawyers have turned to fighting each other in order to gain advantage for their clients. It is commonplace today to hear lawyers in court accusing one another of the most shabby conduct—lying, cheating, deception."[19] Seymour's outrage itself reflects the norm for professionals to protect one another's public reputation whatever they may know about their real deficiencies of competence or character.

Some of the reasons are obvious. The reputation of my profession and by reflection my own reputation depend on the reputation of my colleagues. In protecting them I protect myself. Moreover, if I criticize others, they will be encouraged to criticize me. If I snoop into their practices, I concede their right to snoop into mine. More subtly, if I criticize a colleague before nonprofessionals, I am acknowledging the public's capacity for informed judgments about professional practice and this undercuts the ground on which the claim to professional autonomy rests.[20]

The reach of formal disciplinary bodies is limited and public criticism of colleagues is discouraged. If collegial control exists, it must operate behind the scenes of professional practice in the informal influence that workers have on each other through their example and respect. The effectiveness of such influence should not be minimized. The question is whether this influence is stronger in the professions than in other occupations and whether the structure of professionalism is responsible.

Millman's *The Unkindest Cut* is a study of the "backrooms" of American medicine and "features of the everyday world of the hospital that adversely affect the quality of patient care." Her charges are serious. She documents them by careful case studies of three hospitals, which she maintains are typical. She concentrates on the ways that doctors define, perceive, and respond to medical mistakes. She concludes that these tactics are geared to "systematically ignore and justify medical errors, or treat them as if they were inconsequential." She finds, for example, that Medical Mortality Review conferences provide "professionally sanctioned justifications and excuses for mistakes . . . ritualized in institutional ceremonies" to relieve doctors from feeling responsible for patients' deaths.[21] A list of chapter titles in Millmans's section on Overlooking Medical Mistakes reveals the drift of her analysis: Medical Mortality Review: A Cordial Affair; I Just Work Here: Excuses for Not Intervening in Physician Incompetence; and Keeping the Patient Uninformed and Closing the Ranks.

Millman focuses on the way incompetence is covered over,

rather than immorality as such, but almost all professional codes incorporate injunctions to maintain state-of-the-art competence and to practice only within one's area of competence. Conceal-ment of avoidable incompetence is concealment of immorality and is itself immoral.

It should be noted that Millman is no muckraker. She does not castigate persons or even the system of hospital care. The motives she points out that lead hospital personnel to short-change patients are ones generally excused as "only human nature" responding to stress. She takes pains to point out that doctors and all professionals whose work entails risks to them-selves or others need defense mechanisms against anxiety and guilt.[22] It can be argued that defenses are necessary if profession-als are to do their work boldly and confidently and if able people are to be retained in the professions. The difficulty lies in assuag-ing anxiety without harming clients. The rationalizations that Millman identifies militate against the best care of patients.

The hospital example is crucial because, among all profes-sional settings, here individuals work in view of colleagues.[23] Furthermore, the consequences of mistakes and misconduct are severe and visible. If collegial control falters under these condi-tions, it is not likely to be effective in settings where practices are screened from other professionals and the consequences of mistakes are indirect and nebulous. My personal observation is that peer control is weak indeed in academia. Peer control of hiring, task assignment, promotion, raises, and tenure are de-fended jealously as faculty rights. Customer satisfaction (of stu-dents, conference audiences, journal editors, etc.) is taken seri-ously, but professors have only the vaguest idea of how hard or well their colleagues work. Hyperspecialization and classroom autonomy keep them effectively sealed off from one another's daily activities.

The qualities of professional work claimed as a basis for immunity from lay control militate against collegial control. Professionals pride themselves on their originality. The problems they deal with require creative application of theoretic principles to unique circumstances. They demand freedom from the time-clock because creativity cannot be forced. They enjoy immunity from standardized evaluation since their services and products cannot be reduced to common measure. It is granted that other professionals would be the best judges of performance if judges were to be admitted at all; but colleagues seldom get to see the work being done, and when they do, they are reluctant to apply their own standards. Millman reports that a major rationalization among physicians for refraining from criticizing one another is that medicine is an art rather than a science. Something like this notion is found among professionals in general. They do not pass judgment on one another's work for the same reason that Toscanini, Walter, and Furtwangler would not criticize one another's performance of Beethoven's *Ninth*.

The net effect is the weakness of the professions' control over their members compared to other influences. As the number of professions and the number of members in each profession grow and as an ever greater proportion of professionals work in bureaucratic settings, the professions are likely to move even further away from genuine community and self-rule toward the condition that Rothstein describes for present day engineering:

> engineers are usually members of primary work groups that have norms and values developed by the groups, which may be composed of engineers and non-engineers. If engineers, as primary group members, deviate from those norms and values, they will be punished by their fellow group members. Engineers are also members of formal organizations and are subject to the organization's rules, which are probably not devised by engineers. If they violate the rules, they are likely to be punished by their organizational superiors, who may not be engineers. Because engineers work in thousands of different work groups and organizations, they are subject to thousands of sets of norms, values, and rules, many of which are undoubtedly dissimilar and even conflicting.[24]

Larson believes that this trend profoundly alters occupational dynamics. The increase in educational requirements for more and more occupations and the demand for professional status among those that require advanced education causes both "diffusion of professionalization as a model for the collective improvement of status" and "proletarianization of educated labor," since most of these people work in subordinate roles in large organizations and share the work experience of the proletariat. This further reduces the relevance of the functionalist model. Larson wonders whether "the ideological effects of professional consciousness can resist the forces which objectively undermine the privileges of professional work."[25] In particular, a strong tension is generated when the self-image of "free" and "personal" professionals is extended to salaried workers with narrowly circumscribed jobs in large bureaucratic organizations. Here the myths of professionalism appear as a "last-ditch defense against subordination."[26]

It is a delicate task to draw a moral from these facts. At the least, we can say that the picture of professions as integrated collegial communities is mythological. Autonomy in the strong sense of collective self-rule, like orientation to service, is a free-floating ideal in search of a mooring in professional structures. The professional ethos praises service, competence, and peer review; and the professions take measures, wholehearted but halfway, to promote them. Many obstacles stand in the way; some inevitable for the organization of specialized work in mass society, others the result of self-interest. Professions pretend to be autonomous communities dedicated to providing expert service for human welfare. They in fact are loose congeries of individuals with similar training and culture and varying expertise, dedication, and integrity, whose influence on one another is shifting and adventitious.

Professional schools and associations provide a façade of integration, but their control over practitioners is slight. Members of the same profession may cluster into miniature communities in local areas and large organizations, but these are a far cry from the professionwide communities advocated by Durkheim and posited by Goode. Professions as communities within the community remain an unrealized ideal, one whose viability remains in question. The myth that they exist provides an ideological justification of unmerited privileges.

Myths of Person

9. *There is a distinctive professional conscience:* The functionalist model presents professions as structures that effectively cultivate competence and conscientiousness. It says that a profession develops its own standards and ensures that its members adhere to them. It implies that rules of professional conduct occupy a central position in the professional's moral life by defining obligations such as competence, diligence, loyalty, candor, and confidentiality.

In criticizing these propositions, we will utilize Mill's

thoughts on the connection between the concepts of moral wrong and punishment.

> We do not call anything wrong, unless we mean to imply that a person ought to be punished in some way or other for doing it; if not by law, by the opinion of his fellow creatures; if not by opinion, by the reproaches of his own conscience. This seems the real turning point of the distinction between morality and simple expediency.[27]

It is otiose to apply moral rules to actions unless sanctions can be devised to give them acceptance, that is, to motivate most people to follow them. Although moralists should propose codes that have not yet been accepted and criticize codes that have, their ultimate aim should be to gain acceptance for a favored code. They should condemn both codes that cannot gain acceptance and systems of action that do not accept their professed codes.

Mill distinguishes three sorts of sanctions: formal sanctions, applied by agencies established by explicit legislation; informal sanctions, in the form of social pressure from fellow members of one's community; and self-imposed sanctions, in the form of the individual's conscience. We have observed that the formal sanctions at the disposal of professions and the informal sanctions of collegial review are limited and must contend with contrary pressures in the workplace. If the rules of the professional ethic are effective, it can be only because most members of the profession have internalized them. The justification of a professional's claim to moral autonomy thus turns on the existence of a special conscience among its members.

The indifference of sociologists to this point is surprising. It bears on their central assumption of the collective orientation of professions to service. While this notion pertains to the net effect of professional practice, any such orientation would be reflected in effects on the individual level. That is, an occupation oriented to service would attract, encourage, and develop an unusual proportion of practitioners with an unusually strong vocational conscience. The absence of evidence for this impugns the premise that professions are collectively oriented to service.[28]

Apart from citing the protestations of the professions themselves, sociologists do not adduce evidence of a special conscience. In criticism, Larson charges, "there are no data about the proportion of professionals who do, in fact, manifestly follow a service ideal; nor do we know how intense this orientation is, or how predominant, relative to other professional orientations; finally, we do not know if the service ideal is more widespread and intense, in general, among professionals than among other workers." She cites Freidson's data.[29]

Proposals to assess the service orientation scientifically, such as Ritzer's test, go no further than to ask individuals where their values lie. The possibility of ideological illusion compromises such data. People are hardly reliable witnesses who have been taught that their goal is human welfare and that lip service to this goal is expected, who are habituated to use the rhetoric of service to explain their actions to themselves and others, who are persuaded that service is the cause of professional practices apart from personal motives. Protestations of service count as evidence for the ideological image of the professions rather than their actual orientation.

There is an interesting parallel here between the discomfort of professionals and that of business people. Professionals feel compelled to apologize for self-interest and pretend that self-serving practices actually are in the public interest. Business people feel compelled to apologize for public service and pretend that it actually benefits themselves or their organization. The myth must be sustained that the invisible hand of the service orientation will take care of the interests of professionals while they single-mindedly pursue the welfare of others, just as the invisible hand of the market sees to the public welfare as business people single-mindedly pursue their own interests. The discordant facts—that professionals often are selfish and business people often are public spirited—cause dissonance for both groups. Such is the result of subjective illusions and ideological mystification.

It is quite possible that the service motive *is* stronger among professionals than other groups. We pray that our physician, nurse, lawyer, accountant, psychiatrist, social worker, professor, or military officer has our interest at heart. We know and admire many humane professionals and we know and condemn many nonprofessionals preoccupied with self-interest. But, we also are acquainted with the opposite type in each group and we have no hard empirical evidence as to which type predominates. I am not questioning the existence of a distinctive professional conscience.

What I question is that it is universal, powerful, and directed to the highest standards of service. To maintain that it is in the absence of adequate evidence is mythology.

10. *Professions attract and educate the best people for the job:* Direct evidence of the role of conscience in professional practice is lacking, but perhaps some facts can be brought to bear on the matter. If we could show that acculturation effectively fosters the professional conscience, we would have reason to believe in its universality. A profession's rules and the professional's dedication to them allegedly distinguish the profession from other occupations. If collegial control is to have a concerted effect (i.e., if it is to bring real pressure to bear on the individual to follow common rules in the face of contrary pressures of the workplace), the rules must occur during professional socialization prior to practice. The training of the preprofessional, therefore, is crucial in implementing the moral autonomy that professions claim.

In *The Credential Society,* a well-documented study of the role of education in social stratification, Collins discusses the rise of professional schools in terms of what he labels the 'myth of technocracy.' The essentials of the myth are that the growth of technology has transformed America (and other industrial nations) from a society of ascription to one of achievement. Where power and privileges once were assigned according to family or political connections, the needs of technology now require them to be earned by the performance of socially useful, scientifically sophisticated tasks. The educational system is pivotal in the new system because it identifies ability and develops the skills that people need for their social function.[30]

There are ample data to show that the main determinant of success in modern society is education and that the amount of education required for admission into particular occupations is growing. These facts are used to support what Collins calls the "meritocratic myth", which is part and parcel of the functionalist account of social stratification. He observes,

> The explanation for these trends has commonly been treated as obvious. Education prepares students in the skills necessary for work, and skills are the main determinant of occupational success. That is, the hierarchy of educational attainment is assumed to be a hierarchy

of skills, and the hierarchy of jobs is assumed to be another such skill hierarchy.

But, he contends,

> the technocratic model crumbles at virtually every point where one can test it against empirical evidence in a more detailed fashion. The educationocracy, which is its backbone, is mostly bureaucratic hot air rather than a producer of real technical skills. Whichever way we look at it—comparing the performance of more educated and less educated people at work, finding out where vocational skills are actually learned, examining what students pick up in the classroom and how long they remember it, examining the relationship between grades and success—the technocratic interpretation of education hardly receives any support.[31]

Briefly, Collins's alternative account[32] is this.

A. Occupational mobility is limited in modern organizations. Advancement is possible within the slot in which one begins work, but the slots are sealed off and individuals rarely change slots. Organizational practices ensure this despite cliches of personnel directors: "There are no dead-end jobs, there are only dead-end people!" "There are no artificial barriers to advancement in this company. A man can go as far as his talents will take him." Such pronouncements are ideological self-deception. "Although the prevailing rhetoric of meritocracy emphasizes the openness of career possibilities, the reality is closer to a castelike separation among major occupational blocs."[33]

B. Management relegates the determination of who will be allowed into each slot to the educational establishment. Where one lands and one's chances for advancement are determined by one's educational credentials.

C. The amount of knowledge required to perform tasks is exaggerated and more of the knowledge people need is acquired on the job than in school. The curricula of technical schools are designed to see that the right people enter the higher occupations and prepare them to fit in socially.

> What evidence is available . . . suggests that schools are very inefficient places of learning. Many of the skills used in managerial and professional positions are learned on the job, and the lengthy courses of study required by business and professional schools exist in good part to raise the status of

the profession and to form the barrier of socialization between practitioners and laymen.[34]

There are two elements in the thesis that Collins propounds here. First, much of professional education is designed to acculturate individuals to the ways of the profession rather than to impart knowledge necessary for the technical aspects of the job. This claim reminds us of Goode's description of the effort of professions to create real communities. Community requires a shared identity, values, role definitions, and language, setting members apart from the larger community. Intensive adult socialization is required to cultivate these. Goode observes, "Three professions—the clergy, the military, and medicine—almost isolate their recruits from important lay contacts for several years, furnish new ego ideals and reference groups, impress upon the recruit his absolute social dependence upon the profession for his further advancement, and punish him for inappropriate attitudes and behavior."[35] Something like this occurs in other programs of study. Students are so submerged in studies that their social contacts are limited to fellow students and faculty and the opinions and values they encounter daily are those of the profession.

Second, Collins suggests that professional training also is protracted to justify the professions' status. Professionals persuade the public that their services are worth a high price *because* the training is so extensive. Critics of the professional ideology claim that students are "overtrained" or taught more than they need to know.[36] Goode observes that aspiring professions typically demand of their members as much education as the market will bear; that is, as much as society will subsidize and prospective income will induce preprofessionals to indebt themselves for.[37] Many professionals end up with routine tasks for which extensive training is unnecessary or in specialties for which their training is useless. Yet the professions have resisted certification of technicians to take over routine work unless there are institutional guarantees that these will be supervised by "real" professionals, thus ensuring that the profession will retain control of its domain of service.

Larson spells out this second claim in Marxist terms. In mobilizing to control a market, a professionalizing occupation seeks to standardize its product in order to assure the public that all its members will provide the same (high-quality) services. To do so it must capture the gate-keeping function with the authority to set standards, design education, and test achievement. The ideological formula is that responsibility for public service requires standardization of the product (professional services) *via* standardization of producers (professionals) *via* standardization of the production of producers (professional education). This concatenation ties in with income and status in that the profession ostensibly establishes a fair price for services in proportion to the labor-time required to produce standard competence. In Larson's judgment, the equivalences here are spurious. The price or exchange-value of professional services is not a true measure of their use-value because it is only ideologically tied to the length of education.

> While both years of schooling and credentialing are related to the market value of specific professional services, the relation appears to be ideological: indeed, it functions more as an implicit justification for the price of the professional commodity and for the privileges associated with professional work, than as the actual quantitative translation of 'average socially necessary labor time' into market value.[38]

Professions typically use their monopoly over education to protract the period of training as a way of holding down the supply of professional service and thereby raise its price.

Third, the last proposition in Collins's account of occupational stratification is that the persons admitted into the professions by the credentialing process are the offspring and cultural heirs of those already in professions and other superordinate social positions. Culturally subordinate groups are accultured not to aspire to higher education and they are denied the skills necessary to succeed when they slip in. Hence, they lack the opportunity to acquire the academic credentials to rise in the world of occupations whatever their native ability. Social stratification is perpetuated.

In summary, the functionalist model justifies professionalism by claiming that its mechanisms select the most able individuals for professional training and provide them the precise skills to do their work effectively. The conflict theorists point out that the actual system diverges from this ideal in a way that protects existing class privileges and reduces the contribution of the professions to general human welfare. Hence, the functionalist picture of professional education is a myth.

11. Professional schools inculcate the professional con-

science: A protracted period of formal education with isolation of recruits for resocialization is precisely what would be needed to cultivate an orientation to service and inform the professional conscience with relevant norms. This is part of the ideological justification given for overtraining. Exposure to all the aspects of professional work is supposed to give the practitioner what Larson calls the "intelligence of the whole," by which she means an understanding of the whole field and its evolutionary dynamics.[39] This kind of breadth of vision would equip professionals to determine how their profession could best serve humanity. Thus, Parsons defends the place of professional schools in the university by ascribing to them a liberalizing function. While conceding that the professions sometimes fall short of their ideals, he maintains that

> the very antithesis which is commonly drawn, not only by professional men themselves but in the general public, between the 'professional' and the 'commercial' attitudes, would indicate that in the professions and their great traditions is to be found one of the principal reserves of defense against the false conception of utility, in its close connection with the love of money.

He argues that to master the intellectual content of the professional tradition a liberal spirit with its ideal of learnedness is essential.

> The man who is dominated by only the more sordid motives of gain or even the immediate success of his practical task alone is incapable of it. The valuation of knowledge for its own sake is an integral part of the professional spirit . . . The ideal professional man is not only a technical expert in the sense transcending special skills; by virtue of his mastery of a great tradition he is a liberally educated man, that is, a man of general education.[40]

The notion that a professional education is a liberal one is astonishing. The traditional professions have recognized otherwise. They have been aware of the narrow focus of the training for which they are willing to take responsibility and have encouraged a liberal education prior to entrance into professional training, though critics charge that this is designed to develop gentlemanly qualities to set the professional apart from skilled workers and prepared him for social intercourse with genteel patrons rather than to provide the wisdom necessary for moral leadership.

In any event, newer professions that recruit from lower socio-economic segments of society, notably engineering, cannot afford this luxury, and liberal education falls by the wayside. Professional education becomes ever more specialized, focusing ever more strongly on the narrow objectives of the occupational group. Where undergraduate degrees are required as prerequisite to professional training, no concerted effort is made to see that they instill the moral qualities we have been discussing and the pressure is to concentrate on a narrow range of technical knowledge. This was bound to occur as success in professional school became the prime requisite for entry at desirable points in the occupational structure. Overtraining legitimates the status of professionals in relation to ancillary workers, to whom "dirty work" or the routine aspects of service are delegated, and of elite professionals in relation to their journeyman colleagues. It is another means to fortify stratification among and within occupations rather than a means to instill a social conscience, which indeed may be a handicap in the drive for success.

There are efforts at moral education within professional schools. These include indoctrination in the codes of professional societies and examples of professionalism provided by the faculty. The limitations of these efforts are obvious. Few schools devote entire courses to professional ethics. The major exception are law schools, but the emphasis is on ABA's disciplinary rules, which have the force of law rather than of conscience. Hearteningly, medical schools have instituted studies in medical ethics, but students do not give the attention to them that they do to "real" courses in scientific medicine. Other professional curricula assign a few days or minutes to ethics in courses devoted to other purposes. Moral training takes the form of instruction in the profession's code, not a searching and critical inquiry into ethical problems from diverse points of view. As for the example provided by the faculty, students are in a position to observe their professionalism in teaching and research not in handling the moral dilemmas of practice.

The net judgment that emerges from the foregoing criticisms is that the principal theses of the functionalist model are myths designed to promote the interests of the professions ideologically. Certainly, they are grounded in actual practices, many of which

produce real if less than maximal benefits for humanity. There *is*
an operative professional ethos. But, it is not strong enough to
overcome counter pressures in society, it is internally self-con-
flictive and vague, and it is better designed to make professionals
faithful servants of their patrons than of humanity at large.

Notes

1. See "Myth" in Harvey, *A Handbook of Theological Terms.*
2. Feuer sees a residue of mythic elements in political ideologies (*Ideology
and the Ideologists*, p. 961). It stretches his thesis to maintain that professionals
think of themselves as chosen people and their elites as leaders to the promised
land (the Jacobic and Mosaic myths); but his warning that civilization depends on
the ability of intellectuals to transcend the role of mythmaking ideologues should
be taken to heart by social scientists and ethical theorists alike.
3. *Nicomachean Ethics*, Bk. I, Ch. V, p. 30.
4. *The Rise of Professionalism*, p. 243.
5. *Ibid.*, pp. 234–236.
6. Bayles summarizes these in *Professional Ethics*, pp. 30–43.
7. *Ibid.*, p. 140.
8. "Price Discrimination in Medicine," pp. 33–42.
9. *Ibid.*, pp. 45–46 and 53.
10. *Ibid.*, p. 51.
11. Larson, *The Rise of Professionalism*, p. 226. She links stratification in
professions with social stratification (pp. xv, 8, 18, 67) whether the latter be
traditional (pp. 10, 12, 118, 127), enterpreneural and managerial (pp. 28, 122–123),
or technobureaucratic (pp. 147–148, 158, 179).
12. *The Rise of Professionalism* deals with distances established from "manual" occupations (pp. 77, 148), especially those devoted to routine aspects of the
profession's own work (pp. 31, 34) and with rejection of unionism (pp. 101, 156).
13. *Ibid.*, pp. 220–221.
14. *Ibid.*, p. 215.
15. Rothman maintains that the clinicians in the infamous Tuskegee syphilis
study did their best to follow good medical practice despite the racist overtone of
the research. ("Were Tuskegee and Willowbrook 'Studies in Nature'?" Rothman
cites Jones' *Bad Blood* and Ettling's *The Germ of Laziness*.)
16. "The Study of Occupations," "Professions," and "The Making of a Physician," *The Sociological Eye*, pp. 288, 376, and 397–399.
17. "Doctors and Lawyers."
18. Westin, *Whistle Blowing*, p. 3.
19. *Why Justice Fails*, p. 16.
20. Hughes, "Mistakes at Work," *The Sociological Eye*, p. 320.
21. *The Unkindest Cut*, pp. 9–11.
22. *Ibid.*, p. 91.
23. *Ibid.*, pp. 127–128.
24. "Engineers and the Functionalist Model of the Professions," pp. 86–87.
25. *The Rise of Professionalism*, p. 232.
26. *Ibid.*, p. 219.
27. *Utilitarianism*, pp. 303–304.
28. Moore makes the connection between collective and individual orienta-

tions explicit (*The Professions*, p. 15) but ignores the insight and proceeds with the functionalist model.

29. *The Rise of Professionalism*, p. 59. See Freidson, *Profession of Medicine*, p. 81.

30. *The Credential Society*, pp. 1–2.

31. *Ibid.*, pp. 7–8.

32. *Ibid.*, pp. 12–21.

33. *Ibid.*, pp. 43 and 44.

34. *Ibid.*, p. 17.

35. "Community within a Community," p. 196.

36. Larson, *The Rise of Professionalism*, p. 230.

37. "The Theoretical Limits of Professionalism," p. 286.

38. *The Rise of Professionalism*, p. 212.

39. *Ibid.*, p. 231.

40. "Remarks on Education and the Professions," pp. 365 and 366.

❏ PART III

STRUCTURAL CHANGE

□ 8

CHARTERS, CONTRACTS, AND COVENANTS

We now turn to the normative issues with which this study is primarily concerned. In this chapter and the next, we examine elements in the structure and ideology of professions that ought to be preserved and possibilities of change in those that ought to be reformed. In the following chapter we will examine professional codes in two lights, as instruments of the institutions discussed in prior chapters and as expressions of ethical norms, which are discussed in the last chapters of the work. We have, then, two things to consider, proposals for the reconstruction of professions as institutions (Part III) and the ingredients of the professional ideal that is the lasting legacy of the professions whatever their fate as distinctive institutions (Part IV).

The Normative Contribution of the Models of Profession

The sociological-philosophical inquiry of the first part of this work was designed to prepare the ground for practical proposals in the last part. A realistic picture was sought of the social and intellectual context in which the norms and ideals of professionalism must be put into effect. Unfortunately, a realistic picture proved hard to come by. Popular ideas and the functionalist model proved to be ideological. They distort the nature of professions under pressure of competition for social goods.

Distortion is a relation between a picture and reality in which elements of the picture corresponding to elements of reality are altered for special effect. To discover the key to the distortion, one must not only discriminate elements in the picture; one must have independent access to the reality depicted and the motives of those responsible for the distortion. But what if one's only access is through other pictures with their own distortions? We utilized the model provided by conflict theorists to provide us the key to the distortions of the functionalist model. Now we must play functionalism off against the conflict model to expose the latter's distortions.

As it turns out, this leads us directly into normative issues. Both models purport to be descriptions of social life rather than prescriptions for conducting it. However, like all social theories, they are underdetermined by empirical data. There is no way to decide between the two models by simply arraying facts and statistics for and against them. We are forced to choose between sophisticated versions of the two, versions equally adapted to the hard and indisputable facts, on the basis of the value judgments each makes possible. Indeed, the construction of each model is controlled by implicit evaluations. The functionalist model represents professions as measuring up to a certain ideal—they are depicted as something like moral organisms, as these were defined in Chapter 3—and the model emphasizes the traits that justify this judgment. The conflict model criticizes professions precisely for falling short of that ideal and emphasizes the traits that justify this contrary judgment. The ideal will be taken as our point of departure. That is, elements actually in professions or that could be developed to bring them nearer to the ideal will be sought, and the ideal tailored to make it attainable or more nearly attainable under existing circumstances.

Conflict theorists, no more than functionalists, make explicit the value judgments that control their analyses. For example, the closest Larson comes to expressing personal feelings about the professions are brief comments on the first and last pages of her book. At the outset, she explains how she came to undertake her inquiry out of puzzlement at the reluctance of lower-strata professionals to organize and strike on an occasion in which they had so much to gain.

> What made professors and architects—not to mention physicians, lawyers, and engineers—feel that the tactics and strategy of the industrial working class would deprive them of a cherished identity?

What is there, in the attributes of a profession, that compensates for subordination, individual powerlessness, and often low pay?[1]

At the end of her book, she asserts abruptly,

Dissatisfaction with the structural limitations of one's work and the social uses of one's productive activity need not remain a private crisis of conscience. . . . To separate the progressive human meaning of one's work from the ideological functions inscribed in one's role is a task of personal salvation. This questioning has been attempted and is taking place today, however silently, however timidly, in schools and work places. Breaking with ideology, finding new norms for the social production of knowledge and the social use of competence demands passion, vision, and hard work. This major historical task can only be sustained by a solidary collectivity, aware of its part and of its place in the overall struggle for human liberation. In a historical perspective, abandoning the "subjective illusion" and the seductions of bourgeois individualism become the premise of personal freedom.[2]

We may infer from comments like this that the conflict theorists hope to dispel the illusions of bourgeois individualism in order to enable everyone to exercise personal freedom and implement "new norms for the social production of knowledge and the social use of competence."

The premises that justify this ambition are these: Class structure based on economic position has become more definite and rigid over the last two centuries. Professionalism has contributed to the trend.

As the labor force tends to become totally subsumed under the formal relations of capitalist production, the real and the ideological privileges associated with "professionalism" legitimizes the class structure by introducing status differentials, status aspirations, and status mobility at practically all levels of the occupational hierarchy.[3]

The primary myth of bourgeois individualism is that there are no classes or class exploitation, but only differential privileges that are the rightful result of individual achievement. A corollary is that the solution to social ills lies in individual effort and responsibility. The need for class struggle is covered over.[4] The professional ideology is part and parcel of this myth.[5]

Larson explains the creation of ideology by "contradictions" in the social system. The contradictions that she cites are so variegated that it is difficult to determine why they are labeled by the same term. Apparently, they are all discrepancies between the social system that elites defend and ideals that have a hold on the popular mind.[6] Elites must misrepresent their social position to justify it by the ideals. Thus, the professions represent themselves as oriented to human welfare rather than vulgar commerce. Elites within professions represent the work of routine practitioners as higher in intellectual quality than other occupations.

It is one thing to accept an exposure of falsehoods in an ideology. It is another to swallow a substitute. The premises of the conflict ideology must be examined with equal care.

At the outset, we must reject Larson's division of society into just two classes in regard to interest and viewpoint and of intellectuals into spokesman for the dominant ideology and critics "secreted" by a revolutionary class.[7] Some intellectuals belong in each of these categories, but there is little reason to credit revolutionary intellectuals per se with more insight than reactionary ones or to think that their pragmatic interests make them any more objective about human welfare. Are the ideas of a revolutionary class any less ideological than those of a dominant class? Does being exploited cause one to be any more careful with the truth in attempting to escape exploitation than being an exploiter does in justifying exploitation? We, I and hopefully many of my readers, aspire to rise above the social conflict to survey it as objectively as possible with a view to the ultimate human good beyond classes and the rivalries of ideologues. We can do so only by sympathetically participating in the opposing points of view.

What then is valid in the functionalist model? What survives the assaults of conflict theory? After admitting that the failings of professions "have been legion," Marshall stoutly maintains, "professionalism is an idea based on the real character of certain services. It is not a clever invention of selfish minds."[8] The conflict emphasis on the economic aspects of the professional project systematically discounts the positive features of the professional ideal and the extent to which it has functioned to inspire professionals in modern societies, noncapitalist as well as capitalist. There should be no argument that contributing to human welfare through expert service to those who need it is the proper ideal for work of every sort. It is questionable whether the ideal is as powerful in the professions as they claim or whether it functions at an acceptable level anywhere, and it is obvious that the structures of capitalist society exert strong pressures on the individual to diverge from the ideal; but these facts do not gainsay that the desire to serve is a real motive for many professionals and declarations of service are not all hypocrises and self-deceptions. Ideals can have a real effect, even when they are misused ideologically, and there are influences in professional institutions, albeit wavering and weak, that encourage individuals to live up to the professional ideal. The practical problem is to strengthen those influences.

Utopian Visions and Practical Proposals

In an organic society, important occupations would be chartered under a social covenant accepted by all. The charter would state the duties and social responsibilities of the occupation. Necessary rules would be spelled out and remaining aspects of the work would be left to individual judgment. A system of accountability would ensure that individuals followed rules and exercised judgment responsibly. Institutions would be designed to equip them to do so competently.

We will sketch the steps necessary to reach this goal. However, these steps cannot be taken all at once and it would be disastrous to try. Hence, we must reason back from the ideal to what is feasible. Some steps would be beneficial in themselves even if the final steps to reach the ideal were not taken. These can be recommended without reservation. Other steps would temporarily exacerbate present failings of professions. We have to decide whether progress toward the ideal is worth the price.

We have observed that the claim that professions are collectively oriented toward human welfare falls before two facts. Professions are less integrated than they pretend, and the control they exercise over their members is directed toward maintaining discipline in the project of controlling the market rather than for the public good. If the institutions of professionalism are to be organized so as to make the service ideal effective, it is necessary to integrate professions more fully and ensure that their instruments of control are used for the desired purpose.

The professions do not have any effective collective orientation, and assuredly not an orientation to service, because they are not genuine communities. They are analogous to what Quine calls "scattered objects," rather than integral entities.[9] 'Profession' is a singular term that denotes something more integrated than a mere set of people (physicians, lawyers) or similar activities (healing, counseling); its parts (members) behave as they do partly because of their interaction with one another. However, the integration is not complete. Most of the parts interact directly with only a few other parts (professional with other local professionals) and only indirectly and weakly with the ruling elements of the whole (elites, leaders, officers of professional associations, educational administrators). Hence, the corporate influence of the profession on the individual is swamped by other influences such as the pressures of the market place, work group, or employing organization.

Tightly knit communities are not likely to evolve naturally from groups with tens of thousands and in some cases hundreds of thousands of members scattered across a vast country, competing in thousands of markets and employed by thousands of organizations. Integration would require elaborate formal organizations. The obvious way to achieve this would be to strengthen the organizations that already exist, the professional associations, schools, and licensing agencies.

The influence of existing professional associations over the rank-and-file is minimal. Bar and medical associations are exceptional in numbering the majority of practitioners among their members. Only a minority belong to associations in most professions and they are often scattered among several. Furthermore, in all associations most members are passive. Concern for corporate social responsibilities is confined to a few officers and committees.

One way to enhance the role of the professional association would be to charter one for each occupation in the way in which corporations are chartered by the state. Membership in the professional corporation would be mandatory as a condition for the license to practice. Dues would be converted into a form of taxation. (As a dues-paying member of the American Association of University Professors, it has always seemed to me unfair representation without taxation for nonmembers to benefit from AAUP's efforts to promote academic freedom, the tenure system, economic interests of the profession, etc.) If members of an occupation were forced to contribute to the support of its governing body, they would be not only paying their fair share for its maintenance, but they would be motivated to see that it discharged its functions properly. Finally, once all practitioners were members of the corporate organization, it would be easy to give appropriate elements of its ethical code the status of law and the organization could be provided material and political resources to enforce them effectively.

The Professional Charter

We would certainly not want to enhance the power of professional associations in this way if their orientation to monopolistic self-aggrandizement were left untouched. Insurance that professional corporations would use their power for the purposes we have in mind would depend first of all on the right kind of charter. The primary function of a charter would be to define responsibilities. In an organic society, lawyers would be assigned special, though not exclusive, responsibility for the preservation and improvement of the legal system; medical professionals, for the system of health care; engineers, for protection of the environment and conservation of resources; etc. Existing professions give mere lip service to these responsibilities. An effective system of responsibilities would define exactly who is responsible, for what sort of actions, for what groups of people or aspects of peoples' welfare, and to whom.[10]

In respect to who is to be responsible for what acts, the professional charter would define the responsibilities of individual practitioners in their work and the corporate responsibilities of functionaries of professional institutions. The responsibilities of practitioners would be spelled out in codes of conduct that might be adapted from present professional codes and either made part of the charter or perfected by processes mandated by the charter.

The designation of responsibilities for functionaries requires something quite different from anything found in present codes. At most, these declare the responsibility of "the profession" for such matters as improvement of the legal system or protection of the public health, safety, and welfare without imposing specific duties on anyone in particular. The concept of the social responsibilities of a group entails the notion of the group acting as a corporate unit. Groups do not act in the literal sense, only individuals can act; but an individual can act for the group if he or she is authorized to commit its reputation and resources to specific ends. For a group to discharge responsibilities, then, individuals must be assigned the responsibilities by virtue of their positions in the group. Its social responsibilities must become their role responsibilities. If other members of the group recognize the legitimacy of the assignment, the individual can be said to be carrying out the will of the group and the group can be said to act through them. Thus, if professional corporations are to have social responsibilities, provisions in the charter must assign specific responsibilities to offices in the corporation to act in the name of the corporate whole.

Effective responsibility requires not only assignment of tasks, but accountability to someone for their performance. In the present system of professionalism, practitioners are accountable mainly to themselves, a bit to their immediate colleagues, and almost not at all to anyone else except in the case of egregious malfeasance. There would have to be mechanisms of enforcement for the rules of professional corporations to make members accountable to their colleagues. The democratic form of the corporations (discussed later) would make their officers accountable to their members.

However, experience shows that accountability of members of a profession to one another is not sufficient to protect the public interest. Designated representative members of society with no material interest or psychological identification with the profession would have to be charged with reviewing whether it is doing its job and empowered to impose effective sanctions if it is not. We will explore the possibility of a formal governing body for occupations in the next chapter. Whether true accountability can be achieved short of this extreme measure is questionable.

Professional Covenants

How professional charters are developed is as important as what they contain. They will be effective only if they are viewed as voluntary agreements between professions and society, agreements to which every individual professional is a party. The idea of a contract is useful here, but it has to be adapted to the diffuse nature of occupational groups. No individual or organization can speak for all practitioners, present and future, or sign a document that will bind everyone. Complex procedures for simulating the contractual relationship must be developed. Some of the possibilities will be discussed shortly, but here hope is expressed that if professionals were to understand that they are given a monopoly over an occupation under contract to meet specific obligations, they would come to recognize practice as a privilege rather than a right of birth, initiation, or conquest. They would acknowledge that society rightfully expects dedication beyond loyalty to particular patrons or employers.

If entry into a profession were to require formal agreement to a contract, practitioners could be more certain of their rights and privileges, as well as their obligations. The actual rights and duties implicit in the present traditions of the professions, not to mention those that ought to exist, are by no means evident to all or accepted by all. A contract could spell them out. Moreover, the contractual element of a social charter for a profession would add the force of promise to the individual's obligation to follow the professional ethic. The professional's limited role in formulating the ethic of his or her profession provides a convenient rationalization for picking and choosing provisions to follow. To agree to a contract would be to promise to follow the entire ethic conscientiously. Such a promise would not be absolute—the individual would retain the right to dissent out of personal conscience—but promising is an important step psychologically. It is a formal act in which one commits ones self, publicly and in advance, to terms spelled out in a formal document.

Contracts would provide the basis for definite expectations among parties to the professional relationship and for evaluating their performance. They would facilitate intelligent planning and a system of accountability. These advantages could not be achieved fully without codifying the contract down to the last detail, securing universal acceptance, and giving it formal legal status. However, this kind of pettifoggery would stifle initiative and deaden moral judgement, so reasonable limits to codification would have to be observed.

We may note that there is no danger of excessive detail in existing rules. Only a small portion of the functioning ethic of any profession is formalized in civil statutes. A somewhat larger portion are formulated in codes of professional societies, but their provisions tend to be nebulous and debatable. When the typical client comes to the typical professional, each's understanding of what to expect from the other is fragmentary and vague. Relations are negotiable but frequently go unnegotiated. More systematic codification of the rights and duties of both parties would help remedy this.

The notion of a contract is both more legalistic and less far-reaching than what is needed as a foundation for relations between professionals and the rest of society. Some have suggested the notion of a covenant instead. Veatch in applying contract theory to medical ethics argues for the need for "social relationships among lay people and health professionals built upon complex layers of mutual loyalty, fidelity, respect, and support."[11] Professionals must invest more of their person and fate in their work than the term 'contract' implies. The very notion implies that obligations are limited to those defined by its provisions. Contracts, moreover, do not have the solemnity and moral force conveyed by the religious connotations of covenants. We should observe, however, that the moral force cannot be generated by merely labeling a professional charter a covenant. Basic reforms in the acculturation of professionals are needed to bring them to regard it as one.

Veatch's Triple Contract

Whether or not the obligations of professionals are to be established by state charters, the advantages of formal agreements are patent. The complications that the attempt to achieve agreements would entail are many. They will become evident through a critical examination of Veatch's proposals for a contractual medical ethic.

Veatch argues that present relationships between lay people and health professionals fall short of the ideal because the only principles available to regulate them are those of the "folk ethic" or mores of physicians and the codes that they unilaterally create and enforce, notably, AMA's principles and the opinions of its Judicial Council. There is no reason why other health professionals or lay persons should accept these principles, yet each of these groups has an important role in medical decisions. Furthermore, each of them have a stake in the way physicians make decisions— not only a stake, but a rightful claim in view of the monopolistic character of the physician's role. All elements of society, therefore, should have a say in the formulation of medical ethics.[12]

The same argument holds for other professions. Veatch defines 'professional ethics' as sets of norms unilaterally devised and enforced by an occupational group.[13] By this definition, no professional code can bind anyone besides professionals, nor is anyone else obligated to respect the professional's fealty to a code, nor indeed should professionals themselves follow a code when it requires conduct that violates common morality. To establish mutual obligations, all of society must be involved in formulating and adopting norms for both professional and lay roles in the professional relationship. Professionals and lay persons must make pledges to each other, not just professionals to professionals.

Veatch's opinions on the problem of moral consensus and mutual obligations and the inadequacy of unilateral professional codes are well taken. Nevertheless, the "new foundation" that he proposes for medical ethics is not sound or practical. In the absence of a general social contract, medical and other professional contracts would be much weaker than he envisions. The potential contribution of the professional ethic to the development of an organic society correspondingly is limited. A number of difficulties stand in the way of effective professional contracts, which will be laid out by criticizing Veatch's theory.

Veatch speaks of three contracts: a basic social contract in which the members of society agree on principles of social interaction; a covenant between society and the health-related professions (the second contract); and agreements between individual physicians and patients (the third contract).[14] The provisions of the second contract are derived from the first, and contracts of the third kind are derived from the second.

Veatch describes his conception as a "synthesis contract theory" and tries to show that it should be acceptable to the major traditions in medical ethics. These he divides into theories that maintain that morality must be *created* by convention and those that postulate an objective moral order, divine or natural, to be *discovered* by revelation, reason, or the moral sense. At the end of his argument, he claims,

There is a convergence between the vision of the people coming together to discover a preexisting moral order—an order that takes equally into account the welfare of all—and the vision of people coming together to invent a moral order that as well takes equally into account the welfare of all. The members of the moral community thus generated are bound together by bonds of mutual loyalty and trust.[15]

Veatch's argument fails because he neither demonstrates the convergence of the traditions on his concept, nor the soundness of the concept itself. He creates the illusion of convergence by dismissing theories in the discovery tradition that do not find in the objective moral order a requirement for the impartial treatment of everyone and theories in the creationist tradition that do not make the factual judgments that self-interest requires a stable social order and that only an order that treats all impartially will be stable. He claims tautologically that the theories left in each tradition (i.e., after excluding those who do not stipulate impartiality) will "converge" on the principle that the welfare of all members of society should be considered impartially.

In truth, we would want to negotiate covenants only with those from various traditions who share this much of the moral point of view. It may be we could negotiate lasting covenants only with such persons. However, Veatch must assume more to demonstrate the logical convergence. Thinkers in the different traditions would have to arrive at similar conclusions about the character of "welfare," "impartial treatment," and the conditions of these, and they would have to agree on the principles to be incorporated in the basic social contract necessary to realize these values, whether they rely on revelation, practical reason, the moral sense, or computations of self-interest. The history of ethical theory provides no basis for expecting this to happen. The sources one consults for insight inevitably lead to different conclusions about right behavior.

It would be highly convenient if there were a basic social contract. It would mean that the members of society had freely bound themselves to common principles. The problem of devising professional covenants would reduce to deducing the implications of the principles for the professional context. Unfortunately, nothing like a social contract exists. What we have in its stead is a plethora of mores and ethical traditions with many common elements and many differences, followed conscientiously by some people, expediently by others, and flaunted by many. Most members of society "consent" only to the extent of failing to rebel against its morality, emigrate from its jurisdiction, or strenuously attempt to reform it. People acknowledge moral obligations, even common ones, for many different reasons. Nothing is gained by pretending that this congerie of accommodations represents a contract. At most, mores might be transformed into a contract by a long, strenuous, concerted effort by a sufficiently philosophical society. There is no likelihood that this will happen in any society of the present ilk.

At points, Veatch does not appear to require an actual social contract to provide a basis for a medical covenant. In arguing for particular provisions of his own Draft Medical Ethics Covenant[16] (e.g., that physicians should not be required to prolong life under all circumstances and that particular breaches of confidentiality should be mandatory), he appeals to what *would* be in the ideal social contract. Perhaps he considers it sufficient justification for an actual medical covenant that it be derivable from an imaginary social contract.

It is impossible to defend this position. Veatch maintains that the thought-experiment of drawing up a social contract has heuristic value for the ethical theorist. The question is What does the experiment add to the general philosophical enterprise of trying to determine the principles by which people ought to live by reasoning from a certain perspective (i.e., the moral point of view)? Well, it requires imagining ourselves negotiating with like-minded people to devise a contract. The fantasy might point out the need to disregard our special interests and take seriously only the opinions of ethical theorists who do likewise. It also would remind us that our reasoning is fallible, so we should listen to the arguments of others. Finally, it would remind us that we are seeking principles that will be worthy of adherence by all rational people, not just tailored to our own use. Unfortunately, this heuristic exercise does not bring into play any new source of moral principles nor any content for the hypothetical social contract. Imaginary ideal observers or "rational contractors" are not independent oracles whom we can consult. They think what we have them think and speak to us the words we put in their mouths. What they see as rational is precisely what seems reasonable to us.

To illustrate the limitations of the maneuver, consider Veatch's argument for the deontological claim that keeping a promise is per se a "right-making characteristic independent of the consequences" of an action.[17] He contrives an example in which a drug-befuddled patient extracts a promise from a physician by a sort of deathbed blackmail (who wants to distress a dying man?). Honoring the particular promise would be harmful to innocent persons. Veatch tries to eliminate from the example all of the usual utilitarian reasons against violating promises. He feels that, nevertheless, there would be something wrong about violating the promise. I infer from Veatch's comments elsewhere that he would justify this feeling by an appeal to "our moral intuitions."[18] However, he does not express *my* moral intuitions. I feel differently about the promise and I am forced to attribute his feeling to a habit of disapproval carried over from cases where breach of promise is wrong on grounds of utility. He no doubt would attribute my feeling to moral blindness. The point is that the heuristic device of the social contract does not resolve our differences. My "rational contractor" would differ with his precisely on the point in question and they would dismiss one another's arguments precisely on the grounds to which Veatch and I would appeal against one another.

Imaginary contracts, therefore, do not provide a more secure grounding for ethical claims than appeals to what seems reasonable (to the speaker). Indeed, they are mythological expressions of personal senses of reasonableness. Actual contracts at least represent consensus among those who are trying to settle ethical questions.

The Congress of Medical Morality

An imaginary contract establishes only an imaginary community, not a real community bound together in reciprocal pledges of mutuality and loyalty. A real contract negotiated by its signers would be required to establish a real community. Our health system is nationwide, so an actual social contract and an actual medical covenant would have to embrace all Americans. What are the prospects accomplishing this? The problem of consensus is mind-boggling.

Veatch requires that a social contract be only "accessible in principle" to all citizens, that it be one to which all "can and should subscribe." However, he adds that it actually must be "perceived by all as morally legitimate."[19] When he discusses who would draw up the contract, he includes everyone in "the common community of moral discourse" on the ground that there are no moral experts. He dismisses two sorts:

> There is little evidence that training in the science of ethics improves one's ability to know what is moral. There is also little evidence that training in the nonmoral components of a decision-making area gives one expertise in the morality of a problem.[20]

In drawing up the social contract and professional covenants, the opinions of all citizens are to be considered equally. No special weight is to be given to ethical theorists or professionals.

Since it is impractical to convene all citizens of the United States, let us suppose that the social contract and medical covenant are drafted by randomly selected delegates, say 1000, at a Medical Morality Congress at the Checkerdome in St. Louis, July 4, 1988. The drafts will be submitted for ratification to the entire populace via telecommunications and will be negotiated with this in view. Proceedings at MMC will be carried by television.

According to my computations,[21] samples of 1000 from the American population (men, women, and children of all backgrounds, interest, IQs, etc.) would average one physician and 1/40,000th of a professional philosopher. (Thus, in one of 40,000 samples there would be one chance in 5000 that a delegate would be Veatch).

Such a process would obviously be insane. Veatch tries to make his version more reasonable by requiring negotiators to use "the heuristic device of thinking of themselves as impartial contractors." Impartial or rational contractors, according to Veatch's specifications, will put on Rawls' veil of ignorance so as to ignore their prospective position in the social order they are devising. This is supposed to prevent them from favoring rules that would benefit themselves and enable them to apply the test of reversibility, according to which rules "must be acceptable to one standing on either the giving or the receiving end of the transaction." This, Veatch contends, ensures that principles will be acceptable from the moral point of view.[22]

Veatch's requirement for delegates to MMC or any actual contractors to mimic perfect contractors amounts to an injunction to be as rational and impartial as possible. To improve the chances that the delegates will try their best to think straight, let us imagine that they are subjected to a crash course in ethical thinking. This would require considerable practice in dealing with cases as well as instruction in principles and reasons. Mr. Veatch might be called in to teach the course.

Let us now suppose that we now have well-tutored delegates, sincerely trying to devise a social contract and medical covenant from the moral point of view. We find that their fellow delegates disagree with them on some particulars. They, unlike imaginary rational contractors, may be real sources of insight. Shall they defer to one another's judgment? Not necessarily. We must be aware of the possibility that some have chosen Machiavelli's maneuver (cynically pretending to don the veil of ignorance and arguing speciously for rules biased for their social position) or succumbed to Sartre's syndrome (deceiving themselves in bad faith that they are thinking impartially). Well and good, delegates will accept other delegates' opinions only if their arguments are rationally convincing—according to their personal sense of rationality, impartiality, and human welfare.

Each of us has to rely on his or her own reason as a last resort, but the congress at least would be helpful developing alternatives, and the dialectic would help the sincere person conceive of more ideal contracts than he or she could alone. As Veatch urges, those who think there is an objective moral order ought to recognize the limits of their insight and come together to compare divine revelations or the deliverances of their practical reason or their moral sense, and those who believe that morality must be created ought to assemble and negotiate from a common point of view. But, as history shows, strenuous efforts to think rationally starting from diverse premises typically arrive at contrary conclusions. What shall we do if factions at MMC, whether sincerely, cynically, or in bad faith, favor different drafts of the basic social contract and the moral covenant? And what about the probability that none of the drafts will please the public or even a substantial part of it? After all, the public will not have been put through the crash course in moral thinking and only a part of it will have followed the course of MMC debate on TV.

The results of a process of this sort are predictable: If contracts are adopted, they will contain a mixture of requirements imposed by the strong on the weak, compromises in which all agree to follow rules not entirely pleasing to any, pseudorules sufficiently vague to allow people to follow their preferences under the appearance of a common morality, half-baked practices sanctioned by one or another tradition, and perhaps some provisions that are really valid from the moral point of view. In other words, a MMC would come out with something like the melange of mores under which we already live.

The Medical Morality Congress no doubt is a parody; but if Veatch is not calling for a formal assembly to draft a social contract and does not consider existing moral traditions to be a tacit one, it is hard to see what his proposal to base the medical covenant on the social contract amounts to. In his book, he imagines himself at the negotiating table and proposes articles for the social contract as well as the medical covenant. Perhaps his aim is to contribute to agreements that will be reached through publications, conferences, and conversations among small groups of individuals. However, the "will" here can only refer to the indefinitely remote future in respect to the social contract and a fortiori any covenant based on it. Philosophers have debated the foundations of morality for centuries. Despite indifferent progress toward consensus, their efforts have been noble. If Veatch is merely urging us to keep up the effort, his proposal is unexceptionable but also unexceptional. *Of course,* we should, but this does provide a new foundation for medical or professional ethics.

Prospects for Real Covenants

With all of its problems, the idea of professional covenants is not a foolish one. But in the absence of a clearly stated, consensual social contract for our society, on what would they be based. If a profession or elements of the public set out to develop a covenant, what might they use as its foundation? The dialectic of the centuries has not been fruitless. Competing moral traditions have become more articulate and systematic. The more irrational ones have been laughed off the intellectual stage. Popular mores, while unorganized and insecurely grounded, have become more civilized. Knowledgeable people have a greater opportunity to become aware of the content and options of rational morality. Some points of consensus have emerged. These developments provided grounds for hope that at least those who seriously reflect on professional ethics could find enough convergence in rationally criticized moral traditions to hammer out provisions for professional covenants. It is not inconceivable that national consortiums of such persons might reach agreement on drafts for actual covenants.

A consensus among experts, however, would not be a contract. Where would one begin in trying to establish their drafts as actual charters for professions and covenants into which professionals and lay persons would enter voluntarily? How can a theoretical list of rights and duties be transformed into a real framework of mutual trust and fidelity?

Surely, the process would have to begin with public criticism of the norms according to which present professions conduct their affairs. Public criticism of actual practices catapults us from the dream world of rational contractors into debate with key people in the institutions we aim to reform. Our immediate purpose would be to persuade professionals to modify their operational ethic in order to make their behavior better conform to the reasonable expectations of the public and to make their principles acceptable for the behavior of others with roles in their professional life.

If our analysis of the professional ideology and the subjective illusions it cultivates is valid, the arguments of ethicists with points of view not shaped by the professional subculture are essential to this program. Indeed, such arguments and the more diffuse pressures of popular opinion have already contributed to it. Veatch overstates his case when he describes physicians' codes as unilateral. They are indeed written by physicians, but they incorporate values from the larger society, and they are responses, moral as well as ideological, to external criticism of scandalous practices. The acquiescence of society to professionals' behavior reflects at least its partial assent to their professed principles. It is this partial assent that must be nourished into fully informed agreement by all parties.

A perfected charter for a profession would include not only rules and norms for the individual practitioner derived from a rational ethic, but specifications for institutions to support ethical behavior. The charter would state the rationale for the rules and institutions in the functions of the profession for human welfare. The language of the document would be clear, unequivocal, and logically organized; and the myths of ideology would have been swept away. There would be no vagueness or ambiguity to conceal differences among signatories. They would know what they were signing and outsiders would know what they had committed themselves to.[23]

These requirements make the task of securing consensus all the more difficult. In any actual effort to achieve it, the temptation would be to soften the rules, lower the ideals, take refuge in obfuscation, in order to achieve the appearance of agreement. But let us assume that these hazards could be braved and explore further what would be necessary to secure acceptance of perfected covenants.

At the outset, the "public" that would be prepared to participate in the creation of covenants would be the most informed, rational, and concerned sector. The hope would be that eventually it would be possible to persuade the entire populace to accept them through a program of moral education. Such a gradualist approach would have some prospect of success in contrast to the patent impracticality of the Moral Congress and the vacuity of the social contract. It would have common moral traditions to draw upon and professional codes as first drafts. It would have expert opinion available in the form of the perennial debates over ethical theory. It would have forums for communication and instruments for implementation in the form of professional associations and schools. It would have a point of contact with society in the units of government that legislate for and license professionals. The gradualist approach at least has a place to begin and some leverage for progress.

Lest the prospects seem too rosy, however, we should remind ourselves of the institutional constraints under which it would be conducted. To understand the resistance that would confront meaningful reforms, let us imagine draft covenants that significantly modify the role of professionals as auxiliaries of socioeconomic elites. Let us suppose that they seriously qualify the principle of service to society through single-minded service to patrons by provisions that require the public interest to be put ahead of client interest under specific circumstances (q.v., whistle-blowing). Let us suppose that the covenants impose important corporate responsibilities on professions: for example, on all professions to see that their services are distributed justly; on specific ones to guarantee the integrity of the environment, justice under law, free and open education, a fully informed public, etc. Let us suppose that the covenants guarantee professionals rights necessary to discharge these burdensome responsibilities even though this curtails traditional powers of clients and employers. Let us suppose, that is, that the covenants require sacrifices by both professionals and their patrons for the common good. What institutional obstacles would they encounter?

The primary channels to reach potential signatories would be the professional associations and schools. It would be best to approach persons of experience first; students in school have not yet earned the right to enter into the professional covenant. So we approach practicing professionals through their associations, perhaps working with their committees on professional ethics. But we immediately find that the associations' contact with the rank-and-file is limited, and the biases of professional elites are responsible for the ideological distortion of professional ethics in the first place. The likelihood of persuading these elites to transcend corporate interest to view their profession from a strictly moral point of view appears slight. We would be asking these to don the veil of ignorance, to mimic ideal contractors! They are the least likely in a profession to do so. It might be possible to bring morally sensitive and reasonably self-critical ethical committees, conservative though they be, to see flaws in their ethic, but the reforms they might endorse would be eviscerated by compromises and evasions when brought to the floor of professional coventions, leaving the status quo complacently undisturbed. (At this writing, the fate of the modest reforms proposed by ABA's Kutak Commission is uncertain. It appears that the more far-reaching ones will be rejected. This is the result of more than 6000 hours of work and a half million dollars expenditure, according to an apologist![24])

Suppose a wave of moral enthusiasm, or shame at the involvement of professionals in major scandals such as the Maryland public works bribes and Watergate, or a crisis requiring radical changes in social institutions were to make professions receptive to fundamental changes in their practices. This would not ensure that they would accept our draft covenants. We would still need a forum to communicate with them. We have decided that it is impractical to bypass professional associations by convening a Moral Congress. Our alternative is to draw all practitioners into associations so that they would be involved in the debate when the associations undertake to revise their codes.

Some indication of the difficulties with which this effort would have to contend is found in the attitude that professional ethics is a compendium of advice of older people to the young. An author of a manual on professionalism observes, "A young man leaving college is plunged frequently into a life so different from his previous experience that he needs advice from the men who have already had the experience that is about to become his." He expresses the wish to protect such men from corruption by imparting the lessons of fifty-six years of professional practice in the "school of experience and 'hard knocks.' "[25] Disregarding the author's inability to imagine women as professionals, note his assumption that experience teaches us what is right and older people do not have to worry about such questions. Young people have little to contribute. Theirs is to listen and learn. This is hardly an attitude that encourages vigorous debate.

The elders so generous with their experience and prejudices compose the very elites with a material interest in *not* democratizing professional associations. The officers and active participants in present associations are successful self-employed professionals and professionals who have advanced to the top managerial ranks of employing organizations. It is they who can afford to attend meetings and devote resources to association business. It also is they who have benefited from alliance with the socioeconomic powers of society.

To engage the rank-and-file would require radical changes in professional associations and other institutions. Some of these will be considered in the next chapter, but we must continue to remind ourselves that changes that would give more power to the professions could be harmful without the right kind of charters. Since changes are necessary to secure a hearing for possible charters, we are in something of a circle. We must lay the groundwork for charters by cautious changes in institutions and hope to perfect the institutions once the charters are in place.

Involving the Public

Covenants would be agreements between society and the professions. The public must be involved in drafting and adopting them. Lay persons as well as professionals would be asked to abide by their provisions.

We need not linger over the claim that only professionals are qualified to determine the content of professional ethics. It confuses the esoteric character of technical work and the exoteric character of its role in human affairs. The aspects of professional work discussed in here, for example, certainly fall within the ken of any educated person. Veatch points out the absence of any epistemological basis for a claim of greater moral insight by professionals and he argues that professionalism biases one as to the importance of the values involved in one's work.[26] Bayles responds to the "peer argument" as follows.

> Laypersons are competent to judge professional conduct and would provide a public perspective to the development of norms that is presently lacking from self-regulating systems. One might claim that professionals should be judged only by other professionals because otherwise they would not receive judgment by their peers. This claim is defective because it sets professionals above others in society and implies that laypersons are not the peers of professionals who essentially constitute a nobility not to be evaluated by commoners.

He points out that the same considerations apply to establishing norms as for judging performance under them. "If [as he argues] professional norms are to be evaluated by their promotion and preservation of liberal values, establishing and enforcing norms of professional conduct should rest with the public. This requires that legislatures should adopt the norms or authorize commissions with lay membership to do so."[27]

What is the chance of engaging the public in drafting the covenants? Let us suppose that we can persuade a state legislature or perhaps the U.S. Congress to appoint a blue-ribbon commission to recommend a covenant for a certain profession. We wish to involve the most informed, rational, and concerned sector of the public, that which could best be trusted to view things from the moral point of view. Where would we look? Besides representatives of the profession, the commission might include humanists, social scientists, and theologians from the universities; prominent professionals from occupations other than the one under consideration; and leaders from politics, business, and labor. No doubt many of these would accept the professional ideology. Let us suppose, however, that we can bring them to see the need for reform. Now they are ready to accept the draft covenant we provide—or better, to participate in developing one that incorporates reforms such as we may have imagined. The commission submits a report to the legislature with or (more probably, in view of the considerations adduced earlier) without the endorsement of professional associations.

The usual fate of reports of high-minded commissions cannot make us optimistic. In legislative assemblies, the popular will rules only when the populace is aroused and of one mind. On most matters a minority prevails. Ours is a system where interest groups win concessions in matters of intense preference by giving way to other interest groups in matters of less preference.[28] Even if a profession were to want to change its role, it is unlikely that its patrons would let it. These are the most powerful socioeconomic elements of society. The commission would be asking members of the legislature, most of whom are beholden to these elements, to break up a sweetheart arrangement that ensures the expertise necessary to dominate society. It would ask legislators to turn against their own influential constituents in a matter in which the public has little interest or knowledge.

The result is predictable. The report of a commission of the usual sort would be shelved or proposals based on it amended beyond recognition, and the professions left much as they are. A group charged with effecting charters of the sort envisioned here somehow would have to acquire real political clout. This will not happen until the general public is convinced—not merely convinced but aroused to the fact—that our social and economic institutions are incapable of dealing with the lethal problems that confront us. It also must be persuaded that reconstitution of professions along the lines we have discussed is one realistic way of addressing the problem.

The effect of charters and covenants depends on the existence of organizations to implement them, both the organizations that the charters themselves would establish and supporting organizations in the economy and body politic. It is to these structural matters than we turn next.

Notes

1. *The Rise of Professionalism*, p. x.
2. *Ibid.*, pp. 243–244.
3. *Ibid.*, p. 239. See p. 243.
4. *Ibid.*, pp. 147, 156, 236, and 241.
5. *Ibid.*, pp. xi–xii, 55, 157, 216, 227, and 241.
6. For examples, see *ibid.*, pp. 137, 213, and 234.
7. This assumes a class affiliation for all intellectuals, despite Larson's

observation that "Marxist thought concedes to intellectuals a measure of autonomy and detachment from any predetermined social group" (*ibid.*, p. xiv).

8. "The Recent History of Professionalism," p. 337. Larson herself acknowledges that "experts and professionals do possess cognitive and technical competences which are important, if not always essential, for the social development of productive forces and the full satisfaction of human needs. By choice and socialization they are often deeply involved with the intrinsic value of their callings." (*The Rise of Professionalism*, p. 243)

9. *Word and Object*, pp. 98–99.

10. These are the elements of Baier's "rational reconstruction" of the ideas of responsibility and task responsibilities in "Responsibility and Action."

11. *A Theory of Medical Ethics*, p. 7. I have examined this theory at length in "Veatch's New Foundations for Medical Ethics."

12. *A Theory of Medical Ethics*, pp. 6, 16–17, and 132.

13. *Ibid.*, pp. 6, 16, 83, and 91.

14. *Ibid.* This theory is worked out in Chapter 5, "The Triple Contract: A New Foundation for Medical Ethics." I shall be referring to the argument on pp. 110–126 unless otherwise indicated.

15. *Ibid.*, p. 125.

16. *Ibid.*, pp. 327–330.

17. *Ibid.*, p. 183.

18. *Ibid.*, p. 177. See pp. 170, 173, and 175.

19. *Ibid.*, pp. 6, 88 and 134.

20. *Ibid.*, pp. 117 and 121.

21. Based on 200 million citizens in the United States, 200,000 members of the American Medical Association, and 5000 members of the American Philosophical Association.

22. *A Theory of Medical Ethics.*, pp. 119–120 and 183.

23. See my "Evaluating Codes of Professional Ethics" for a discussion of these standards applied to engineering codes of ethics.

24. Alexander-Smith, "Commentary," p. 72.

25. Mead, *Manual of Engineering Practice*, p. 11.

26. *A Theory of Medical Ethics*, pp. 98–99.

27. *Professional Ethics*, pp. 138 and 139.

28. See Dahl, *A Preface to Democratic Theory*, Chapter 5.

□ 9

RECONSTITUTION OF INSTITUTIONS

The social ideal of maximum welfare fairly distributed will not be brought into being by preachments. What are needed are not voices in the wilderness but ways to make them heeded in the workshop and marketplace. It is not enough, therefore, to articulate the professional ideal. People must be induced to pursue it, and this requires moral engineering as well as moral theory.

The term 'moral engineering' raises the specter of pallid puritans drafting detailed blueprints for the lives of others. What we have in mind is rather an intelligent effort to design institutions that will foster moral practices, perhaps moral horticulture as we suggested in Chapter 3, though this term also is misleading in its way. In any event, since genuine morality presupposes autonomy, manipulation has no place. Rational persuasion is the tool. Nor can moral reformers be drawn from a separate professional class, such as ministers of the gospel or professors of philosophy; they must be persons in a position to affect the shape of institutions, such as leaders of professions and politicians. The purpose of a study such as this is to counsel those with the power to act, those who can determine the conditions under which rank-and-file professionals make their decisions and act morally or immorally.

Piecemeal engineering must work with the materials at hand. Moral reformers can only criticize and improve existing institutions, codes of conduct, educational programs, and other instrumentalities of the moral life; they cannot create them de novo. We will analyze the principles that they would need to follow in the circumstances described in the first part of this study.

Professional Corporations

The major and, it appears, unavoidable step toward involving all practitioners in the corporate business of a profession so as to orient their activities collectively to human welfare is to organize them under a state charter. This step must be taken with diffidence in view of the concentration of power and organizational problems it would entail.

The obvious way to establish a corporation for a profession would be to charter one of its existing associations. In some professions it would be obvious what association this should be; for example, the American Bar Association, the National Association of Social Workers. In others, there are several small associations with overlapping territories: for example, the American Psychological Association, American Personnel and Guidance Association, and American Psychiatric Association; the National Education Association, American Federation of Teachers, and American Association of University Professors. The National Society of Professional Engineers might seem the logical candidate for engineering, but the profession is so sprawling that it might be necessary to charter associations for different disciplines: for example, the American Institute of Chemical Engineers, American Society of Civil Engineers, Institute of Electrical and Electronic Engineers, American Society of Mechanical Engineers. We might be tempted to designate the American Medical Association as the corporation for health care professions, but the American Nurses Association and the organizations of medical technicians would object, since it would fortify the place of physicians on the top of the medical hierarchy.

In some professions, existing associations with elitist structures and inveterate biases might have to be bypassed altogether and corporations created from scratch. This would encounter bitter resistance because present practitioners think they have proprietary rights over their professions and they would necessarily be the initial members of newly constituted bodies. It would be easier to persuade them to accept new responsibilities and restrictions by the promise of new powers for favored old organizations than to shift their loyalty to new organizations. Nevertheless, new organizations would be necessary were the old ones too unreceptive to the proper kind of charter or were organizational problems among them too tangled.

Once a corporation was established, ways would be designed to engage all practitioners in its activities. Membership could be made a condition of licensure to practice. Financial contributions would be mandatory. This, supplemented by public support (tax revenues, service surcharges, etc.), could provide resources for important responsibilities. These responsibilities would involve the corporation in the work of ordinary practitioners and give them a stake in its behavior.

The corporate powers would be extensions and consolidations of powers now exercised weakly by some associations in some professions. The powers would be assigned to the corporation and to other institutions such as schools and state agencies coordinated with the corporation. The profession would be charged with initiatives in various areas, but would require concurrence of and be accountable to state bodies (legislatures, regulatory agencies, review commissions).

The responsibilities of the professional corporation would fall in the following areas.

1. *Standards of competence:* These would include educational requirements, tests for admission to practice, periodic reviews to ensure that practitioners maintain expertise. A licensing agency would need the power to penalize malpractice, to censure, fine, suspend, or revoke license. General standards for products, services, facilities, and resources for competent practice also would be necessary.

2. *Standards of conduct:* These would include a code of professional behavior, rules, laws, and their enforcement. The corporation would have to define the profession's ideals and aspirations and support ethical practitioners against pressures to violate standards through sanctions against clients and employers who exert pressure.

3. *Educational requirements:* These would include the educational policy in general; review of curricula and accreditation of training institutions; and cultivation of a rational professional ethic as expressed in the standards of conduct.

4. *Research:* This would be geared toward the expansion of the cognitive and technological base of the occupation, including general policies for research, allocation of resources through grant review, and influence on funding agencies.

5. *Representation:* This would cover counseling the public and other bodies in the name of the occupation, bringing

its special resources to bear; and providing expert testimony, proposals for legislation, and criticism of public policy and corporate practices.

We should remind ourselves at this point that the aim is not for the corporation to regulate everything practitioners do but to give direction to individuals who have been assigned clear responsibilities and broad discretion. The assumption is that the functionalist ideal would have been made to function—that ordinary practitioners would not only be technically competent but fully socialized into a code of conduct that would be valid from the moral point of view.

The power of the professional corporation would not necessarily make it responsive to its members. Its power would be intolerable unless its leaders were accountable to the rank-and-file and the rank-and-file had a say in its business. Ways would have to be devised to enable the lower strata of a profession to participate in its activities and protect them from undue influence from economic superordinates. Attendance at meetings could be subsidized by corporate funds. Employment contracts could guarantee practitioners time for participation. Those not actually involved in the management of the corporation could participate in deliberations over policy, ethics, and social responsibilities. Channels would be provided for debates, referenda, and communication of instructions to elected representatives. The present house organs of professional associations would be supplemented by sophisticated electronics. All of these measures would give the average practitioner the means as well as the incentive to participate in the corporation. Something like a genuine communal life would emerge.

Such a community would be equipped morally as well as practically to elicit desired behavior from its members much more effectively than the present voluntary and elitist associations. The fact that the rank-and-file had a voice in formulating its covenant would give the latter moral as well as legal force. Though new members would pledge obedience to a covenant already in place, the opportunity to work for changes in it would make their acceptance more voluntary. Assuming that the covenant was valid morally, they could be brought to see its wisdom by rational socialization.

Professional Estates: The Ultimate Solution

Pressure groups that are democratically organized are pressure groups nonetheless. Their internal structure does not ensure that they will transcend corporate egoism and tunnel vision. A democratic professional corporation might devote itself single-mindedly to the interests of the profession or special patrons. Even if its members could break free of the illusion of the professional ideology that service to patrons is equivalent to service to humanity, they might continue to exaggerate the value of the human needs they serve compared to those served by other occupations. Corporate self-importance is the typical bias of specialists isolated from other sectors of society by a unique subculture.

Institutions must be devised to combat corporate egoism and hubris. One way would be to incorporate all occupations, nonprofessional as well as professional, into a single governing body with power to allot social resources according to human needs and to hold each occupation accountable for the way it carries out its mission. Since the powers of such a body would rival that of the present arms of government, it might have to be established as one itself. In the states of this country, perhaps parliaments of work or occupational senates could replace present senates as branches of the legislature. The other house of the legislature could continue to represent localities. The new senate would be composed of delegates from occupational corporations. Naturally there would be problems of representation and procedure—we would not want the large number of engineers and engineering technicians to swamp the psychologists and counselors, or affluent physicians to intimidate hospital orderlies, or brash marketeers to outglitter staid academics—but we could expect that these problems would not be insoluble for a pragmatic experimental approach.

More difficult would be the task of making the body responsible to the public for rationally organizing the essential work of society. The occupational senate would need extensive powers to discharge its functions: to initiate legislation, fund and monitor appropriate executive agencies, and make the final decisions on policies proposed by the corporations respecting health care, administration of justice, engineering, the educational system, social welfare, and the other functions of occupations. The mere creation of an arm of government charged with the coordination of work would not guarantee its orientation to human welfare. Interest groups would lobby it to promote their causes, just as they lobby the present arms of government. Corporate egoism and the specialist's bias would continue to influence the scramble for resources and the control of the occupational senate over its corporate members. But by formalizing and holding up to public scrutiny the role of professions as pressure groups, some degree of accountability could be established. They would be forced to argue their causes before skeptical competitors, to adduce arguments to show the connection between their demands and the public good. This would make functionaries of the professions more self-critical and provide a milieu in which the moral point of view could compete more effectively with narrow self-interest and tunnel vision.

What we are contemplating is a deliberate effort to create professional estates of the sort Durkheim had in mind. Nothing short of making them integral parts of the governing framework of society seems capable of converting professions as we know them into the moral milieus cultivating civic virtue that Durkheim imagines them already to be. If the project succeeded, we also might hope to advance toward Whitehead's vision: Our example might inspire other societies to establish comparable estates. The ground would be laid for transnational communities of scientists, engineers, physicians, lawyers, managers, social workers, academicians, etc. Common values might emerge to mitigate the terrible ravages of national rivalry and suspicion.

The establishment of vocational estates under an arm of government would be a radical solution to the problems of society in the sense that it would get at one of the deep roots of such problems, the almost total subordination of expertise to special economic and social interests. All radical solutions have the disadvantage that their byproducts and remote consequences, and even the probability that they will solve the problem for which they were designed, are incalculable. The present solution need not even be considered unless I have convinced the reader that the problems are grave and the establishment of professional estates is designed to solve them.

The second difficulty with radical solutions is that it is hard to get others to accept them or keep a steady course in carrying them out. To be candid, the proposals advanced here are not likely to be adopted unless our society approaches collapse. The remainder of this chapter will be devoted to measures that professional estates would undertake and that could be approximated by professional corporations, by professions under less stringent charters or covenants, and even by professions as presently constituted. It is possible that an accumulation of small steps would move toward what we would hope to accomplish through a monumental one, and at less risk.

Equal Access to Certification

As conflict theorists have pointed out, the patronage of the rich and powerful was not forced on occupational groups. The bell-weather professions in the nineteenth and twentieth centuries eagerly locked themselves into a system of educational and vocational privileges that both results from and reinforces inequities in their delivery of services.

Membership in these professions was drawn from the elites who were served. The United States has not had a hereditary aristocracy or (except for slavery and its aftermath) caste system. But it has developed a shifting elite with an interest in perpetuating its status and conveying it to offspring, friends, and others "like us" (with the same culture, religion, attitudes, ancestry). The elite has maintained its identity in the face of waves of egalitarian sentiment and the extension of formal political rights to new groups. One of its principal measures was to make education the prime credential for position and provide special educational opportunities for its members. It gained acceptance for this arrangement by the ideology that opportunities are open to all. People are taught that those who are uneducated and uncredentialed are that way because of personal deficiencies rather than social barriers.[1]

The result has been some social mobility and the illusion of much more, for individuals by entering privileged occupations and for occupations by entering the ranks of the professions.

To maintain class identity, the economic elite had to control entry into the professions. They did so, Collins argues, primarily by control of education. Utilizing Weber's concept of status groups as self-consciously exclusive groups within society, he claims,

> Status groups are formed on the basis of common and distinctive experiences, interests, and resources. . . . Class-based status groups derive from occupational experiences, common interests in struggles for power and wealth, and differential resources for life style, for group mobilization, and for cultural idealization. . . . Professions are occupational communities; they are thus a type of class-based status group except that the community is organized explicitly within the realm of work itself rather than in the sphere of consumption.[2]

Professional education has been elitist in two respects: One must have the cultural background provided by elite families to enter and do well in professional schools—the elite have a disproportionate share of what Collins, following Bourdieu et al., calls "cultural capital." And much of professional education is devoted to further acculturation to maintain the identity of the status group, though it pretends to be strictly technical in a class-neutral sense.

The particular form that the professions in America took was greatly influenced by the "nativist" defense of white Anglo-Saxon male values and cultural identity against waves of immigrants (more than 24 million between 1880 and 1920). The trend toward free entry into the occupations since the Revolutionary War was reversed.

> The shift back to professionalism began in the atmosphere of a nativist counterattack in the late nineteenth century against the influx of culturally alien immigration and political reform in defense of the local powers of the Anglo-Protestant middle class; the revival of closed professional enclaves went hand in hand with the consolidation of the culturally elite universities in control of an expanding educational hierarchy . . . far from indicating the triumph of technocratic meritocracy, the development of the modern American profession is only a new variant on the familiar processes of stratification through monopolization of opportunities.[3]

Collins traces this process in detail for medicine, the legal profession, and (where it was less successful) engineering.[4]

The heritage of this historical process has been a restriction of opportunity for blacks and a succession of ethnic minorities. The waxing, alternating with waning, of affirmative action programs and a growing political awareness of minorities has produced some progress toward equal opportunity; but the cultural deficits of the poor and ethnic groups and the recalcitrant attitudes of the ruling elite is enough to make optimism about the inevitability of equality foolish.

It would be the responsibility of an arm of government of the sort we have described to see that admission to the professions is open to all groups equally. It would also be its responsibility to insist on the aggressive recruitment of underrepresented minorities.

The problem of cultural deficits would be more difficult. Contrary to the one-sided account of the conflict model, the functions of professional schools are not limited to overtraining intended to intensify cultural differences and credentialing to perpetuate the hierarchy of occupations. It has been a truism since Plato that every society needs a sorting mechanism for its essential functions. It must identify people with natural aptitude for particular kinds of work. It needs incentives to entice them into the fields where they are needed. It must provide them relevant knowledge and skills and assign them to jobs for which their aptitude and training suit them. Only in this way can it hope to realize Plato's idea of justice as each tending to his own business for the good of the whole. Surely in modern society it is true more than ever that specialized knowledge and skills, for which some have more natural aptitude than others, are necessary for complex tasks. The intellectual activities of the professional require special nurture. Standards of competence must be set and education provided to enable practitioners to meet them. The university is society's prime credentialing agency and purveyor of ideology, but it is far from being nothing but these. Standardized training is necessary if society is to benefit from specialized work and native ability is relevant to the absorption of that training. Whoever is to be served, some individuals must be selected to receive training that others do not and certified as ready to practice once they are trained.

What is required is relevant training available to the largest pool of talent, which means true equality of educational opportunity. Equality of opportunity means first of all open admission to everyone on the basis of ability to complete the training. It also means full material support for all who are admitted so that the more affluent will have no greatr chance to complete the training than the less affluent. The means to this end are well known. The will to implement the means is lacking. Even public institutions of higher education are becoming ever more expensive and exclusionary, and this is especially true of professional schools. Cultural biases in admission and retention have been identified but not eliminated. We can hope that a society structured to exercise real control over its system of work and really committed to distributive justice without the ideological illusion that such justice already had been achieved would have the will as well as wherewithal to act.

Finally, once society has debated and adopted charters for the major occupations, has criticized its institutions in the way necessary to do so, as a consequence has a lively sense of the need for a combination of equal educational opportunity and high levels of educated competence, and has a spirit animated by a recognition of the importance of work for which one has aptitude to the happiness of the individual, we could expect that society to see the need for acculturation of all its citizens from the first years of life to take advantage of educational opportunities. Schooling would be open to people with diverse backgrounds and they would be provided the cultural capital to take advantage of it.

In retracing this familiar territory, I am not blind, as conflict theorists sometimes appear to be, to efforts to provide equal educational and vocational opportunities, nor do I suggest that a parliament of work would remove all the obstacles that have turned up in the path. I only point out the need for progress and the urgency of these particular steps whatever institutional forms are used.

Professional Sexism

The one exception to the privileged access to the professions among the socioeconomic elite is women—if 50 percent can be considered an exception. Our patriarchal culture has limited vocational opportunities for middle-class women as it has for economically and ethnically disadvantaged men and women. The dramatic rise in the percentage of women in professional schools in the last decade gives hope that attitudes and structures are changing. Still, Lorber's profile of women physicians holds for most professions.

> Fairly consistently, American women doctors have been urban, upper-middle-class, highly qualified academically, and children of pro-

fessional or managerial parents. . . . And yet these elite women have, compared to male doctors, substantially lower incomes, fewer hospital appointments, and few memberships in professional societies, even though their publications are comparable. . . . They are also overrepresented in less-prestigious specialties, such as pediatrics, psychiatry, and public health.[5]

Women are in the minority in the more prestigious professions and do not fare as well in most of them as men. Furthermore, the professions in which women predominate, such as nursing, social work, school teaching, and librarianship (the semiprofessions or quasiprofessions, as sociologists denigratingly label them), do not rank high in prestige, income, power, or autonomy.

These facts do not require excessive statistical proof. I shall only add anecdotal data that illuminate the attitudes behind the patterns of discrimination.

Until the 1960s and 1970s, professional codes typically referred to the professional by masculine pronouns (and, consistently, the 1968 Code of the American Nurses Association refers to the nurse in the feminine). The fashion in more recent codes has been the plural (psychologists, engineers, journalists do so-and-so), obviating the choice between masculine and feminine and the use of awkward locutions such as he or she and men or women. However, ABA and AMA still use the masculine for lawyers and physicians and their clients or patients. No doubt all professions will come around as gender-neutral language becomes customary in official statements. One wonders, however, whether the attempt of professions to clean up their speech act represents a real change in attitude or merely a fashion of the times.

Codes are prepared with a view to public relations and so sexist language is likely to be avoided in them. The assumption that professions are a male domain is more evident in unguarded remarks. Typical, I imagine, are the hortatory materials distributed as late as 1979 by the now defunct Engineers Council for Professional Development under the title "A Professional Guide for Your Engineering Career." The following are phrases from W. E. Wickenden's 1949 address, "The Second Mile": "professions to which any man may aspire within the bounds of his talent . . . What is the distinctive mark of the professional man? . . . As men mature they come to value professional rewards." These are from W. J. King's "The Unwritten Laws of Engineering":

> Occasionally a man will worry unduly about where his job is going to get him . . . Every young man should read Emerson's essay on "Self Reliance." . . . What if he [your boss] turns out to be somewhat less than half the man he ought to be . . . What Every Executive Owes His Men . . . Make it a rule to help the other fellow . . . Engineering is essentially a gentleman's profession . . . On the other hand, there is no reason that a man should be afraid to say "damn".

King describes the attire of the engineer in male terms (pressed trousers, a tie, etc.) and, in reference to the "design and development of good engineers," he quotes Pope, "The proper study of mankind is man." Also in the ECPD packet, the pamphlet "The Young Engineer: A Professional Guide" speaks glowingly of "the dramatic endeavors the profession has made to serve man and improve his environment and quality of life." All of the pictures of engineers in the handsome brochure, "The 2–4 Program for Professional Development" are pictures of men. (In fairness, I should report that the packet contains an attractive booklet written by Sara Jane Neustadt and entitled "WOMENGINEER." It makes a strong appeal to women to enter engineering and seeks to dispel the myth of female incapacity. It refers the reader to The Society of Women Engineers for further assistance.)

The ideological seduction of social scientists should warn us that they are no more immune to sexist thinking than the professionals whose self-images they accept uncritically. This is reflected in the dearth of attention to women, their work, and their absence from professions and professional elites in scholarly writing. Sociologists, mainly men, consistently use masculine pronouns except when discussing the occupations dominated by women. Statements such as these are common:

> [A profession is a] group of men who are trained by education and experience to perform certain functions better than their fellow men.

> The professional man is distinguished by the fact that he does not give only his skill. He gives himself.

> The professions are described in dictionary definitions as dealing with the practical affairs of men . . . The practitioner's activities . . . impinge radically upon the most basic concerns of man.[6]

Goode generally refers to the "men" who perform various kinds of work and to them and employers and clients by masculine pronouns; but when he comes to the schoolteacher, he shifts to the feminine. Thus, he refers to the intellectual shallowness of "her" knowledge-base for both curriculum content and pedagogic technique. Hughes talks exclusively in terms of "professional men" and "a man's work" except when he refers to the social worker, who is "she." This is the more striking because he is one of the few older sociologists who acknowledge that women work.[7] The following are some of his more discordant remarks:

> [Y]oung people must choose their occupations, as they do their wives, largely on faith . . .

> [Referring to the nurse:] She is the right-hand man of the physician, even and especially when he isn't there.

> A great deal of our ambition takes the form of getting training for kinds of work which carry more prestige than that which our fathers did.

> Thus a man's work is one of the things by which he is judged, and certainly one of the more significant things by which he judges himself.

> At best, we professors have a wonderful and stimulating life . . . with a good chance of marrying women of great intelligence and charm and great powers of sympathy and support.

> [Remarking that students are quick to detect contradictions between our words and behavior:] "You are not in high school now. You are in college. Be a man. You are on your own," say we professors. [Then we treat them like children.][8]

Finally, we may note the titles of two books that suggest the framework that sociologists take for granted, Hughes' *Man and His Work* and Reader's *Professional Men*.

Ideally, the expansion of opportunities for women in the (paid) work force will proceed independently of the structural changes that we are describing. The prospect of the alleviation of this age-old injustice is one of the more encouraging social developments of our time. However, the end of sexual discrimination will not necessarily mean the end of social discrimination. Structural changes will still be needed to eliminate the obstacles that prevent individuals of native ability who lack material and cultural resources from gaining access to the professions.

Justice in the Distribution of Services

Abstractly defined, the justice of a just action consists in equality of contribution to the happiness of all those affected by it. Since one cannot *make* others *be happy* or *distribute happiness*, this means that an action is just insofar as it distributes goods and burdens at the agent's disposal in such a way as to facilitate more or less equally each person's autonomous pursuit of happiness.

Knowledge is one of the most important social goods. It is socially produced in that everyone in society provides material support for inquiry even if he or she does not engage directly in it. What is socially produced should be socially appropriated, so the stock of knowledge is a collective possession of humanity. The whole stock cannot be appropriated by anyone, but its fruits can be shared. A just society would be organized to share it with everyone equally. Professionalism provides skills based on knowledge that people cannot acquire for themselves, so justice demands that these skills be available to everyone in a way that will contribute equally to the happiness of each.

To realize justice in a complex society, institutions are required that maximize the probability that benefits and burdens will be distributed fairly. The institutions of professionalism must be judged by this criterion as well as in terms of their contribution to the aggregate utilization of knowledge by society. That is, they must be judged by the distribution of knowledge as well as the quantity of knowledge utilized.

The major arena of action for individuals is the network of institutions that composes their society. Justice boils down to doing what one can to make just institutions work, to reform unjust ones, and to compensate for injustices that cannot be avoided. The scope for justice is limited for isolated individuals confronted with a social structure that has evolved over millennia with only sportive attention to justice. Professional corporations and a coordinating arm of government would make possible for the first time a comprehensive social policy for the organization of work and the practical utilization of knowledge in which justice would factor as an essential value.

Many moralists seek a definition of justice that would make it morally indefeasible; that is, a definition under which it would never be right to act unjustly. The concept adopted here countenances the abridgment of justice for other values, though rarely.

The ultimate principle of morality is that one should perform the act that promises to maximize benefits and distribute them fairly. On occasion, we are forced to choose between the two clauses of this principle. We should try to maximize benefits if the possible increment in benefits is large and the unfairness not extreme and we should sacrifice small increments that require gross inequities. Where the costs of the alternatives appear to be in balance, we must choose intuitively or randomly.

This mixed principle partially, though not entirely, escapes the standard criticism of utilitarianism as stated by Petit:

> The embarrassment with the utilitarian criterion is that under a particular, not implausible circumstance it would have us recommend the unequal allocation of a certain good. The circumstance is of course that such a distribution produces more aggregate happiness than the alternative.[9]

It is not, however, my intention to defend utilitarianism. I think we must concede that it is necessary in boundary situations of life to sacrifice ourselves and to ask others to sacrifice themselves for the general welfare, while in normal situations we frequently must forego opportunities to add to the aggregate benefit in order to see that available benefits are distributed fairly. Still, critics exaggerate the conflict between justice and utility. Justice itself has high utility in that the marginal utility of benefits is greater when they are widely distributed than when they are concentrated for a privileged few. If I provide the first of two units of a good (automobiles, appendectomies, legal counsel, sewer service, the news) to A, I usually will create greater aggregate utility by giving the second to B. Brandt defends the use of the progressive income tax to meet the needs of the poor in these terms.

> The utilitarian justification . . . is that a dollar taken in taxes from the wealthy would have done the wealthy far less good than the same dollar spent providing food stamps, medical care, and so on for the poor or handicapped. All this the utilitarian can defend, and it is easy to see that application of the utilitarian criterion for optimal institutions moves in the direction of economic equality for all.

Utilitarians do not take equality as an end in itself. They advocate moves toward equality, because such moves usually maximize utility, but they oppose moves that would diminish utility just for the sake of equality. Brandt remarks, "when we see how far a utilitarian theory does take us toward economic equality, we can well wonder how much farther the critics of utilitarianism would like to go."[10]

In addition to the greater marginal utility of justly distributed goods, just acts develop socially desirable habits and precedents and unjust acts do the reverse. Furthermore, just actions are naturally pleasant (q.v., Aristotle) because they afford pleasure involving the higher human faculties (q.v., Mill) and realize the self as part of the moral organism (q.v., Bradley). Thus, justice has more utility for the doer than injustice.

Quite apart from the satisfactions of justice for those who do it and its benefits for those to whom it is done, it is demanded by egalitarian ideologies across the world. Inequality is resented and breeds discord. The social planner who seeks a stable social order in the name of utility must see that it promotes justice.

The principle of utility and a fortiori our mixed principle dictate the social policy of distributing professional services so as to make as nearly as possible an equal contribution to the happiness of all members of the community. This does not require the same services for everyone. The physician's attentions have greater value to one who is ill than to one who is well. A person without legal problems finds no value in the services of an attorney. The aim must be to make services equally available to all who need them. This suggests one abridgment of justice as a matter of policy. Society should institute welfare rights to entitle injured, deprived, and handicapped members of society to professional help beyond the limits defined by strict justice. A unit of service may move two persons equal distances up the scale of happiness, but leave one in the depths of misery because of the point from which he or she began. Society should extend more help to that individual. If the person's misery is socially inflicted, this is compensatory justice; but if it is due to nature or accident, special assistance and the burden it imposes on others is a matter of compassion rather than of justice.

Arguments parallel to those for the utility of justice hold for compassion. Whether they suffice to justify welfare rights or it is necessary to qualify our mixed principle further to advocate a society that is compassionate as well as utilitarian and fair depends on complex factual issues concerning the effects of different policies, need not be addressed here.

Professional Injustice

From the perspective of conflict theory, we can see that there is systematic injustice not only in unequal opportunities for members of different sectors of society to enter professions, but in the excessive share of social resources that the professions command and, most of all, in the inequitable distribution of professional services.

Factual data about the distribution of services are complex and their significance may be disputed on the basis of different conceptions of justice. There is agreement about gross inequities, at least, among observers sharing something like our conception. Groups defined by irrelevant characteristics receive far less than an equal share of services in our socioeconomic system. First and foremost are the poor. Overlapping these are ethnic groups, the culturally deprived, and people living in certain areas (rural, inner-city).[11] We will take this inequity as an obvious given. The question is What can and should be done about it?

The need for distributive justice and the degree to which it is lacking are acknowledged most explicitly by the legal profession (whose business, of course, is justice). The ABA is unique among professional associations in recognizing a responsibility in this area, though it carefully circumscribes that responsibility to protect the economic interests of the lawyer. It asserts,

> The legal profession cannot remain a viable force in fulfilling its role in our society unless its members receive adequate compensation for services rendered and reasonable fees should be charged in appropriate cases to clients able to pay them. Nevertheless, persons unable to pay all or a portion of a reasonable fee should be able to obtain necessary legal services, and lawyers should support and participate in ethical activities designed to achieve that objective. (Model Code)

This declaration is worth something. However, that equality is not achieved is obvious. Auerbach states flatly, "the recipients of the best legal services have remained consistently identifiable in the twentieth century along class lines," and "In the United States justice has been distributed according to race, ethnicity, and wealth, rather than need. This is not equal justice."[12] He explains the situation by the formation of the elite in the legal profession. Seymour draws the same conclusion.

> The impact of the legal system touches the lives of most Americans one way or another, but it falls most heavily on those poor and lower middle income families who are caught up in criminal prosecutions, collection suits, and other enforcement proceedings without friends, resources or adequate legal representation.[13]

Crimes of the poor are more likely to be detected, the quality of professional help for them is low, and sentences imposed by the courts are severe. In civil proceedings, they are not guaranteed legal counsel and the laws and courts are biased against them in respect to such matters as collection of debts. The justice of particular processes may be debated, but that something is fundamentally wrong is starkly evinced by the fact that 40 percent of the prison population and only 12 percent of the nation is black, and the creditor class (large business, public utilities) are represented by lobbyists in legislatures whereas there are none for the poor.[14]

The ABA at least recognizes the right of everyone to legal counsel. The American Medical Association makes no such admission about health care. It takes pains to absolve the physician of responsibility. "A physician shall, in the provision of appropriate patient care, except in emergencies, be free to choose whom to serve, with whom to associate, and the environment in which to provide medical services" (Principles of Medical Ethics). "A physician has a duty to do all that he can for the benefit of his individual patients without assuming total responsibility for equitable disbursement of society's limited health resources" (Opinion of the Judicial Counsel). It does lay down guidelines for the physician about how to treat those who are already patients, but by the time these decisions must be made, institutional economic, ethnic, and geographical biases have taken their toll. As Beauchamp and Childress note, macroallocation of medical resources set the parameters for microallocations.[15] The latter cannot be just if the former are not.

Critics have harped on facts from which the AMA has turned its eyes. Beauchamp and Childress, for instance, point to this line of criticism:

> Some writers have claimed that our health policies are unjust because we do not allocate more of our resources for preventive measures aimed at protecting those who cannot defend themselves against the onslaughts of disease. They admit that preventive measures will

place new burdens and restrictions on the controlling social classes, who have thus far resisted such measures.[16]

Munson speaks broadly of "the crisis in American health care." In documenting the charge that "we live in a system in which there are still two kinds of medicine—one for the rich and one for the poor," he observes:

> Despite the great economic investment in health care, some 12 percent of the population of this country (one out of eight people) receive no medical care at all. Others frequently lack access to care even when they can afford it, and a large number of people cannot receive the proper kind of care.[17]

Among the factors contributing to this situation are overspecialization by physicians, underfunding of community clinics and care centers, lax enforcement of Hill-Burton regulations requiring hospitals to provide reasonable volume of free and reduced cost care, paucity of family-care doctors, and concentration of physicians in metropolitan centers.

Engineering societies do not mention justice at all. They put a premium on loyalty to the employer and are disposed to think of engineers as technicians at the service of others rather than authors of policies and actions that broadly affect human welfare. Furthermore, in contrast to critics of the legal and health care systems, external observers seldom evaluate the delivery system for engineering in terms of justice. Yet engineers occupy strategic positions in the administration of public works and management of private industry, and some facts about their role stare us in the face. Take a modern metropolis—Dallas is an archetypal example. The city center is a marvel of architecture and engineering, a gleaming maze of stone, steel, and glass. The affluent live in pleasant homes among trees and grass in the suburbs. They commute to work sealed in soundproof comfort, their attention occupied by the automobiles around them on the expressway and the FM radio, oblivious to the miles of squalor in which lower-income persons live with cluttered sidewalks, untended lots, potholed streets, and malfunctioning sewers.

The poor in this country enjoy a trickle-down of engineering services through public works. A more fundamental injustice is the cavalier disregard of the interests of people in underdeveloped countries and future generations. The greater the expansion of engineering techniques and tools, the more rapid is the consumption of irreplaceable energy and the irreparable destruction of the environment.

If the moral community comprises *all* persons, not just those of one country or generation, and if *each* member of the moral community has an equal right to the material conditions of happiness, it is painfully obvious that the economic system works injustices on the poor, on other nations, and on future generations. Engineering and technology as value-neutral amplifications of whatever relationships the economic system generates contribute to the net result in the face of the best of intentions on the part of the individual engineer.

Similar indictments could be issued against other professions. The professions are organized to serve patrons of a limited class with constraints only against the most egregious harm to others. Where unjust discriminations exist, professionalism magnifies them by its very efficiency. It is true that an aggregate increase in productivity sometimes justifies the increase in inequality. Though discrepancies in advantages widen, the least advantaged receive more from a professionalized society than they would from an unprofessionalized one. Yet this is hardly the case in every instance, and where it is, the benefits of professionalism could have been spread more equally by an alternative institutional structure. That the least advantaged group benefits from advances in knowledge despite the inequitable social structure does not gainsay that they would benefit more from advances in an equitable one.

A few professional groups and many individual professionals are aware of the injustice of the system and their collusion in it. They make an effort, sometimes passionate, usually half-hearted, to alleviate it. The remainder bury themselves in their professional task and ignore its larger meaning in the complacent illusion that the system is not only the best devised by man, but the best devisable.

Invisible Injustice

Professionals staff delivery systems that provide more and better service to some segments of society than others. The opportunity to enter these most privileged of occupations is afforded individuals from some segments more than others. Professions profess to serve humanity, but serious inequities exist, the efforts of professional groups to rectify them are half-hearted, and professionals individually tend to resist social change. What in the pattern of professionalism blinds most professionals to these injustices?

Our perception of the treatment of socially defined groups is determined by the conceptual framework that we bring to experience. This is doubly true of the interpretation of statistics and other public data. The conceptual framework of the typical professional reflects the professional ideology, inculcated during professional socialization, reinforced by the professional subculture, and shielded from challenge by the public's acceptance of the same ideology. The ideology is functionalist. It emphasizes the functions performed by the professions and dismisses dysfunctions as the unimportant aberrations of a few deviants not integral to the system itself. Functionalist beliefs make for political and social conservatism. Social action is directed toward control of the deviants rather than changing the system. The functionalist fears to tamper with the system for fear of disrupting its functions.

Due to the false elements in the professional ideology, the typical professional perceives the social world as more fair than it is. Subjective illusion conspires with corporate self-interest and hubris to prevent professionals from projecting fundamental reforms. Somehow, the larger society must take the initiative and escape the professional ideology in doing so. This is why a forum in which occupations would have to compete for social resources is necessary. Only there could we hope for a just social policy to emerge.

Fair Pay

Nothing has bred cynicism about protestations of public interest more than the unconscienable exploitation of human need by some doctors and lawyers. Professional avarice not only belies the ideology of service; it seduces practitioners into obeisance to the economic elite and, where they do serve the wider public, it syphons off disproportionate shares of social resources. For justice to be served, therefore, a ceiling needs to be imposed on professional income. I envision a ceiling closer to the present (1987) *average* for academics of about $30,000 than that for physicians of over $100,000. The opposition which this would face is suggested by the groans that arise from preprofessionals when I broach it in my course on professional ethics. Students smile benignly as I review the most radical reforms until I come to this. Their indignation indicates why many people want to become professionals.

Excessive incomes are defended on the twin bases of fairness and incentive. It is said to be only fair to reward highly arduous work that requires special talent and extensive training and contributes to so much to human welfare. And it is said that rewards are necessary to recruit people for these tasks.

Both claims are undercut by the professional ideology that speaks glowingly of the intellectual character and special dignity of professional work. Larson scoffs at such talk in discussing the "proletarianization of educated labor"; but the fact that the conditions under which many professionals work (e.g., engineers in a large electronics firm or social workers and counselors in a welfare agency) resemble those of skilled labor more than self-employed practitioners with affluent clients does not mean that the work itself does not have intellectual interest and intrinsic satisfaction or that it would not have much more if it were rationally directed to human welfare. The conflict model tends to denigrate professional work when it should emphasize the intrinsic dignity (at least potentially) of other kinds of labor.

We have the right, therefore, to dream, to hope, to strive for conditions in which professionals would work hard to perfect their art and work hard at practicing it primarily for the satisfaction of doing so. They would have to be paid a sufficient wage to live comfortably and work effectively. But success would be rewarded but in terms of service rendered not recipients' ability to pay.

The fairness requirement is easily met. There is nothing unfair about asking people to work for a living wage when the work is interesting, satisfying, and gratifies their moral sense. The incentive factor, however, might require short-term compromises. We are designing a system for people who still view life from the prudential rather than the moral point of view. To induce a sufficient number to undertake training and lifelong dedication to practice at the state-of-the-art level of competency to meet urgent human needs in stressful situations requires greater rewards than strict justice demands. There is no justification, however, for the extremes of income resulting from professional monopolies in a market economy.

It is open to serious question whether the measures we have considered could nurture true moral organisms into existence in a capitalist society. There they would become instruments for harmonizing the moral obligations of professionals with demands of employing organizations and clients, whose aim is not the welfare of humanity. It might seem that the conflict would be resolved if the employer and the agency that defines obligations were one and the same, that is, if all professionals were employed by the state. However, merely broaching this possibility calls objections to mind. Whatever its economic form, the planning-implementing mechanisms of the modern state are overloaded. The unity of "the state" as employer-and-governor in socialized societies is spurious. It resolves itself into a loose interrelation of bureaucracies, each with its vested interests and the whole not coordinated for the public good. The educational-credentializing-monopolizing institutions of traditional professions can be used to gain the same privileges in a state bureaucracy as they do in capitalist corporations.

The conflict theorists do not spell out the nature of the social system that would replace the present hierarchical and exploitive one. Presumably, they do not wish to return to tribalism. The new society would be industrial. It would coordinate the activities of masses of people and utilize bureaucratic institutions. Position in its organizations could create status differentials as effectively as entrepreneurial success or the patronage of the social elite. If status corrupts, it will not be automatically eliminated by public ownership of the means of production or formal dedication of economic activities to "public interest" by agencies acting in the name of society.

Therefore, rather than tying our proposals to a particular economic program, it seems preferable to pitch them at a more abstract level so as to make them compatible with alternative systems. What is needed in any system are institutions to adjudicate the claims of occupations against one another in terms of some overarching conception of human good and to review the practices of each occupation to ensure that it meets its special responsibilities. Chartered professional corporations and occupational senates would be such institutions. But they would have to be tested to see whether they would work and whether perhaps less extreme measures would work as well.

Limited Measures

In an attempt to conceive of ways to create a genuine orientation of professions to the public good, we have imagined consolidations that would enhance their power. The result could easily be the opposite of what we desire. Professional estates could stifle the initiative of practitioners and they could be used to advance corporate interests even further at the expense of society.

In these proposals we are grappling with the ancient problem of balancing justice, welfare, and liberty. The institutional reforms require a change in habits of thought among professionals and the public alike. I shall concentrate here on the place of moral training.

Traditionally, ethics have been taught in professional schools, when they have been dealt with at all, as a matter of training in what professional codes say and how they apply to specific decisions. Students are required to learn the codes and identify the provisions that settle specimen cases. In other words, ethics is taught as another technical discipline. Thus, the American Personnel and Guidance Association publishes a casebook in which a set of examples illustrate right and wrong actions under each provision.[18] The University of Texas Law School Foundation publishes a problems book in which the author appends to each case a list of citations of the ABA Model Code and court decisions governing the case.[19] Such texts convey the impression that there is a correct solution in the code for every ethical problem though the solution may seem paradoxical to the uninitiated.

On the other hand, a new style of education is emerging. Some texts attack ethics in a genuinely dialectical manner, for example, Munson or Veatch in medical ethics, Thompson and Thompson in nursing ethics, and Baum and Flores in engineering ethics. They present hard cases whose solution is problematic under existing codes. They push the student to reflect on foundations.[20]

Unfortunately ethics is a minimal part of most professional curricula and the traditional approach dominates. If the new approach were taken seriously, we would hope to produce a generation of questioning professionals who would take a lively interest in the professional covenant and insist on its periodic review.

Only if critical ethics is taken seriously by professionals can we expect professional ethics to become a concern for the general public. If it were taken seriously, we could hope that its issues would be addressed in ethics courses in colleges and values-clarification programs of lower schools and churches and come to be dealt with by ordinary people at a deeper level than those issues are treated in the mass media.

Let us suppose that a professional code has been revised to be valid from the moral point of view, that it obtained sufficient acceptance to be considered a covenant, and that most practitioners have been so embued with critical ethics that they can be relied on to make decisions from the moral point of view in light of the covenant. In the present economic system, they would be under the usual pressures to compromise to please clients and employers. If they refused, the latter still would have unscrupulous practitioners to use. What measures short of professional corporations and estates could be instituted to protect the moral practitioner? To control malfeasance, professional associations and certification agencies of the state would have to be strengthened. Once again, this requires a dangerous concentration of power, but we are presupposing that the associations have been reformed sufficiently to have a valid covenant. Assuming their commitment to the public interest, they could develop mechanisms to protect the ethical practitioner from the employer. Associations might be able to develop sanctions to induce employers to recognize the right of professional conscience and institutionalize respect for the professional ethic. Once again, opposition could be anticipated because this would curtail the traditional right of employers to discharge at will. As Ewing points out, this right is sanctioned by law.

> To leave absolutely no doubt that employers and senior managers can demand complete loyalty from subordinates and get it, the common law says the employer may discharge his employee at any time for any reason, so long as there is no statute or agreement limiting such right or discharge. *A fortiori,* the employer can transfer, promote, demote, or otherwise change an employee's status at any time. It does not matter if the boss is arbitrary or even wrong in taking such action. He doesn't have to give a good reason or any reason. For an employee to have a paycheck *and* rights of speech, conscience, and

privacy, says the common law, is tantamount to running with the hare and hunting with the hounds.[21]

Ewing reviews tentative and very modest efforts of legislatures and courts to protect employee rights and argues that it would benefit all concerned, employers as well as employees and society, to make a strong bill of employee rights part of the legal structure of this country. One route would be amendment of the Constitution. Ewing proposes this amendment:

> No public or private organization shall discriminate against an employee for criticizing the ethical, moral, or legal policies and practices of the organization; nor shall any organization discriminate against an employee for engaging in outside activities of his or her choice, or for objecting to a directive that violates common norms of morality.[22]

(He adds other provisions relating to privacy and due process.) Ewing is hopeful that his aim can be achieved without a Constitutional amendment by more limited legislation, voluntary contracts, and internal procedures instituted by enlightened employers.

We are considering here a body of laws and voluntary practices to guarantee protection of professionals against penalties not only for objecting to, but refusing to obey directives that violate their professional ethic. It would significantly limit loyalty to the organization by key personnel, loyalty that the professions have taken pains to *guarantee* by faithful-agent, conflict-of-interest, and confidentiality clauses of their codes and by punishments they have added to the penalties inflicted by employers and the state on whistle-blowers, bribe-takers, and "unfair" competitors. Employers are not likely to see this change in their relationship with professional employees to be in their interest.

This employer reluctance is understandable in view of the status of professions as economic interest groups. We are seeking a way to make professions into strong countervailing forces against pressures exerted by employers and the market to violate professional norms. Any addition to the power of the professions could be used to exact economic concessions under the present social system. It is hard to imagine employers welcoming this. It could be initiated only if the professions were transformed so as to have a genuine and palpable orientation to the public good.

In this chapter we have considered changes that might divert professionalism from service to the narrow interests of the professions and their patron groups to the common welfare and create a mutuality of trust and obligation between professionals and the rest of the community. The changes require a reformation of professional institutions across the board. In honesty, we must recognize the improbability that society will undertake such a radical experiment.

Few share the apocalyptic vision of the present social order that makes it reasonable to contemplate fundamental changes. Society is a ponderous barge drifting with the current toward deadly shoals. We do not know whether it could be steered into safe channels. Who can tell? The passengers are unconcerned. They are content with easy progress downstream. They praise the professionalism of the crew members who busy themselves with routine shipboard tasks. They leave the navigation to the captain. But he is nowhere in sight. He may be astern, fishing, or below, drunk. He may have jumped ship. A few visionaries amidship are charting a new course. They are met with amusement and irritation when they cry alarm. When they try to seize the helm, they are locked in their cabins or thrown overboard.

However, some of the more reflective passengers may heed warnings. The steps we have proposed forward reforming the professions may obtain a hearing. At least, they must be voiced.

Notes

1. Larson, *The Rise of Professionalism*, pp. 34, 51, 136, 210, 221, 239, and 242.

2. *The Credential Society*, p. 134.

3. *Ibid.*, p. 131. See p. 173.

4. *Ibid.*, Chapter 6, particularly pp. 145–146, 154–155, and 169. For a more detailed study of the nativistic counterattack in the legal profession, see Auerbach, *Unequal Justice*, Chapters 1 and 2.

5. "Women and Medical Sociology," p. 76.

6. Taeusch, *Professional and Business Ethics*, p. 5; Marshall, "The Recent History of Professionalism," p. 328; Cogan, "The Problem of Defining a Profession," pp. 35–36.

7. "The Theoretical Limits of Professionalism," p. 286.

8. Hughes, *The Sociological Eye*, pp. 295, 308, 338, 357, and 358.

9. *Judging Justice*, p. 130.

10. "A Defense of Utilitarianism," p. 43.

11. Bayles refers matter-of-factly to the "economic, racial, and geographical maldistribution of services." *Professional Ethics*, p. 27.

12. *Unequal Justice*, pp. 5 and 12.

13. *Why Justice Fails*, p. 7.

14. *Ibid.*, pp. 44 and 54.

15. *Principles of Biomedical Ethics*, p. 171.

16. *Ibid.*, p. 191.

17. *Intervention and Reflection*, pp. 447 and 448.

18. Callis, Pope and DePauw, *APGA Ethical Standards Casebook*.

19. Matthews, *Problems Illustrative of the Responsibilities of the Legal Profession*.

20. Munson, *Intervention and Reflection;* Veatch, *Case Studies in Medical Ethics;* Thompson and Thompson, *Ethics in Nursing;* Baum and Flores, *Ethical Problems in Engineering*. The critical approach is analyzed in the *Hasting Center Monographs on the Teaching of Ethics*.

21. *Freedom Inside the Organization*, p. 30.

22. *Ibid.*, pp. 234–235. See Ewing, *Do It My Way or You Are Fired*.

☐ 10

PROFESSIONAL CODES

The primary reason to cut through the screen of ideology for a realistic view of the dynamics of professional life and to institute reforms in its institutional framework is to foster the observance of the professional ethic. But *is* there *a* professional ethic in any sense of the word? The term 'professional ethics' has several meanings. It refers, first, to the norms required by the moral point of view for the kind of work that professionals do, that is, an ideal rational ethic. This is what moral theorists try to formulate. It does not yet exist in perfected form acceptable to everyone. 'Professional ethics' means, second, common norms actually followed by most professionals. Sociologists describe widespread practices; an ethic exists to the extent that professions regard such practices as morally obligatory. Since the norms for these practices are not necessarily acceptable from the moral point of view, this sense of 'professional ethics' differs from the first. The term means, third, common elements of codes of professional associations. Many such codes exist, but they do not always conform either to rational norms or actual practices, so this sense of 'professional ethics' is distinct from the first two. Finally, the term refers to a prospective compact between the professions and society. The institutional reformer seeks to create such an ethic, but with the proviso that it conform to rational ethics and the hope that its principles will gain currency among professionals and become incorporated in their codes.

Only with the convergence of the first three senses of 'professional ethics' can there be a harmony between pretensions, practices, and the legitimate expectations of society. The present work scouts the territory that will have to be crossed to create an ethic of the fourth sort as a means to promoting the convergence of the other three.

It is prudent to begin with the existing codes of professional associations, treating them as hypotheses to be criticized with a view toward the final ethic at which we aim. To utilize codes in this way, we must attend to three things: how the codes must be perfected from the moral point of view; how acceptance can be gained for perfected codes among professional groups; how institutions can be developed to ensure that the codes will be followed in practice. We have discussed the problems of gaining consensus and restructuring institutions in prior chapters. Here we will discuss the task of perfecting codes.

Evaluating Existing Codes

Many professional associations arrogate to themselves the function of moral engineering for the entire occupation. At an early stage in the professional project, the association sets up a committee to draft a code. It duly debates and adopts the code and revises it from time to time. It imposes it with more or less force on all who work in the occupation whether or not they belong to the association. The result is a plethora of codes across the spectrum of occupations, some careful and detailed, others vague and perfunctory. Some of their elements are intended to shape practices to conform to ideals; others are ideological masks better suited to cover over practices than to improve them. To evaluate codes as instruments of moral persuasion, therefore, we need first of all to examine their actual uses.[1]

We will not examine the major codes in detail but develop a strategy for evaluation, using their provisions as illustrations. The strategy will be consequentialist. One is prone to assume that any ethical code is *a good thing*, but are these? What are the consequences of having codes at all and what are the consequences of codes of this and that character?

The concepts of function and dysfunction are basic to this analysis. A function is a set of consequences that either explain or justify a rule, practice, or institution. A dysfunction is a set of consequences that does or should inhibit its observance or support.

The definitions cover two kinds of functions and dysfunctions. What will be termed social functions are the actual consequences that explain the existence of rules, practices, and institutions. Sociologists have developed the notion of social functions to understand the way systems of action are kept in equilibrium with their environments or propelled forward in certain directions. Thus, among the social functions of professional codes are their corporate functions in maintaining the status of occupations as professions and their societal functions in strengthening the network of institutions in the existing society.

What will be termed human functions are the consequences of possible rules, practices, and institutions for human welfare that would warrant their observance or support from the moral point of view. They are the consequences such things ought to have and must have to justify their existence. Socially functional rules, etc. are not necessarily humanly functional. They may be exploitive and may be promoted by those who profit from the exploitation. They may be inefficient yet tolerated in the absence of anything better. They may serve no purpose but endure because other practices take care of the survival of the society or the institution. Practices can last a long time without meeting human needs, just as the organs or behavior of a biological species may be maladaptive as long as they are compatible with features of the species that do ensure its survival.

The concept of function in the second sense is appropriate for ethical evaluation. The ethical question is not what enables a society to survive as it is, because that society may be evil, but what discharges human functions and dysfunctions and what are those of the alternatives.

The present inquiry is ethical rather than sociological, but we have to consider the social functions of professional codes for two reasons: to distinguish them from human functions, for which they are often mistaken, and because social functions sometimes obstruct and sometimes facilitate human functions. The moralist needs to understand why social functions exist and how they can be made to serve human functions.

Social Functions of Professional Codes

The ostensible function of codes is moral. That is, their professed aim is to raise the level of professional practices. They employ the rhetoric of morality and appeal to conscience. When they have social functions antithetical to the moral one, these are disguised. They are latent and underground.

Ideology is a set of ideas promulgated in order to promote a social objective. The social functions of codes primarily are ideological. Corporately, codes communicate ideas that promote the professional project of the particular occupational group. Societally, they fortify loyalty to the institutions that the group serves.

Codes contribute to the professional project in two ways. The professional ideology maintains that every genuine profession has an ethic. An occupation's code conveys the impression that this is true for it and hence that it is a profession. Second, the code formulates what leaders of the profession would have the public think its operative ethic is. This is intended to instill trust in its actual practices.

Ideologies are not necessarily false. Codes with ideological functions may codify actual practices or those that leaders actually want to foster. But the ideological function also may be served by false descriptions and pretended norms. The main ideological requirement is that the code be simple and plausible to a wide audience.

Codes are instruments for persuasion both of members of the profession and the public. They enhance the sense of community among members, of belonging to a group with common values and a common mission. The effectiveness of codes varies greatly for this function. Every lawyer is aware of the ABA's Code of Professional Responsibility. Few engineers are familiar with the numerous engineering codes and few professors with AAUP's Statement on Professional Ethics. Some professions have no codes, though they may profess adherence to the rules of ordinary morality. Thus the Society of Automotive Engineers says rather haughtily:

> While fully subscribing to ethical guides, SAE has no formally enunciated code of ethics. The members have generally felt that they know what ethical behavior is and have lived up to it as well as any other engineering group; they refuse to adopt a code merely to be numbered among Societies having such a Code.[2]

Ethical codes are notably missing in business professions other than accountancy. This may be due to the popular conception that business and ethics do not mix. It contributes to perpetuating that prejudice.

Rank-and-file familiarity with codes is greatest where provisions are enforced by the state as a condition for licensure or by professional associations with strong disciplinary powers. Some moralists would deny that enforcement induces *ethical* behavior on the grounds that it removes rules from the realm of conscience. This is the notion that principles cease to be moral when they become laws. Though false, the notion itself may replace the sense of sharing common values with that of being under common sanctions.

The sense of common values is enhanced when codes are taught in professional schools. They are taught either because familiarity is a condition for licensure or because ethical behavior is conceived to be part of professional competence. For example, the American Psychological Association and the National Association of Social Workers warn against sexual intimacy with clients because they impair objectivity and hence effective service. Social distance is taught as part of professionalism.

Another practice that promotes group identity is the ceremonial use of codes or adumbrated versions such as the Faith of the Engineer of the Engineers Council for Professional Development and the Engineers' Creed of the National Society of Professional Engineers. The latter reads,

> As a Professional Engineer, I dedicate my professional knowledge and skill to the advancement and betterment of human welfare. I pledge:
> To give the utmost of performance;
> To participate in none but honest enterprise;
> To live and work according to the laws of man and the highest standards of professional conduct;
> To place service before profit, the honor and standing of the profession before personal advantage, and the public welfare above all other considerations.
> In humility and with need for Divine Guidance, I make this pledge.[3]

Individuals may be asked to pledge fealty at graduation from professional school or induction into an honorary fraternities or professional society. Ceremonies have little bearing on conduct, but they nourish the impression of membership in a coherent group in which everyone observes high standards and hence are set apart from ordinary humanity.

A second ideological use of codes among members of a profession is disciplinary. The aim here may be moral as well as ideological. Leaders genuinely are concerned to deter malefactors and encourage conscientious behavior. No doubt many are concerned for morality for its own sake, but all are highly concerned with appearances, the reputation of the profession, the honor and dignity of professional.[4] Of course, one of the better ways to maintain dignity is to respect oneself and one of the better ways to gain honor is to act honorably; but these are not always the most effective ways, and truly honorable persons are not overly concerned with reputation. Strictures in codes relating to dignified conduct appear to have more of a public relations function than a moral one: They aim at making professionals good advertisements for the profession.

In all but a few cases—the law, medicine, and the military—the enforcement agencies of the profession are not sufficient to bind its members together into an integrated self-governing community. Most professions are composed of individuals following personal ethical standards. The influence of integrating organizations (professional schools, associations, licensing boards) is weak. Where there are significant powers of enforcement, professional associations and the governmental agencies they dominate are preoccupied with the economic behavior of their members. Garceau comments, "Ethics has always been a flexible, developing notion in medicine, with a strong flavor of economics from the start."[5] Layton reviews cases from 1908 to 1932 in which the American Society of Mechanical Engineers and the American Institute of Electrical Engineers disciplined members for raising social issues, such as air pollution, and for attacking the behavior of fellow engineers in private industry. He generalizes:

> the history of the ethical codes of the traditional learned professions is anything but reassuring. The contemporary verdict is quite clear: these codes benefit the professions, but the public probably loses more than it gains. It is rather notorious that internal policing is minimal. But these codes, particularly that of the American Medical Association, have been used with great ruthlessness to punish dissidents who have taken the public's side on issues such as group medicine.[6]

On an anecdotal level, Jack McMinn reminisces about Bill Ellison, a revered senior engineer: "I particularly remember him for the very candid response he gave to my expressed concern about whether [certain] business contacts were ethical. Ellison looked me straight in the eye and said: 'Ethics are rules old men make to keep young men from getting any business.' "[7]

If we are not to impute cold cynicism to the promulgators of codes, we must remember their proneness to confuse corporate prudence with morality. Most officers of professional associations are not narrowly self-interested. In serving the association, they set aside considerations of personal income. But their loyalty is often to the group rather than to humanity. They tend to identify ethical behavior with behavior that benefits their group.

The disciplinary utility of codes is limited because enforcement mechanisms are weak. The most obvious way to gain currency for a rational professional ethic would be to strengthen those mechanisms. However, the efforts of courts to limit the control of associations over the economic behavior of their members deter them from strengthening their ethical influence.

Even without effective control over its membership, an association can use a code for public relations. It may make an attractive version available for professionals to frame in their office. (People who really use lists of rules for personal guidance do not hang them in public places; they keep them in their desk or paste them on the bathroom mirror.) Codes may be broadcast in house publications, advertisements, public ceremonies, etc. Thus, the mayor of Columbia, Missouri, was induced to proclaim National Insurance Week in 1980 and the Columbia Life Underwriters Association published a picture of him signing the proclamation in the presence of officers of the association together with NALU's Code of Ethics. This code declares "the position of the Life Underwriter is unique [in that] as a life insurance advisor he owes a high professional duty toward his client, while at the same time, he also occupies a position of trust and loyalty to his company." The advertisement thus conveyed the message that the insurance agent is a skilled and trustworthy advisor because he (sic) is a member of a tightly knit group with high ethical standards despite the fact that he is a self-employed entrepreneur with obligations to his parent company.

Such efforts are designed not only to instill trust in the public; they enable the members of the profession to say (and think), We must be ethical—just look at our code! I do not maintain that the efforts are studied or very successful. If professionals are not aware that they have codes, how much less so is the public? Still, codes fit neatly into the program of occupations to persuade society that they deserve the status and autonomy of professions and this explains the perpetuation of codes that are ineffectual operationally.

Human Functions

We have defined social functions of codes as those uses that serve to sustain the system of action of which they are a part whether or not the results are beneficial in terms of human welfare. Human functions are such beneficial uses. Let us examine first the human functions of rational codes or codifications of those forms of professional behavior that, as best we can determine, would actually promote human welfare. What is the value of codification?

The most obvious function is guidance for those practitioners who have not thought through moral issues. Codification would be otiose if the obligations of professionals were always obvious and could be met without sacrifice, if professionals never faced difficult dilemmas or always did what was right as a matter of course or could handle every question on the basis of common morality. Debates over confidentiality, conflict of interest, bribery, paternalism, whistle-blowing, credit for the work of others, social responsibilities, etc. show that these conditions are not met. Hard thinking and searching dialogue are necessary. A rational code would contain the results individuals would have reached for themselves if they had reasoned objectively long enough on an adequate base of experience. If such a code is available, it relieves professionals of most of the burden of ethical inquiry. After all, their primary responsibility is to heal, counsel, minister, design, etc., not to puzzle over ethical questions. Most in matter of fact do not reflect on ethics until faced with difficult questions, when the pressure of action prevents careful thought. It would simplify their moral universe to have solutions at hand which had been worked out on the collective experience and wisdom of the moral community.

Not that codes of this sort would eliminate the need for personal judgment. Individuals have to see that proposed rules are the ones they would have reached had they pursued the issues. They have to judge how close a proposed code comes to the ideal and where it falls so short that they should fall back on personal conscience. Every code must be treated as a hypothesis to be tested and adapted while following it. Nevertheless, codes are useful as guides. No code can make decisions mechanical, but adherence to tested rules under ordinary circumstances reduces the occasions when one is obligated to think about alternatives and flounder through their problematic consequences.

An ideal code would be a consensual one, rationally valid and accepted by both members of the occupation and the public. If one can convince oneself that the official code of one's profession meets these specifications, one can go about one's business most of the time in conformity with accepted practices. One can be assured that one's efforts will be complemented by those of others who follow the same code. There is a common basis for advice and support. Suppose I am under pressure from a client or employer to use my expertise for a dubious purpose. Refusal based on professional norms will carry more weight with others than my purely private conscience. Suppose I come under fire from colleagues for unprofessional conduct. I can appeal to a common code for justification, whereas without one I can only pit my opinion against theirs. A consensual code provides colleagues an objective basis for judgment and enables the individual to anticipate what that judgment will be.

Few of us act from purely moral motives. One who would establish a functioning public morality must exploit prudence and inclinations to induce many members of the group to perform the actions that morality requires. The professions are staffed by persons of ordinary conscientiousness and limited good will; that is, people who do what they think is right if the cost is not great and they are convinced that others will do likewise. Therefore, as we have insisted, practicable codes must be accompanied by institutions that make heroism unnecessary by sanctions that deter malfeasance. A degree of control is necessary to establish standard practices. But a rational and consensual code is necessary to make those practices moral. To the extent that we can endorse a code that governs behavior through the control mechanisms of the group and the conscience of the individual, we can also endorse the behavior itself. One of the benefits of valid codes is that they provide the individual the satisfaction of participating in a moral organism and having the opportunity to live among other moral persons.

These various human functions are properties of *valid* codes for which *consensus* has been gained. They include moral guidance for individuals, collegial support, and a basis for objective judgment in disciplinary proceedings. These functions are important and worth a considerable cost. The difficulties in achieving them have been emphasized in previous chapters, but the values at stake are so high that a concerted effort is justified.

The Hermeneutic Hurdle

We have distinguished between human and ideological functions. Need these war with each other? Why can't the professions both eat their conceptual cake and put it in the window for show? Why can't codes be both effective tools of morality and good public relations? There are reasons why the one gets in the way of the other.

Codes are texts that communicate ideas, express attitudes, and direct behavior. Identification of the functions of a code must be predicated on an understanding of what it says to those affected by it, since their understanding, not the analyst's, produces behavior and the consequences categorized as functions.

The hermeneutic task appears easy, since codes are written in plain language. The analyst is prone to assume that their words mean to others what they mean to him or her as an adept speaker of English. However, words mean different things to different audiences. What will be termed the interpretive community of professional codes is heterogeneous. It is quite possible that the formulas of a code mean something different to their authors, to the leaders of professional associations, to practitioners in the field, to the public, and to ethical theorists.

Differences in interpretations of principles can have disastrous consequences for the individual. Consider the misfortune of the three engineers in the infamous BART (Bay Area Rapid Transit) case. As sanctioned by the "notify proper authority" provision of the National Society of Professional Engineers code, these engineers went over the heads of their superiors in the professional staff to report what they judged to be dangerous defects in design to the authority's political board. When the public media got wind of the story, the engineers lost their jobs. Not only did fellow engineers in NSPE fail to support them, they were criticized under the very same code of ethics for insubordination and excessive ambition; that is, for unprofessional behavior. The authors of *Divided Loyalties* ask, "Did [the three engineers'] actions follow inevitably from a specific code of ethics governing the behavior of a particular professional association, or is the code so ambiguous that several courses of action were possible and permissible?[8] A code that means different things to different people can do more harm than good.

Interpreting a text requires working with hypotheses about its meanings for the community that uses it. Our own understanding of the text and even the intentions of its authors are only clues to what it means to those who act on it.

Discussions of codes in the literature focus on the denotations and connotations of content-words, such as 'confidentiality' and 'conflict of interest.' They neglect what I call semiotic virtues, which also affect the meaning of codes for various audiences. These virtues can be divided into the semantic features of a text, its logical structure, and the context of presuppositions that control its interpretation. By semantic features, I have in mind such matters as the clarity, precision, and univocity of individual words and phrases, and the opposites of these properties. Semantic defects allow different audiences to read different meanings into a text or prevent them from finding any definite meaning in it at all.

By logical structure I have in mind the consistency of code's provisions, the tightness of their interrelations, whether one can tell which provisions take priority over others, whether implications can be derived from provisions alone or in combination with plausible factual propositions or normative postulates, and whether the structure of the whole is perspicuous. Deficiencies in structure may allow different audiences to draw different implications from a text or prevent definite implications from being derived at all.

By presuppositions of a code, I mean values and beliefs in terms of which audiences make sense of it. Variations in presuppositions can cause the interpretive community to read different meanings into a text and gain false ideas of the world from it.

Clarity, consistency, and veridical presuppositions are virtues of a text; vagueness, inconsistency, and illusion are vices. In an ideal world, all communications would have the virtues and none of the vices. In this world, the virtues are important, but we cannot take for granted that they serve every purpose. There are reasons why codes of ethics are infected with some of the vices.

In discussing techniques for cultivating the semiotic virtues in codes, I will use the following as illustrations:

(AAUP)   American Association of University Professors: Statement on Professional Ethics

(ABA)   American Bar Association: Model Code of Professional Responsibility

(AICPA) American Institute of Certified Public Accountants: Rules of Conduct

(AMA)   American Medical Association: Principles of Medical Ethics; and Current Opinions of the Judicial Council

(APA)   American Psychological Association: Ethical Principles of Psychologists

(ECPD)   Engineers Council for Professional Development: Code of Ethics for Engineers, with Guidelines

(IEEE)   Institute of Electrical and Electronics Engineers: Code of Ethics

(SDC)   Sigma Delta Chi (Society of Professional Journalists): Code of Ethics

The Problem of Presuppositions

The emergence of codes was concurrent with the development of the professional ideology. Authors of codes have generally constructed them with the functionalist model in mind and the model provides the conceptual background for most people's understanding of them. To encourage readers to interpret codes in this way, their authors utilize the professional terminology (codes of ethics define "professional conduct" and "professional responsibilities"). However, the functionalist model does not ensure the same understanding among all the interpreters of a code because ideological concepts are protean. They change from context to context and mind to mind for people situated at different points in the network of professional relationships. A couple of examples will show how this affects interpretation.

Codes ordinarily refer to the profession in the singular as if it were an integrated whole. Outsiders may take this literally and assume that the rules of the code are enforced in an effective manner. If the content of the code seems valid, this reinforces their respect for the profession's autonomy. However, insiders know that "the profession" is a scattered object. They view the code at best as a compendium of aspirations and at worst as window dressing. They approach matters such as criticism of colleagues in a different spirit than the outsider. The illusion of unity also permits professions to pretend that they discharge macrosocial responsibilities, while the looseness of organization enables everyone to dodge personal obligation. The pretense deters external regulation; the reality prevents action internally.

Until recent times, codes were drawn up with self-employed consultants who enjoy upper or upper-middle socioeconomic status in mind. The "dignity" that the codes promote is the dignity of the gentleman. It encourages the elite to arrogate to themselves ethical decisions for the profession and for professionals working under them as assistants or employees. It excludes subordinate employees from the moral sphere and encourages cynicism about professional practices and general sense of ethical impotence. The view from below supports a different model of professional life than the view from above. It shoves into the corner some of the most acute moral problems and leaves them to the tender mercy of economic and political forces.

Differences in images of professions stand in the way of consensus on the import of codes. Effective codes await a realistic understanding of professional life. Society must appreciate the internal complexity of particular occupations and the differences among occupations. The fog of ideology must be dispelled for all to see the actual practices.

The sociological study of occupations is creating such an understanding despite its sometime seduction by ideology. Code builders also can contribute. Every code should be accompanied by a rationale, one that expresses the sense of the public as well as the profession, in which the nature of the occupation is spelled out in detail, candidly, accurately. Obstacles in the way of moral behavior should be assessed and the way the profession tries to overcome them explained.

I have in mind that the rationale would be part of the charter for the profession and hence an authoritative basis for interpreting the code. It may be expected that a rationale that candidly acknowledged the deficiencies of the profession and the obstacles to moral behavior would encounter opposition from many of its members. They would not want to pay the price of being *that* honest. Candor runs counter to the ideological impulse.

A start toward official rationales is provided by the preambles of some codes, but these are brief and reflect the views of the professional association, not necessarily the whole profession or society. The only major code with a substantial preamble is that of the ABA.

Opinions of advisory and judicial organs of some associations, such as ABA's Committee on Ethics and Professional Responsibility, AICPA's Professional Ethics Division, AMA's Judicial Council, and the National Society of Professional Engineers' Board of Ethical Review, provide commentary for codes and an accumulation of case decisions. However, the explanatory value of these is limited. They interpret particular provisions of the codes and indicate their rationale implicitly, but they are fiats issued from the top and do not represent an argued consensus among the membership of the association or the profession, not to mention the public.

One harmful unconscious presupposition that has been noted, that professions are male domains because they have been populated by men, can be combatted by altering the language used in professional codes.

Several rationalizations are available for sexist language. Traditional grammarians have declared that such words as 'man' and 'he' have a generic as well as gender sense and that no prejudice is implied when they are used generically for a mixed group ("mankind," "the professional man," "when the doctor prescribes for the patient, he should follow his instructions"). Thus, Fowler endorses the convention that "where the matter of sex is not conspicuous or important *he* and *his* shall be allowed to represent a person instead of a man or a man *(homo)* instead of a man *(vir)*.[9] However, as Miller and Swift observe, "sex is always important when the accomplishments of one sex are being coopted by another.[10] They advance the empirical thesis that when the name of a species is used for the genus, the speech community takes the members of the species to be representative of the genus and members of other species to be deficient, deviant, or subordinate. By referring to humanity as "man," we affirm the humanness of men and throw doubt on that of women. Miller and Swift supported this principle with evidence that the linguistic practice shapes the attitudes of both men and women toward women. The habit of referring to professionals in male terms makes us expect a man when we hear 'doctor,' 'lawyer,' 'engineer,' 'manager,' 'journalist,' etc. We check to see what is wrong or odd or untypical when the person proves to be a woman. The phenomenon works in reverse, of course, when we hear 'secretary,' 'nurse,' 'house-wife' (sic), 'schoolteacher,' etc. (Miller and Swift report with glee the anguish of male teachers who attribute their poor public image and low pay to the practice of referring to schoolteachers as 'she.'[11]

Miller and Swift trace the process by which gender-neutral and even feminine-agent words (such as 'obstetrician') were pre-empted by men over the centuries. Arbiters such as Fowler call for feminine forms (e.g., 'actress,' 'authoress,' 'aviatrix,' and on (?) to 'doctrix,' 'lawyeress,' engineerette') to ensure that the customer would know that he (sic) is getting an odd kind of professional for his money.[12] Miller and Swift conclude, first in general terms, "The use of *man* to represent the human species reinforces the erroneous notion that the species is male or at least the male is more representative than the female."[13] Specific to our purposes, they maintain,

> Throughout its history, as English made the gradual change from grammatical to natural gender, words denoting occupations or professions could be and from time to time were used for females and males without distinction. But because males are consciously or unconsciously considered the norm, new feminine designations were introduced and accepted whenever the need was felt to assert male prerogatives. As the language itself documents, once certain occupations ceased to be women's work and became trades or vocations in which men predominated, the old feminine-gender words were annexed by men and became appropriate male designations. The new endings were assigned to women, quite possibly, in Fowler's phrase, to keep a woman from "asserting her right" to a male's name (or his job).[14]

While, therefore, use of the masculine as a generic term is sanctioned by the traditional grammarian, it is freighted with disutility from the moral point of view. It reinforces the obstacles to vocational mobility for half of the species. It limits the pool of talent for the professions. The commands of grammarians carry little weight before the demands of justice.

The second excuse for using "professional men" acknowledges its gender-specific connotation. It claims that this is appropriate since most professionals are in fact men. The excuse hardly holds water. Some professionals are women and more will be soon if sexual barriers are overcome. Hence, 'professional men and women,' 'professional persons,' or just 'professionals' are more accurate than 'professional men,' if indeed accuracy is our concern.

The third excuse is that 'he or she' and the use of the plural and passive voice are awkward and inelegant. Why not sacrifice a bit for style, if one declares his (sic) antisexism in unequivocal terms? The answer is threefold: First, awkwardness is due to change of habit; we will soon become at ease with new habits. Second, there is a sexist bias to standard English and it affects attitudes regardless of the speaker's intentions and declarations. Third, the fact that an author will not take the trouble to clean up his (rarely her) language is evidence that he does not take sexual injustice seriously.

The remedies for sexist language are simple. The more awkward ones, locutions such as 'he or she' and 'the professional man and woman,' call attention in a time of transition to the rightful place of women in professions. An easier solution is to speak in the plural, as engineering codes do when they say, "Engineers sign only work they have done or supervised." Of course, nonsexist language does not eliminate sexist assumptions—engineering associations still organize outings for *wives* at annual meetings while the *engineers* are in working sessions.

The Utility of Vagueness

The vagueness and ambiguity of the professional terminology contribute to the ideological use of functionalist models in the struggle for status. What might be called the ideological enthymene distills the essence of this use. It works by equivocating 'professional':

1. The *[ideal typical]* professional is a distinguished man, the master of a science, who counsels important people and ministers to the needy and consequently deserves status, power, and wealth.

2. We are professionals *[members of an occupation called a profession]*.

3. Therefore, we are distinguished . . . and deserve our status, power, and wealth.

(It is expedient to suppress most of the conclusion so that the audience will not examine it closely.)

Semiotic vices may have ideological utility. This is not necessarily by design. There are factors that make for vagueness and inconsistency for authors who have the best of intentions. It is simply hard to think out a perfectly structured code, and words inevitably mean different things to their authors as careful thinkers than to casual readers, to elite professionals than to workaday practitioners, to self-employed consultants than to bureaucratic employees, to public than to private functionaries, to management than to subordinates, to traditionalists than to reformers, to members of professional associations than to outsiders, to professionals than to the public, to corporate employers than to clients, to upper than to lower socioeconomic classes.

Codemakers cannot be sure that provisions of their code will be taken in the way they intend. Furthermore, ideological instruments must be palatable to groups who differ on substantive issues. To gain wide acceptance, provisions are written in general and often vague terms. Professional codes are not adventures in exploration. They express the lowest common denominators in the norms of persons of ordinary conscientiousness with a wide spectrum of prejudices. They are, consequently, products of compromise and discreet vagueness.

We have noted the generality of the protestations of public service in major codes. Where they try to spell out the social obligations that service entails, such as protection of the environment, distributive justice, or education of the public, they do so in much less detail than when they spell out obligations to clients and employers and to the profession and fellow professionals. A casual glance such as a member of the public might direct toward a code would suggest that the profession takes its social obligations seriously. Careful scrutiny by a troubled practitioner seeking guidance would disclose few specific or demanding duties.

While there is an important moral component in obligations to clients and colleagues, there also is a strong prudential component. The obligations are self-interested in that they help the professionals get business by assuring the client of their loyalty. They serve corporate self-interest by obliging professionals to engage in "fair practices" in competing for business; that is, practices that maintain fee levels and befit the dignity of the profession.

In some circumstances the moral and prudential components of a code reinforce one another—prudence counsels what morality demands. In others they are antithetical and there is internal tension, if not arrant contradiction, among provisions. There is a tension between provisions regarding whistle-blowing and employee loyalty and between peer review and criticism of colleagues. To ease the tension, many codes are simply silent about practices that might jeopardize the professional's position, e.g. whistle-blowing, the avoidance of paternalism. Codes choose self-interest over the interest of the public.

The net effect of vagueness is to convey to the casual reader that the profession is dedicated to high ethical standards without imposing stern and arduous duties on practitioners. Highly conscientious persons will be challenged by codes, but this comes by reading duties into them rather than from them. Less conscientious persons will find a legitimation of practices no better than those required by the ordinary mores of society.

The looseness of logical structure of codes contribute to their ambiguity. Where provisions conflict, they lack clear guidelines to determine which take priority. The indeterminateness in the relations among provisions facilitates the use of codes for rationalization. A reasonable person cannot fail to approve of most provisions of the code and the whole appears to be an ethical document. The unethical practitioner can then pick provisions at will to justify actions performed for other purposes.

Unger observes that inevitable limitations on the content of codes also exposes them to this use. He counsels against the attempt to detail all situations calling for ethical decisions, especially in a dynamic profession:

> One problem with overspecific codes is that few will care to read them. Another is that omissions, which are inevitable, become significant "loopholes." For example, suppose the code contains a detailed list of the hazards that the public is to be protected against. Then if a question should arise about some hazard *not* on this list, it might be inferred that there is no obligation to protect against it. A more general provision would avoid this problem. An additional drawback of lengthy codes is that important points may be buried in a mass of less significant items, thereby losing much of their impact.[15]

He concludes that codes should be limited to a few general provisions and he follows this advice in his own model for electrical engineering. He settles for a very limited role for codes in fear that stronger ones will be misused.

This is a counsel of defeat. If the ethical stance of professions is to be improved, detailed codes clear and precise enough to read the same way to everyone must be developed.

Clarifying Individual Terms

Semantic perfection is an exacting ideal. Establishing common and valid presuppositions in the interpretive community is a necessary preliminary. Explaining the special meaning of words and phrases in the context of the code is a follow-up. The few codes that incorporate formal definitions do so for brevity and convenience in judicial proceedings, not for clarity. This seems to be the case with the AICPA definitions of 'client,' 'firm,' 'practice of public accounting,' etc. Perhaps the fact that codes are formulated in ordinary language persuades their authors that any educated speaker of English can understand them. This ignores the need for definitions not only to attach meanings to neologisms, but to fix meanings of familiar words that shift in use.

In the absence of explicit definitions, one must take the provisions of a code as contextual definitions of its terminology. That is, one must construe terms in the most sensible way to fit the concrete applications stipulated in the provisions. Unfortunately, the context is not always sufficient to pin down their meaning. It is another reason why we cannot follow Unger's advice to keep codes brief.

Let us consider some examples. Take the term 'ethics' itself. I can only guess what engineers mean when they remark, "That is not a question of ethics, but of morality." Perhaps they mean to distinguish role norms (the ethics of the profession) from norms for the rest of life (ordinary morality) or norms that ought to be enforced by the professional association from those that should be left to individual discretion.

In our group of codes, only the AMA attempts a definition. Its success in clarification is negligible, but it promulgates an important distinction:

> Historically the term "ethical" has been used in the opinions of the Judicial Council and in resolutions adopted by the House of Delegates

to refer to matters involving (1) moral principles or practices; (2) customs and usages of the medical profession; and (3) matters of policy not necessarily involving issues of morality in the practice of medicine.

AMA states that violations of (1) and (2) call for disciplinary action, but members are guaranteed the freedom to disagree with (3). It also remarks that ethical standards "may exceed but are never less than, nor contrary to, those required by law."

The ABA uses the term 'ethical' to distinguish aspirations and objectives toward which every lawyer should strive ("ethical considerations") from the minimum level of conduct below which no lawyer can fall without being subject to punishment ("disciplinary rules"). Thus ethics for the AMA is what is enforced; for the ABA, what is not enforced.

SDC paradoxically labels a special provision of its entire Code of Ethics as "Ethics." This provision deals with the journalist's duty to be "free of obligation to any interest other than the public's right to know the truth." Do the remaining provisions not have ethical force?

The rationale for a code ought to make clear what the code is for, its scope, how ethical norms are distinguished from nonethical norms and professional norms from other norms, the relation of ethical rules to legal rules, etc. Existing codes make no effort to do so.

'Dignity' is a popular word. It carries at least two distinct meanings in codes. IEEE advises its members to "Advance the integrity and prestige of the profession by practicing in a dignified manner and for adequate compensation." ECPD specifies that engineers may advertise their services only in a dignified way and "shall act in such a manner as to uphold and enhance the honor, integrity and dignity of the profession" by avoiding association with fraudulent, dishonest, and unethical business. Dignity here appears to have to do with decorum and reputation (a reflection of engineers' struggle to rise to the middle class?).

On the other hand, the AMA, ABA, APA, and SDC enjoin the professional to respect the dignity of others. This emphasis may be due to the fact that these professions involve direct intervention into the lives of individuals, whereas engineers affect people indirectly in groups. The APA's effort to articulate this difference is inadequate. It observes,

As practitioners, psychologists know that they bear a heavy social responsibility because their recommendations and professional actions may alter the lives of others. They are alert to personal, social, organizational, financial, or political situations and pressures that might lead to misuse of their influence.

Respect for human dignity in a more specific sense than caring about the way one affects the lives of others is an important ideal for some professionals. It was literally a matter of life and death in the case of Frank Tugend, an old man who quit eating rather than endure helpless senility, as reported in Mark Jury's photo-essay, *Gramp*. Dr. Ben Kline, explaining why he and the family did not intervene, is quoted as saying:

> What he did that wasn't unusual was make up his mind that it was time to die. And it's my opinion that there should be some dignity in death; and if he made up his mind that he was no longer going to endure the indignities of living, then it wasn't up to us to sustain life. I think that's cruel, because man is deserving of dignity. Not only in life but in death.
> When he took out his teeth and said, 'I don't want to live'—then no way am I going to force IVs and medications and so forth on him. I'm going to let him die with dignity.[16]

Apparently it was Mr. Tugend's right to choose death over the "indignities" of living that was respected, it being assumed that he had made up his mind in a rational way.

The AMA's very first principle is that the physician should provide medical service "with compassion and respect for human dignity." Unfortunately, the word 'dignity' is not used again in the AMA Code or Opinions. I am guessing that statements that bear on the concept are those that refer to the patient's right to choose a physician; the desirability of obtaining informed consent in terminating life-prolonging treatment and in the selection of therapies; safeguarding patient confidences and restricting public discussion of a patient's condition. These provisions imply a concern for patient autonomy and the privacy that is a condition of autonomy. They fail to specify what the physician is to do when a patient's wishes stand in the way of urgently needed treatment and what kind of wishes (informed, rational, self-regarding, etc.) should be honored.

The APA begins its code with the ringing declaration, "Psychologists respect the dignity and worth of the individual and strive for the preservation and protection of fundamental human rights." The term 'dignity' is used only once again. We are left to guess that it bears on that part of the "welfare" and "best interests" of clients and consumers that entails a right to know the results of psychological assessments or research involving them, and informed consent to being used in research and the right to withdraw, though the APA conceives that some research justifies deception of subjects and harm that may have to be rectified later. (These provisions reflect a struggle to reconcile respect for the individual's autonomy with the need of society to know more about human behavior.) The APA's code, like most others, promises confidentiality and respect for privacy, but again with limitations to permit effective therapy and research. As we would hope, APA is more sensitive than other professions to psychological dependence on the part of clients and so warns against client exploitation, especially sexual, as well as exploitation of students, research subjects, employees, etc., again especially sexual.. (Sexual harassment is defined as "deliberate or repeated comments, gestures, or physical contacts of a sexual nature that are unwanted by the recipient.") Finally, the code contains warnings against invidious treatment of persons on the basis of age, sex, ethnic origin, socioeconomic class, and other group characteristics, in respect to the impact of research on social policy, acquiring special competences to serve different groups, and hiring, training, and promoting them. Antidiscrimination policies customarily are justified by respect for the individual, so I read these as evidence of concern, if not clarity, about the elements of dignity.

The ABA associates dignity with democratic institutions and the rule of law. It begins its code by stating,

> The continued existence of a free and democratic society depends upon recognition of the concept that justice is based upon the rule of law grounded in respect for the dignity of the individual and his capacity through reason for enlightened self-government. Law so grounded makes justice possible, for only through such law does the dignity of the individual attain respect and protection. Without it, individual rights become subject to unrestrained power, respect for law is destroyed, and rational self-government is impossible.

The code explicitly derives the fundamental obligation of the lawyer to "represent his client zealously within the bounds of the law" from these grounds. "In our government of laws and not of men, each member of our society is entitled to have his conduct judged and regulated in accordance with the law, to seek any lawful objective through legally permissible means, and to present for adjudication any lawful claim, issue, or defense." I hope I am not imagining connections in seeing the Preamble as the basis for the notions that everyone has a right to legal counsel; that the lawyer has the obligation to promote the informed choice of counsel (but not to solicit business) while acknowledging the individual's right to defend himself; and that the attorney-client relation is personal and fiduciary, requiring strict confidentiality and entailing that "the authority to make decisions is exclusively that of the client."

The AAUP does not refer to dignity, nor hint at the concept except in its statement regarding students. It says there that the professor

> demonstrates respect for the student as an individual, and adheres to his proper role as intellectual guide and counselor . . . He respects the confidential nature of the relationship between professor and student. He avoids any exploitation of students for his private advantage and acknowledges significant assistance from them. He protects their academic freedom.

"Respect for the student as an individual" resonates with complaints about the impersonality of mass education. We can imagine professional abuses that the authors of others parts of the statement had in mind, but they are not spelled out. The reminder that students as well as professors have the right to academic freedom is useful and ties respect for the individual to respect for autonomy. In general, the statement is too terse to impose specific duties.

SDC maintains, "Journalists at all times will show respect for the dignity, privacy, rights, and well-being of persons encountered in the course of gathering and presenting the news." The articles under this provision pertain to irresponsible charges, correction of errors, pandering to morbid curiosity, and invasion of privacy. It does *not* connect dignity with autonomy or confidentiality. What dignity does mean in this context is unclear—perhaps the opposite of public humiliation and a low reputation.

What do these examples show?

1. Professions that intervene in the lives of individual people conceive that their central obligation is to the individual rather than to society as a whole. While the AMA says in its Preamble, "a physician must recognize responsibility not only to patients, but also to society, to other health professionals, and to self," very few of its Principles or Opinions countenance sacrifice of any of the individuals mentioned to the interests of "society." The APA allows more serious encroachments on individual autonomy for the sake of psychological research but tries to provide adequate safeguards. Only the SDC appears to put an abstract value (Truth) systematically ahead of the individual in pursuit of the news.

2. The codes recognize autonomy as an important value. They assure the client freedom of choice in entering the professional relationship and a say in selection of services. The professional retains the right, in the name of autonomy, to refuse service that is immoral or inferior in quality according to professional standards. However, provisions protecting the client from exploitation are more definite than those prohibiting paternalistic encroachments on autonomy.

3. Respect for autonomy is connected with client rights. The practical import of the connection is obscure, however, because none of the codes articulates a theory of rights. Individual, human, legal, and civil rights are mentioned in various places, but no effort is made to state what those rights are or how they are grounded.

4. The codes for the most part leave the connection between dignity and autonomy implicit. Hence, the references to dignity at the beginning of the codes (except for the ABA's) resemble Wittgenstein's wheel that meshes with nothing in the machine—they are ideological adornments that do no moral work. Still, they *could* be put to work. The term 'dignity' has emotive power and there is a rich tradition associating it with autonomy, privacy, and human rights. Good codes could exploit this tradition by explicitly deriving provisions relating to the latter from their initial obeisances to human dignity. In so doing they would usefully explicate the latter concept. The ABA and APA codes do some of this. This is the sort of connection that should be spelled out in rationales for codes.

Confidentiality

All the codes deal with confidentiality but few make clear what the term covers. Professionals might be morally obligated to keep secret only what the client or employer deliberately confides to them or any information they acquire as a result of the professional relationship. The information might pertain to the client's business or condition or it might extend to other aspects of his or her life. Confidentiality might terminate with the professional relationship or after a period or continue indefinitely.

The AICPA's code is unilluminating. "A member shall not disclose any confidential information obtained in the course of a professional engagement except with the consent of the client." The stark restriction of the code to business matters and absence of any reference to humane values suggests that 'confidential information' pertains only to financial affairs of the client. Thus narrowly restricted, however, the rule is very stringent. It allows no exceptions.

The focus of the engineering codes is similarly narrow. They enjoin confidentiality in regard to the business secrets of employers. They see problems only in respect to the proprietory right to discoveries made by the engineer while employed and the use of knowledge acquired in one employment when the engineer moves to another.

The AMA says tersely, "A Physician shall . . . safeguard patient confidences within the constraints of the law." It deals with confidentiality only in respect to release of information about the patient's medical condition—what information and to whom; communications media, the patient's attorney, insurance company, and the courts. It addresses the issue of confidentiality of medical information and the computer in a serious way. It does not refer to other information a physician might acquire about a patient. Perhaps the AMA thinks this is unnecessary because of the long tradition of discretion in the medical profession. (The Hippocratic Oath: "Whatever, in connection with my professional practice, or not in connection with it, I see or hear, in the life of men, which ought not to be spoken abroad, I will not divulge, as reckoning that all such should be kept secret.")

The APA describes with greater care procedures for the sharing of sensitive information with colleagues in counseling and publication of the results of research while safeguarding the individual. I infer that the scope of confidentiality must be broad since psychologists probe deeply into people's private lives. Candor can be assured only by confidentiality. It would help to say this explicitly.

The ABA spells things out in greater detail, though it concentrates on confidences in the narrow sense of what the client confides and on information pertinent to the problem that brings the individual to the lawyer. The code makes an effective argument for protecting these (to encourage people to employ lawyers and to be open with them so they can do their work properly). It makes clear that confidentiality extends to other secrets and that the obligation continues after termination of the relationship. The conditions allowing breach of confidentiality are spelled out.

The AAUP's statement that the professor "respects the confidential nature of the relationship between professor and student" is next to useless. It does not refer to confidentiality elsewhere in its code. Perhaps, it feels that the professor's duty "to seek and state the truth as he sees it" is antithetical to secrecy of any sort of that there is nothing peculiar to the professorial role besides the relation to students that requires confidentiality.

The SDC maintains, "Journalists acknowledge the newsmen's ethics of protecting confidential sources of information." The aim is to protect sources of information, not those to whom the information pertains. The Fair Play rule does not specify the bounds of privacy. It is a weak protection in a profession whose job it is to probe and expose. I would not trust a reporter with intimate details about my life any more if I were convinced that he or she conscientiously abided by the SDC code than if he or she merely appeared to be a person of ordinary morality.

Despite these reservations, we must admit that the codes explicate 'confidentiality' more successfully than 'dignity.' The other codes could well emulate the ABA's and APA's thoroughness.

To draw some general conclusions about the semantics of the illustrative codes: They do not utilize explicit definitions, nor do they derive their norms from explicitly stated assumptions to make their terms clear. The more complex codes make a few passing gestures at doing so; the simplest ones apparently see no need to do so at all. There is voluminous literature by members of professions and outsiders that clarify concepts in different (often contrary) ways, but these discussions are not official interpretations. Inclarity hides diversity to create the illusion of common principles. Correlatively, if the professions were truly serious about achieving a common ethic, more elaborate attempts at clarification would be necessary.

Logical Structure

The rules of many professional codes have been devised piecemeal in response to transgressions that have brought opprobrium on the profession. Rules against conflicts of interest, misuse of trade secrets, bribery, and the like read like compendia of scandals. The entire code of the American Football Coaches Association reads this way. Scandal and external criticism are threats to the professional project. The practices involved must be combatted— or at least verbally condemned.

Codes typically begin as congeries of ad hoc rules, which is reasonable enough on an empirical and pragmatic approach to ethics, but rules need to be systematized under general principles. A tighter logical structure is demanded than existing codes display. Particular rules sometimes are presented as specifications of principles and principles represented as canons; that is, systematically interrelated and as covering all areas of professional responsibility. Nevertheless, it is unclear which principles and rules take priority, and gaps in coverage, particularly in respect to the more difficult questions such as the limits of professional loyalty to clients and employers, are filled by vague and toothless injunctions.

I shall document this criticism by a brief analysis of the ECPD Guidelines for engineers. Canon 1 reads, "Engineers hold paramount the safety, health and welfare of the public in the performance of their professional duties." It is a modification, for unexplained reasons, of Principle I, "Engineers uphold and advance the integrity, honor and dignity of the engineering profession by using their knowledge and skill for the enhancement of human welfare." Canon 4 reads, "Engineers shall act in professional matters for each employer or client as faithful agents or trustees and avoid conflicts of interest."

The first thing to notice is that there are only six guidelines for Canon 1 as compared to fifteen for Canon 4 (not to mention further guidelines relevant to employee loyalty under the remaining canons, and the entire Canon 5 with guidelines equal in number to those for Canon 4, which deals with the economic practices of self-employed engineers).

The second thing to notice is that the guidelines for Canon 1 are less specific than those for Canon 4 and the other canons. Guideline 1.a merely enjoins engineers to recognize that their decisions do indeed affect safety, etc. Guideline 1.b instructs them not to sign plans that are not safe. Guideline 1.e is a bland injunction to participate in civic affairs.

The remaining guidelines are more instructive ethically. Guidelines 1.c and 1.d relate to whistle-blowing.

> Should the Engineers' professional judgment be overruled under circumstances where the safety, health, and welfare of the public are endangered, the Engineers shall inform their clients or employers of the possible consequences, and notify other proper authority of the situation, as may be appropriate.

> Should Engineers have knowledge or reason to believe that another person or firm may be in violation of any of the provisions of these Guidelines, they shall present such information to the proper authority in writing and shall cooperate with the proper authority in furnishing such further information or assistance as may be required.

Each guideline has specific requirements under these general ones. Here, at least, are provisions relating to the public interest that have some bite. The engineering profession has acknowledged that whistle-blowing is a duty for the engineer and that support of whistle-blowers is a desideratum for professional associations.

I do not minimize the importance of this, but it is a half-way measure. What is proper authority? If engineers' judgments are overruled, need they only protest to the overruler or are they obligated to appeal to the latter's supervisor, executives of the organization, government watchdogs, or society at large through public media as needed to rectify the situation? The risks involved are progressively more serious as the engineer marches through these steps. The profession is understandably reluctant to instruct the individual how far to go toward martyrdom; hence, it leaves the determination of what is proper authority to the individual. By so doing, it opens a moral escape-hatch for well-intentioned but less than heroic individuals while still conveying to the public that it has imposed an arduous duty.

Guidelines 1.c and 1.d are vague because the key term 'proper authority' is left unexplicated. Guideline 1.f suffers not only from this defect, but from what I call vagueness of placement. It reads, "Engineers should be committed to improving the environment to enhance the quality of life." This reference is unique among engineering codes and a late addition to that of the ECPD. Presumably it responds to the challenge of the environmentalist movement. We should be heartened that the profession has acknowledged, however belated and obliquely, that engineering in technological societies systematically damages the natural environment when precautions are not taken. However, the placement of the provision as well as its unfocused wording cast doubt on how seriously the profession takes the responsibility.

Most codes do not contain instructions as to the relation of their provisions to one another. The reader is left to infer their priority in terms of their sequence and content. Thus, one is prone to infer from the content of the Principles of the ECPD code that provisions listed earlier take priority over those listed later, since obligations stated in later provisions (and exceptions likewise) are justifiable as ways to implement earlier provisions. Thus, enhancement of human welfare (Canon 1) is the reason why engineers are obligated to be honest, truthful, loyal to their clients and employers (Canons 2, 3, and 4) and fair to their competitors (Canon 5), and the promotion of these qualities imposes the obligation to serve their profession (Canons 6 and 7). But consider what we must infer about the guideline respecting the environment if we identify logical order with order of listing. Guideline 1.f is the last in the list of guidelines for Canon 1, following even the toothless exhortation to be active in civic affairs. The implication seems to be that the basic obligation of engineers respecting human welfare is negative—not to sign plans that directly endanger individuals. Whistle-blowing is enjoined for rare occasions where this negative duty is grossly violated by others. If engineers have time left over from serving their employers, they (some, but not necessarily all) should work to better their communities. Concern for the environment is an afterthought. Lip service is paid to an attractive ideal, but there is no serious investment of moral capital.

Instructions to the engineer concerning whistle-blowing could be made more detailed and rigorous and still not be arranged logically. At most the principles of a code should be arranged in a sequence so that it is evident that the earlier take priority over the later or vice versa. Alternatively, a code should contain ordering principles that indicate priorities. They might state ends for which other principles state the means; for example, human welfare is the end for which service to clients and employers is a means; fair practices among colleagues, continuing professional development, and support of professional associations are means to serve clients and employers; etc. Laying this out would make clear that obligations pertaining to means become inoperative when the means cease to contribute to the ends. It would combat role-fanaticism, which, to adapt Santayana's epigram, is to redouble professional practices when one has forgotten their purpose.

An alternative ordering principle specifies the relative importance of prima facie rights and duties. For example, the professional's attention ordinarily is focused on the duty to serve clients not on the negative duty to avoid violations of the law and basic principles of morality. Neither of these duties is a means to the other, and they can conflict. Some codes remind the professional through exceptive clauses to "faithful agent" rules that the positive duty ends where it conflicts with the negative. The AMA observes that its ethical standards are never contrary to law whatever one might think from the way they are stated and it enjoins medical societies to report law breakers to the authorities. The AICPA and ABA allow breaches of confidentiality under valid court order, the ABA cautions against any violation of law by a lawyer and adds to the primary obligation to represent clients zealously the qualification 'within the bounds of the law.' None of the codes countenance civil disobedience, though it may be significant that the AAUP and SDC are silent about the duty to obey the law. Rights of expression and obligations of inquiry may demand disobedience on occasion.

As for faithful agent actions that conflict with ethical principles, the IEEE limits the engineer to "such actions as conform with other parts of this Code." The ABA lamely observes that "it is often desirable for a lawyer to point out to a client those factors which may lead to a decision that is morally just as well as legally permissible."

To summarize, some codes definitely assign priority to legality over client interests; a few hint at the priority of ethical principles; most leave priorities indeterminate.

Exceptive clauses deal with particular conflicts within a code. Some of the codes hint at a general ordering principle that would apply across the board. It is not always clear whether a teleological or deontological principle is intended and the order is not consistently followed in any of the codes.

In some cases the principle is stated in the preamble; in

others, in the first of the list of substantive principles. The ABA, in the statement from its Preamble quoted earlier, sets as its goal the "rule of law grounded in respected for the dignity of the individual" and declares that lawyers' obligations derive from their role as "guardians of the law." Most of the obligations it lists pertain to service to clients and implementation of the legal system. Only one provision, buried toward the end, acknowledges that laws may be unjust and lawyers have an obligation to seek their improvement. We must infer that ABA considers the lawyer's central obligations to be procedural—to make the system function as intended even where the laws are not good ones. It builds something of a logical structure in its code by showing how many of special provisions contribute to the "rule of law."

The APA in its Preamble states *two* primary obligations, the aforementioned "respect for the dignity and welfare of the individual" and the enlargement of knowledge of human behavior. It indicates the derivation of some other obligations (competence, objectivity) from these and tries to adjust the two obligations to each other. It is unable to do so and leaves an area of uncertainty; but at least it grapples with the problem.

SDC prefaces its provisions with repetitious statements that it is the duty of journalists "to serve the truth," that the mass media have a "Constitutional mandate and freedom to learn and report the facts," that it is journalists' "Constitutional role to seek the truth as part of the public's right to know," and that "the public's right to know of events of public importance and interest is the overriding mission of the mass media." It asserts that "those responsibilities carry obligations that require journalists to perform with intelligence, objectivity, accuracy, and fairness." How the first three are required in the pursuit of truth is evident; how the last is required is not. There is no explanation of the limits that the Fair Play rule to guard against "invading a person's right to privacy" places on the pursuit of information.

The Prefaces of the AMA and IEEE codes are not helpful as ordering principles. The AMA asserts the primacy of the welfare of the patient and provides no ground for the qualifications subsequently introduced for this obligation. The IEEE calls for engineers to recognize their impact on "the quality of life for all people in our complex technological society." This phrase is too vague to indicate how specific obligations follow.

The AAUP and ECPD lack preambles but their initial provisions are formulated as if they were first principles. However, it is hard to believe that the AAUP intends for professors to place their subject ahead of the interests of their students and institution or consider the latter only means to developing the former. We have commented on the limited implications of the ECPD's injunction to hold paramount public health, safety, and welfare. It must be intended only as a negative obligation, perhaps an application of the No Harm principle (in serving your employer, profession, or self, do no harm to others) or Prevention or Rectification principle (prevent impending harm; rectify harm that you have done). It limits, rather than grounds or orders other principles.

The Organization of Content

These examples indicate the ideal that the provisions of a code should provide an objective basis for major ethical questions confronted by the professional. A related ideal pertains to both the form and content of the code. It is the ideal of systematic completeness—the code should have provisions to cover all major problems and it should organize them perspicuously.

Such labels as 'Canons' (ABA, ECPD) and, less strongly, 'Principles' (AMA, APA) and 'Articles' (IEEE) promise a systematic classification of obligations. This promise is not honored. Two bases of classification are used, neither consistently. The AAUP and IEEE segregate obligations (except for one set in each code) according to the group toward which they are directed. Professional codes generally deal with duties toward clients, patients, students, employers, or employing institutions; colleagues, the profession, and professional associations; third parties, the public, society, or community, directly or through some abstraction such as Truth or Justice; and, in some instances, to themselves.

The remainder of the codes classify obligations in terms of types of action, with provisions thrown in here and there focusing on the group affected. Table 1 is a compilation of the actions treated in the illustrative codes. This content is typical of professional codes in general. The actions have been rearranged to display some coherence.

A model of professionalism may be behind the content of some of the codes, but one does not find a well thought out conception of human action or social practices underlying any of them. Here, as elsewhere, the same discouraging possibility

Table 1. Content Analysis of the Codes

	AAUP	ABA	AICPA	AMA	APA	ECPD	IEEE	SDC
1.	X	X	X	X	X	X	X	X
2.						X	X	
3.	X				X			X
4.		X						X
5.	X	X	X	X	X	X	X	X
6.	X							
7.	X			X	X			
8.					X		X	
9.	X	X	X	X		X	X	
10.		X		X	X	X		X
11.		X	X			X	X	
12.					X	X	X	X
13.					X	X		X
14.	X	X						
15.	X			X		X		

1. Competence; objectivity; honesty about qualifications.
2. Continuing professional development.
3. Enlargement of knowledge; research; publication.
4. Making services available to those who need them.
5. Loyalty to client, employer, or institution; avoidance of conflict of interest; bribery.
6. Respect for autonomy; privacy; confidentiality; trade secrets.
7. Nonexploitation of clients, students, research subjects, and animals.
8. Proper treatment of subordinate; fairness; encouraging professional development; giving credit.
9. Territorial rights of colleagues; cooperation; giving proper credit; fair competition.
10. Monitoring colleagues; reporting malfeasance; preventing unauthorized practice.
11. Protecting honor and dignity of profession; publicizing its merits.
12. Avoidance of harm to outsiders, the public, the environment.
13. Truthfulness in public statements.
14. Effort to reform institutions that bear on profession.
15. Involvement in community activities not related to profession.

emerges: To make a code effective, one must get an entire profession to agree on its foundations. The advocacy of a particular normative conception of the profession that settles important disputed questions such as the limits of confidentiality and employee loyalty is likely to shatter such superficial agreement as does exist. We must wonder whether group solidarity in a competitive society can be achieved without obfuscation.

Boundaries of the Moral Community

The moral community is composed of all of those beings toward whom we have moral obligations. Contemporary normal human adults are paradigm members, but future generations, children, defective and impaired adults, and higher animals also belong. Justice requires the same treatment of all members of the community who are alike in relevant respects and differential treatment according to relevant differences. Thus, animals have rights under professional ethics because they, like humans, have interests that can be harmed by professionals and the No Harm principle is basic to professionalism. Yet they have lesser rights because their interests are less important.

A few codes evince a vague awareness of the problem of boundaries of the moral community by provisions for special categories of individuals. The American Psychological Association is one of the few to devote significant attention to animals. It says that they are to be handled "humanely" in research, though it countenances pain, stress, injury, and death if they are necessary. The American Veterinary Medical Association barely mentions relief of suffering of animals as an obligation and is silent about research with animal subjects and the circumstances under which animals are raised for food and used for labor. Other professions whose work affects the animal kingdom say nothing at all, for example, the American Medical Association and engineering professions whose work endangers the survival of species.

A larger number of professions recognize special responsibilities to legally and medically incompetent humans. The American Psychological Association enjoins special care for "those that are not capable of voluntary, informed consent" and mentions children, people with impairments, and people under the authority of the investigator. The American Bar Association observes that the lawyer's responsibilities are graver when the client has "any mental or physical condition rendering him incapable of making a considered judgment on his own behalf" and mentions children, illiterates, and incompetents. The National Association of Social Workers urges special care for the legally incompetent. The American Medical Association instructs physicians to obtain consent from legally authorized representatives of incapacitated patients such as minors and incompetents, defective infants, and unconscious persons. It urges physicians to pursue the best interests of such individuals within the limits of discretion it allows them.

The AMA treats fetuses as persons, presumably with rights, in speaking of their legally authorized representatives and enjoining physicians to keep risks to them at a minimum; but it permits physicians to perform abortions and engage in fetal research.

These examples are exceptional in codes, they deal with limited cases, and they impose minimal responsibilities. An even more fundamental deficiency is apparent when we view the matter from the perspective of more comprehensive ethics for the various spheres over which professions claim jurisdiction. Lay persons make medical, legal, psychological, theological, and even engineering and journalistic decisions for themselves, their families, and their friends. In many of these, professionals are auxiliaries; in others, they are not involved at all. Professional codes are constructed by professionals and usually by a minority within a profession. They are unilateral rules made by professionals for professionals. Quite understandably, they do not undertake to determine the obligations of laypersons, though sometimes they render lay judgments moot by the obligations that they impose on professionals. In other cases, especially in relation to the legally and mentally incompetent, the professions are willing to concede the power of decision to legal guardians or the court. This leaves a gap not filled by the rules of ordinary morality.

We might put the matter in these terms. Laypersons as well as professionals have role responsibilities in the spheres of action with which the professions are concerned. Medical ethics comprises norms that ought to govern medical decisions whether by physicians or laypersons; legal ethics, norms for legal decisions whether by lawyers or laypersons; etc. But physicians' codes, lawyers' code, etc. provide no guidance for lay decisions nor do they bind laypersons morally. The norms of ordinary morality, on the other hand, are not role-specific. Hence, there is no consensual system of norms for a large part of the actions that fall in the domain of professional ethics. The existence of special groups in the moral community demanding special treatment by persons in professional roles aggravates the problem and exposes the uncertain foundations of the norms that now pass as the professional ethic.

I have argued for the involvement of the public in formulating norms for the various spheres of work, including those tailored to the professional's role, those for the amateur acting without professional help, and those for the client or employer acting in concert with professionals. I also suggest, however, that the professionals have the special obligation to take the initiative in proposing norms and social policies to make them effective.

In respect to the treatment of special groups in the moral community, the medical and psychological professions should propose norms to govern experimentation on helpless animals and humans in total institutions such as mental hospitals and prisons. The medical profession should recommend the proportion of medical resources to commit to the terminally ill, congenitally malformed, and irreparably injured. The legal profession should devise new ways to extend legal aid to the incompetent and sociopathological. Educators must suggest the amount of attention that is due to the intellectually limited, emotionally disturbed, and culturally deprived. Each profession within the limits permitted by the social structure must determine the focus and extent of its pro bono publico efforts and society must decide the portion of its resources to commit to the support of such work. And professions should take the leadership in promoting changes in social structure that would result in a better distribution of services to those who need them. Individual professionals pursue these aims vigorously and feeble efforts at corporate action are evident in some professions. There is no evidence of a concerted and energetic program. The first step to initiating one would be to take cognizance of the obligation to do so in ethical codes.

Ethical Norms

Three kinds of standards are relevant to professional life: technical, economic, and moral. It is obvious that ethical codes should be restricted to moral norms, but the intrusion of self-serving rules for doing business, what is sometimes euphemistically called matters of etiquette, shows that we must belabor the obvious.

Many associations have scrubbed business norms from their codes for legal, ideological, and (we may hope) moral reasons. Two reservations must be made about the effort. First, some economic practices are clearly unethical; for example, claiming credit for another's work to gain employment or promotion. Prohibitions of these belong in codes, though it is especially important that there be a cogent demonstration in the rationale for the code that each rule of economic behavior is justified ethically.

Second, professions as corporate entities have the right to promote the economic interests of their members as long as these are compatible with the general welfare, but prudential aims should be kept strictly separate from ethical obligations. This may be done a couple of ways. Professional associations tradition-ally have attempted to discharge three functions: maintaining standards of competence and providing continuing education; exerting moral control over their members; and regulating busi-ness practices and lobbying for rights and privileges for the profession. Independent trade organizations might be established for the third function. This would free professional associations to concentrate on the first two. At the very least, ethical and economic codes should be distinct documents with clearly distin-guished objectives. The Guidelines to Professional Employment for Engineers and Scientists, endorsed by more than thirty engi-neering societies, is an example of a prudential economic code. The stated aim of the guidelines is "to establish a climate con-ducting to the proper discharge of mutual responsibilities and obligations" of employees and employers. Interestingly, this is said to require "A sound relationship between the professional employee and the employer, based on mutual loyalty, coopera-tion, fair treatment, ethical practices, and respect" and "Recog-nition of the responsibility to safeguard the public health, safety, and welfare." The guidelines spell out employee responsibilities in provisions similar to those of engineering codes of ethics. Engineers appear to want to make their adherence to the profes-sional ethic a contractual obligation. One wonders why they do not try to exact a complementary pledge from employers, that is, to adhere to a comparable code of business ethics as well as to guarantee the right of professional employees to adhere to professional codes.

The reference to ethical practices in the engineers' Guidelines to Professional Employment pertains only to employer-employee relations, not to relations with the outside world. The guidelines fail to make an overall ethical climate in the organization a condition for accepting employment. They are unique in mentioning ethics at all in connection with employment. We may indict the professions in general with passing up an opportunity to exert moral leverage on society and help make their codes a practicable program of action for their members. One can only guess that it is because they fear that ethics might reduce their opportunities for employment.

Ethical codes should concentrate on ethical norms. The norms of professional codes typically comprise rules and ideals. The two kinds of norms have specific roles to play.

Rules are prescriptions and prohibitions of specific behavior in concrete situations (e.g., Report dangerous clients to the police; Do not accept bribes from your employer's suppliers). Violations are punished by moral censure by colleagues and the public and, in the case of legislated rules, formal penalties inflicted by the professional association or civil authorities. Following the example of the ABA's Model Rules, rules should define the minimum level of conduct acceptable for continued membership in the profession.

Besides prohibitions and prescriptions, codes sometimes have permissive clauses. The AMA asserts, "A Physician shall, in the provision of appropriate patient care, except in emergencies, be free to choose whom to serve, with whom to associate, and the environment in which to provide medical services." The ECPD declares, "Engineers may accept an assignment requiring education or experience outside their own fields of competence, but only to the extent that their services are restricted to those phases of the project in which they are qualified." The AAUP declares, "As a member of his community, the professor has the rights and obligations of any citizen." The codes, however, do not always articulate the ideals that ought to guide the individual in the permitted behavior. This might be the task of the rationale provided for the permissions.

The rules and ideals of codes ordinarily specify role duties and responsibilities of the professional. If codes are to be treated as contracts, they should also state professional rights; that is, the conditions necessary for professionals to discharge their obligations. For example, if "Engineers shall not affix their signatures or seals to any engineering plan or document . . . not prepared under their direct supervisory control" (ECPD), they should be guaranteed the right to refuse to seal without penalty from their clients or employers.

Rights impose duties on others, so effective codes would state duties for clients and employers as well as for the professional. For example, if it is the duty of the physician to secure informed consent from patients, it is the patient's obligation to inform himself or herself to the extent necessary for intelligent judgment. And if the recognition of rights by society rouses the right-holder to demand that others discharge their obligations and this strengthens the moral system, client and employer rights should be clearly stated in codes; for example, the rights of employers that complement the obligations of the professional under "faithful agent and trustee" rules.

We noted that some codes do enjoin the professional to respect client rights, but they do so in a vague general way. The rights appear to be ones already sanctioned by law or custom, not role rights or specific rights that obtain by virtue of the individual's position in the professional relationship. These are what need to be spelled out explicitly in codes. A model for this sort of thing is the American Hospital Association's A Patients' Bill of Rights.

A professional ethic is not the sole concern of the profession. It should represent a consensus between the profession and the public. This is patent if the ethic is to cover rights and duties of laypersons in the professional relationship. Most social relationships are reciprocal. The norms that govern the actions on each side would be acceptable to the other in an ideal society.

Codes do not generally pay attention to differences in roles within the profession. We have commented on the emphasis in long-established professions (law, medicine, the older engineering specialties) on the ethical problems of self-employed practitioners. More recent codes (e.g., AAUP, IEEE) deal with employed professionals. On their part, these fail to distinguish sorts of organizations and the roles professionals play in them. For example, excepting the APA and, of course, the AAUP, few mention the special obligations of teachers and researchers. Few address the special obligations of employees of governmental and eleemosynary institutions. Some mention duties of professional employees and others, of professional employers when they supervise professional and nonprofessional subordinates; none regulate both relationships in detail. As a result, most lists of rules apply to only a portion of the members of the profession.

We should make a particular point of the obligations that attend to the so-called social responsibilities of professions. If professions are to be an independent force for human welfare, they must be chartered to do more than provide the services covered by their monopoly. They must be held responsible for improving the institutions administering those services.

Some claim such responsibilities. The ABA charges lawyers with strengthening the rule of law. The SDC views itself as a protector of freedom of thought and communication for everyone. The AAUP declares that "the professor has a particular obligation to promote conditions of free inquiry and to further public understanding of academic freedom." It attempts to do so itself by recommending guidelines and investigating and censuring institutions that violate them. We can imagine the medical profession being assigned a responsibility for the fair allocation of health resources and a systematic program of prophylactic medicine. The engineering profession could be assigned the responsibility for protecting the environment and conserving scarce resources. Professors could be empowered to plan and govern higher education on a national scale.

Whether occupational groups should be chartered to deal with global matters is open to debate. I view the prospect with trepidation, but I assert that it is ideological decoration for a group to pretend to a corporate responsibility when it does not assign the obligations necessary to discharge it to the roles of specific individuals. Logically, these obligations would be assigned to the leaders of the occupation, perhaps the functionaries of professional associations where these are an effective force.

Rules and Laws

The distinction between rules and ideals partly turns on the economy of sanctions. Society has and should exercise only limited instruments to control the behavior of individuals. We ordinarily reserve positive sanctions (rewards) for people who live up to ideals—it is low praise to say, "Well, at least X never broke the rules." Negative sanctions, on the other hand, are reserved for violations of rules, and rules are norms that can be enforced by punishment. The dividing line here is not sharp, of course. Condemnation, peer pressure, ostracism, and boycott are all punishments. We certainly want to criticize people for low ideals or failure to live up to accepted ideals. Ideals thus are a segment of a continuum that overlaps the segment of rules when the kinds of norms are arrayed in terms of the sanctions that would be effective in creating a moral society.

The fact that ideals fall at one end of the continuum suggests that a special kind of rules—laws—fall at the other. Laws are rules for the violation of which more formal and severe penalties are inflicted under the authority of the state.

It seems to some professional associations that a natural complement to its ethical code is a model set of laws. The American Bar Association provides a set in its Disciplinary Rules. These have been adopted by most states, so lawyers can be disbarred for violating them. The National Council of Engineering Examiners follows the ABA's example in proposing a Model Law for licensing professional engineers. It enjoins state registration boards to enforce a list of rules (formulated as NCEE's Model Rules of Professional Conduct). It recommends that boards be empowered to "suspend, refuse to renew or revoke the certification of, or reprimand any professional engineer who is found guilty" of violating the rules. The rules, however, are less detailed than those of the ABA. Registration boards' control over engineers is much less than bar associations' over lawyers, and the influence of the rules is correspondingly weaker.

Should a rational code of professional ethics be supplemented with a legal code? Before those who design institutions utilize the law as a tool, they should reflect on its effect on the moral life; that is, on the utility of laws from the moral point of view. Do we really want professional conduct to be legally regulated beyond the statutes already in place for negligence, fraud, breaches of contract, and similar misdeeds of citizens in general? The power of the state is limited. It should not be squandered on unimportant matters. Furthermore, every new law curtails some form of freedom. Those who already wish to act as the law requires lose the opportunity to decide voluntarily because the threat of punishment shuts off alternatives.

Of course, some laws *are* justified, not only to protect other values, but to enlarge freedom of choice itself, either choices of agents protected against those who are restrained from interfering or of those who are restrained from some choices by empowering them to perform other actions that the restraints make possible. Laws requiring credentials for the license to practice protect the public against incompetence. Laws guaranteeing confidentiality enable professionals to involve themselves in their clients' affairs in a way that greatly magnifies the area for professional work.

Limits in the desirable powers of enforcement of society and the inherently undesirable features of laws do not mean that there should be no regulation of professional behavior. They mean that there should be exacting criteria for such laws. The aim of legislation is to establish conditions that will allow people of ordinary conscientiousness and limited good will to follow their moral impulses in the professional context. This suggests the following criteria for the legislation of moral rules: (1) Only rules that are important to the maintenance of the moral system should be enacted as laws. Venial sins can be tolerated in the name of individualism and liberty and left to dissuasion by peer contempt. Only mortal sins of professional misconduct should condemn one to the exterior darkness of decertification. (2) Only enforceable rules should be made laws. Laws that do no good do positive harm, and a façade of unenforceable laws breeds cynicism and hypocrisy. (3) There should be a consensus on the moral validity of the rules that are made laws. The law depends on voluntary obedience of the great majority to control the immoral few through fear.

Laws on the books and decisions of the courts give legal status to some professional codes and practices. Let us refer to actual statutes and the rules of formal organizations that take on the force of law by virtue of enforcement sanctioned by society as "regulations." As we have seen, some professional associations try to control the conduct of practitioners of the particular occupation by a complex apparatus of ideals, voluntary rules, and enforced regulations. Final evaluation of these apparatuses is extremely difficult, because they are used for both ethical guidance and corporate self-interest. On the other hand, it is difficult to imagine what society would be without them. Hence, I have confined myself to recommendations of piecemeal improvements in their content and form and the institutions that implement them.

We have now sketched a comprehensive program for moral engineering. For each occupation, a comprehensive document is needed with content derived from the moral point of view and a realistic understanding of the social world and perfected semiotically. The document would include an ethical code, model laws, basic ideals, and a rationale for all of these. Correlative with such a document would be a plan to reform institutions to ensure that individuals will internalize the norms and to protect those who do from those who would disregard them.

Notes

1. Much of this material appears in my "The Ideological Use of Professional Codes" and "Evaluating Codes of Professional Ethics."

2. Clapp, *Professional Ethics and Insignia*, p. 260. I take this to be a quotation or a paraphrase.

3. *Ibid.*, pp. 257–258. Observe the atavistic invocation of the deity to help in the mastery of nature.

4. Webster defines 'dignity' as "Quality of being esteemed; degree of estimation; as the *dignity* of one's profession."

5. *Political Life of the American Medical Association*, p. 106.

6. "Engineering Ethics and the Public Interest," p. 26.

7. "Ethics Spun from Fairy Tales," p. 30.

8. Anderson et al., *Divided Loyalties*, p. 14. The California Society of Professional Engineers and eventually the national Institute of Electrical and Electronic Engineers provided assistance to the engineers, who later received the first Award for Outstanding Service in the Public Interest from IEEE's Committee on the Social Implication of Technology. See Kinn, *The IEEE Role in Engineering Ethics*," pp. 8–9.

9. *A Dictionary of Modern English Usage*, p. 392.

10. *Words and Women*, p. 85.

11. *Ibid.*, p. 30.

12. *Dictionary*, p. 176.

13. *Words and Women*, p. 144.

14. *Ibid.*, p. 45.

15. *Controlling Technology*, p. 33.

16. More recently, the physicians of Barney Clark, the first human to be permanently attached to a mechanical heart, made a point of announcing that he "died with dignity." This seemed to make the experimentation and pain in Clark's treatment more palatable to the public.

❏ PART IV

THE PROFESSIONAL IDEAL

☐ 11

IDEALS AND CHARACTER

Imagine a tribe of people living in a habitable but harsh environment. A traveler brings word of an idyllic uninhabited land not many miles away but guarded by a high and perilous mountain ridge. It can be reached by scaling the mountains or an arduous journey up one long river and down another. The tribe debate whether to emigrate. If they try the mountains and fail, they will be left in desperate straits. The river route is so long they would have even less chance of reaching the New Eden, but at least there would be places to settle along the way. As the tribe review the alternatives, they begin to reflect on their way of life, their practices for dealing with each other, outsiders, and the environment. Improvements are possible whether the tribe stays put, risks the mountains, or undertakes the grinding trek upstream.

This is an allegory for the circumstances examined in this work. Consider the professions as tribes in the demanding environment of a competitive society. Part I hypothesized what perfect professions in a perfect society would be like. Part II explored the realities of actual professions in actual society, the way they now function. Part III examined possibilities for structural change, either wholesale by a radical reshaping of society or piecemeal by changes in its elements, including the professions. Part IV will focus on viable ideals for professionals. It is possible for professions to change their ways even if society remains pretty much as it is.

In Part III, fundamental changes in structure could not be proposed without reservation because, as things look now, the ideal society is not likely to come into being and perfect professions are not possible. Should piecemeal reforms fall short, the professions might function even less well than they now do. Should society as a whole turn bad, they would become powerful forces for evil and additions to their power would turn out to be a monstrous mistake. Though we have been able to describe some changes that would obviously be improvements, the full consequences of others would depend on too many incalculable external factors to evaluate. The conclusions of Part III, therefore, were cautious, tentative, provisional, encumbered with qualifications.

The ethical import of professionalism as an ideal and a determinant of individual character is easier to evaluate. The professional ideal properly abstracted and refined is one of the major moral inventions of Western civilization with roots back to Greek and Roman times. Our endorsement of it can be categorical and unqualified.

High ideals often cohabit with venial practices. Despite the failings of professions, professionalism is a vital influence in the lives of not only professionals but workers in other occupations, and normatively the professional imperative is categorical: Everyone should do his or her work as professionally as possible.

Barriers to Universality

Status differentials stand in the way of universalizing the professional ideal. They deny some groups not only an equal share in the benefits of society, but an equal share in the satisfaction of producing them in a morally elevating and socially respected way. Universalizing professionalism would help to erase the status distinction that exists between occupations that are organized and identified as professions and those that are not. It would distribute more fairly the satisfactions of participating fully, with appropriate recognition, in the economic life of the group to members of all occupations. Professionals take pride in their work. Other workers can share in the same pride by developing professional attitudes and habits. Conflict theorists propose to overcome status differentials and promote solidarity by proletarianizing the professions: The higher road would be to professionalize the proletariat.

Some sociologists question the viability of such a program. They maintain that there is a natural limit to professionalization.[1] Their judgment, however, is predicated on the functionalist emphasis on structure and implicit claim that only occupations with a certain structure can perform the functions for which they exist. What the functionalists actually show is that the professions' way of organizing cannot be universalized not that the professionals' way of doing work cannot. Professions are interest groups struggling for position by seeking a monopoly over services and putting it at the disposal of socioeconomic elites. The structure of professions and their ideology are designed to secure external benefits—exceptional status, power, and income—whose nature entails scarcity. In contrast, the dignity of useful work done well and equal shares of status, power, and material goods can be enjoyed by all.

Regulations, Rules, and Autonomy

A limited role has been acknowledged for *rules* and *regulations* in cultivation of ethical practice, I shall now argue the teleological primacy of professional *ideals*. The purpose of rules and regulations, aside from the limited protection they afford the public, is to provide an orderly community in which conscientious practitioners can act as they see fit under the ideal. As much scope as practicable should be reserved for the autonomous pursuit of the ideal by the individual worker.

The problem with this thesis lies in showing what is practicable. An ideal must be articulated that can be put into practice yet is high enough to be worth pursuing. And ways must be described in which people of ordinary conscientiousness can be inspired to pursue these ideals with sufficient dedication to approximate the result—maximal benefits fairly distributed in society—that the moral engineer vainly tries to assure by rules and enforcement. The remainder of this chapter and the next two will be devoted to an attempt to synthesize the normative ideas turned up in the preceding parts of this work into a single coherent ideal. The last chapter will reflect briefly on the problem of instilling the ideal in average practitioners of various occupations.

To be clear exactly what ideals are sought, let us examine a bit further the interplay between enforced and voluntary norms in the cultivation of the moral life. The first point to note is that the two sets, enforced and voluntary, are not mutually exclusive. It is true that some regulations settle morally neutral matters for administrative convenience, but if the regulations are created legitimately, following them becomes a moral obligation. Moreover, few regulations rely on formal sanctions alone for their effectiveness; all are backed—and legitimate ones should be backed—by the forces of opinion and conscience. This is particularly obvious for regulations that incorporate norms that have moral status before their enactment.

Cases in point are the norms for professional conduct the observance of which is made a condition for licensure or membership in professional associations; for example, regulations mandating confidentiality or treatment of those who need it in emergencies and prohibiting false advertising, acceptance of bribes, and intervention in individuals' lives without their consent. Violations of these norms do not cease to be morally reprehensible just because society punishes them.

Regulations are intended to restrain immoral or amoral agents, those who act primarily from self-interest, in order to create an environment in which persons of at least ordinary conscientiousness can follow norms voluntarily without undue sacrifice or heroic virtue. On the other hand, the existence of formal sanctions or even peer pressure stimulate concern for self-interest and threatens to convert people from the moral to the prudential point of view by rendering moral principles superfluous. The issue must be faced, therefore, of how much behavior to regulate and how much to leave to the conscience of the individual. The answer is given partly by the difficulties and disadvantage of enforcement and partly by the possibility of widespread cultivation of strong and informed consciences by the proper kind of moral training.

We have insisted that the number of regulations for professional life and the extent of their enforcement should be set as low as possible, while still protecting the public and the moral practitioner. More than minimal regulations would require intolerable enforcement powers, open to abuse by those in control. In addition, the autonomy of those subject to such regulation is to be considered. By adding sufficient penalties to violations of norms to kill them as options, society effectively makes choices for the individual. The individual is denied the opportunity of choosing what is right for its own sake, since all reason for choosing what is wrong is removed.

Among the ethical premises of Part I of this work was the claim that the intrinsic quality of actions and the satisfaction they bring to the agent are integral to the consequences in terms of which the actions are to be evaluated. It also was noted that a person's work occupies much of one's time and incorporates some of the most important decisions one makes in life. One's opportunity to enjoy true moral dignity would be severely curtailed no matter how beneficial the conduct may be for others, unless afforded scope for moral choices including choices rewarded by no more than by the satisfaction of making them because they are right—even including, some would argue Kantwise, choices that entail sacrifice of other elements of self-interest. Indeed, this constriction of the moral sphere appears to be a primary deficit of competitive society as measured against the cooperative organic society postulated.

This, then, is another reason to limit the regulation of professional life. Not only is the cost of overregulation too high for society, it is unfair to the individual.

We can go a step further. In the continuum of norms discussed in Chapter 10, civil laws were singled out at one end and ideals proposed for the loyalty of the individual at the other. Between them were consensual rules proposed by the group and backed by peer approval or disapproval. The emphasis has been on the desirability of such rules over regulations, when they can be made to work. Brandt makes a similar point about the rules themselves, perhaps in comparison to open ideals or situational discretion for the individual. "We must remember that it is a serious matter to have a moral rule at all, for moral rules take conduct out of the realm of preference and free decision. So, for the recognition of a certain moral rule to have good consequences, the benefits of recognition must outweigh the costliness of restricting freedom."[2] To put this in positive terms and for professions, professions should foster higher aspirations in their members than they can or should enforce. In particular they should inculcate ideals that impose open obligations. Such obligations include those unenforceable by nature, supererogatory, more likely to be observed if left to personal conscience, requiring individual initiative and insight, or simply providing opportunities for the individual to acquire moral dignity by going beyond what is required by law.

Internalization of Ideals

As observed, resounding declarations of ideals are hollow and ideological if they are not internalized by the majority of those who practice an occupation. The recommendation that rules and regulations for professionals be limited despite the power invested in them can be taken seriously only if we can describe how valid ideals can be brought alive.

Ideals are not abstract forms to be admired from afar. To be effective in the world, they must be incorporated in the lives of individuals who act on the social scene. The professional ideal, as conceived here, is a pattern for what we want people to *be* who do our work. One's nature is expressed in one's acts but is something prior to them. The ideal professional can be relied on to perform the acts required by the rules of the professional ethic, but more—he or she can be expected to go beyond rules to accomplish more than they require, to act creatively within their framework and even, when extraordinary circumstances demand, contrary to it.

Fidelity to the professional ideal by even the limited group of people who populate the recognized professions would be no minor matter in view of what was noted in Chapter 1 about the central importance of the professions in modern society. Professionals (in the narrow sense) not only have custody over important segments of the lives of other people, they provide models for the way many others play their roles. They do so de facto by virtue of their prestige, even if their example is not entirely edifying. They would so do de jure if they were to realize perfectly a perfect ideal of professionalism.

We may apply here some of MacIntyre's notions. He maintains that a few roles specific to each culture play a crucial part in its formation. He refers to the occupants of these roles as the 'characters' of the culture, playing on the dual meaning of the term as it refers both to actors in a drama and the moral dimensions of personality. MacIntyre maintains that characters "are, so to speak, the moral representatives of their culture and they are so because of the way in which moral and metaphysical ideas and theories assume through them an embodied existence in the social world." Characters are supposed to live according to central moral and metaphysical ideas of the culture and, hence, express in their actions and provide a graphic illustration to others of what those ideas entail. They are expected to *be* what their actions express. "A *character* is an object of regard by the members of the culture generally or by some significant segment of them. Hence the demand is that in this type of case role and personality be fused. Social type and psychological type are required to coincide. The *character* legitimates a mode of social existence."[3] Characters play a central role in what MacIntyre labels 'practices.'

> By a 'practice' I am going to mean any coherent and complex form of socially established cooperative human activity through which goods internal to that form of activity are realized in the course of trying to achieve those standards of excellence which are appropriate to, and partially definitive of, that form of activity, with the result that human powers to achieve excellence, and human conceptions of the ends and goods involved, are systematically extended.[4]

Thus, characters must measure up to standards of excellence appropriate to the activities required of them—standards, we may add, which the pioneers of the character created in the process of developing a new role for society.

MacIntyre uses the traditional term 'virtue' for the qualities that a role occupant must develop to achieve excellence in his or her appointed activity. In this context he provides this tentative definition: "A virtue is an acquired human quality the possession and exercise of which tends to enable us to achieve those goods which are internal to practices and the lack of which effectively prevents us from achieving any such goods."[5]

The important characters of our culture, according to MacIntyre, include the rich aesthete, the bureaucratic manager, and the psychological therapist. Since he finds much to disapprove in the ideas informing their roles and hence in their activities, their standards of "excellence" and their "virtues," they hardly embody ideals of the sort we have in mind. However, when we adapt MacIntyre's categories to our case, the matter is different. Professionals are central characters in the drama of social life in a technological culture. There is no question that professional practices provide important internal benefits for those who engage in them and external benefits for those served by them. The professional ideal defines the virtues that must become part of the being of the characters who perform the practices, their second nature, if they are to carry on the practices entrusted to them and provide a model for work in general.

In saying this, I do not retract what has been said about the shortcomings of actual professionals and the operative norms of their behavior. Few live up to the professional ideal perfectly and many fall far short of it. But I am expressing the conviction that a valid and important ideal can be extracted from the practice of the best professionals and that the example of the best can become contagious. If this is so, the professional character, as an ideal type in society, can live up to its potential and become a determining factor in the moral climate of the age.

Service Revisited

On the assumption that it is possible to make professional ideal a living force in the lives of average people, we turn to the content of the ideal. The remainder of this chapter will discuss two keystone elements: the ideas of dedication to service and proficiency. In addition, there will be further comment on the extent to which these elements are recognized or neglected in actual professions. The succeeding chapters will trace subsidiary elements that these two entail and that flesh out what is *done* by the professional whose life *is* dedicated to proficient service.

It has been argued that considerable autonomy is necessary if professionals are to enjoy moral dignity in their work. This should be combined with the claim that it also is necessary if professionals effectively are to serve their clients, employers, and the public. Recall that it is a cardinal tenet of the professional ideology that professionals should be more autonomous than ordinary workers because of the technical character of their work. They alone are capable of judging competent and ethical practice. We have seen that this claim is self-serving and the forms and limits of professional autonomy must be assessed critically. After all, where one person's autonomy begins, another's ends. Professional autonomy must be curtailed where it encroaches on the legitimate interests of employer or client or where service to employer or client threatens harm to outsiders. (More problematic are the limits of autonomy for professionals when they act in the interest of employers, clients, or the public without their consent—cases of professional paternalism, which will be examined in the next chapter.)

Complaints have been echoed against the professions for taking advantage of their monopoly status. Recall that the professional ideology justifies monopoly by the myth of noblesse oblige and gentlemanly disinterestedness. Parsons connects these with the allegedly scientific basis of professional disciplines: He pictures professionals as serving all in need with an even hand in terms of the objective requirements of their condition without regard for their social position. Critics point out, to the contrary, that professionals provide more and better services to the affluent and powerful and receive special privileges in return.

The critics have not proved that a maldistribution of services would not have occurred but for professional monopolies or how expansion of the knowledge base for technical occupations and uniformity of competence could have been assured without the monopoly. In any event, we may be assured that monopolies of expertise will continue, whether in the context of individual enterprise or bureaucratic organization, or capitalism or socialism. We can only hope that structural reforms—for example, a limitation on the income of the traditional professions, the universalization of the category of profession (as proposed in Chapter 14), the institution of charters for occupations and transmutation of professional institutions (as described in Part III), effective protection of ordinary practitioners against the unfair competition of the unscrupulous, and reform of professional education (Chapter 14)—will suffice to free up the psyches of individuals for the spirit of service. The existence of a charter would be a crucial first step. Professionals must be made to understand that their status is socially defined and supported, that law and custom grant them privileges and rights for which they owe a great deal in return. One of the first articles of a professional covenant should be a guarantee of service to all in need rather than restricting it to those who can afford it.

The ideal, to serve all in need, is simplistic. Neither the entire profession nor the individual is required to do more than resources allow. Some human needs are too great to be met. Nor are professionals obligated to scurry about and force their services on people who do not want them, though the professions should recognize their obligation to educate the public as to its needs and collaborate with society in imposing some services (medical treatment, psychotherapy, legal representation, safety engineering, minimal education) on individuals who need but do not want them.

The obligation to meet human needs, then, must be cut down to manageable size. Respect for client autonomy provides the key. People, though frequently mistaken about their needs, should be allowed to define them. The professional covenant might require practitioners to accept anyone who approaches them for help and mandate the profession to see that there is a sufficient supply of practitioners to meet the aggregate demand.

This still is impractical. The principle of service on demand also requires qualification. The professional is not obligated to take on new clients when this prevents adequate service to those already clients or to perform immoral acts at any client's behest or to collaborate with a client's self-harmful behavior. Cases such as these, plus a possessive concern for professional autonomy, have caused professional associations to draw back from the obligations to serve all who ask for service and to educate those in need to ask for it. Their commitments in these areas are vague, half-hearted, and discordant.

Recognition of the Ideal in Professions

The American Bar Association speaks in the firmest voice. It states in its Model Code, "A basic tenet of the professional responsibility of lawyers is that every person in our society should have ready access to the independent professional services of a lawyer of integrity and competence." It recognizes that this is a burden that individual lawyers cannot carry alone.

> A lawyer is under no obligation to act as an adviser or advocate for every person who may wish to become his client; but in furtherance of the objective of the bar to make legal services fully available, a lawyer should not lightly decline proffered employment. The fulfillment of this objective requires acceptance by a lawyer of his share of tendered employment which may be unattractive both to him and the bar generally.

It spells out the obligation by listing a number of reasons that do not justify refusal of employment, including the unpopularity of a client or a cause, avoidance of adversary alignment against judges or influential persons, the burdens of court-appointed representation of indigent persons, and repugnance at the subject matter of the proceedings. The ABA recognizes an individual and corporate obligation to educate people about legal resources. "The legal profession should assist lay-persons to recognize legal problems because such problems may not be self-revealing, and are not timely noticed." However, it limits lawyers to communicating information in a way that does not solicit business, misinform the public, degrade the profession, or generate unnecessary litigation. The restrictions severely circumscribe the obligation to inform and one wonders whether a large percentage of people who need legal representation may not know enough to seek it, not to mention be able to afford it.

I have quoted the ABA at some length because it is the one profession that deals with the problem in any important way. The Opinions of the Judicial Council of the American Medical Association affirms the right of individuals to choose their physicians and medical care plans and declares, "Limited health care resources should be allocated efficiently and on the basis of fair, acceptable, and humanitarian criteria" rather than on the basis of "utility or relative worth to society." However, the responsibility that the Judicial Council assigns to physicians is nebulous. "A physician has a duty to do all that he can for the benefit of his patients without assuming total responsibility for equitable disbursement of society's limited health resources." These guarded comments assign a limited duty to physicians to treat those who chance to come to them. The duty is not strong or definite enough to override the right posted as one of the seven Principles of Medical Ethics, "A physician shall, in the provision of appropriate patient care, except in emergencies, be free to choose whom to serve, with whom to associate, and the environment in which to provide medical services." The AMA apparently does not believe it morally reprehensible for physicians to concentrate in affluent areas of the country or screen patients on the basis of their ability to pay.

Other professional associations shy even further from recognizing an obligation to serve all in need or all who seek help. Engineering societies speak only about the responsibility to inform the public of the accomplishments of the profession and lay ground rules for solicitation of employment under a conception of fair competition; they are silent about the responsibility to respond to society's needs. The American Psychological Association in its Ethical Principles enjoins its members to "protect the welfare of those who seek their service," but it does not indicate that 'protecting' means accepting for therapy.

Service implies that professionals aggressively should seek out those who need their help and serve those most in need first of all. Professional associations, however, studiously avoid drawing this implication. They steer clear of a meaningful obligation to provide service under conditions other than those that aggrandize their members. In their scheme, the "right" to choose clients or employers overrides obligations to humanity. This is not surprising given the role of professional associations as ideological mouthpieces and economic lobbyists, but it subverts their authority as moral guides. An independent ethic would impose more stringent obligations than do the associations in their formal codes.

It is a primary obligation of the professional to accept those who come to him or her in need within the limits required for competent service, a reasonable workload, and economic survival. Taking the obligation seriously would entail a significant amount of charitable or other pro bono work and a ceiling on the professional's income. In addition, the principle imposes the corporate responsibility on the profession to ensure an adequate supply and fair distribution of practitioners, while limiting its claim to social resources in such a way as to allow other occupations a fair share. In other words, the obligation to serve must be rigorous enough to impose sacrifices of convenience and income and restrictions on the freedom of choice of professionals. It also presupposes mechanisms other than the market for the allocation of resources.

In Part II, the toothlessness of service requirements by professional associations was treated as evidence that their protestations are ideological masks designed to persuade the public to trust them in the exercise of their monopoly. But, there must be an element of truth in ideologies to make them effective. In the case of service, a valid ideal is involved and it is attractive to many members of professions as well as the public.

Surely, the desire to serve is an important element in the social dimension of human nature. We do not find it surprising or particularly problematic when it expresses itself toward family, friends, or others with whom one has ties of affection. But why would anyone dedicate his work life to service rather than self-aggrandizement, since the recipients are strangers, at least until ties are created by act of service itself, and work is the major avenue to acquiring the resources to gratify self-interest? Serving others often must mean neglecting oneself and those near to one.

The answer seems to be that the desire to serve springs from two basic sources in human nature, which also lie at the root of the moral point of view. These impulses are capable of generalization in the domain of work, as in the broader domain of social interaction as such. One is the complex of reactions aroused in us by the spectacle of lives of other people, the interplay of empathy, sympathy, and compassion at the sufferings of others and vicarious satisfaction at their triumphs. These can be directed not only to individuals with whom one has established intimate relationships but toward all members of the moral community. When one acts on such feelings, one enters into relationships such as those that would permeate a truly organic society and experiences the satisfaction of membership in the society, though that society be realized only imperfectly as yet.

Exactly which among these generous feelings is dominant depends on the particular occupation, the needs it meets and the relationships it requires between the worker and the other. Something like generalized compassion is at work in those who are truly dedicated to the helping professions (medicine, social work, psychotherapy, and the like) and something like vicarious satisfaction in the achievement of others, in the facilitating professions (engineering, teaching, management, and the like). The impulse that leads us to generalize attitudes and live in terms of fitness to belong to something as abstruse as the perfect society is reinforced by the actual communal relations it creates and, of course, the gratitude returned for our service to specific others. While friendship is defective as a model to represent the obligations of the professional to client or employer,[6] professional relationships precipitate something like friendship when they involve sharing of problems, successes, and failures.

The second source of the desire to serve through useful work is justice. The sense of justice causes us to direct the impulse to serve toward all in need, operationalized as service on demand. One feels obligated to return to society something commensurate with the opportunity to do interesting and remunerative work, an opportunity that professionals enjoy in a preeminent degree. This one can do by providing services of maximal benefit to members of the moral community. Justice also demands that one spread those services equally or, more precisely, to see that they, in the context of services by other workers and forms of work, contribute as equally as possible to the quality of life of all.

Generous feelings and justice combat self-regarding desires, equally natural, that motivate people to use work for personal prosperity or to provide for those near to them and consequently to put themselves at the disposal of those who can best reward them. The many examples of dedicated professionals, not to mention conscientious workers in other occupations, show that generous feelings and justice can dominate self-regarding desires. We can hope to make this the rule rather than the exception by constructing the right sort of social environment.

However, a note of realism is needed here. We must not imagine that dedication to service excludes all thought of self. The professional ideal should not be pitched so high as to place it beyond the reach of ordinary people. The true professional should not be asked to forego all thought of personal gain. And a measure of corporate prudence is morally obligatory for those with the opportunity to shape the conditions under which their colleagues work. They must see that all in the occupation are compensated fairly, that it is possible for them to live decently while serving others, to prevent those who are more competent and industrious from being penalized. The aim is to make service the direct and controlling object of professionalism, to prevent profit or wages from being so by making them its routine byproducts.

We are asking for institutions that will create an environment in which it is realistic to expect service to humanity, beyond service to special patrons, to be the paramount consideration that determines the nature of work. Where clients or employers have a legitimate claim to service, the controlling consideration must be What is the most effective way to provide it? Not, What will the compensation be? From this follows all of the usual obligations of competence: Professionals ought not to undertake work beyond their range of ability. They ought to opt for less costly measures where these are effective. They ought to refer clients to other specialists when they are not equipped to handle those clients' problems. They ought to defer to clients' wishes in balancing the level of service against its cost. The ideal of service is viable if we construe it in the sense of a disposition on the part of the professional to allow the interests of those served to control the choice of means, whatever the source of that disposition. In this way, we avoid the unrealistic demand for extraordinary altruism.

This ideal is viable for all occupations. It need not be restricted to elite occupations, which may fall just as short of realizing it as those of inferior status. It is not too much to ask of all workers that they do the job for which they are hired, do it well, do it for the purposes for which they are hired, and do it within their limitations.

We should not put the ideal negatively. Ideals are not burdens but challenges to our deeper selves. Where not stifled by a hostile environment, there is a craving in us all for a vocation that will engage our talents and interest, that we are equipped to do well, and that will serve others. Unless alienated or exploited by the actual conditions under which we work, we all desire to do as well as possible for the benefit of others. The professional ideal articulates the fundamental human need for a meaningful occupation. Since this occupation occupies most of one's life, this is integral to the need for a meaningful life. The professional ideal incorporates the personal qualities one must develop to meet this need. Professionalism is a key to meaningful life.

Competence Revisited

Good intentions ineptly implemented may be as harmful as bad intentions. Dedication to service is not enough; the ideal professional must be competent or proficient. The point here is that these concepts must be construed more broadly than they usually are. To be professional is certainly to be proficient in the technical details of one's work but, from what has and will be said, it also requires moral proficiency. Skills are required to carry out any moral intention, whatever the technique required for the specific job. These skills involve influencing people to act as they ought—the arts of communication and persuasion, for example—and skills in determining what ought to be done—in practical reasoning and a cultivated attentiveness to the needs of others, for example. Hence, standards of professional proficiency are moral and psychological as well as technical.

Moral standards are more general than technical standards. Technical standards are specific to particular forms of work;

moral standards are more nearly the same for all. Technical standards are more precise and detailed and harder to master; though moral standards are not as easy to master, validate, and apply as technicians imagine.

Because what distinguishes forms of work is expertise, one's professionalism is measured ordinally by technical standards. The professional is one whose proficiency is a quantum leap above that of the amateur. Level of proficiency marks the difference between a vocation and an avocation, because it is a level that can be attained and maintained only by lifelong practice and a resolute attempt to learn everything there is to know about a job. We have argued that, in addition, the professional must know everything there is to know about the ethical standards and the social obligations of his or her occupation.

Specialized skills are predicated on bodies of thought, whether these be developed by experiment as in science, trial and error as in the practical arts, deductively as in mathematics and some aspects of the law, or speculatively as in theology and the application of psychological theory to human problems. The differences among the skilled occupations lie in the kinds of thought they involve, not in the difference between thinking and unthinking action. The level of abstraction of the thought of the plumber or electrician is low compared to that of the nuclear engineer, to be sure, but so is the thought of the lawyer, journalist, and (in regard to pedagogy) the professor. All degrees of complexity, all quantities of knowledge, and all mixtures of theoretical study and practical experience are required by various occupations. Nevertheless, a single ideal is relevant to all: Skilled workers must know what they are doing. The level of their knowledge as much as their skill transcends that of the amateur.

The critic considers professionals to be overtrained and can think of no reason for this except to put a social distance between the professional and other skilled laborers. The critic sees protracted professional education as an exclusionary process, a rite of passage that is not necessary for doing the job but that restricts the opportunity to do it and fortifies the tight monopoly of a small elite over a service. This view of professional education denigrates human curiosity and its soul-expanding power. It is the mission of anyone with a true vocation to put knowledge and skill at the disposal of others. Such an agent is anything but an unconscious tool, an automatic computer-manipulator. It is stultifying and inhuman to require anyone to devote an entire life to a field without a lively interest in every aspect of it and its relation to the rest of life. Once stimulated, intellectual curiosity carries the professional far beyond the information necessary for the routines of practice. Professionals want to understand all of the dimensions of the concrete situations with which they are called to deal though a narrow sector has been marked out as their special responsibility.

Professional knowledge is eclectic. Professional problems are variegated and fluid. Professionalism requires an imaginative and probing mind, not that of a drudge or mere instrument of others. Such a mind can be expected to take an interest in everything pertaining to its work. The educational system should encourage and nourish such minds even if this requires it to impart knowledge never directly put to use.

Professionals should know as much as they can about their field. It is too much to expect all of them to contribute new knowledge. If this were required, there would be very few professionals even in the "professions." Some specialists (scientists, scholars, theoreticians) professionally search for new knowledge. Most specialists apply knowledge discovered by others. Both types of specialist are professional to the extent that they dedicate themselves to the ideal of theoretically informed skill and do their part to marshall the collective resources of humanity for the solution of its problems.

Professional mastery has negative and reflexive as well as positive and substantive aspects. Professionals not only know what there is to know; they know the limits of their knowledge and scrupulously confine their claims to competence within those limits. They not only estimate the probability that causes will have effects within the domain of their expertise; they estimate the likelihood that their estimates are correct. The reflexive sense of one's limits is demanded by respect for the autonomy of one's clients, employers, and the public. The latter must know the scope and reliability of one's expertise if they are to make rational decisions about whether to follow one's advice. Professionals put their intelligence and knowledge at the disposal of those whom they serve to the extent compatible with the moral exercise of their own autonomy. This takes much more self-knowledge than discharging their responsibilities paternalistically.

I have incorporated much from the professional ideology in this characterization of professional competence, but I am denying that the ideal of competence is the exclusive province of traditional professions. More importantly, I refuse to glorify technical competence and unswerving loyalty to the employer without regard to the uses to which the competence is put. A narrow view of professionalism idealizes means in detachment from ends; but true competence is not only the ability to do , but to know what X is for and to see how X accomplishes it. It includes the ability to recognize that X should be refused in circumstances where it does not accomplish its end or has negative consequences that outbalance its end. Furthermore, competence entails the ability to understand ends set by clients. The end is something that contributes to clients' welfare as they see it, though, if the professional is not to be reduced to a *mere* means, the end must fall among those states of affairs judged professionally to be morally acceptable. The professional must value client autonomy and contribute to it as well as to other elements of the good life for the client.

Objective Concern

This discussion of dedication to proficient service will be concluded by sketching the attitude toward the other that follows from it. What is the proper term for an attitude that results from combining the affective and volitional impulses behind the desire to service—empathy, sympathy, compassion, altruism, generosity—with high standards of competence? The traditional name for the combination of emotion and intellect in the service of others is 'practical love,' but this is too strong for modern ears. One should not expect from the professional the same attitude toward clients, employers, and the public as toward intimate friends and members of the family. I suggest instead the term 'objective concern.'

Concern implies care. True professionals care what happens to those whom they affect, both clients and outsiders. They are charged in particular with the care of clients and they come to care for them. Hence, clients engage their compassion, generosity, and benevolence.

But professionals are also objective. They keep their emotions under control so that emotion will not distort their practical judgments or prevent them from applying their entire expertise to their clients' problems. Professionals make hard decisions and demand hard decisions of clients. While sentiment is the driving force behind their commitment to rationally informed measures in the service of others, sentimentality has no place. Professionals, like true friends, are concerned about the needs of clients, but with a detachment that allows an objectivity not always welcome or even appropriate in friends. Indeed, objectivity together with skill is what makes the professional more helpful than the typical friend. In this regard professionalism is a partial model for enlightened friendship.

To put the conclusions of this chapter in a nutshell, what the professional ideal requires is that anyone who does work that affects the interests of others *be* a person dedicated to service to others and effective in providing it by virtue of having acquired the intellectual virtues of technical knowledge and skills and the moral virtues of generosity and justice. Being such a person, the professional consistently *displays* objective concern toward others. He or she normally *acts* within the consensual rules of coworkers and supports the regulations that help provide a hospitable environment for his or her efforts but goes beyond, and if necessary against, rules and regulations to serve more effectively than they require, for *qua* professional that is his or her primary concern.

Notes

1. Wilensky, "The Professionalization of Everyone?" and Goode, "The Theoretical Limits of Professionalism."
2. "Toward a Credible Form of Utilitarianism," pp. 118–119.
3. *After Virtue*, pp. 28–30.
4. *Ibid.*, p. 187.
5. *Ibid.*, p. 190.
6. See Bayles, *Professional Ethics*, p. 64.

□ 12

PATERNALISM AND CLIENT AUTONOMY

The ideal of dedication to proficient service for all in need asks professionals to transcend self-interest. Under favorable conditions, which society should provide, their own interests will be served fairly in the course of serving others; but the needs of clients, employers and the public determine the way they do their work, not their own needs and certainly not their wants. The power they have been granted by society must be used to the benefit of all as far as they are able to ensure this, not to exploitation of some for the benefit of others and themselves.

Professionals, however, must not only want to serve; they must know how. The very dedication to service, together with the proficiency that sets them apart from those whom they serve, may tempt them to cross another boundary into improper behavior. The attempt to serve can easily turn into illegitimate forms of paternalism.

The term 'paternalism' has floated about in the discussions of moralists for about a century in search of a stable meaning as its users exploited one and then another analogy between the parent's relation to children and other forms of human interaction. Inspired by Mill's *On Liberty* to propose categorical bans on some patently offensive patterns of behavior, the first authors employed a narrow definition, concentrating on coercion as a means of protecting the coerced from harm. As similarities were noted between the intentions behind this and other ways of promoting the welfare of persons without their consent, the concept of paternalism was broadened. In the process, it came to cover some patently desirable actions. We now realize that a categorical ban on paternalism is out of the question. Some of its forms are justified and even obligatory, and a fairly complex set of principles is required to distinguish between justified and unjustified forms.

Indictments of Professional Paternalism

Attention to professional paternalism has been fairly recent, since professionalism only lately has come to be a dominant force in social life. Once recognized, however, it has been subjected to broadside attacks. We will consider two examples and prepare the way for a more balanced view by noting their excesses. These are the assaults of Lieberman and Illich.

The professions define human needs the areas under their jurisdiction and professionals subtly shape the goals of the individuals whom they serve. Professionals thereby take the lead corporately and individually in constructing social reality for the rest of society. Lieberman and Illich see this as a threat both to political democracy and individual autonomy.

Lieberman charges that self-aggrandizement and paternalism lead professionals to systematically and deliberately mystify the character of their work.

> Professionals are dividing the world in spheres of influence and erecting large signs saying "experts at work here, do not proceed further." The public respects the signs and consequently misses the fact that what goes on behind them does not always bear much relation to the professed goals and activities of those who put them up. Professionals frequently say one thing and do another and assert that the layman's inability to find consistency between talk and action is caused by his inherent lack of insight into the professional mysteries. But the gap exists, and it has important political, economic, and social consequences; the public is losing its power to shape its destiny.[1]

Lieberman believes that the public acquiesces to this grab for power out of frustration at the complexities of modern life.

> A principal feature of our managerial, affluent, post-industrial, frenetic, and compulsive life is a willingness to delegate most facets of it to others. We are trained, but unschooled; lettered but unlearned, intelligent but undisciplined. We have turned over to others the power to make legal, medical, aesthetic, social, and even religious decisions for us.[2]

The professions have exploited the distraction of the public to usurp functions of government "without public debate and without the possibility of compromise or change." Lieberman comments mildly, "The management of public affairs by groups not representative of the public is not an ideal ardently sought by democratic or open-society political theorists or by common men, but it is a reality being achieved by professionals."[3]

Illich indicts modern society in similar terms. This century has relinquished individual decision to dominant and domineering professions, producing a total institutional control over the individual's life plan.

> The transformation of a liberal into a dominant profession is akin to the legal establishment of a state church. Physicians transmogrified into biocrats, teachers into gnosocrats, morticians into thanatocrats are much closer to state supported clergies than to trade associations. The professional as teacher of the currently accepted brand of scientific orthodoxy acts as theologian. As moral entrepreneur and as creator of the need for his services, he acts the role of priest. As crusading helper, he acts the part of the missioner and hunts down the underprivileged. As inquisitor, he outlaws the unorthodox: he imposes his solutions on the recalcitrant who refuses to recognize that he is a problem.[4]

Paternalism disables its subjects and the professions are paternalistic by nature. Since the twentieth century is the era in which the professions have come to power, this is the Age of Disabling Professions. Illich charges, "The Age of Professions will be remembered as the time when politics withered, when voters, guided by professors, entrusted to technocrats the power to legislate needs, renounced the authority to decide who needs what and suffered monopolistic oligarchies to determine the means by which these needs shall be met."[5] Criticizing the myths of service and disinterestedness, he traces the source of the professions' power to their affiliation with elites.

> A profession, like a priesthood, holds power by concession from an elite whose interests it props up. As a priesthood provides eternal salvation, so a profession claims legitimacy as the interpreter, protector and supplier of a special, this-worldly interest of the public at large. . . . Neither income, long training, delicate tasks nor social standing is the mark of the professional. Rather, it is his authority to define a person as client, to determine that person's need and to hand

the person a prescription. This professional authority comprises three roles: the sapiential authority to advise, instruct and direct; the moral authority that makes its acceptance not just useful but obligatory; and charismatic authority that allows the professional to appeal to some supreme interest of his client that not only outranks conscience but sometimes even the *raison d'état*. . . . In any area where a human need can be imagined these new professions, dominant, authoritative, monopolistic, legalized—and, at the same time, debilitating and effectively disabling the individual—have become exclusive experts of the public good.[6]

Illich maintains that the rise of professions spells the end of individual autonomy over the major departments of life and democratic determination of collective ends.

The public acceptance of domineering professions is essentially a political event. Each new establishment of professional legitimacy means that the political tasks of law-making, judicial review and executive power lose some of their proper character and independence. Public affairs pass from the layperson's elected peers into the hands of a self-accrediting elite.[7]

These strident indictments are unfair. The record of professions is mixed. They perform many important functions and they have shown some capacity for restraint in response to criticism. Nevertheless, professionalism is available as an instrument of domination, paternalistic as well as exploitive. The drive to use it for paternalistic purposes is obstructed only by the uncertain forces of consumer skepticism and individual professionals' respect for client autonomy.

The Anatomy of Paternalism

Definitions of paternalism typically refer to the identities of the agent and the subject of the paternalistic action; their relationship, involving the mental and physical state of each; the aims and measures of the paternalist; and the response to the act on the part of the subject. For brevity we will refer to the paternalist (e.g., the paternalistic professional) as *P*, the subject (e.g., the professional's client) as *S*, and the paternalistic action (e.g., a professional practice) as *A*. What general conditions of *P*, *S*, and the *P–S* relationship make *A* paternalistic?

The authors who first treated paternalism as a moral category, such as Dworkin and Feinberg,[8] were interested in legal paternalism, which they define as the use of the law to coerce individuals, usually to prevent self-harmful actions. The paternalist agent is a legislature or an official mandated to exercise this power. The moral question is Should the state stand in loco parentis toward its subjects?

The concept of paternalistic agent subsequently has been enlarged to cover any person or group with the power to act on others. P includes people in customary social roles (e.g., friends, neighbors, relatives) and those charged with role responsibilities by law (e.g., licensed professionals). The relevant factor is P's power to affect S. It may come from any source.

The subject of paternalism must be in some condition of need and impotence. S includes individuals who are so temporarily (e.g., the sick, ignorant, accused) or permanently (e.g., the handicapped, retarded, insane, impotent). Any individual can be treated paternalistically as the occasion arises. Fixed classes of individuals are treated institutionally in a paternalistic way on standard occasions.

The aim that is conceived to be essential to paternalism has been extended from protection of S from self-harm to protection from any kind of harm and promotion of any kind of good. P acts for S's welfare, whether it be to prevent or eliminate an evil or protect or promote a good. It should also be noted that it is P's *aim* that matters not whether act A *actually* benefits S. P must desire to benefit S, believe that A will do so, and do A because of the belief that it will do so.

The concept of paternalistic measures has been widened in the literature to accommodate these expansions in the categories of P, S, and the P–S relationship. Initial attention was directed to coercion, in which P tries to force S to do or abstain from something. Analogous considerations are involved in justifying acts *on* S when S is passive (e.g., unconscious, catatonic, distracted) and acts *in behalf of* S when S is incapable of acting (imprisoned, disenfranchised, absent). We will use the term 'intervention' to cover coercion, acting on, and acting for. What makes intervention paternalistic is the lack of S's consent—or rather P's belief that S has not consented or indifference to whether S has consented. Note also that the lack of consent at the time of A is essential. Prior and subsequent consent pertain to the justification of paternalism not its definition.

Rules for paternalism are designed in the first instance for the use of the would-be paternalist. Moral rules are to be followed in the responsible use of autonomy, so they must be applicable to the subjective conditions (of purpose and belief) in terms of which agents apprehend situations, both the conditions under which they ought to act and the conditions into which they should bring themselves before they act. P should perform A only when P believes that A is the best way to help S and the belief is well-grounded. Thus, the definition that follows is couched not in terms of objective variables, but in terms of the status of the variables in P's mind.

Action A is paternalistic if and only if

1. P believes that A is an intervention in S's life;

2. P does not take into consideration whether S consents to A;

3. P believes that A will contribute more to S's welfare than not performing A or performing another action incompatible with A; and

P performs A for this reason.

Obviously, A will usually *be* an intervention when P *thinks* it is. This also holds for P's belief that S's consent is lacking. Unbeknownst to P, S's wishes may have changed. Greater divergence is to be expected between what P thinks A will contribute to S's welfare and what it actually will contribute.

The Alleged Absolute Right to Autonomy

The expansion of the category of paternalism to cover a wide range of cases and the resulting complication of the principles required to govern it distresses those who are outraged at its more egregious forms. They worry that the pejorative connotation of the term and the negative force of the category are being weakened. They fear that this will undermine the barrier being raised against the practice. Since utilitarianism teaches us to see both good and evil in most practices and justified and unjustified varieties of them, the most vigorous antipaternalists, except for Mill, have been antiutilitarians. They have proposed deontological grounds to derive a categorical ban.

The most favored ground is the alleged absolute right of

persons to autonomy. It is claimed that paternalism violates the subject's autonomy and hence is wrong whatever its consequences. Advocates of this view have sought definitions of autonomy and paternalism that would make the calculation of benefits and harms of different forms of paternalism irrelevant to a negative judgment against it in any form.

There is very little to commend in this extreme view. Rejecting the notion of absolute rights, we fall back on utilitarian calculations. Respect for the autonomy of the subject provides a prima facie case against paternalistic acts, but countervailing considerations under special circumstances are sufficient to defeat the case.

To see this we need to look closely at the nature of autonomy. It enters our discussion of paternalism at four points: as a value for S that may be diminished by P's paternalistic action A; as a condition of S that may be curtailed prior to A, making it easier to justify A; as a feature of A itself that is worthy of respect; and as exercised in S's consent or dissent from A, which bears on A's justification.

Rights theorists have utilized minimal and maximal concepts of autonomy in considering its value to S. At the minimum, autonomy is the power to decide between physically possible alternatives, however irrational the decision or odious the alternatives. Some antipaternalists write as though the exercise of this power is so precious as to prohibit any paternalistic intervention. Thus, Arneson takes Dworkin and Feinberg to task for "qualifying to death" what Arneson thinks to be Mill's absolute ban on paternalism by allowing P to intervene to promote S's future autonomy (Dworkin) or to protect S from irreparable harm (Feinberg) when S's choice is substantially irrational.[9] This position is not appealing intuitively. In the first place, it is hard to imagine a paternalistic act depriving anyone of autonomy in this minimal sense. As Sartre says, human consciousness is not sometimes free and sometimes not; in the sense of aiming at one perceived possibility in preference to others, it *is* freedom.[10] Paternalist P may change S's alternatives, their costs, or S's perception of them, yet S will retain the power of election among alternatives. The only conceivable cases approaching the total elimination of autonomy would be where P caused S to react unconsciously or, if it were possible, totally controlled S's consciousness. These are surely not the cases with which the ethic of paternalism has to deal. The hard cases involve not elimination of S's autonomy, but its diminution from some significant point above the minimum. The question, therefore, is quantitative: Does the paternalistic act gain enough in the way of value for S to compensate for the reduction in some aspects of S's autonomy? It depends upon the *amount* and *type* of reduction. One surely does not want to say that no reduction of any sort or any amount is ever justified.

Reference to S's autonomy *at the time of P's* intervention introduces a second point. Autonomy is not an instantaneous achievement; it is something to be realized and expressed by successive actions over a lifetime. We should not say either that *S is* or *is not* autonomous and certainly not that S's autonomy is *eliminated* when it is *diminished* on occasion; we should only say that S is *more or less* autonomous in the aggregation of occasions of his or her entire life and that an action by another *adds to* or *subtracts from* that aggregate autonomy. What is at issue with paternalistic interventions is whether a subtraction from S's autonomy at the time of A and perhaps subsequently by the effects of A—a minute fraction of S's lifestream of acts—is justified by a gain in other values. Indeed, as Dworkin reminds us, an act may be paternalistic in reducing S's autonomy and yet be justified by enhancing S's subsequent autonomy. We should add that A is much easier to justify if P knows that S has ample opportunity to act autonomously on occasions not affected by A. The absolute rights theorist mistakenly treats every intervention as though it destroys autonomy or least expresses a fundamental disrespect for it.

The Dimensions of Autonomy

Those who talk of an absolute right of autonomy ignore its complexity and its degrees along several dimensions. I will suggest the following, all of which have been noted in the literature on paternalism.[11] They comprise both external or physical and internal or psychological conditions.

To be autonomous S must possess externally (1) the resources to act, such as wealth, position in society, friends, bodily health and strength, and freedom from physical and social restraints. P can curtail S's autonomy by reducing these or enlarge it by increasing them, in either case paternalistically if P does it for S's welfare without S's consent.

Also externally, (2) each action that S can perform entails opportunity costs or sacrifices of values.[12] It also has an opportunity income in terms of values that it would gain. These negative and positive values, multiplied by the probability that they would be realized through the action, constitute the action's "expected value" according to the familiar calculus of decision theory. P may intervene in S's life by altering S's expectations.

Psychologically, an autonomous act requires (3) a schedule of preferences. Everyone has preferences, but not everyone has thought them through, compared them with alternatives, and ranked them consistently. By "thinking them through," I have in mind an accurate grasp of the contribution that they would make intrinsically or instrumentally to happiness. If by 'values' we mean what is truly desirable for the individual (as distinguished from what he or she desires or prefers), the perfectly autonomous person may be said to prefer true values in the order of their importance to happiness. P can enhance S's autonomy by contributing to S's self-knowledge and diminish it by interfering with it.

(4) An autonomous act requires beliefs about the means, instruments, and actions that will produce those things, states, relations, and processes that the subject desires or desires to avoid. What are the consequences of these means? Their costs? Their remote effects? An agent must have an opinion about these to draw implications from his or her preferences for available actions. Let us refer to these opinions as S's causal beliefs. If we mean by knowledge something like true beliefs grounded on adequate reasons, we can say that people are more autonomous the wider their range of causal beliefs and the closer these beliefs approach to genuine knowledge. P can enhance or diminish S's autonomy by contributing to or blocking S's causal knowledge.

Benn labels the ability to act on preferences informed by beliefs 'autarchy' and saves the term 'autonomy' for persons who develop their preferences and beliefs by critical inquiry.[13] Almost all natural persons possess autarchy. This suffices to give them the dignity of personhood and the consciousness of being originators of actions. Only a few persons approach autonomy, but it is an ideal toward which all should strive.

Benn proposes a "principle of respect for autarchy" to the effect that "manipulating [a person's] actions by means that short-circuit his decision-making capacity do him wrong, unless overriding justification can be found."[14] The principle does not ban absolutely paternalism since many interventions do not short-circuit S's decision-making capacity in a radical way or do so only temporarily and do not rob S of a sense of personhood. Furthermore, Benn recognizes that there can be an overriding justification even for those that do. However, his primary aim is to defend the principle of respect for autarchy by pointing out the "conceptual sacrifice" involved in valuing it for oneself while denying it in others. This conceptual sacrifice constitutes a considerable barrier to extreme forms of paternalism.

(5) Informed preferences and well-grounded causal beliefs, together with the ability to draw practical conclusions from them—all are ingredients of what we ordinarily consider to be rationality in the pragmatic sense. One more ingredient is self-control. Autonomous persons are authors of their own rules as dictated by their beliefs, but in addition, they have the power to make themselves obey those rules. The self that obeys is the self that acts as it should on occasions when there is a strong pressure or temptation to diverge from the agent's life-plan. The self that rules is the enduring self that develops a life-plan in times of leisure and rationality and sustains the plan though the succession of actions that, in the self-controlled persons, implement it. Self-control and autonomy thus are proportionate to the stability and firmness of character and personality. The person lacking self-control is one who cannot adhere to a steady life-plan but veers in one direction and then another under the pressure of circumstances. Such a person is deficient in autonomy, however sound his or her preferences and beliefs may be. P can enhance S's autonomy by measures that strengthen S's character and detract from it by measures that sap it.

To draw all of this together, if we refer to the magnitude of S's resources and the breadth of S's repertory of actions with high expected values as S's 'power' and S's ordered preferences, well-grounded causal beliefs and self-control as S's 'rationality,' we may say that S is autonomous in proportion to his or her power and rationality and that P's intervention encroaches on S's autonomy to the extent that it reduces either of these. Note, however, that an action may increase some elements of S's autonomy while reducing others, so it is not easy to assess what respect for autonomy entails in evaluating a given case of intervention.

Forms of Paternalistic Intervention

I should like to make a special point of the fact that it is possible under our definition of paternalism for a paternalistic agent to *increase* a subject's autonomy. *P* may add to *S*'s resources or reduce the exorbitant cost of some of *S*'s alternatives without *S*'s consent. This is a possibility because it is *S*'s perception of these matters that affects *S*'s preferences and hence *S*'s disposition to consent to *P*'s action. *P* may alter objective conditions to enlarge *S*'s autonomy before *S* sees that the action does so and *S* may resist in jealous defense of autonomy. This could happen when an attorney accepts a court appointment to represent an unwilling prisoner or a physician gives medical assistance to a delirious accident victim. On the other hand, *P* can thrust autonomy upon a subject who fears and resists it on the assumption that autonomy has a value whether *S* realizes it or not. For example, *P* can challenge *S* to shape his or her values more critically, face up to unpleasant facts, practice arduous character-building or intellect-developing disciplines, etc. These are standard role responsibilities of parents and professional teachers, psychiatrists, and journalists. Opportunities for such measures arise from time to time for other professionals such as lawyers, doctors, engineers, and accountants. Any professional can take the initiative to break the deference and dependence of a client, employer, or public.

Once paternalism is defined broadly as intervention in another's life, we need to distinguish different sorts in terms of the effect on autonomy. In Heidegger's terminology, solicitude or care for other people *(Fürsorge)* takes two forms:

> It can, as it were, take away 'care' from the Other and put itself in his position in concern: it can *leap in* for him. This kind of solicitude takes over for the Other that with which he is to concern himself. The Other is thus thrown out of his own position; he steps back so that afterwards, when the matter has been attended to, he can either take it over as something finished and at his disposal, or disburden himself of it completely. In such solicitude the Other can become one who is dominated and dependent, even if this domination is a tacit one and remains hidden from him. . . . In contrast to this, there is also the possibility of a kind of solicitude which does not so much leap in for the Other as *leap ahead* of him in his existential potentiality-for-Being, not in order to take away his 'care' but rather to give it back to him authentically as such for the first time.[15]

Note three things. First, Heidegger considers care to be the essence of being human *(Dasein)*, so that by taking all care of others from a person, we rob that person of his or her humanity. Second, Heidegger observes that in caring for others, we can help them shoulder their burdens and live an authentic care-ridden (careful, caring) existence. And, third, this form of solicitude can be paternalistic if being authentic is a value (Heidegger does not commit himself on this), since the other does not always welcome it. Autonomy is not an easy state. Many people shy from its anxieties and are blind to its satisfactions. They try to evade it. Yet if it is a fundamental value, the paternalist is justified in thrusting it upon them.

It is clear from these considerations that there should be no categorical ban on paternalism. Even absolute respect for the right to autonomy does not forbid all paternalism, since paternalistic acts may enhance the subject's autonomy. In that paternalistic acts, by definition, are performed without S's consent, they diminish S's autonomy by at least the amount of the act of consenting, but at the same time they may increase its net amount by facilitating later acts for S or enhancing the autonomous features of acts that S will proceed to perform.

In view of the complexity of autonomy and the degrees that it admits along its various dimensions, it is absurd to consider every paternalistic intervention that diminishes autonomy to be an absolute breach. There is a minimal level of autonomy or autarchy, below which no one should be pushed for whatever paternalistic reasons, but few if any interventions of professionals do this.

The Value of Autonomy

It is a mistake to impose an absolute ban on paternalism out of respect for autonomy. Yet autonomy should be respected and curtailments of it are prima facie wrong. Paternalism is wrong unless there are overriding reasons for it. What is the positive value of autonomy?

We will center the discussion around reasons that Mill marshals against encroachments on people's liberty in self-regarding matters. Neither paternalism nor autonomy are Mill's categories, but we can construct a view about them from his defense of liberty and individualism in acts that primarily affect only agents themselves, while accepting limits on acts that affect the welfare of others. The elements in autonomy he values are the process of choosing, the rationality and morality of some choices, and the success of actions (in the sense of contributing to happiness) that rationality and morality promote. For each of these (to follow Arneson's account),[16] Mill stresses the value of the uniqueness and diversity of persons, the development of human traits to their fullest, and the self-cultivation of these traits. He also stresses the value of the individual's autonomy not only to the individual, but to society. If we are interested in the happiness of all, we will want to promote the happiness of each, since the happiness of all is the aggregate of the happinesses of each. At the same time, we will want each to contribute as much as possible to the happiness of others, for the happiness of all. Autonomy plays an important part in the happiness of each, though it is sometimes injurious to its possessor; and autonomous persons in the long run contribute more to the happiness of others, though they sometimes abuse their autonomy.

In respect to the aspects of autonomy that are valuable to its possessor, Mill observes, "it is the privilege and proper condition of a human being, arrived at the maturity of his faculties, to use and interpret experience in his own way" and "If a person possesses any tolerable amount of common sense and experience, his own mode of laying out his existence is the best, not because it is the best in itself, but because it is his own mode."[17]

Note, however, that Mill already is hinting that the value in an action's being ones own is proportionate to the involvement of the person's higher faculties. Mill makes this point more clearly in his praise of diversity.

> It is not by wearing down into uniformity all that is individual in themselves, but by cultivating it, and calling it forth, within the limits imposed by rights and interests of others, that human beings become a noble and beautiful object of contemplation; and as the works partake the character of those who do them, by the same process human life also becomes rich, diversified, and animating, furnishing more abundant aliment to high thoughts and elevating feelings, and strengthening the tie which binds every individual to the race, by making the race infinitely better worth belonging to.[18]

Mill makes the point fully explicit in commenting on why a "being of higher faculties" will accept frustration and discontentment rather than allow himself to sink to a lower grade of existence. He maintains that, while this may be attributed to pride or love of liberty, power, or excitement,

> its most appropriate appellation is a sense of dignity, which all human beings possess in one form or another, and in some, though by no means exact, proportion to their higher faculties, and which is so essential a part of the happiness of those in which it is strong, that nothing which conflicts with it could be, otherwise than momentarily, an object of desire to them.[19]

Note that dignity is a variable. Those who have more of the higher faculties by birth or cultivation have a greater share and greater happiness. This is why Mill puts so much stress on the importance of education as the complement to libertarian institutions and allows education to be paternalistic in its initial phases—children are to be educated by compulsion until they are able to exercise the higher faculties.

Mill explains that his antipaternalism does not extend to children, to "backward states of society in which the race may itself be considered as in its nonage," to civilizations surrounded by enemies, or to people who are "delirious, or in some state of excitement or absorption incompatible with the full use of the reflecting faculty."[20] This concedes too much, since some of these groups are not irrational and even when people are less rational than their paternalistic would-be benefactors, they may still take care of themselves more successfully. As Mill himself says, "with respect to his own feelings and circumstances, the most ordinary man or woman has a means of knowledge immeasurably surpassing those that can be possessed by any one else." Furthermore, the individual "is the person most interested in his own well-being: the interest which any other person, except in cases of strong personal attachment, can have in it, is trifling, compared with that which he himself has."[21] This, of course, is the more true in proportion as the person measures up to the conditions of full autonomy.

Persons with unique styles of life have both intrinsic and instrumental value for others. Mill notes that they can be "noble and beautiful objects of contemplation." We may speak of the aesthetic value of individuality in the sense the delight provided by its sheer diversity and the specimens of excellence which it includes. When excellence is produced or cultivated, it may be appreciated as a work of art. Mill exclaims, "Among the works of man, which human life is rightly employed in perfecting and beautifying, the first in importance is surely man himself." We would not exchange humans for automatons even if the automatons could get all our "houses built, corn grown, battles fought, causes tried, churches erected and prayers said."[22]

Mill devotes the bulk of his attention to the more obvious external utility of individuality. Individual differences produce experiments in living from which others can profit, new ideas for our common stock of knowledge, new practices and customs, etc.

Thus, Mill makes a powerful case for the liberty of individuals to run their lives as they see fit, the more so as they achieve maturity and rationality; but his principles leave room for intervening under special circumstances in consideration of overriding interests of the subject and to develop conditions for the subject's future autonomy.

Professional Paternalism

Parsons's concept of specificity of function is the myth that professionals scrupulously confine themselves to devising technical means to ends set by clients, employers, and the public. In actual fact, they often shape the goals of their clients by controlling their flow of information and exploiting their dependence, and professions corporately define the needs of society. To expose the myth is not to say that professionals and professions should not have a voice in such matters, but it does enable us to see that they can and sometimes do illegitimately use control of technical means to take the power of decision from subjects by acting upon or for them without their consent or by manufacturing consent.

The myth of specificity of function is disingenuous at best. Insofar as it disguises the use of power to take advantage of others, it is exploitive. Insofar as it disguises paternalism, it is an obstacle to informed consent or dissent. In both cases, it shields actions from critical evaluation.

What conditions make professional paternalism prevalent? The paternalistic agent must have power over the subject and the subject must be in a condition of impotence and need. Social institutions bestow power on professionals as an adjunct of the role assigned to them. Because of their monopoly, people in need are forced to go to them and follow their directions. The professional–client relation and even to an extent the professional–employer relation, therefore, is one of socially enforced dependency.

The dependency is far from absolute. After all, professionals need clients for fees and employers for salaries. The client or employer often has a choice among professionals from the monopolistic group. However, professions are geared to conceal the character of practice from lay scrutiny, so people frequently do not know who will provide the kind of treatment they want, for instance, nonpaternalistic treatment. They can move from professional to professional in search for the kind that will satisfy them, but this has an excessive cost. It disrupts what needs to be a stable relationship and there is little assurance that the new professional, a product of the same socialization as ones already tried, will prove more suitable. The question of paternalism is neglected particularly by consumers of professional services, because they have not been schooled to be on the lookout for it or to object to it.

The power of professionals could be limited if consumers would insist. Why don't they? The primary reason seems to be psychological rather than legal or social. The acquiescence of clients is encouraged by what has been called the mystique of professionalism. As apologists and critics alike insist, professionals utilize complex and esoteric knowledge. They speak a special language and think according to special logic. They solve or appear to solve problems on the basis of lore that their clients do not have, cannot acquire, and may not entirely appreciate.

This circumstance places professionals in a position somewhat like that of sorcerers: They obtain results that others desire ardently by powers that pass understanding. In connection with this, Moore advances the "tentative evolutionary hypothesis" that the shaman is the protoprofessional or prototype of the modern professional in nonliterate societies. Shamanism is an art "relying prominently on alleged spiritual forces directed toward practical vicissitudes of a harsh human existence." The shaman is a specialist set apart from ordinary folk by unique personal attributes and esoteric training. Elements of religion, science, magic, and even politics, psychology, and jurisprudence are incorporated in his work. It is inviting to view him not only as a protopriest and physician, but protoengineer, psychiatrist, and attorney.[23]

If the shaman is the protoprofessional, the professional is the postshaman. It is not surprising to find superstition intermixed with experimental principles in medicine and other specialties in literate societies. Moore observes that, since we continue to live "in a world in which non-rational forces seem to prevail but ordinary activities work with some variable efficacy," there is not "an absolutely sharp and inviolate distinction among purely technical and efficacious controls" even in highly differentiated social systems. There continues to be a "reliance on spurious technical controls, the attempt to command unseen and mostly purely imaginary forces, and the seemingly simple, essential stance of facing the inevitable."[24] This is speculative, but there is no doubt that there is a mystique to professionalism. Hughes refers to the "charism of skill." He maintains that there is a psychological and moral division of labor in society as well as a technical one. We delegate some matters to professions "not merely because we cannot do them, but because we do not wish to run the risk of error. The guilt of failure would be too great." When we do this, we want to believe absolutely in the agent to whom we have delegated our responsibilities, and we are correspondingly resentful should the agent fail. Our resentment motivates the professional and his or her group to conceal failures in order to preserve the trust they need for autonomy.[25] Concealment ordinarily is an opprobrious act, but the professional ideology rationalizes it on the grounds that it serves the interests of clients. To help clients, the professional must be able to count on their willingness to carry out instructions. A mystique, it is argued, is necessary to generate an illusion of infallibility. Trust and deference are alleged to redound to the benefit of the client.

Here are the seeds of paternalism. Deference feeds professional hubris. The offshoot may be indifference and even antipathy toward client autonomy rationalized in terms of the latter's own good.

Devaluation of Client Autonomy

Professionals rightly take pride in their skill. To utilize such skill to the fullest they think they must be "in charge" of situations. However, the rational purpose for being in charge is to cultivate *all* the values at stake and these include the client's autonomy. Professionals are prone to take a narrow view according to which to share authority is to relinquish control. Client autonomy is excluded from the benefits pursued because power sharing is ego threatening. It is dismissed as unprofessional.

Millman's conclusions about physicians can be generalized to other professions. She reports, "There are two kinds of information that doctors routinely withhold from patients: one kind has to do with facts about the patient's illness; the other kind has to do with evaluations of the competence of performance of the other doctors involved in the case, or the wisdom of the treatment that other doctors have recommended."[26] She analyzes a whole gamut of strategies by which this is accomplished, for example, redefining and disregarding patients' expressions of distrust and anger. The strategies effectively exclude patients from the management of their illness.[27] They also dispose the physician to construe any question or initiative by the patient as a challenge to his or her competence. To the extent that he or she, nevertheless, is dedicated to the patient's welfare, the practices nurture a chronic paternalism.

While this syndrome is most evident among physicians, it is found among other professions, though, as Rueschemeyer suggests, it is harder for practitioners in professions relying on human relations skills, such as the law, to treat their clients as children than professions that rely on esoteric science, such as medicine. Clients of the former are more likely to know what the professional is doing for them.[28]

I suspect that there is another, more subtle reason for professionals' indifference toward client autonomy. Since practice is problem-oriented, professionals are accustomed to justify decisions exclusively in instrumental terms. They profess to choose their actions according to technical standards. In operation, this means according to the external consequences for the client and the public. This colors the professional's perception of the client. If the consequences of the client's behavior are bad, it seems proper to create a new environment that will elicit different behavior from him or her. This ignores the intrinsic value that self-initiated behavior may have for the client, the satisfaction of being the author of one's actions.

The denigration of client autonomy is paradoxical, since professionals are so jealous of their own. Their unusual degree of autonomy should make them appreciate its value for others.

The tendency to neglect client autonomy is reinforced by the narrow utilitarian ethic that stresses external consequences in evaluating actions. The action-oriented professional may adopt this ethic in reaction to nebulous deontological criteria for evaluating actions entirely by certain formal characteristics, particularly those predicated on the notion of autonomy as an absolute value regardless of the consequences for the agent. The broader consequentialism adopted in the present study figures the effect of the professional's actions on the quality of the client's actions into the same equation with their effect on the client's health, treatment before the law, education, financial interests, etc.

The mystique of professionalism fosters the hubris to which professionals—and everyone who thinks of duties in terms of noblesse oblige—are victim. At the same time, it creates a stagnant passivity in clients. It is only human to intervene in the lives of those pliant enough to allow it or needy enough to invite it. It is only human to persuade oneself that one is qualified to do so when one finds oneself on a pedestal of infallibility.

To counter the excesses of professional paternalism, it is not enough to rail against it nor, as we have seen, should it be forbidden categorically. What are needed are strong prima facie prohibitions together with a careful exploration of the exceptional conditions under which paternalism is justified. The most effective antidote to the temptation of professionals to slip into wholesale paternalism is to impose a burden of justification on those who practice it and provide realistic but demanding criteria for doing so.

Justifying Paternalism

What considerations override the prima facie objection to paternalistic acts? What variables should the prospective paternalist assess? We cannot hope to develop a formula for mechanical computations but we can develop a checklist of aspects of any situation that a conscientious moral agent will review, estimate, and intuitively combine to rank a proposed action against alternatives.

The first consideration obviously is the magnitude of the benefits to be gained and evils to be avoided by the action, less any evils that may ensue or benefits that may be lost as its byproducts. The probability of each of these must be estimated and an expected value determined for the action. The expected value of the paternalistic action must be compared to the expected value of its alternatives, including that of not doing anything at all. A melioristic judgment is required, since the choices are typically between actions that are better or worse, rather than actions that can be determined to be absolutely right or wrong on a formal or a priori basis.

Paternalism is an issue in the professions because important values in addition to the client's autonomy are at stake. Professionalism originated as a way of organizing work to service areas of life such as health, safety, freedom, fair treatment, prosperity, mental and spiritual well-being, etc. Only recently have occupations that deal with more superficial values claimed to be professions. In developing policies for paternalism, we will concentrate on cases where S comes to P or is brought to P because an important value for S is in jeopardy or an important opportunity is open and S thinks P is able to help. S does not consent to the course of action, A, which P judges to be the most effective to solve S's problem. P has the power, based on special knowledge, institutional position, psychological dominance, etc., to carry through with A without S's consent. The importance of the values to be achieved for S—more precisely, P's estimation of the importance of those values—constitute a reason to perform A in face of the prima facie reason not to perform it because it encroaches on S's autonomy and because performing it would reinforce paternalistic practices.

A number of moralists consider it to be either a necessary or a sufficient condition for the justification of A for it to be necessary to prevent irremediable harm to S. The same reasons that are given for this position can be extended to cases where A prevents the loss of an irretrievable opportunity. Thus, similar justifications are relevant to the psychiatrist who would forcibly prevent a manic-depressive from committing suicide and the academic who would require a student to take courses essential to success in a chosen vocation during the student's one and only tenure at the university. However, in my judgment, neither the prospect of preventing irremediable harm nor that of taking advantage of an irretrievable opportunity is *sufficient* to justify paternalism, since the harm or opportunity may be trivial compared to the encroachment on S's autonomy. Nor is either *necessary* to justify paternalism, since the curtailment of autonomy by the paternalistic act may be trivial and the harm that S may bring about through the exercise of autonomy may be important enough to warrant the encroachment, even though harm could have been remedied at a later date. Irremediability and irretrievability are dimensions of the magnitude of harms and benefits, not necessary or sufficient conditions of justification in themselves.

It is nevertheless worthwhile to single them out in connection with autonomy. If an action only temporarily deprives S of autonomy, and especially if it enlarges S's future autonomy, it is more likely to be justified than if it terminates an important form of autonomy for good. On the other hand, even an irretrievable curtailment of autonomy may be justified if it is necessary to protect S from some other very serious irremediable harm. Situations of this last sort, however, are hard to find in the professions or anywhere else in real life.

In the case of highly specialized activities, it is important to make explicit the principle that *all* the benefits and harms related to the activity must be reviewed. Professionals tend to focus on values of their subjects specific to their mandate (health, justice, national defense, etc.) and neglect those affected by a wide range of other activities. Having been engaged to deal with a specific problem, the professional is disposed to concentrate on its solution in the name of efficiency and ignore side effects, such as curtailment of the subject's autonomy. To counteract this cast of mind, professionals must be reminded to consider the impact of their work on the autonomy of clients, employers, and the public.

Professional Codes and Paternalism

The first place one looks for barriers to paternalism is the professional codes. Codes, as we have noted, are histories of scandals. They also are inventories of the professions' self-understanding. Their strictures against exploitation of clients and betrayal of employers reflect a recognition of the power of the professional and some of the opportunities for its abuse. The dearth of strictures against paternalism reflect a lack of awareness that the power can be used to encroach on the autonomy of clients and employers. The injuries inflicted by paternalism are more subtle than those of exploitation and, since some paternalism is justified, cases are more problematic. These may be what causes injunctions against paternalism to be indecisive but they are the very reasons why codes should speak out clearly.

Most professions attempt to erect barriers against exploitation or at least wish to appear to. The American Medical Association though, rather perfunctorily, condemns unnecessary treatment that costs the patient or society. "It is unethical for the physician to provide or prescribe unnecessary services or unnecessary ancillary facilities." The American Bar Association, while emphatically endorsing zeal on the part of the lawyer, seeks to limit burdens imposed on clients, adversaries, and the courts by urging realistic advice about the probabilities of success of actions and prohibiting frivolous positions in litigation and participation in actions intended to harass or maliciously injure. Engineers are instructed by the Engineers Council for Professional Development to be faithful agents and dissuage employers from unpromising ventures: "When, as a result of their studies, Engineers believe a project will not be successful, they shall so advise their employer or client." The American Psychological Association states in comprehensive terms, "Psychologists are continually cognizant of their own needs and of their potential influential position vis-a-vis persons such as clients, students and subordinates. They avoid exploiting the trust and dependency of such persons." Specifically, "Psychologists terminate a clinical or consulting relationship when it is reasonably clear that the consumer is not benefitting by it." The American Personnel and Guidance Association is less explicit: It requires termination of the relationship only when the counselor "cannot be of professional assistance to the counselee or client either because of lack of competence or personal limitation." The American Psychological Association also judges that "Sexual intimacies with clients are unethical" and reiterates, "Psychologists do not exploit their professional relationships with clients, supervisees, students, employees, or research participants sexually or otherwise." The National Association of Social Workers is sensitive to the whole range of these abuses. It states, "The social worker should not exploit relationships with clients for personal advantage" and in particular "should terminate service to clients, and professional relationships with them, when such service and relationships are no longer required or no longer serve the clients' needs or interests." The social worker "should under no circumstances engage in sexual activities with clients."

In contrast to strictures against exploitation, only a few professions warn against paternalism and then obliquely. Mental health and social welfare professions proclaim client self-determination as a principal objective, though they are not as clear on the point as one would like. The American Psychological Association only declares, "Psychologists respect the dignity and worth of the individual and strive for the preservation and protection of human rights." The American Personnel and Guidance Association observes, more to the point, "A counseling relationship denotes that the person seeking help retain full freedom of choice and decision and that the helping person has no authority or responsibility to approve or disapprove of the choices or decisions of the counselee or client." The National Association of Social Workers says emphatically "The social worker should make every effort to foster maximum self-determination on the part of clients." In professions without explicit warnings, it is only too easy to construe dedication to the welfare of clients to sanction paternalistic incursions on their freedom.

The attitude of the American Bar Association is complex. While noting that "In certain areas of legal representation affecting the merits of the cause or substantially prejudicing the rights of a client, a lawyer is entitled to make decisions on his own," it notes that otherwise "the authority to make decisions is exclusively that of the client and, if made within the framework of the law, such decisions are binding on his lawyer." The lawyer is only allowed to ask for *permission* to forego actions that seem in the client's interest but are unjust. The rationale for reducing the lawyer to a mere instrument who is not morally culpable for carrying out the client's wishes as long as he stays within the bounds of the law is that the legal system guarantees everyone's right to counsel and this would be curtailed by holding lawyers ethically responsible for their actions under client instructions. If this is so, the Bar Association is not primarily concerned with the client's right of self-determination or expressing a distaste for paternalism. Indeed, it endorses a limited form of paternalism when "any mental or physical condition of a client . . . renders him incapable of making a considered judgment on his own behalf." We may assume that even well-intentioned lawyers interpret this permission liberally.

One would infer from engineering codes that this profession recognizes no problem of paternalism. The most relevant provisions of the codes are those that demand candor and objectivity in engineers' public statements and frankness in their advice to employers. These are important in helping others make informed decisions; but the codes do not contain strictures explicitly against acting on the client's or employer's behalf without his or her consent.

The blindness of engineers to their brand of paternalism may be a function of vision constricted by training and responsibilities. It seems hard for them to see that technically impressive plans for worthy objectives sometimes should give way to other human needs. To see how this produces paternalism, consider the following case as seen by a politician. Metropolitan Sanitary District of Chicago Commissioner Joanne Alter reported the resistance of staff engineers to altering plans for the ambitious Tunnel and Reservoir Plan (TARP) to control flooding and pollution caused by storm sewer overflow, when changed economic conditions caused their governing board to seek cheaper alternatives. Alter saw in their strategy a well-intentioned attempt to do what was best for the public against its transient wishes as expressed by elected representatives. She viewed TARP as an illustration of a widespread tendency of technical experts to determine the best course of action for their organization or clientelle and then present cost-benefit options in a way that magnifies the benefits of the favored courses and the costs of the alternatives.[29] This is sometimes called delegation upward, of the implementation of decisions made at a subordinate level to a formally superordinate level of an organization. Nothing in the standard engineering ethic calls attention to this subtle form of paternalism and little in the ethic puts a brake to it.

Medical paternalism has attracted the most attention among critics. The practice incidentally enhances the physician's power over patients. Until recently the American Medical Association seemed to give carte blanche approval to paternalism by insisting that physicians should rely on their own judgment in advancing the health of their patients. This is consonant with the tendency of professionals, as seen in the case of the TARP engineers, to value the particular goods in their care above autonomy or other values that their clients may rank higher for themselves.

Possibly in response to criticism, the AMA now takes a fairly forthright stand against paternalism:

> The patient's right of self-decision can be effectively exercised only if the patient possesses enough information to enable an intelligent choice. The patient should make his own determination on treat-

ment. Informed consent is a basic social policy for which exceptions are permitted (1) where the patient is unconscious or otherwise incapable of consenting and harm from failure to treat is imminent; or (2) when risk-disclosure poses such a serious psychological threat of detriment to the patient as to be medically contraindicated. Social policy does not accept the paternalistic view that the physician may remain silent because divulgence might prompt the patient to forego needed therapy.

Escape clause (2) is a major one and has rationalized much paternalism. Nevertheless, I have the impression that physicians are becoming more sensitive to complaints about paternalism, which gives some hope that practices of professions can be affected by moral criticism.

The Professional's Autonomy

Preservation of subjects' autonomy is a reason to prohibit paternalistic acts; but moral inhibitions and, even more, legal sanctions against paternalism curtail the would-be paternalist's autonomy, which is a reason to avoid them. In the usual case, the negative value of the curtailment of the subject's autonomy outweighs the positive value of the paternalist's exercise of it. It is not too much to ask people to limit themselves to actions that do not seriously infringe on the autonomy of others, since this leaves them many outlets for action in normal circumstances. Furthermore, we are calling for abstention from paternalism under valid moral principles to which the agent freely subscribes. Voluntary abstention is itself an autonomous act. Respect for client autonomy is a responsible use of professional autonomy.

Nevertheless, it should be admitted that restrictions on professional paternalism require professionals to abstain from actions that are very important to them. They pledge to provide service to people in need at a high level of competence. Their work is one of their most important theaters of action. To serve clients in accord with high standards, professionals sometimes have to intervene in areas where informed consent is difficult or impossible to obtain. The actions appear dictated not only by standards of competence, but by the ideal of service. To ask professionals to refrain on the basis of an abstract and nebulous "absolute right" of clients to autonomy is not convincing. More persuasive reasons are needed, reasons which explain what is gained by respecting the right. On some occasions, there are no such reasons available and then professionals should act paternalistically.

We are seeking to delimit paternalistic practices that would maximize happiness were they to become established under existing or a reformed set of institutions. The prospective paternalist must evaluate the act in terms of the effect on happiness of universalizing it in comparison with universalizing a contrary practice of abstention and leaving client autonomy intact. This is not in itself sufficient to determine whether the act is right, so it is not the Kantian test of whether one who imagines the universalization of a rule suffers self-contradiction or conflict of will. Rather, we require the agent to reflect on whether his or her action would contribute to the actual currency of the rule and take this consequence into consideration. Actions instill habits that carry over to situations where the action may be performed unthinkingly with harmful results. The example of the action may lead others to act likewise without considering the consequences in different circumstances. The precedent can provide a rationalization for actions with evil intentions. These results are the more likely as the agent is a prestigious person, such as a successful professional. Professionals must be especially concerned about their actions contributing to practices.

These dangers pertain to justified as well as unjustified actions. They do not suffice to condemn an action out of hand. The point is that they must be considered seriously in evaluating any action and a fortiori any practice.

The precedent factor in the case of many actions is a mixture of good and bad. Where it is mostly positive, this is a good reason to establish the action as a practice. Where it is mostly negative, this is a good reason to prohibit the practice. Where the positive and negative effects are balanced, this is a good reason to leave the decision to the discretion of the agent on the given occasion.

That most acts of professional paternalism set bad precedents is patent. In a climate of respect and deference, it is easy for the professional to fall into paternalistic habits and for the professional subculture to take paternalistic practices for granted. Paternalism also provides a lovely rationalization for unlovely actions. ("After all, it's for your own good!") It is convenient to think one is concerned for the other's good when one's motive is ego-gratification or profit.

Yet some forms of professional paternalism are justified. Pater-

nalism is permissible or even required at times under the obligation of service. What is needed are demarcations, boundaries,
barriers that will block slippage from justified acts into unjustified practices. These would be provided by consensual rules
negotiated between society and the professions. Paternalism in
general should be condemned and discretionary paternalism limited. Only under exceptional circumstances is paternalism to be
permitted, and those circumstances must be spelled out in the
professional code, charter, or covenant.

To make limitations on paternalism work, however, a strong
central ideal of maximizing client autonomy must be inculcated
during professional socialization. Skills for strengthening client
and public autonomy must be developed as components of professional competence. The professional must be taught to take pride
in this function. This kind of training is almost totally absent
from formal professional education and has no significant place
in most professional subcultures.

Reflexive Obligations in Paternalistic Decisions

Most of the proposals offered here are restraints that professionals
would observe voluntarily, not ones to be enforced by law. They
are principles to guide the conscience in its search for reasons. In
that search, agents are required not only to make objective judgments about the world, but reflexive judgments about the quality
of their objective judgments.

Paternalism is the intention to aid a subject in the conviction
that the intervention will benefit the latter though he or she has
not consented to it. These beliefs on the part of the agent may be
mistaken and the action still be paternalistic. This fact has
implications for the question of justification.

The moral community makes its members accountable to
each other under common principles and instills those principles
in their conscience in order to motivate actions with desirable
consequences. Properly motivated actions are more likely to
contribute to the ends of society when they are based on beliefs
shaped by sound education, experience, and reasoning—ignorance and error are as dangerous to the well-formed society as
malice. Hence, to maximize actions that are desirable from the
moral point of view, the community must hold its members
responsible for the grounding of their beliefs. It must insist that

they seek evidence and reason logically and that they act in the way appropriate to the strength of weakness of the grounds that are available. These principles belong to what has been called the ethic of belief. I shall refer the logical standards one ought to follow in reaching practical decisions as the epistemic ethic. I advance the meta-ethical thesis that we ought to make the epistemic ethic a prominent part of our comprehensive normative ethic.

Specifically, norms governing paternalism should require would-be paternalists to assess the grounds for their belief that a contemplated action will indeed benefit their subjects. What evidence do they have that they understand subjects' needs and that their belief that the action will meet those needs is correct? We made the point earlier that to justify a paternalistic act, it is necessary to determine on objective grounds that its expected value, figuring in a deduction for its abridgment of the subject's autonomy, is significantly higher than those of alternative actions. We are now maintaining that this is not sufficient to justify the action. The proposition is a consequence of putting the burden of proof on the paternalist. When the grounds for thinking that a paternalistic act will help are slender, the action should be shunned even though the grounds for preferring alternatives may be equally slender. Under our principles, there is a rational bias, if it may be so put, against paternalism. It is reinforced by the precedent factor, whose principle, when there is little evidence about the consequences of an action, is to avoid setting a bad precedent. In the absence of strong evidence that a paternalistic action will help, refrain from it. The burden of justification is on paternalism; abstention seldom requires justification.

The medical profession provides a paradigm because paternalism is rife in medicine and because medical ethics have been analyzed so extensively. I will utilize Buchanan's data from surveys of medical practices and representative statements of physicians. These show that physicians routinely withhold information from patients and their families about diagnoses, prognoses, options for treatment, and their risks. They rationalize these practices as necessary to prevent harm due to the patient and family's inability to understand technical matters and an alleged contract with patients to minimize harm by any available means. The harm from which the patient may be protected include depression at bad news, refusal to accept proper treatment, and the stress of making vital decisions. Families are protected from stress and the guilt of making wrong decisions.

While not condemning all forms of medical paternalism, Buchanan makes a strong case against most. He expresses a preference for arguments based on "a theory of moral rights rooted in the conception of personal autonomy," but he employs a utilitarian argument which he thinks will "meet the [medical] paternalist on his own ground and then attempt to cut it beneath him by showing that his arguments are defective."[30] He thinks that this will have a more practical effect than a deontological argument.

Buchanan argues that medical paternalists would need extensive psychiatric knowledge to determine whether information would indeed have the effects (depression, irrational decisions, guilt) that they assume. Objective data show that the effect is frequently the opposite of what physicians assume. Physicians lack the training, not to mention the extensive data about individual patients and their families, for reliable judgments. Furthermore, the value judgments involved (how a patient should use her last days, whether he should risk surgery or live with an incapacitating condition, whether she should rear a deformed child) deal with the value of life. They are moral rather than psychiatric or medical, so they are to be made by the persons themselves, not by "experts." Little in physicians' special intelligence, training, or perspective equips them to make better decisions about such matters than patients or their families, and there is nothing in any tacit professional contract that transfers the right of decision to the physician. The point that I want to single out is, in Buchanan's words, the

> tremendous weight which this paternalist argument places on the physician's powers of judgment. He must not only determine that giving the information will do harm or even that it will do great harm. He must also make a complex comparative judgment. He must judge that withholding the information will result in less harm on balance than divulging it. Yet [none of the physicians] even mention this comparative judgment in their justifications of withholding information. They simply state that telling the truth will result in great harm to the patient or his family. No mention was made of the need to compare this expected harm with harm which might result from withholding the information, and no recognition of the difficulties involved in such a comparison was reported.[31]

The empirical studies show that "the evidential basis for such comparative judgments was remarkably slender." One must suspect they were rationalizations that reflected the doctors' exaggerated estimation of their knowledge and insight and, more insidiously, an egotism nurtured by the professional environment. In any event, physicians who make vital decisions for patients on the basis of inadequate evidence violate the epistemic ethic.

This is not to deny that medical paternalism is justified in exceptional cases. The physician may have detailed information about the patient and family and the harm to be prevented by intervention may be grave. But exceptions must be recognized as such and not used to rationalize wholesale paternalism, and they are becoming rarer as medicine becomes more specialized and physician–patient relations less intimate.

If physicians are the worst offenders in the realm of unreflective paternalism, the reason lies in the fact that medicine is the most professionalized occupation. Medical paternalism is a lens through which we can detect incursions upon the autonomy of clients in other professions. It teaches the disheartening lesson that critical standards of reasoning learned in technical areas are not automatically carried over to nontechnical decisions. Professionals need to be taught to follow the principles of the epistemic ethic in moral questions as well as in technical questions. The problem of paternalism shows how difficult this will be.

Justified Professional Paternalism

Paternalism is intervention in another's life for the latter's own good without his or her consent. Professional paternalism is intervention in the life of a client, employer, or the public in one's capacity as a professional, made possible by power bestowed by society. The factors relevant to justifying professional paternalism are the following:

1. The magnitude of the benefits to be bestowed and harms prevented by the intervention, less any benefits foregone and harms produced, in comparison to alternative actions. The reversibility of harms and retrievability of opportunities are dimensions of this magnitude. In the case of professional paternalism, special attention should be paid to the values assigned by society to the care of the profession, but

the effect of professional decisions on other values must not be neglected.

2. Among the benefits and harms are the increase or diminution of autonomy by the intervention. In the case of the professional paternalism, these include the autonomy of the client and that of the professional. The intervention may curtail the client's autonomy temporarily or in a particular respect while leaving the power to make autonomous decisions intact or expanding it for the future or in other respects, in which case the evil of curtailment is less. The client's autonomy usually is to be preferred over the professional's, since the raison d'être of professionalism is to serve the client. But the professional must retain enough autonomy to follow high standards of competence and serve most clients, though on occasion not particular ones.

3. The effect of the action in setting a precedent and reinforcing a habit is important. Actions performed in the professional role fortify or weaken practices. Practices have to be evaluated in terms of the way they may be abused and their consequences in a variety of settings.

4. The paternalist must reflexively review the reasons available to ground the judgment about the probable benefit of the action. Professionals must have adequate evidence that their actions will benefit the client so that their judgment clearly is more reliable than that of the client or client's guardian.

We can say loosely that a paternalistic act is justified if and only if its expected value computed according to these four measures is appreciably greater than any alternative, including the refusal to act. The qualification, appreciably greater, is included because paternalism is prima facie wrong. The burden of proof is on one who claims that it is justified in a particular instance. If there is doubt about the sufficiency of the justification, one should err on the side of inaction.

To combat the excessive paternalism characteristic of professionals, we should authorize it only when the justification is especially strong. Examples of professional respect for client autonomy are important because of the role of professionals as models in modern society. There are positive reasons to avoid paternalism, so there must be even stronger reasons to warrant it.

An opposite point also should be made. Justified actions are either permissible or obligatory. What might be merely permitted for a nonprofessional may be obligatory for the professional because of socially assigned role-responsibilities. These conceivably could include care for certain individuals or groups when they do not consent to the care. For example, in our present way of doing things, physicians, psychiatrists, and lawyers make decisions for the legally incompetent. Journalists decide what is fit to print. Ministers declare God's will on matters of faith and morals. Public works engineers design structures that they presume society needs but not always with a popular mandate. Statesmen decide matters of war and peace that they deem the public too emotional or uniformed to handle rationally.

As these examples show, many actual paternalistic role-responsibilities are problematic. There is a tendency among professionals to pretend that there is a social contract where society tolerates practices out of ignorance or inertia. There is a tendency of professions to interpret their mandate broadly to encroach on human lives where they should not. Paternalistic obligations, therefore, must be spelled out in publicly debated and approved codes, charters, or covenants. They must meet the stringent requirements sketched earlier. Paternalistic obligations should not be sanctioned in professions where profound respect for human autonomy has not been demonstrated.

The positive emphasis, therefore, should be on that respect. It should be incorporated as a central element in the ideal of service and in the personal traits to be cultivated in individual professionals. The reason for being for the professional is to provide services to others that they cannot provide for themselves. Service is enhancement of the quality of existence of the other, of his or her life as a person. Autonomy is essential to personhood. Respect for the autonomy of the person one is serving, therefore, is integral to serving that person. This almost always means not encroaching upon the client's autonomy and frequently to extend it by supplementing the client's knowledge or power.

Notes

1. *The Tyranny of the Experts*, p. 3.
2. *Ibid.*, p. 9.
3. *Ibid.*, p. 8.
4. *The Disabling Professions*, p. 20.
5. *Ibid.*, p. 12.
6. *Ibid.*, pp. 17–19.
7. *Ibid.*, p. 20.

8. Gerald Dworkin, "Paternalism"; Joel Feinberg, "Legal Paternalism."

9. Richard Arneson, "Mill versus Paternalism," p. 473.

10. *Being and Nothingness*, pp. 475–480.

11. I have adapted the framework provided by S. I. Benn in "Freedom, Autonomy and the Concept of a Person," adding distinctions from other authors and embellishments of my own.

12. *Ibid.*, p. 111.

13. *Ibid.*, pp. 113 and 124.

14. *Ibid.*, p. 117.

15. *Being and Time*, pp. 158–159.

16. "Mill versus Paternalism," pp. 478–481.

17. "On Liberty," in *Utilitarianism, On Liberty, Essay on Bentham*, p. 197.

18. *Ibid.*, p. 192.

19. "Utilitarianism," in *ibid.*, p. 260.

20. "On Liberty," in *ibid., pp. 135–136, 139, and 229.*

21. *Ibid.*, p. 206.

22. *Ibid.*, p. 188.

23. *The Professions*, p. 26. My discussion is adapted from pp. 25–33. Other speculations about the prehistory of professionalism may be found in Carr-Saunders and Wilson, "Professions," and Thomas, "The Relation of the Medicine Man to the Origin of Professional Occupations."

24. *The Professions*, pp. 32–33.

25. "Mistakes at Work," *The Sociological Eye*, p. 318.

26. *The Unkindest Cut*, p. 137.

27. *Ibid.*, Chapter 9.

28. "Doctors and Lawyers."

29. See Vivian Weil, *Report of the Workshops on Ethical Issues in Engineering*, pp. 5–6.

30. "Medical Paternalism," p. 370.

31. *Ibid.*, pp. 377–378.

□ 13

THE PEDAGOGICAL IMPERATIVE

The obligation to serve all in need clashes head on with respect for client autonomy when clients do not consent to intervention in their lives, yet lack the power or rationality to care for themselves. When vital interests are at stake, paternalism is an option. Something is lost whatever the decision. Therefore, it is an obligation of the professions to minimize occasions when it is necessary. The obvious way is to seek consent from clients to the actions judged to be in their interest. Consent, however, can be manufactured, it can be misinformed or illogical, and it can support decisions that ought to be resisted or rejected. Not every form of consent makes an action nonpaternalistic or contributes to its justification, only the right kind of consent secured by the right kind of measures.

Such consent cannot always be secured and some paternalism always will be necessary. However, much can be done to prepare people to take part in professional decisions and it is the obligation of the professions to see that this is done. I shall develop this theme under the metaphor of the professional as a teacher. The pedagogical imperative is essential to achieving the proper balance between the obligation to serve and respect for client autonomy.

The Athenian Stranger in Plato's *Laws* explains why a legislator should append a preface to every law that defines terms and gives reasons. The Athenian remarks, "[Is the legislator to offer] never a word of advice or exhortation to those for whom he is legislating, after the manner of some doctors?" He proceeds to contrast two sorts of doctors and two sorts of patients. The slave-doctor does not understand the principles behind medical treatment and never discusses the complaints of slave-patients with them.

> The slave-doctor prescribes what mere experience suggests, as if he had exact knowledge; and when he has given his orders, like a tyrant, he rushes off with equal assurance to some other servant who is ill; and so he relieves the master of the house of the care of his invalid slaves.

The legislator should emulate another type of doctor:

> the other doctor, who is a freeman, attends and practices upon freemen; and he carries his enquiries far back, and goes into the nature of the disorder; he enters into discourse with the patient and his friends, and is at once getting information from the sick man, and also instructing him as far as he is able, and he will not prescribe for him until he has first convinced him; at last, when he has brought the patient more and more under his persuasive influences and set him on the road to health, he attempts to effect a cure.[1]

The professional should be like the freeman-doctor, who seeks causes before he prescribes cures and tailors his cures to the individual. Too many professionals treat clients in the manner of slaves or, in the modern equivalent, as machinery in need of service.

Our critique of paternalism rejects the slave-doctor attitude though allowing limited forms of the behavior that follows from it. We must explore the implications of the conception that professional service is an interchange among equals and how it follows that the role of the professional is that of teacher as well as partner and agent. Since good teachers are also good students (of the needs and circumstances of their students as well as the latest developments in their discipline), the pedagogic model also represents professionals as learners and those whom they serve as teachers.

The Teacher as Paradigm Professional

The place and limits of paternalism are perhaps is more problematic in the schools than anywhere else in contemporary society. Teachers are expected to stand not only in loco parentis, but in loco civitatis. Reminiscent of the educational philosophies of Plato and Aristotle, they are expected to inculcate right opinions before children are able to think critically, both for the children's own benefit in adjusting to society and for society's benefit by making them good (i.e., obedient) citizens.

Some paternalism is integral to good pedagogy but less than sanctified by the expectations of society. If discipline is imposed, it is to enable students to learn self-discipline. If it is true that teachers know what is better for students, they should equip students to know what is better for themselves. If students must be ruled for their own good, it is to prepare them for self-rule. Of all professions, teaching most obviously demands respect for the client's (student's) autonomy. Its whole purpose is to provide the information, skills, principles, and questions necessary for an independent existence. Teachers who do not respect student autonomy are teachers in name only; in reality, they are propagandists and manipulators, ideologues and mythologizers.

When we say that the teacher is the paradigm professional, we mean the ideal teacher in an ideal learning situation. The ideal educational system would be designed according to principles that strictly circumscribe legitimate paternalism. Coercion would be minimal, even coercion for the student's own good. Let us review some of the familiar implications of this ideal.

Where students are properly prepared by home and culture to make responsible choices, curricular requirements may be converted into guidelines and directions into advice. Students choose their studies, class attendance is voluntary, time is set aside for independent study, and grades are for self-appraisal rather than to rate, rank, motivate, or certify.

Ideal teachers learn from ideal students. They learn new insights from the innovative, and the dialectic with all students helps them shape their ideas by seeing them from the standpoint of others. Assisting one another in the pursuit of knowledge, teachers and students develop mutual respect and fidelity. Fairness and kindness flourish naturally; they are not strained or shammed.

Under such conditions, the teaching-learning process disengages itself from the credentialing function. Students seek to learn what they want and need to know, not what is a badge for admission to employment and status. The authority of teachers rests on their ability to learn and teach, not on their power to open the doors of commerce and bureaucracy. Where they must impose requirements in the interest of students, they give reasons and students and the public play an active role in perfecting the requirements. It will be for the teacher as expert to propose and the public as client and consumer to dispose—after public debate in which teachers of wisdom and fortitude declare clearly what is required for genuine education.

Individualism is not only tolerated in the open educational system; it is demanded. Independent thought is a role-responsibility of students and teachers alike. Open schools can fulfill their mission only in an open society where all sorts of freedom—personal, moral, religious, and political—are protected. In the open society, the bold and venturesome teacher is the paradigm of the responsible use of expertise. What this shows about paternalism is that, paradoxically, the better the teacher and the teaching environment, the less the need to intervene in the lives of students; and by analogy, the better the professional and the more open the society, the less the need to take over areas of decision from clients, employers, and the public.

Unfortunately and shamefully, our educational system falls far short of the ideal. The teaching of skills for ends that are uncriticized, to be used in conformity to community mores, is the rule. The public, sensing the debasement of the professional ideal in this form of pedagogy, meet the clamor of teachers for professional identity with polite scepticism. Teachers are good and faithful servants of society but not very bright or very ambitious. Their work is routine and they deserve their menial status.

Consent and the Justification of Paternalism

To build a bridge from the discussion of paternalism to the pedagogic ideal, let us look carefully at the role of consent in justifying actions. Clearly, informed consent is a desideratum. It is a basic obligation of the professional to seek it aggressively; that is, to teach the client whatever is necessary to see the wisdom of the best course of action. The professional has the complementary obligation to teach clients and the public how to care for themselves so as to reduce the need for help so that, even if a dependent relationship is necessary, it will be terminated as quickly as possible.

Paternalism is intervention without consent in a person's life for his or her welfare. The absence of consent has been seized upon by those who consider paternalism wrong as an infringement of autonomy. What they have in mind is informed consent, since the paternalistic character of an action and its wrongness are not relieved by consent "manufactured" by playing on the client's ignorance or psychological dependence.

It is argued that informed consent makes an action nonpaternalistic by transforming the agent into an instrument of the subject's will and the action into an extension rather than an abridgment or substitute for the subject's will. Since infringement on the subject's autonomy is what makes paternalism objectionable, informed consent makes the action nonpaternalistic and inoffensive.

This conclusion is too facile. The intrinsic value of doing for yourself and having another do for you are in no way equivalent. Treating them as equivalent comes from lumping together different forms and degrees of autonomy. The satisfaction we get from autonomy comes from the sense of authorship of our actions. It is the awareness not only of setting a course of action in motion toward a goal, but of taking steps to carry it out and exercising our faculties in doing so. Though we get vicarious pleasure from the success of our agents and congratulate ourselves on our intelligence in selecting them, this hardly matches the satisfaction of doing for ourselves. We use agents because they achieve our ends more successfully than we, not because we get the same enjoyment from their powers as we get from our own.

Consenting to something is itself an autonomous act, but a low-grade one. Its intrinsic value is correspondingly slight, though its instrumental role in relation to the subject's welfare may be significant. An agent who really wants to act for a subject's benefit is obligated to ascertain what are the subject's interests. The most direct way is to consult the subject, to ask whether the course of action is correct in his or her judgment—correct, we must remind ourselves, not in producing consequences that seem good to the agent, but consequences that meet the subject's true needs. Paternalist P who acts without consulting S foregoes an important mode of confirming P's own judgment. The paternalistic action may still be justified, since P may not be able to consult S or may have good reasons to trust his or her judgment over S's; but the absence of consent is a mark against the action.

This much is relatively straightforward. The fact that there are several forms of consent complicates the issue. The consent whose absence is a defining condition of paternalism is consent at the time of the action or concurrent consent, as distinguished from prior and subsequent consent. With each of the three we may distinguish consent that actually is given (occurrent consent) from that which would be given under different circumstances (dispositional consent). Thus, one who did not consent would have, if asked; another, if conscious; a third, if not intimidated. A significant form of dispositional consent is that the person would have given if rational or that a rational person would have given in the first person's shoes.

Some authors on paternalism have placed a good deal of importance on dispositions, but it is hard to see why. An unexercised disposition produces none of the satisfaction or the results of its exercise. It might be argued that S's disposition to consent is at least evidence of S's values and hence of the correctness of P's judgment, but what evidence can P have of S's disposition in lieu of its expression in occurrent consent, except by already knowing S's values? Hence, knowledge of S's disposition to consent is otiose in respect to the justification of the action.

A special instance of this point is connected with prior consent. Suppose that S has authorized P at time t_1 to perform A at time t_2, and P has good reason to infer from this consent and other evidence that S's values at t_1 would be sufficient to justify A. In the absence of clear evidence that S's values have changed, P has the right to assume that S would have consented at t_2 given the opportunity. Many authors consider prior consent to be equivalent to concurrent consent and declare the actions sanctioned by prior consent to be nonpaternalistic. By our definition the actions are paternalistic, but they can also be justified if P's knowledge of S's values at t_1 is an adequate basis for justifying the action and P has reason to believe that the values are the same at t_2. It is S's values, not S's dispositions to consent, that justify the action.

The justificatory force of subsequent consent or, more accurately, endorsement of an action by a subject who did not consent at the time of action also is evidentiary. We feel that the fact that S approves of A having been done somehow counts in A's favor. We are tempted to think that S's autonomy has not been seriously abridged, particularly if the action has been successful and S's approval is well considered.

In criticism of this attitude, it has been argued that later events cannot retroactively make A right if it was wrong when it was performed. However, if a later event has some value in itself and can be anticipated as a consequence of A, it is part of A's expected value and contributes to its justification. Unfortunately, S's subsequent approval has only a minor value as an exercise of autonomy, for S can hardly view an action to which he or she did not consent as an extension of his or her agency. Hence, the fact that P anticipates S's endorsement does not justify A, if A is objectionable on other grounds. S's approval might assuage P's guilt if A goes wrong or assure P that the encroachment on S's autonomy was not so great as supposed at the time, since S was not thinking clearly, but the evidential value of consent here is quite limited. It helps P determine ex post facto whether the action was well designed to meet S's needs and enlarges P's basis for judging whether future acts will meet S's needs or those of similar subjects. That is, S's subsequent approval helps P choose better, though it does little to justify P's earlier choice.

If existing professional relationships in fact are tacit contracts, they are indefinite as to the responsibility of clients to participate in the solution of their problems and the responsibility of the professional to assume any portion of this responsibility. Therefore, the principles of paternalism must become a part of the public understanding of professionalism. Such an understanding would take the form of widespread expectations, shared by clients and professionals alike, as to the obligations of each party in the relationship. The principles might be spelled out formally as provisions in professional codes or in statements of responsibilities provided clients by professionals. Engagement of a professional then would be an authorization to take the initiative in serving the client, but it would be retracted when client no longer consents. This could be formulated so as to allow the professional to take urgently needed actions while preserving for the client the right to withdraw from the relationship under certain conditions (e.g., after a delay to meet an emergency, recover sanity or civil liberties, etc.). Depending on how the professional contract was developed, some of what are now debatable paternalistic acts would become definitely prohibited and others definitely sanctioned.

Client Rationality

In most cases where professional paternalism is justified intuitively, the client (less often, the employer) is incapacitated from thinking clearly or acting effectively, that is, is deficient in rationality or power, the two essentials of autonomy. Such deficiencies are relevant to justification in two ways. On the one hand, they make it more likely that subjects will injure themselves, fail to avoid injury, or miss important opportunities. On the other hand, the subjects' autonomy is already curtailed, so paternalistic intervention infringes less upon autonomy and is easier to justify by other gains.

Client deficiencies in power seldom are the occasion for paternalism. People utilize professionals because they lack resources of time, opportunity, or knowledge to do for themselves or because the opportunity costs for what they want to do are excessive. It is their intention to utilize the professional's expertise to enlarge their power. This, of course, does not obligate professionals always to do as clients bid. Clients may demand immoral services or services harmful to others. Refusal to provide these can be paternalistic to the extent that the professional protects the client from legal penalties, social condemnation, or immorality. In most cases, however, there is ample justification to refuse apart from the paternalistic consideration.

A bit more problematic are cases where the client, while otherwise appearing to be rational, solicits services which are self-injurious. If no other professional is available who is willing to provide the services, refusal to provide them is paternalistic. Paternalism by inaction, while not blocking the autonomy the client already exercises, prevents the actualization of potential autonomy. In such cases, the considerations already stipulated for justification become relevant; viz., the magnitude and probability of the injury to be averted, the professional's grounds for trusting his or her own judgment of the client's interests over that of the client, the possibility of setting a harmful precedent, and the provisions of any sort of contract or prior consent.

This last case leads naturally to cases where the client is deficient in rationality. The professional who thinks a course of action favored by a client is patently self-destructive must suspect some defect in information or reasoning on the latter's part. Such suspicions do not justify a hasty leap or complacent slide into paternalistic practices endemic to one's profession. Rather, the professional is obligated to delay action long enough to test the client's rationality. He might be obligated to delay long enough to repair clients' deficiencies, especially in respect to information or sound beliefs, or to allow clients to right themselves, calm down, or regain self-control. But if clients persist in demanding self-injurious courses of action or refusing help, the professional must evaluate his or her course of action on the bases provided earlier.

The elements of rationality include a well thought-out and logically ranked set of values, adequate causal knowledge relative to the pursuit of alternative objectives, and the self-control to follow the dictates of one's values and beliefs. Some professions, such as law, engineering, and accountancy, are equipped primarily to enlarge or supplement the client's causal beliefs. Professionals may be justified in exerting pressure on clients or employers to defer to professional judgments about how to achieve their objectives. There seldom is a justification for professionals to exploit their strategic position to countermand client decisions that flow from misguided values or lack of self-control.

The opportunity to do so is not unusual. Professionalism is a way of making specialized knowledge usable for nonspecialists and professionals can control information to shape clients' view of possible ends and their costs. They can achieve the aims of paternalism by persuading clients to value what the professional thinks they ought to value or to sanction the professional's pursuit of ends that clients lack the self-control to pursue. The element of persuasion creates an illusion of client autonomy. The client *is* consenting; the professional *is* acting as the client's agent in accordance with the way the client is now viewing the matter; the client *does* enjoy a sense of participation in the professional's actions. This justification, however, founders on the deception involved. The consent is manufactured and manufactured consent contributes no more to justification than informed dissent. Indeed, informed dissent is the more autonomous act and an action in the face of informed dissent may be more justified than one for which consent has been manufactured.

Rational Consent

In the discussion of paternalism, the emphasis has been put on the difference between informed and manufactured consent. For consent to be informed, however, is not enough. Irrational persons can be induced to consent to wrong actions by correct information and irrational consent to helpful actions hardly constitutes an important act on the consenter's part or converts the paternalist into his or her agent.

This consideration introduces another uncertainty into the paternalist's calculations and should serve as a further brake on paternalistic impulses. Should S consent to a proposed course of action, P must assess how informed and rational S is. If P has played a role in developing S's consent, P must judge whether this was accomplished by appealing to some lurking irrationality. Should S object to the action, P must judge whether the dissent reflects a better insight into his or her needs than P's. Such judgments are subtle and difficult and one should be extremely self-critical in making them. This is one more reason for P to be cautious both about overruling S's wishes and accepting S's expressions of consent as removing an action from the category of paternalism.

Some moralists have a different concept in mind under rational consent. They maintain that P's action can be justified if a rational subject would have consented to it or if S would have consented if rational. This appeal to the rational consenter is spurious. The rational subject (RS, as distinguished from the actual S, who we assume to be irrational) exists only in P's mind. RS thinks only in the way P assigns. RS is not an independent oracle whom P can consult; RS speaks only the words P puts in RS's mouth. RS's rationality is what P takes to be reasonable. The rule perform a paternalistic act only if a rational subject would approve amounts operationally to the rule think through the reasons for your actions and act only for what you take to be good reasons. It is an application of the principle that epistemic norms are part of rational ethics, not a technique for finding new grounds for an action.

There may be heuristic value for P to think in terms of what the hypothetical RS would want. The thought-experiment reminds P that paternalistic actions are prima facie suspect. They require good reasons; good intentions are not enough. The experiment also reminds P that the appropriate reasons lie in S's needs, not in P's or what P's would be if P were in S's shoes.

To the extent that P must consider S's values in deciding upon a course of action, P must overcome personal bias and imagine what it is like to be S. This may not be easy when P is removed from S's life experience by training and mode of existence and when biases about human needs are endemic to P's subculture. This is often the case with professionals in relation to their clients and the public.

A favored way to overcome bias is to consult the judgment of others. Professionals are accustomed to confer with colleagues on technical problems and develop technical standards corporately through commissions or committees of peers. Unfortunately, when the question of what is good for a client is a matter of the client's values rather than of the technical means to meet them, colleagues are likely to reinforce the professional's prejudices rather than correct them. The colleague's judgment is shaped by the same influences. He or she equally is removed from the client's life experience and subject to the same biases of the professional subculture. It is urgent in difficult cases, therefore, to solicit advice from competent persons with perspectives resembling those of the client and knowledge about him or her individually; for example, guardians, relatives, and friends.

Paternalism has been discussed in relation to the professional with individual clients. A parallel point can be made about paternalistic attitudes toward the public. The professions' claim to autonomy amounts to the plea, trust us! Not just to carry out your wishes, but to decide what is best for you. We have urged the involvement of the public in the governance of professions to ensure their orientation to service. Here I want to insist that a profession will keep better informed about the needs of society if it involves the public in the development and administration of its charter. Steps by the professions to involve the public have been modest and we have catalogued obstacles in the present social system. "Public" control turns out to be control by representatives of the profession or representatives of the public co-opted by the profession. To break the social paternalism of the professions we can appeal only to the understanding of morally sensitive and self-critical persons in their ranks, to persuade them that people do not *need* certain kinds of "service."

The Pedagogical Dimension

To understand the precise educational obligation of the professional, let us consider a case where paternalism is at issue. S comes to P or is brought to P with a serious problem, but is disinclined (or would be if fully informed) to let P perform action A that, in P's judgment is best suited to solve the problem. P has the power, bestowed by institutions of society and reinforced by the professional mystique, to bully or deceive S into accepting A or to carry out A regardless of S's wishes. P must choose between performing A without S's consent or refusing to serve S at all. The first alternative is paternalism. The second violates the obligation to serve on demand.

Professionals are not often confronted with dichotomous choices. Many lines of action usually are open that are less effective than the ideal one but better than not serving at all. Several types of treatment usually are available to the physician. If the patient can be persuaded to accept one that is less than ideal, its expected value, including preservation of patient autonomy, must be compared with that of sending him elsewhere for treatment. Similar choices face the lawyer whose client is bent on a line of defense that would land her in the penitentiary or a contract that would entangle her in a disastrous business venture; the teacher whose students detest courses essential to their educational objectives; and the engineer whose employer wants to undertake a large and unpromising project, adopt an inferior design, or buy from an unreliable supplier.

In these cases, we are assuming that the professional has the power to do what he or she wants. All that stands in the way are professional scruples, which are characteristically weak in regard to client autonomy. It helps to justify a paternalistic action that it has a high probability of achieving important values for subject and there is no effective alternative that preserves the subject's autonomy. The obverse is that prospective paternalist P should actively seek alternatives that engage S's autonomy and, if P must proceed with A, P should supplement it with measures that develop S's autonomy. P should explain the reasons for A even if this does not persuade S to consent to it. Professionals should help clients acquire the knowledge, skills, self-control, and discipline necessary to do for themselves. Every professional should be an educator. This is an obligation of the individual professional vis à vis individual clients and the profession vis à vis the public. Ideally, professions eventually would put themselves out of business. (Of course, they need not fear this in view of the growing complexity of modern life.)

There are problems aplenty with our injunction. Helping others to autonomy is time-consuming and time is money for professionals. Taking the time to educate clients and lay the groundwork for informed and intelligent consent would reduce the number of clients served and fees collected. Respect for client autonomy, if it were universal among professionals, would reduce the services needed as more people became able to care for themselves.

The following item expresses a typical attitude that rationalizes paternalism for many professionals. In his newspaper column "Health," Lawrence E. Lamb, M.D., responds to an inquiry regarding a low-sodium diet that a doctor had prescribed for high blood pressure without explaining its purpose:

> I'm sure most doctors know the proper medications for their patients, but it would help if they would explain things so the patient understood a little better why he is required to do certain things and why he is taking medicines. Like what the medicine does to help when you take it and what would happen if you didn't. Sometimes it's difficult to just take medicines on blind faith.

Dr. Lamb replies,

> It would be wonderful if all doctors had the time to discuss the details of each illness with each patient. If they did, they wouldn't be able to see but a limited number of patients. That would significantly increase the cost per patient as well as result in a significant shortage of medical help.
>
> The public has to realize that the doctor cannot give individualized instructions to each patient. Even if you use medical assistants for this purpose and if they're qualified to do it, you still have the problem of the expense involved. Most doctors would like to have the time to explain more things to their patients, particularly those who are truly interested as you seem to be.[2]

Dr. Lamb then explains the reason for a low-sodium diet, thereby helping the medical profession to discharge its educational responsibility. For this he should be praised. However, his apology for uncommunicative doctors is smug and exasperating. He treats informed consent and the educated participation of the patient in his or her therapy as a trivial good compared to improvement in physical condition. Paternalistic treatment is preferred, since it is more efficient; that is, it gets more patients healed in less time. (It incidentally increases the physician's income.)

Mitigation of professional paternalism would entail real costs for the client as well as the professional. Initially, it would require the regulation, if not the breach, of professional monopolies to ensure more practitioners (with lower incomes), who would have more time to treat clients as autonomous persons. It might reduce the need for professionals in a society whose members were equipped to care for themselves. More likely, it would enable the same number of professionals to undertake more difficult tasks by consigning routine ones to laypersons and technicians. Before that, however, clients would have to accept less care in order to enjoy the sort of care that enhances their autonomy.

Public Education

The natural extension of the obligation to educate the individual client or employer is the corporate responsibility to educate the public. Public capabilities of self-help in routine aspects of professional services would utilize knowledge more fully and free the profession for more difficult tasks.

By and large the professions have not acknowledged the responsibility to educate the public. The American Medical Association expresses the opinion (in response to what question?) that "Physicians are free to engage in any teaching permitted by the law." This is weak; teaching is permitted rather than enjoined and the AMA probably has in mind the teaching of physicians and health professionals rather than laypersons.

Sigma Delta Chi confesses that journalists have something to learn from the public when it states, under Fair Play: "Journalists should be accountable to the public for their reports and the public should be encouraged to voice its grievances against the media. Open dialogue with our readers, viewers, and listeners should be fostered." This does not quite say, however, that journalists have an obligation to inform the public about journalism.

The engineering associations refer to education in a perfunctory way. They urge engineers to extol engineering and its accomplishments; they say nothing about schooling the public to be protoengineers. The Engineers Council for Professional Development declares, "Engineers shall endeavor to extend the public knowledge of engineering, and shall not participate in the dissemination of untrue, unfair or exaggerated statements regarding engineering." The Institute of Electrical and Electronics Engineers makes clear that it is concerned about public relations rather than substantive education. "Members shall, in fulfilling their responsibilities to the community, seek to extend public knowledge and appreciation of the profession and its achievements."

The American Psychological Association goes a bit further. It takes note of popularized psychology and seeks to impose standards on the way it is presented. For example, it states,

> Individual diagnostic and therapeutic services are provided only in the context of a professional psychological relationship. When personal advice is given by means of public lectures or demonstrations, newspaper or magazine articles, radio or television programs, mail or similar media, the psychologist utilizes the most current relevant data and exercises the highest level of professional judgment.

The APA does not define public education as a social responsibility. Perhaps, it does not need to because pop psychology is much in demand and very profitable. A systematic program of public education on the part of the professional might help drive the charlatans from the market, but psychology is less exclusive than other professions.

The American Bar Association comes at the problem from another angle and deals with it in more detail. Under the principle that "A lawyer should assist the legal profession in fulfilling its duty to make legal counsel available," it announces, "important functions of the legal profession are to educate laymen to recognize their problems, to facilitate the process of intelligent selection of lawyers, and to assist in making legal services fully available." It recognizes that the public must be made aware of some of the content and procedures of the law to recognize problems and intelligently select counsel, so it stipulates, "lawyers should encourage and participate in educational and public relations programs concerning our legal system with particular reference to legal problems that frequently arise." It insists that advertisements and educational programs "should be motivated by a desire to educate the public to an awareness of legal needs and to provide information relevant to the selection of the most appropriate counsel rather than to obtain publicity for particular lawyers." It then goes into detail about such matters as proper advertising, volunteered advice, etc. with a view to discouraging solicitation of business and the incitement of litigation. And it gives advice similar to APA's that discussion of matters in public lectures should be couched in generalities so as not to give advice to individuals about specific problems. The ABA, however, appears to see a moral limit to the educational function. Its obligation to make educated legal representation available to the public requires the lawyer to assist in preventing the unauthorized practice of law. Hence, while recognizing the right of laymen to represent themselves at their peril, it does not recognize any obligation of lawyers to help them become competent to do so. Rather, it argues, "the legal profession should help members of the public . . . to understand why it may be unwise for them to act for themselves in matters having legal consequences."

The professions thus have varying views about the responsibility to educate the public, but all consider that it falls within narrow limits. The psychologists acknowledge that laypersons can be taught to handle some of their own problems—or at least the professional association tolerates efforts of its members to do so. Most professions, like the ABA, are concerned to facilitate the intelligent choice of professional help. Some education in the rudiments of their field is necessary but it is not thought to equip the layperson to handle his or her own problems.

I suspect that something like a concept of a critical mass of knowledge is behind this attitude. A little knowledge is deemed to be dangerous. One must master a field to a minimum degree to be competent and one will do more harm than good for oneself or others if one is incompetent. Professional training is necessary to attain competence. Society perhaps should tolerate individuals' attempts to care for (and sometimes to injure) themselves if it is to avoid excessive control, but the professions should take a stand against it. They should also seek to prevent amateurs from caring for others; hence, they should fight for licensure legislation and combat unauthorized practice.

The concept of critical mass is the rationale for the tight control that professional associations exercise over the educational process. They and the educational establishment of the professional schools determine the level and content of training for certification and control access to it. By accident or design, this protects the professional monopoly. The point here is that it discourages education at levels below the critical mass and limits the autonomy of the layperson.

Professionals are jealous of their special knowledge and threatened by the prospect of sharing it, since after all it is the source of their status in society. This explains why the professions and most professionals give only lip service to public education and lack the will to sacrifice time, energy, or income to it. They are not at all distressed by the public's dependency.

It is too much to infer a conspiracy. This is not a tyranny of the experts (Lieberman) or a plot to disable the public (Illich). The complexity of modern life reduces everyone to lay status in every field but one. The physician is an amateur psychologist, lawyer, engineer, accountant, personnel manager, marketeer, etc. and each of the others is in a similar position. Esoteric knowledge can be put to use only by professionals, and laypersons need the use of that knowledge to survive. It does not take a deliberate program or devious conspiracy to put us at one another's mercy.

The Specter of Technocracy

Critics of professionalism conjure the vision of a society of narrow technicians each of whose autonomy is confined to the narrow limits of a specialty. The autonomy of each shrinks as new specialties crowd in. One can do little for ones self, though everyone does a great deal for others. Most of the important things of life are done by others; one progressively relinquishes autonomy even where it is available. This important value is lost by default in the pursuit of other benefits; and in the end everyone loses those benefits as well, since no one has the wisdom to rule the whole.

The theory of the critical mass of knowledge leads to this prognosis. One reaction is primitivism. If autonomy is an absolute value and if partial knowledge used autonomously leads to disaster, why not return to a form of life in which very little technical knowledge was needed? In reaction to modern society, few people try to live a self-reliant existence in small groups without scientific medicine, engineered structures, manufactured goods, civil government, or high culture. Even if they were willing to accept the radical reduction in population that would be required for everyone to live this way, most civilized people would find this existence nasty and brutish. The quality of autonomy that they would enjoy would be low indeed.

Primitivism, however, is not the only alternative to hyperspecialization. The theory of critical mass can be challenged. Proper education can provide laypersons the rudiments of knowledge in fields in which they perforce remain amateurs, while seasoning them with an awareness of their limitations, so that they may seek professional help when they need it and cooperate with the professional in utilizing it. Occupations that provide this kind of education are *enabling* professions. They enable the members of society to become more autonomous by the art of self-care and by sharing in the mounting store of knowledge amassed by civilization, rather than by abandoning civilization and technology.

At some times in life, we all must commit ourselves to the care of others and defer to their judgment about what is best for us. This does not mean that we abdicate responsibility for our existence. Autonomy is not won or lost in a single act. If we energetically exercise autonomy and abet it in our fellows in every possible way, we can safely entrust our lives to others on occasions of acute need without becoming robots or domestic pets. The good society does not provide autonomy to everyone in every facet of life—we are too interdependent for that. It provides new freedoms to compensate for limitations that must be imposed on old ones and it makes the growing repository of power in its culture and institutions available to all.

Professional Lying

If there is one absolute obligation of the teacher, it is veracity. Knowledge is a commodity that is not exhausted by use or diminished by being shared. It is a benefit that its possessor is always obligated to share. Indeed, it grows by being shared. To learn, one must be exposed to the truth and what others think is the truth—the noble lie is an instrument of the indoctrinator, not the teacher. The teacher also essentially is a learner, and the free exchange that is the milieu of teaching requires one to impart that which one has a right to receive, the candid statement of the truth as one sees it.

The pedagogic model of professionalism comes at this point into conflict with our everyday attitudes toward professionals. We are of two minds. On the one hand, we expect them to be faithful agents, "hired guns" if need be, for their employers. On the other hand, we take their ethical posturing at face value and view them as models of probity. If they depart from normal moral standards, we assume that there is a good reason in the demands of their role.

Our ambivalence extends to veracity. Scrupulous veracity is rightly admired and understandably rare. By our expectations we build duplicity into the role norms of some professions as a condition of effectiveness. Then, we are disillusioned when professionals are caught in lies and we blame the profession as well as the individual.

The reputation of reporters is built on scoops and we gleefully admire thier guile in worming their way into the confidence of unsuspecting informants. The success of trial lawyers is measured by their skill in cultivating desired impressions in juries and judges. Candor in business, diplomacy, and bargaining of any sort is regarded as ineptitude or a betrayal of those whom the professional represents. Some of the most admired research in social science involves manipulation and deceit. Entire vocations are devoted to spying and monitoring suspected enemies of the state.

These attitudes are not the sole province of the public. They are typical of the professions themselves and what they honor in their members. Politics, for example, is the art of dissimulation and the professional politician is one who has mastered the art. The public rewards him by electing him to high office and declaring him a strong leader and a statesman. Not the least of its reasons is that his peers admire him as a "real pro" and eagerly do business with him.

Lyndon Johnson, if we can trust Robert Caro's critical biography, was effective not because his colleagues liked him (he had few true friends) or admired his principles (he had no apparent principles); he succeeded through studied deviousness, secretiveness, and deception. Caro describes his strategy with Roosevelt, on whose coat tails he rode to his early victories: "With older men who possessed power, Johnson had always been "a professional son"—always deferential ("Yes, sir," "No, sir"). Was this the technique that he employed on Roosevelt, and that endeared him to the President?" We may wonder whether Roosevelt, no mean fox himself, was taken in or whether, seeing through Johnson's guile, it was precisely it that he admired. Cato reports, "The President tendered Johnson the ultimate compliment. He told Harold Ickes that Johnson was 'the kind of uninhibited young professional he would have liked to have been as a young man'— and might have been 'if he hadn't gone to Harvard.' "[3] When Johnson used his skills to enact social programs, he was praised. Only when he further mired the nation in an unpopular war was he condemned. When deception leads to catastrophe, we want straight talk; in normal times we do not welcome or reward it. We think it highly unprofessional for politicians to say exactly, clearly, and fully what they really think.

To assess these attitudes we must distinguish between professionals who lie and those whose profession requires them to lie— professional liars, if you will. When we enter a relationship with a doctor, lawyer, engineer, or clergyman, we expect truthful answers to our questions. Yet we employ professionals to lie for us and in some instances we even expect them to lie to us. When we step back from these practices to view them from the moral point of view, we must ask ourselves, Do we want to incorporate a high regard for veracity in the professional ideal and allow departures only under the most extreme conditions or do we want to endorse an instrumental view that sanctions the use of both honesty and deception as neutral tools according to expediency?

I shall make a case for strict veracity. It is hardly a novel position among moral philosophers, but it is by no means a dominant operating norm among professionals. The point of this discussion is to show how it derives from conclusions that we have already reached.

What the Codes Say

Truthfulness does not appear to be a primary professional virtue for professional associations. Some codes enjoin candor and objectivity in particular contexts, but these strictures allow concealment and dissimulation as discretionary tactics in other parts of the professional routine.

The codes of lawyers, psychologists, and engineers deal with areas where, we can assume, egregious malpractices occur. The efforts of the American Bar Association to draw fine distinctions between appropriate and inappropriate communications to the court, juries, and those in adversary relationships in connection with the obligation to represent clients zealously within the bounds of the law show an estimable concern for the workings of the system of justice, but not for veracity per se. The consequence is a legalistic attitude (exactly what is perjury, false evidence, irrelevant statements in court, proscribed communication to adversary clients and juries?) rather than an ardent dedication to truthfulness. I should hasten to say that, if the relegation of candor to subsidiary rank is a venality, it is not the fault of the Bar Association but of the adversary system of justice.[4]

Truthfulness is mentioned more often in the code of the American Psychological Association. Psychologists are urged to conduct research so that its results will not be misleading, for example, by discussing the limitations of their data and preventing its distortion by employers, to teach candidly and objectively, and to present honestly their credentials and that of psychology. However, the APA provides a major exemption for deception in research. This and the provision dealing with informed consent are worth examining.

> Except in minimal-risk research, the investigator establishes a clear and fair agreement with research participants, prior to their participation, that clarifies the obligations and responsibilities of each. . . . Failure to make full disclosure prior to obtaining informed consent requires additional safeguards to protect the welfare and dignity of the research participants. Research with children or with participants who have impairments that would limit understanding and/or communication requires special safe-guarding procedures. Methodological requirements of a study may make the use of concealment or deception necessary. Before conducting such a study, the investigator has a special responsibility to (i) determine whether the use of such techniques is justified by the study's prospective scientific, educational, or applied value; (ii) determine whether alternative procedures are available that do not use concealment or deception; and (iii) ensure that the participants are provided with sufficient explanation as soon as possible.

Bok, for one, challenges the legitimacy of research requiring deception. She argues that most of the information sought can be gained by nondeceptive research and the remainder is not worth the damage that deception does to the profession and the public. She charges that the perspective of the liars (in this case, the researchers and the psychologists on review committees schooled in the same ideology) blinds them to the dangers.[5]

The Engineers Council for Professional Development is relatively straightforward in its treatment of veracity. It assumes that engineers tell the truth as a matter of course, but need to be reminded to speak up on matters where it would be expedient to remain silent. The most critical provisions of ECPD Code concern whistle-blowing, as we discussed earlier. The code also emphasizes veracity in testimony before tribunals and commissions. The health-related and psychological professions could well give more attention to this area. The code also recognizes that truthfulness is involved elsewhere than speech acts. Engineers have an important certification as well as design function and honest communication is integral to it. Careless approval of poor designs can be as harmful as deliberate falsification of data. Hence, there are provisions dealing with signing and sealing documents.

The three associations, ABA, APA, and ECPD, at least grapple with questions of veracity. Other codes give them short shrift. The American Medical Association enjoins physicians in a very general way to be honest with patients and colleagues and expose fraud and deception. It has stringent rules for informed consent of subjects used in clinical investigations and other procedures, but recognizes exceptions.

> Informed consent is a basic social policy for which exceptions are permitted (1) where the patient is unconscious or otherwise incapable of consenting and harm from failure to consent is imminent; or (2) when risk-disclosure poses such a serious psychological threat of detriment to the patient as to be medically contraindicated. Social policy does not accept the paternalistic view that the physician may remain silent because divulgence might prompt the patient to forego needed therapy.

Exception (2) could be construed broadly to justify a good deal of deception; but there seems to be an encouraging shift in actual practice from paternalistic lying and withholding of information to greater candor and respect for patient autonomy. We cannot yet say, however, that the norm is for the physicians to be as candid with patients as they are with each other.

The American Association of University Professors announces in stirring terms that the obligation of the professor is to state the truth as he or she sees it and adhere to high standards of scholarship. Veracity is implied in these generalities, but the code does not come to earth on particulars other than to issue injunctions to foster honest academic conduct among students and to acknowledge academic debts to colleagues.

The most disappointing treatment of veracity is Sigma Delta Chi's code for journalists. It stands foursquare for accuracy and objectivity in reporting the news and correcting errors but not against deceiving people to get information. It advises lamely against communicating "unofficial charges affecting reputation or moral character without giving the accused a chance to reply" and "invading a person's right to privacy."

One may think that it makes little difference what AAUP and SDC say since they have little impact on professional practice in the absence of disciplinary powers. However, codes indicate operative ideals even if they do not shape them. Most professions favor truthfulness as a matter of ordinary morality, but condone guile in pursuit of values specific to their sphere of action (justice, health, etc.) and do not address the knottier problems with veracity that the pressures of professional life raise.

Methods for Assessing Lies

Bok's examination of lying is an exemplary piece of philosophical analysis. If ethical discourse can improve real life practices, this surely will be an instance. I shall rely on her argument to establish a strong presumption against professional deception. Bok does this for lying in general by pointing out that norms of truthfulness are necessary for civilized social intercourse, egregious forms of deception cause great harm, lesser forms cause more harm than is apparent and tend to evolve into worse forms. Bok does not condemn lying absolutely, but she is grudging in her exceptions and critical of the excuses commonly offered. Deception is the last resort after all honest alternatives have proved impossible. Hence, the burden of proof rests on the one who would justify deception and truthfulness need never be justified. (On this last point, she goes too far—the truth-teller surely would have to argue his point in Kant's example of the murderer looking for his victim.)

The legitimacy of particular deceptions are to be evaluated by the familiar consideration of consequences construed broadly:

the intrinsic quality of the act for the deceiver; the prospect of achieving his or her objective; the benefits and evils associated with the objective and byproducts of the action; the precedent it sets; etc.

In calculating values, one must attend to the epistemic ethic to assure oneself that the deception has been examined from all angles. Bok borrows from Baier and Rawls to propose the "public test" or "test of publicity,[6]" which require that reasons be given that will persuade a relevant audience. Personal conscience is too malleable to be reliable on complex questions, and calculations of benefits and harms are too affected by bias, self-deception, unexamined presuppositions, and hasty computations. One is forced to transcend these limitations if one is to persuade others with other biases. (Note that truthfulness is necessary to justify deception—one must discuss one's reasons candidly with the others one would persuade.)

Who composes the relevant audience? Initially, Bok suggests reasonable people in general, but she observes, "The appeal to 'reasonable persons' never has protected the interests of those considered outsiders, inferiors, incompetent, or immature" and the public test "does not work well when there is a question about just how 'reasonable' the available public is."[7] Presumably, one must have arguments that will be persuasive to a potential audience among more rational actual persons. In any case, the audience must be wide enough to include potential dupes as well as liars.[8] Liars are especially prone to mistakes of judgment— about the magnitude of the crisis they face, who is counted an enemy to be combatted by lies, whether others have entered a compact to be lied to, when dupes are likely to approve of lies retroactively, the benefits of altruistic lies, etc. They deceive themselves about the purity of their motives and the extent of their understanding of a situation. And, of course, liars with bad motives pick up the excuses of well-intentioned ones to rationalize self-serving lies. The most effective way to correct the liar's mistakes is to view them from the dupe's perspective. This helps to expose them to the liar as well as to outside observers.

When Bok deals with cases, she is forced to make judgments about what audiences *would* conclude in a public debate, not what any *have*. To determine this, she relies on her own feelings about being deceived. She appeals to what is reported by others in the media, literature, philosophical essays, etc.—sources she admits are not very reliable. And, where data have been gathered systematically, for example, polls about the public's loss of confidence in government and surveys of what dying patients want to learn from their doctors, she welcomes them. But she fails to warn that judgments about harms and benefits of particular forms of lying must remain very tentative until the wants of people are investigated more adequately.

The Harm of Lying

The test of publicity leads Bok to condemn most lying. Her arguments suffice, in my opinion, to condemn almost all professional lies. The objections to professional lying have to do with the direct harm to those deceived and outsiders, their harm to the liar, their tendency to evolve into harmful practices, and the damage they do to trust.

Some professional lies do direct and visible harm to their dupes. Bok criticizes three widespread practices in some detail. She points out that unwitting subjects of behavioral research may suffer from intrusion into their privacy, shame at being duped, and anxiety about facts (and misconceptions) the experiment reveals about them; debriefing cannot be counted on to rectify this psychological damage. Placebos that give temporary relief may cause patients to ignore the underlying causes of their distress, come to rely too heavily on pills and the wrong ones, and grow distrustful of legitimate medical care. Professionals who cover up for a colleague, for example, an alcoholic surgeon, put the public at risk.[9]

More fundamental, and more directly connected with theses we have developed, is the effect of the liar's duplicity on the dupe's autonomy. Bok compares lying with violence and argues that lying often is the worse.

> Deceit and violence—these are the two forms of deliberate assault on human beings. Both can coerce people into acting against their will. Most harm that can befall victims through violence can come to them also through deceit. But deceit controls more subtly, for it works on belief as well as action.

She explains:

> All our choices depend on our estimates of what is the case; these estimates must in turn often rely on information from others. Lies distort this information and therefore our situation as we perceive it, as well as our choices . . . To the extent that knowledge gives power, to that extent do lies affect the distribution of power; they add to that of the liar, and diminish that of the deceived, altering his choice at different levels.[10]

They obscure for the dupe possible goals, alternative actions, their costs, benefits, and uncertainties—in other words, lies sap the conditions of rational choice. The encroachment of violence on autonomy is public and obvious; that of deception is concealed and so harder to combat.

Bok's attack on deception is most eloquent when she discusses the sick and dying. Physicians who conceal the truth rob patients of freedom to "consider one's life as a whole, with a beginning, a duration, and end" and take a "stance toward the entire life they have lived, and . . . to give it meaning and completion." More obviously, such lies prevent patients from disposing of their last days, forcing them into helpless dependence on strangers.[11]

Respect for the autonomy of clients is sufficient to bar almost all professional paternalism. Three further points reinforce this conclusion. First, the altruism of an action does not make it less harmful and it helps hide the harm. Second, the fact that people in need and dependent, such as the sick, mentally disturbed, retarded, and immature, are easier to deceive is a reason to take *greater* care to be truthful, not *less*. They are defenseless. They are in danger of exploitation under the guise of paternalism. Their autonomy needs to be strengthened, not weakened further. Third, society provides guardians and representatives for such persons, who usually know their needs and are personally concerned about their welfare. If there is to be paternalistic deception, these are the people who should exercise it, not those who happen to have a formal and limited professional relationship with them.[12]

The Wages of Mendacity

Bok's remaining lines of attack pertain to the hidden injuries that lying inflicts on the liar and the community. In discussing the liar's biases, she notes:

> Liars usually weigh only the immediate harm to others from the lie
> against the benefits they want to achieve. The flaw in such an outlook
> is that it ignores or underestimates two additional kinds of harm—
> the harm that lying does to the liars themselves and the harm done
> to the general level of trust and social cooperation. Both are cumula-
> tive; both are hard to reverse.[13]

The consequences for the liar will be accepted as harm only if
one agrees with the judgment that being a fit member of the
moral community is a basic satisfaction in life. Duplicity cuts
one off from that satisfaction. Lying should not be a role-obliga-
tion of any professional partly for the sake of the self-respect of
professionals themselves. That it has been taken to be in some
professions, for example, in politics and business, is a serious
source of moral unrest. Furthermore, every lie weakens the inhi-
bition against lying and reinforces the habit of duplicity as a way
out of difficulty. Lies create webs of deception, suspicion on the
part of dupes, and anxiety about being found out on the part of
the liar. Deception becomes a way of life. Liars find themselves
"living a lie." We are all tempted to deceive or lie to ourselves.
Lying to others makes self-deception harder to resist. To justify
their claim of a special right to lie, liars exaggerate their judgment
and objectivity. These powers are perverted. The liar loses the
ability to make moral discriminations, especially about the kinds
of falsehood and their excuses. Where lying is a way of life, so
also is rationalization.

The typical excuses for lying are so weak that one must
suspect that those who resort to them are either illogical or
cynical. A case has been made for the morality of some deceptive
practices in professions. However, the benefits of paternalistic lies
are illusory. Lying to protect colleagues endangers the public and
usually does not benefit the colleague in the long run. Lying to
preserve confidences may be necessary under some conditions,
but it is better for there to be protections for the professional who
remains silent. A more complex problem is posed by the practice
of lawyers who, knowing or suspecting that clients have perjured
themselves, build on that testimony in court. Paradoxically, this
is defended in the name of truth. The adversary system, it is
claimed, requires candor between client and attorney. The truth
will out publicly if attorneys on both sides pursue their case in
every way possible. Bok argues that this excuse ignores the
viewpoint of the deceived. If potential members of juries were

consulted, they would not accept deception as a legitimate technique, nor would the lawyer want juries instructed that he claims this right to lie.

Excuses extenuate or remove the blame from something that would otherwise be a fault. To remove blame entirely, an excuse must provide a justification that appeals to a standard acceptable to reasonable people.[14]

Bok pitilessly exposes most excuses. A few are valid: Some white lies are too trivial to bother about. Deception to save innocent lives in a crisis is legitimate and systematic duplicity is necessary for survival in an utterly corrupt society. In certain gamelike situations, both sides implicitly acknowledge the right of the other to dissemble or even welcome it so as not to have to confront the truth. Informed consent to a deceptive practice can justify occasional subsequent deception of those who have consented.[15]

None of these reasons apply extensively in the professions. Some doctors and soldiers routinely face crises that require lying to save lives or prevent other grave harms, and those whose job involves bargaining may have to dissimulate in order to stay in the game at all. Lying in these cases still is harmful to dupes, the liar, and social trust. An effort must be made to find alternatives, circumscribe the practices narrowly, and change the system that requires them.

Since lying corrupts, most well-intentioned liars eventually abuse the power to deceive. Their example, particularly if they are influential persons such as professionals, generates deceptive practices. Deceptive practices spread more easily than other forms of wrongdoing because the normal controls of detection and accountability are short-circuited. This is one of the great harms of the ideological screens that professions erect before their practices. Moreover, the falsity of the ideology creates a favorable climate for deceptive practices—corporate self-deception makes it easy to view deception of nonprofessionals as useful or even obligatory.

Individual lies often escape detection. Deceptive practices eventually tend to be exposed. This produces suspicion and distrust, if not active resistance and counterdeception. Bok reserves her most scathing criticisms for deceptive behavioral research rationalized as the pursuit of truth. The gap between objective and methods makes this deception particularly scandalous. Bok is aghast at the effect on students "where professors teach them to deceive, where their grades and professional advancement depend on their adaptability and ingenuity in working with deceptive techniques . . ." She also is concerned at the loss of confidence in social science as a profession.[16]

Perhaps, we are exaggerating the impact of professional deception. After all, what is a little lying here and there? Everyone does it. Much professional deception is altruistic and the harm of self-serving forms may not be so grave. Habits and practices do not develop so easily. The social controls of ordinary morality and the legal system deter malfeasance. After all, hasn't this, the greatest and noblest nation on the earth, been built with the help of professionals?

We cannot settle for this cheerful judgment. Even the most uncritical defenders of our society bemoan its rancid stench of distrust. Regardless of whether we assign blame to professions for the social rot, we must lament the ruin of the hope that they would serve as exemplars and milieus for a higher kind of morality.

Positive Duties of Veracity

In view of the pivotal place of professions in modern society, the dangers of professional lying must be taken seriously. They must be countered with an ideal of professionalism that resolutely abjures the easy fixes of deception. Professionals have the obligation to promote integrity of communication in all parts of society. This means that it is their duty not only not to lie, but to ensure that truth is communicated fully and accurately wherever communication is appropriate at all.

Gert points out that the only rules that can be followed always at every hour of the day are prohibitions. "Do not lie" can be obeyed by sleeping and, in waking life, remaining mute.[17] But it is not the charge of professionals to stagnate in inaction or evade the turmoil of life in disengaged purity. They have positive functions. To carry them out, professionals must not just not lie, they are required to communicate actively. Truthfulness is their role obligation. Scrupulous veracity is their ideal.

Is veracity central enough to the professional task to warrant the prominence we are giving it? The models of the professional—client relationship disclose its importance.[18] The agency model reflects the raison d'être of professions, to put to use a body of knowledge and skills for those who have not mastered them. Truthfulness and candor are essential to the acquisition and transmission of knowledge. The fiduciary model recognizes that a bond of trust must exist between professional and client for the professional to do his or her work. Truthfulness and candor are essential to trust. Agency and trusteeship are limited by restrictions on professional paternalism out of respect for client autonomy. The pedagogic model reflects that respect. Antipaternalism prohibits one from encroaching unnecessarily on the autonomy of another; the pedagogic imperative commands one to contribute actively to that autonomy.

The obligations here are derived from the principles of justice and utility *via* the principle of special responsibilities; that is, the principle that the common good is achieved by assigning responsibility for groups of people or aspects of their welfare to people in special roles, with the restriction that outsiders not be harmed by the way role occupants discharge their responsibilities. Effective role responsibilities require accountability. Public exposure of practices is required so that society can monitor professional conduct. The role of professionals is so important that public knowledge is essential to public autonomy; that is, to democratic control of activities that vitally affect everyone.

The relation of the professional to both client and society requires trust and trust is founded on truthfulness. Furthermore, the obligation to expand client and public autonomy entail the positive obligation to impart knowledge. The world of teaching and learning demands honesty and candor as does no other. In the interchange of ideas, it is absolutely essential that each party communicate as effectively as possible what is in his or her mind. It is hard enough for the most conscientious speaker to communicate ideas without having to combat the suspicion that deception breeds. The free and open relation between teacher and student is a paradigm for all professional relationships.

What exactly is the professional to communicate? Certainly no more than others can and will understand. This unfortunately may be limited. The educational system does not prepare people to be informed consumers of professional services and they lack any sense that they have an obligation to learn about professional matters. The information it is the obligation of the client to demand includes what the professional proposes to do and why, the alternatives, and their costs and benefits. It includes an estimate of probability of each outcome and how well grounded those estimates are; that is, some measure of the professional's competence. There must be dialogue in which the professional and client explore the latter's values to help both parties to bring those values to bear on the decision at hand. In a word, professionals are obligated to communicate all that is needed for the client to make a rational decision in terms of his or her own values about the services the professional proposes to render. Clients are obligated to communicate whatever is necessary for the professional to perform this task.

I have urged that, in addition to these obvious obligations, the professional ought to make the transaction a learning experience for clients, to equip them to handle problems in the future. Education of the public at large is an extension of this obligation.

In a larger framework, rational choice is facilitated for clients by open admission of errors by the professional and disclosure of incompetence and malfeasance by the professional community. Lip service is paid to peer review and exposure in professional codes, but their implementation by disciplinary bodies is limited and countered by the reluctance of the professions to wash linen in public and endanger their reputation by exposing the wrongdoing of their members. Many codes urge practitioners to be honest about their qualifications and refer clients to more qualified experts. Only the engineering codes urge practitioners to admit errors.

The sketchy treatment of the obligations of candor in the professional ethic doubtless is connected with the fact that it would dissipate the professional mystique, strip away the charism of skill, and reduce the professional's power vis a vis clients, employers, and the public. It would transform the professional—client relationship into something like an interchange between equals, and power is always hard to give up.

The professional is obligated to communicate as much to the client as the client can absorb and push to the limit the client's willingness to listen. A couple of important complications should be addressed in this connection. The esoteric and technical character of professional knowledge imposes heavy demands on communication skills. Bok discusses the difficulty of communicating with children and the temptation to resort to fictions to create desired impressions or educate desired behavior.[19] This attitude also is prevalent among those with custody of retardates and the mentally impaired and disturbed. The autonomy of the subjects already is diminished, so it is easy to rationalize paternalistic attitudes. But, if paternalism is to be a self-destruct mechanism, if it should aim at its own elimination, such people are due as much help in achieving autonomy as "normals" and perhaps more. The skills of self-care have to be conveyed in simpler terms or bit by bit, but the struggle to communicate correspondingly must be more strenuous.

A particularly subtle instance of the difficulty of translating professional knowledge into lay terms for even normal adults is the experience reported to me by several ministers and ministerial students. They despair at their ability to convey the sophisticated concepts of sin, hell, the Trinity, Jesus, and the character of God's existence that they learned in progressive seminaries. Intricate theological arguments are unwelcome in sermons and Sunday School lessons. The minister falls back on systematic ambiguity, preaching doctrines in terms that will be understood at a lower, more literal, graphic, and emotional level by the congregation. The semiotic virtues are practiced with diffidence. Semiotic vices are indulged for pragmatic reasons but, it is hoped, not to such as an extent as to become corruptive.

Whether this practice is defensible for the professional minister in a fractured society is a difficult question. It is my sense that it is not. It may be rationalized as not lying because there is no desire to deceive, or by a complex doctrine of levels of truth, or by the excuse that dissimulation of ideas promotes a higher truth in living, worship, and action. The transparency of these excuses is apparent when we compare the habit of theological double-talk with the subterfuges of research scientists, trial lawyers, paternalistic physicians, guileful reporters, "noble lie" politicians, and all variety of spies, bargainers, and hired advocates. The altruism of the theological dissembler does not prevent damage to trust and clear thought.

The second complication for the obligation to inform is that the truth often hurts. Truth often is unwelcome and the natural temptation of the professional is to avoid bearing bad news. Yet, if we want professionals to prepare the way for the organic society, we must expect them to insist that their clients face the truth because the truth makes them free—free to act, if not free from care. Professionals cannot avoid value judgments. To serve is to provide something of value. If autonomy is a primary value, to serve you may require me to thrust autonomy upon you. I, the professional, must say, if you want my help, you must listen to what I have to say and you must open your mind to it however painful or burdensome it may be.

It is sometimes a professional obligation to hurt when the hurt is compensated by a benefit society has charged the profession with providing. Still, the truth does hurt and the truth-teller is responsible for the hurt. One should not play the professional role if one is not willing to accept the responsibility.

This unhappy feature of human intercourse imposes the further obligation to keep the hurt at a minimum. Truth should not be administered callously or brutally. Compassion is not excluded by professional objectivity or the limited nature of the professional—client relationship. The truth should be communicated only when it is necessary, at the proper time in the proper way. If it produces anguish or anxiety, guilt or despair, humiliation or painful self-evaluation, it should be communicated gently, diplomatically, constructively—if you will, with love.

But Not the Whole Truth

In the vision of the organic society, we imagine the occupants of all the essential positions voluntarily observing the norms for their roles and approving the behavior of other members. Such a society can be built only by open and veracious dialogue. Integrity in communication also would be essential to the day-to-day workings of the organic society to give each access to the information and points of view they need to serve the public competently.

Unless the ideal is handled carefully, it can evolve into a demand to open every detail of thought and conduct to public scrutiny. Such a demand runs straightway into conflict with the guarantees of confidentiality that compose one of the strongest elements in the traditional professional ethic.

Most professional codes are unclear on the subject of confidentiality. They do not address difficult questions about the extent and basis of the obligation.

Whose secrets must professionals preserve? Clients currently employing them or also those whose employ they have left?

Everyone in an employing organization or only those at the top? What about those with whom the employer is doing business?

What sorts of information are covered? That consciously confided by the client, that the professional chances on by virtue of the professional relationship, or all information whatever the source? Information about the client's affairs or discoveries about the world in which the employer claims a proprietary interest?

What are the exceptions to confidentiality? Are professionals permitted or obligated to disclose secrets when important client interests are at stake? How important? Must potential victims or the authorities be notified when the client plans to harm others? How serious must that harm be? Are reportable deeds restricted to prospective violations of the law? What about information about a client's past crimes? What about crimes of others from which the client benefits?

I shall not address these questions in detail. Our contextual and institutional approach makes it clear that they should be answered differently for different professions according to present or future responsibilities. For instance, the primary reasons for the existence of a professional clergy is to help some people work out their relationship to the ground of being. In the higher religions, a satisfactory relationship requires moral righteousness. The minister must share guilty secrets in order to give moral counsel. I cannot see that anything other than the intentions of a homocidal maniac should be disclosed to anyone else. Likewise, it is the responsibility of doctors to heal, not to enforce the law. They should not be required to report people suspected of crime or whose condition—gunshot or knife wounds—raise the suspicion that a crime has been committed.

On the other hand, some professions are assigned the task of probing in order to publicize facts about the subjects with whom they deal. Medical and sociological researchers experiment with humans in order to make facts about human beings public knowledge. Journalists observe and interview in order to report. The subjects of their investigations are not clients, so ordinary rules of confidentiality do not apply, though moral questions about intrusion into their affairs remain.

The law has proved the most difficult domain for drawing the boundaries of confidentiality. As an agent of the legal system, the lawyer's task is to get aspects of private lives into the public record so that justice will be done. A tortured argument is required to derive the obligation of confidentiality from the duty to promote justice. Hazzard nicely conveys the moral ambiguities here in exploring the implications of the ABA Model Rules, which so define 'secret' as to include "information gained in the professional relationship . . . the disclosure of which would be embarrassing or would likely be detrimental to the client." Lawyers are enjoined not to disclose secrets of clients. What does this mean when they discover that money paid to clients has been obtained by fraud or money paid by clients has been concealed to evade taxes or bribe public officials? Hazzard reports,

> In such circumstances, most lawyers keep silent, even if they have not merely suspicions but solid evidence of the wrongdoing of the nonclient. There are often impelling practical reasons for maintaining silence. If the crime or fraud is disclosed, the lawyer's client might be implicated as a joint or acquiescent wrongdoer. If a negotiation is pending between the lawyer's client and the wrongdoer, disclosure might upset a deal that the client needs, or frustrate a chance to get restitution to which the client is entitled. Furthermore, disclosure may mark the lawyer with his fellows as someone who tries not only to represent clients but to be a public police force as well. The problem of keeping silent about third-party wrongdoing therefore involves the question of what a lawyer may do for his client . . . it is clear that one thing he can do, at least up to a point, is to keep dirty secrets not only of his clients but of others as well.[20]

Similar complications arise for engineers as consultants and employees of firms that have questionable relationships with customers, the government, or their own employees.

We must sympathize with professions that shun policing functions. As one debater argued in the ABA deliberations regarding the recommendations of the Kutak Commission, lawyers have no desire to become the "conscience of the corporation." Nevertheless, they could be expected to give ethical counsel without becoming gumshoes or moles.

In general, however, very strong rules of confidentiality should be observed in most professional relationships, with obligations to disclose only when egregious malefaction or serious harm to the innocent is threatened and all alternatives to disclosure have been exhausted. The effort to obtain informed consent from the one with whom the confidentiality relation obtained would often be crucial.

Strong rules of confidentiality must be examined carefully

because they gain business for the professional by assuring clients of professional discretion. Our suspicions are aroused by the use of the service ideology in their justification. It is argued that society should abstain from monitoring professionals because it would seriously interfere with their ability to fulfill their more proper functions. Unless individuals believe their secrets will be preserved, they will not go to professionals for help or provide them the information to do their job or trust them enough to follow their advice. In view of the delicate role that lawyers play for people in trouble, it is not surprising to find this argument stated in the ABA Model Rules and extended by judges, who are lawyers, to other professional relationships such as medical and counseling ones.[21]

I believe that the ABA argument is sound, but it does not get to the roots of the desire for confidentiality. Bayles is right in tracing the obligation to keep secrets and the virtue of discretion that it delimits to a respect for privacy, which he defines as "the control of information about oneself." Privacy is a primary value and to enjoy it, one must have "freedom to pursue one's business without scrutiny by others unless one consents or they have a need to know."[22]

Of course, "the need to know" is the hooker. We have argued that violations of confidentiality are warranted in rare cases of justified paternalism and when danger to others is clear and serious. The reason for holding exceptions to a minimum is that the whole system of professionalism should be structured to serve individuals without harming others and privacy is an important value for those who are served. Professional acts generally are not directed to the preservation of privacy—they are intrusive by nature. The professional must gain access to the client's or employer's affairs to render service. But it is the professional's obligation to keep the intrusion to a minimum and avoid collusion with outsiders in extending it. The burden of proof, therefore, rests on the professional who would break a confidence.

Privacy as control of information about one's affairs is an exercise of autonomy. We want privacy so that we can make choices with ease and spontaneity, shielded from the pressures of public scrutiny and judgment. Many of us need solitude for meditation, communion with nature, the quiet enjoyment of art. We enjoy the pride of ownership over our thoughts and behavior, as well as our goods, and resent the intrusion of others. There are parts of our lives that might bring us public shame yet cause no great harm to others.

Not the least, privacy itself is a possession. Sharing it with those whom we choose is one of the joys of life; having it dissipated without our consent robs us of something precious. We voluntarily share our privacy with professionals as a condition for their help, which is why the intimacy and trust of the professional relationship is sometimes akin to friendship. As with bona fide friends, we rightfully feel betrayed when they break our confidences without our consent. We feel they have opened our private realm to public exposure.

At the same time that we voluntarily share more and more details of our lives with professionals, uninvited intrusions grow. The planet becomes more crowded and we are thrown against our neighbors. Social control in mass society becomes more difficult and more and more data are demanded to manage people for the common good. Thus, concern for computer, research, and media ethics is prominent in professional codes. The strategic position of the professions tempts society to enlist professionals as agents of control as attested by the duties imposed by some countries on journalists to spy on adversaries of the state and psychiatrists to "treat" dissidents. The professional is asked to sacrifice individuals for the benefit of society and the power of the profession.

The professional's obligation to protect confidences and the client's right to confidentiality are established fairly well in principle, but more could be done to implement them institutionally. Attention has been devoted to mechanisms in large organizations to handle charges of malfeasance properly without the need for external whistle-blowing. Stronger traditions for professionals to give ethical as well as technical advice to employers and clients and to withdraw from unethical relationships would protect all professionals. They would help professionals avoid the dilemmas posed by knowledge of guilty secrets. Professional covenants and effective guidelines for the employment of professionals would reduce the need for violation of confidences and make it easier for persons of limited conscientiousness to observe strict rules scrupulously.

Communicative Integrity in the Organic Society

Confidentiality viewed as respect for privacy is an element in respect for the client's autonomy. We derive the obligation of strict veracity from the same respect for autonomy. Veracity and confidentiality are two sides, the positive and negative, of the same ideal, communicative integrity. The integrity of communication is essential in building a society that is both technical and liberal, where specialized knowledge and autonomy both are enjoyed fully.

The organic society is not unified by controls over its members. It does not require prying and peeking into every cranny of private life. It is the antithesis of totalitarianism. It requires the moral development of individuals so that they, with maximum latitude for free action, will make enlightened choices under common principles using collective knowledge and skills. All have the opportunity to master the portion of knowledge necessary for their jobs and the opportunity to utilize the knowledge of others to meet needs they cannot meet for themselves. This requires the proper balance of protection of the right to privacy, where privacy can be allowed, and insistence on publicity, where publicity is necessary.

The position of the professions in contemporary society imposes on them the heavy burden of promoting communicative integrity. It gives the professional ideal the power to contribute mightily to the transformation of society if only it can take hold and first transform professions and professionals. If it does, veracity and confidentiality will be among its most important contributions of professionalism to civilization.

Notes

1. *The Dialogues of Plato*, 720B–E, vol. II, p. 491.
2. From the *Columbia Missourian*, (30 August 1979). Reprinted by permission of Newspaper Enterprise Association, Inc.
3. *The Path to Power*, p. 668.
4. See the case made by Weinreb in *Denial of Justice*, discussed by Ladenson in "Aversary Criminal Procedure and Ethics."
5. *Lying*, pp. 198–200.
6. *Ibid.*, pp. 96–100.
7. *Ibid.*, pp. 230, 107, and 105.
8. Bok refers to the inclusion of dupes in respect to particular practices on pp. 103, 108, 171, 200, 202–203, and 240–241.
9. These examples are discussed on pp. 66, 69, 161–162, and 200–202.
10. *Ibid.*, pp. 19–21. For other comparisons of force and deception, see. 43, 109, 217, and 225.
11. *Ibid.*, pp. 243, 244, and 250.

12.   Re altruism, see pp. 63, 65, 116, 175, and 224; re protection of the defenseless, see pp. 71, 221–222, and 225–226.

13.   *Ibid.*, p. 25.

14.   *Ibid.*, pp. 78 and 96.

15.   She discusses these exceptions on pp. 43–44, 60, 109–110, 114–118, 136–138, and 186.

16.   *Ibid.*, pp. 206–207.

17.   *The Moral Rules*, pp. 69–70 and 103–104.

18.   The reference is to Bayles's discussion of models in *Professional Ethics*, pp. 60–70.

19.   *Lying*, pp. 217–221.

20.   *Ethics and the Practice of Law*, pp. 31–32.

21.   One of the most discussed cases is *Tarasoff v. Regents of the University of California*, 529 P 2d 553.

22.   *Professional Ethics*, p. 83.

□ 14

PROFESSIONALISM SANS PROFESSIONS

The burden of this part of our discussion has been to establish the priority of ideals over rules in professional ethics and to gather materials to articulate the professional ideal. Rules and the institutional structures that implement them are important, but since one function is to provide an environment for the ideal, they should be designed to shape professionals according to the ideal and create a space in which professionals can act out the demands of the ideal.

It is now time to extract the elements of the ideal from the contexts in which we have found them and integrate them in a summary statement. Once we have done so, we will conclude with some remarks about how the ideal may be cultivated in the present social world.

The Professional Ideal and the Ideal Professional

I have urged that we should think of the ideal as the idea of what professionals should *be* rather than as a catalogue of what they should *do*. The professional ideal represents the ideal professional.

What a person is, however, displays itself in what he or she does. Professionalism as a fundamental formation of personality and character is only a disposition until it is released in a stream of actions. Actions actualize and reinforce dispositions and dispositions are valuable just because they shape actions.

Professionalism is valuable only because it is expressed in action. Indeed, its very existence is problematic until the professional behaves in certain typical ways. Hence, a formulation of the professional ideal must be validated by showing that it leads to the actions we expect of the professional, actions that are required by some comprehensive ideal, such as the organic society.

Valid rules of professional behavior codify the things that the true professional can be relied upon to do *as a rule*. This means that the professional usually will follow the consensual rules of the profession, sometimes even in circumstances that seem to warrant their violation. This is described as being a principled person and doing what is right as a matter of principle. The professional recognizes the importance of precedent and predictability in role behavior, yet without absolutizing rules. The professional has the insight and strength to depart from them when important circumstantial considerations dictate and may even pioneer new practices, resulting in new rules, in the novel circumstances of a rapidly changing society.

In view of the interconnection among ideals, virtues, role responsibilities, rules, and actions, the professional ideal must be defined in terms of the basic pattern of intellectual and moral virtues that disposes a person to act in the ways idealized in codes of professional ethics. However, since there is much to criticize in these codes and practices, the virtues also dispose the ideal professional to act somewhat differently than the norm. The success of our definition will be measured by how intelligible it makes the degree of conformity of the good professional to current practices and what causes departure from them.

For convenience in stating the ideal, I will refer to the professional as she and anyone with whom she deals as he; but of course ideals and virtues are gender-blind. Masculine and feminine words can be interchanged in this discussion without altering its meaning.

Also for convenience, I shall refer to the recipient of professional actions as the client but my statements can be adapted in obvious ways to relationships with patients, students, employers, customers, colleagues, subordinates, and bystanders.

Dedication to Service

The ideal of a professional is that of a person dedicated to providing proficient service to those who need it. Therefore, it will be helpful to summarize the essentials of the service component. The idea of proficiency will flow naturally from the discussion.

Professional service is highly specialized: Its primary focus is a particular human need for which a particular expertise, relatively narrow in scope but deep in content, is relevant. The primary recipients are people distinguished by the specific need, whatever their position in society. The professional's mission is to put expertise at the disposal of those who need it but are unable to acquire or exercise it for themselves.

Needs turn upon either harms or opportunities. Helping professions or helping components of professions are oriented to service for those who have suffered or are threatened with injury or misfortune. For this kind of service, the professional must have compassion, sympathy, concern. She must feel deeply for the anguish of others, yet control her feelings sufficiently to maintain the distance necessary for objective judgment. She must have the strength of character to sustain compassion, to continue to care for a constant stream of clients, without developing emotional calluses or burning out.

Enabling professions assist people in taking advantage of opportunities to achieve positive benefits. The burden on the professional in this kind of service is not as heavy. She needs zest and an ability to take vicarious satisfaction in the successes of others. She must have a general interest in human affairs. These qualities, while sometimes difficult to generate, are pleasant and exciting in contrast to the gruelling demands of compassion. It is less wearing to contribute to victories than to succor the defeated.

The importance of compassion and empathic zest are obvious enough. What is distinctive about professionalism is the difficulty of maintaining them under the circumstances of practice. They must survive the routinization of tasks and constant turnover of recipients. We have labeled these perduring attitudes objective concern—'concern' because it is other-directed, 'objective' because it employs rational and realistic measures.

Objective concern requires a deep-seated friendliness, but in a strictly circumscribed form. It requires the professional to care for and take care of people with whom she usually cannot and often should not establish intimacy.

Limitations on intimacy are imposed not only by the importance of objectivity but by the obligation of distributive justice.

The professional is provided an interesting and satisfying career by society or, to be precise, by institutions supported by levies on everyone in society. A professional career, therefore, is a privilege rather than a right, and the professional is obligated in fairness to provide benefits to all in society in return. She cannot indulge in favoritism.

The obligation to serve all has to be qualified a number of ways because there is no way to serve more than a few members of society, but it clearly forbids the professional from restricting her services to those who can pay or those who have the power to command. It requires her to seek out some of those in need who are not affluent or powerful. It requires her to support efforts by her profession and society to provide for the rest.

The obligation to repay society is supported by the virtue of public spiritedness, a commitment to improving society. The professional does not plead that she is too busy for the ordinary duties of citizenship. Beyond this she makes her expertise available for matters of public policy, legislation, judicial decisions, and education. She devotes time to improving her profession by participating in worthy associations, encouraging colleagues to do so, helping to discipline malfeasants, advancing the knowledge base of practice, raising the standards of competence, sharing her knowledge with colleagues and clients, and so on. Obviously no one professional is called upon to do all of these things, but each devotes a considerable part of her time to some of them in a balance dictated by common sense. The point is that it is not the mark of the true professional to sequester herself from all social interaction besides that involved in professional practice.

We have seen enough of the dynamics of professional life to realize that there are serious structural obstacles to a thoroughly fair delivery of professional services. This does not provide the individual professional an excuse to be less just; it obliges her to be more so. Her *sense* of justice, her *indignation* at injustice, her *desire* to set it right must be the stronger to circumvent the obstacles thrown up by society and fight to remove them.

The passion for justice is a function of dedication to service. 'Dedication' is a near synonym for 'devotion.' The etymological affiliation of 'devotion' with 'to vow' makes it an attractive term in this context. The professional is willing to vow fidelity to a vocation, the occupation to which she feels called by natural endowments and opportunity. Thus, we expect the devotion to others that follows upon formal vows.

The affiliation of 'dedication' with 'to declare' conveys the idea of professing in a weaker sense than vowing. To that extent 'dedication' is a less vigorous term than 'devotion.' But besides sharing with 'devotion' the idea of commitment to a responsibility, 'dedication' has a valuable second sense. It means a setting aside of something for an important, perhaps sacred purpose ("we can not dedicate—we can not consecrate—we can not hallow . . .")

The professional dedicates her career, she sets it aside and reserves it, for a purpose that transcends self-interest; namely, to provide a service that is not freely available elsewhere to those who need it. She consecrates her life to this purpose if she grounds her commitments in religious convictions. Even if she does not, she dedicates and devotes her life to proficient service for those in need.

Fairness requires not only that professional services be equally accessible to all, but that it be impartiality administered to those who receive it. The quality of the professional's actions is controlled by the needs of the client, not by whether or not he is a member of her family, circle of friends, or social caste. It is not that she serves friends less (to avoid favoritism) but rather that she strives to give the best service of which she is capable, the service she would want to give to a friend, even if the recipient is a stranger. Impartiality does not make her treat friends as strangers, but rather strangers as friends.

Dedication manifests itself in the public sphere as a burning sense of justice. Its primary expression in the individual sphere is diligence. The professional works to the limit of her time, energy, and emotional capital to meet client needs. Hard work traditionally has been the burden and privilege of professionalism. Here, we are saying that it does not merely reflect the fascination that good professionals find in their work; it reflects dedication to meeting the needs of others. It, therefore, springs from a fundamental desire to do one's part, to be a fit member of an organic society.

Another way to look at dedication is that it expresses itself in a pledge to the client to be worthy of the trust asked of him. This norm for personal relations echoes the notion of a covenant between the profession and society. The professional accepts employment on the condition that the client entrust an important part of his life to her hands. She implicitly promises to do the best she can to take care of it. This imposes on her the obligation to be as prepared as she can in anticipation of the assignment and to exercise the virtue of diligence when it is under way. Dedicated service, therefore, is a matter of fidelity to promises. It requires trustworthiness and loyalty.

Insofar as dedication expresses the impulse of justice, the desire to do one's part and provide for others in return for opportunities afforded one, it is a matter of loyalty to society. Applying Socrates' metaphor of the state as parent, we may say that the professional carries out responsibilities assigned to her profession in repayment of the nurturance that her society provides in the role of parent. We might refer to the motivation behind service as filial piety or even patriotism, but in view of the patriarchical roots of these terms (*filius* and *patria*) and remembering the attractiveness of the fiduciary model of professionalism, 'fidelity' is probably a better name.

Forms of Nonharm and Helpfulness

The power vested in the professional by virtue of her social position, expertise, and mystique is open to two sorts of abuse. She is in a position to exploit the client; that is, to harm him for her own or someone else's benefit. She also is in a position to treat him paternalistically; that is, to encroach on his autonomy in the hope of benefiting him.

The ideal of service obviously excludes exploitation. The professional, before anything else, takes care not to harm clients or third parties. She can be relied upon not to divide her loyalties or enter into arrangements that will pit them against one another, which may disperse her energy among competing parties, compromise her objectivity, or subject her to pressures or temptations to shift from an other-regarding to a self-regarding stance in her social relationships. These points are all emphasized in professional codes. They instruct the professional to avoid conflicts of interest, association with unsavory enterprises, acceptance of bribes and kickbacks, and the like.

But in more subtle ways the professional is required to be careful in the way she takes care of clients. She must be careful to make her qualifications and limits known before accepting employment. She must not accept assignments for which she is not qualified. She must warn her client when a course of action upon which he is bent is likely to fail. She must take responsibility, admit mistakes, give proper recognition to colleagues, and criticize them when the interests of the client are jeopardized. In other words, she must display the virtues of loyalty and trustworthiness with a clear vision of the priorities among those to whom loyalty is due.

Faithful agency does not extend to assistance to clients in illegal or immoral activities. The professional refuses to collaborate in such activities, she counsels or warns against them, she severs connection with their perpetrators, she blows the whistle. In view of the rewards of going along to get along and the penalities for rocking the boat, these steps involve progressively graver dangers. The scrupulous professional may reduce her effectiveness as agent for clients or even sacrifice her opportunity to practice at all. Paradoxically, the ideal of service may require actions that incapacitate one from service in order to preserve its conditions for others.

The ideal professional is a moral person. She refuses to be an agent in an immoral enterprise or to use immoral means in a legitimate one. However, we need a reminder here. In judging the obligations of the professional, hasty assumptions should not be made about what is moral. Role responsibilities may require different behavior than is appropriate to other roles, for example, silence where one would be expected to speak up or brutal candor where comfort and support might seem to be appropriate. The professional is equipped to make such judgments in view of an overall conception of her mission in society.

Determination not to harm and if possible to help others to achieve such benefits as health, justice, desirable structures and artifacts, education, and solace is the utilitarian dimension of the professional's dedication to service. The deontological dimension is respect for autonomy. To serve means to promote the good of the one served. An important good both in itself and as a foundation for many others is autonomy. This ability to make reasoned choices and carry them out effectively varies with people and for a given person with conditions in his life. The professional frequently has the opportunity to extend or restore—or diminish or block—its exercise.

Dedication to service patently excludes interference with the autonomy of clients to exploit them or the autonomy of others solely to serve the client. A little reflection shows that it also excludes most forms of professional paternalism, as we have discussed. What should be mentioned here are the personal qualities on which the avoidance of paternalism depends.

People are sometimes tempted into paternalism by compassion. We have observed that the professional keeps this emotion in control so that it will not interfere with objectivity. Objectivity in turn takes the subject's autonomy into account in assessing various kinds of intervention in his life.

Greater danger is posed by hubris. Confidence bred of expertise may mislead the professional into thinking that she knows best. Anxiety to get on with the technical task may make her impatient with the slow art of rational persuasion. She may disregard the importance of the client deciding and doing for himself.

The professional's social status reinforces exaggerated self-estimation. This makes the corrective all the more important. The true professional is humble. Not only does she see that there are colleagues who have equal or superior expertise, that she and they fall short of ideal mastery of the art, that there is always more to learn than has ever been learnt, that even what they do know is an inheritance from predecessors—but she also knows that clients have abilities and achievements in which she does not share at all. More important, she realizes that there is a basic identity between her and clients, that they are all moral agents and moral agency sets human beings apart from other creatures. The sameness of human beings and their community of interest are more important than differences in expertise. There is a fundamental egalitarianism in professional relationships. The "professional" who cannot respect her clients is no professional at all because she lacks the requisite knowledgeable dedication to service.

The professional takes justifiable pride in her proficiency and dedication to service. After all, she is also a person and respect for persons entails respect for self. But pride is not hubris and it associates quite comfortably with modesty, self-criticism, and objective self-knowledge, requirements for the professional if she is to present her abilities honestly to those who rely upon her.

Communicative Integrity and True Grit

It is possible to consummate professional transactions only if the integrity of the communicative process is maintained. Integrity of communication requires a complex of virtues on the part of the professional that we have called communicative integrity. Its centerpieces are veracity and candor, but it involves more; hence, the special name.

The professional is uniquely required to communicate accurately in order to do her work. She must share not only technical knowledge, but informed opinions about options, their possible consequences and merits. In other words, she must share what she can of the thoughts that will help clients become equal partners and neutralize the paternalism latent in professional relationships. Egalitarianism, of course, has to overcome the hubris and jealous possessiveness toward the expertise that sets the professional apart.

Strict veracity is essential in professional communication. So also is candor, since the client may not want to hear about his own limitations, possible failure, or moral weakness. He may also not want to accept the autonomy that the professional is obligated to press upon him.

Moreover, communication is interactive: It requires dialogue so that the one who takes the initiative can adjust her successive steps to the understanding of the other and, not incidentally, learn from the other knowledge useful in carrying out the task she has undertaken. Hence, the professional must demand candor and truth from the client. The client may not want to give it, so here again dedication to service requires determination and persistence.

There is more to communicative integrity than veracity and candor. In doing her job, the professional becomes privy to client confidences and facts about his private life. Confidentiality is a keystone of the professional ethic not just for the reasons given in codes (clients will not utilize professionals or provide them necessary information without its guarantee) but because respect for the client as a person demands protection of his privacy. Everyone needs an inviolable domain free of external pressure in which to initiate rational self-directed actions. One of the reasons for the existence of professionals is to help make such actions effective. It is obviously not compatible with this function to expose the client's private domain to public scrutiny without his consent.

Yet the obligation to speak out may take priority. The professional must disclose client secrets when important public interests are at stake; for example, when the client plans seriously harmful acts or tries to keep possession of basic discoveries that belong in the public domain.

The imperative to share thoughts and knowledge truthfully and candidly is primary to the professional's mission. Confidentiality provides a channel to guide communications to their proper destination. The channel is defined by boundaries between the public and private spheres drawn so as to maximize welfare and justice by fostering constructive autonomy and restraining its destructive use. Candor and confidentiality are balanced so as to enable the professional to carry out both special obligations to those whom she serves directly and general obligations to the moral community.

It is the professional's vocation to communicate. We cannot overemphasize how central this is to the kind of work she does. It is the root of the pedagogical imperative. In turn it is an expression of the basic obligation of justice, the obligation of the professional to return to society in proportion to what society has given to her, which also is expressed in dedication to service, diligence, and public spiritedness.

At several points where dedication to proficient service expresses itself in action, we have found serious social and psychological obstacles. Something like courage is necessary to overcome them. However, the kind of strength required in the professional context is more low keyed than 'courage' suggests. We might call it grit or sand. By whatever name, it is the strength to persist in one's commitments despite threats and temptations.

We noted that the professional who insists on doing what is right despite pressure from client or employer risks the loss of commission or employment. The professional who thrusts autonomy on the client exposes herself to his resentment. If she refrains from interfering when the client appears to be making mistakes, she risks the guilt of omission. The professional who accepts agency risks making mistakes that will inflict injury not only on herself, but on the client and outsiders. The vocation of the professional is to involve herself in the affairs of others, yet to do so is to risk mistakes, guilt, and condemnation.

Besides the threats that tend to deter energetic action, the professional also must overcome temptations that would seduce her from it; for example, to coast because of the repetitiveness of her tasks, to indulge in ego trips made possible by the professional mystique and charisma of skill, to go for the money and prestige in accepting employment. The grit necessary to persevere in service despite dangers also is necessary to persevere despite temptations.

Intellectual Virtues

Qualities of intellect and will are intimately interconnected. Certain intellectual abilities are necessary to make moral decisions and carry them out and consequently it is a moral obligation to develop and use those abilities. I have chosen to label the complex of skills of the true professional proficiency. Proficiency is what distinguishes her from the amateur and the professional who does not practice the professional virtues.

A number of synonyms of 'proficient' such as 'expert' and 'adept' would do as well. The root of 'proficient' means to make progress or go forward. The professional is proficient because she has advanced as far as possible in her discipline. The root of 'expert' means to have tried (as reflected in 'experience,' which is built on the same root). The professional is expert because she has tried out her practices and been tried (and found worthy) by their travails. 'Adept' is affiliated with having obtained. The professional is adept because she has obtained the skills necessary to practice well. All of these overtones of meaning are intended in our use of 'proficient.'

Professional proficiency involves both technical and what may be called moral skills. Three comments are in order about both sorts of skills. First, they vary from profession to profession, since they are determined by the nature of the work. We must be careful in our characterization of the professional not to imply that there are no significant differences between the physician, lawyer, teacher, engineer, counselor, and so forth. Likewise, when we characterize the moral skills required of the professional, it should be understood that not all are as prominent in some professions as others; for example, skill in interpersonal relations is not as central to some forms of engineering as to some forms of law.

Second, however, the obligation to acquire appropriate skills is the same for all professionals. So also is the obligation to acquire the specialized knowledge on which the skills are based. It is a *moral* obligation for the professional to be proficient. She must maintain state-of-art competence. She must not practice until she receives the proper training, she must practice only in areas in which she is trained, and she must continue training throughout her career. Being prepared is an obligation of diligence along with working hard on particular assignments.

Third, a profession is an art. Rather than concentrating on a narrow band of concepts under a unified theory, the professional (except, of course, the professional scientist) must master an eclectic group of concepts tied together only by their relevance to concrete problems. Hence, the professional must have broader intellectual curiosity than most pure scientists. To the point here, she must have perceptive powers akin to those of the artist. She must be able to see the universal in the particular as she applies disparate concepts to an endless procession of unique cases.

The fundamental intellectual virtue utilized in moral decisions is traditionally labeled practical wisdom. It is required to decide how to use technical skills. First of all, the professional needs a comprehensive vision of human welfare. She has to understand how the particular benefit in her charge—health, learning, justice, structures, products—is related to others under welfare. I have argued that this is critical for discharging the obligation of justice. The professional cannot know what is due others and what she is responsible for providing unless she is able to place her services in the context of other services.

Besides concepts of welfare and particular benefits, the professional must be able to see how each benefit can be realized in concrete circumstances. This ability is much like the power of perception, as Aristotle observes. It also can be viewed as common sense or good sense if it be recognized that it is not just a natural endowment but can be improved by practice.

Various forms of good sense are required by the moral virtues we have surveyed. Take for example communicative integrity. It requires the professional to share her thoughts on some occasions and conceal them on others. Many times it is no easy matter to decide whether to speak up, answer only if asked, refuse to say, or even dissimulate. Aristotle points out about moral judgments in general, "it is possible to go wrong in more ways that one . . . But there is only one way of being right. That is why going wrong is easy, and going right is difficult; it is easy to miss the bull's eye and difficult to hit it." To adapt his remarks on anger to speech: It is easy to babble irresponsibly, lie unconscionably, or remain stubbornly silent, but to speak the truth to "the right person and to the right extent and at the right time and with the right object and in the right way—that is not easy, and it is not everyone who can do it."[1]

It takes skill to communicate "in the right way." The professional must explain technical issues in nontechnical language that the client can understand. She also needs to know how to listen since she must learn from the client and other laypersons facts about the concrete conditions upon which she is to apply her art and she needs to learn the client's needs and values. She needs to provide the client with conditions for informed consent to the best course of action and determine whether he has given it, which may be difficult if he is inarticulate.

The various judgments required to communicate successfully illustrate need for the basic intellectual virtue of judgment or what we have called good sense. We noted that good sense is required in judgments applying technical rules to individual cases. It is also required in judgments about how types of human benefits enter the client's life as needs and opportunities.

Let us connect these points, labeled earlier as the epistemic ethic. It is a moral obligation for the professional to prepare herself to make the best judgments possible before being called upon to make them and to use the utmost care when she does make them.

There are two levels of judgment to be considered. On the first, the professional has to assess the needs of the client and decide how to address them, either directly applying her own expertise or assisting him to help himself.

At the second level, the professional must assess the soundness of her judgments at the first level. She does this proactively in deciding which assignments to accept. She does it concurrently with deciding upon services by reflecting on how well grounded are her estimates of what will work, what are the likely consequences and their probabilities. The client has a right to know not only the professional's estimate of objective probabilities, but how well founded her estimate is, especially when he risks vital benefits on her decisions. Likewise, the professional must decide how reliable her judgments are in deciding whether to overrule the prima facie objection to paternalism. To do so she must not only believe that her judgment of what is best for the client is far superior to his, but that she has adequate grounds for this assessment. And finally the professional must make judgments similar to her reflexive judgments about her own decisions in evaluating the performance of colleagues, as she is required to do to maintain the integrity of her profession.

To generalize, rational analysis is integral to professional work. The professional is obligated to develop logical virtues both to form objective hypotheses about external states of affairs and reflexive assessments of the credibility of such hypotheses. The virtues enable her to master general concepts, both those at the basis of her art and those that pertain to facts about the external world and the internal states of other people (those to be affected by her work) and herself (the one who must be relied on to do the work). They equip her, finally, to apply technical and moral concepts to the facts to institute changes for the better.

The Universality of the Ideal

The professional ideal has been defined in terms of what a professional should be, singling out virtues or acquired qualities of character and intellect central to the provision of proficient service.

Among the moral qualities of the true professional that lie at the basis of dedication to service are compassion and empathic zest blended into objective concern; justice or fairness expressed both in receptivity toward potential clients and public spiritedness; the courage or grit to persist in service despite dangers and temptations; fidelity to people and promises; respect for autonomy and privacy; communicative integrity; and humility and objectivity.

In respect to intellectual virtues, emphasis has been placed on the ability to think abstractly and use judgment in applying the general to the particular. These virtues are integral to both technical and moral skills, to mastering the art of manipulating the subject matter of one's occupation and the art of helping other people in ways that enlarge rather than curtail their autonomy.

The institutional structure of professions does not develop these qualities to maximal degree in all professionals, nor does it permit the qualities to be fully expressed without cost to those who do acquire them. Measured by the ideal, professions stand in need of improvement. Nevertheless, something like ideal professionals emerge in sufficient numbers to make professionalism a major social resource. The professions must be credited with bringing the ideal of professionalism to the forefront of modern consciousness and making it an option for some members of society.

But is it an exclusive *possession* of the professions? Should they *monopolize* it? Perhaps they *must* in the sense that it can be realized only in the kind of work they do or only under the institutions they provide?

Or, to the contrary, should professionalism not be a model for everyone in every occupation? Would we not want everyone to do his or her work as professionally as possible?

The professional virtues as forms of human excellence can be developed and hence they can be deliberately pursued and cultivated. Our survey reveals that all are relevant to features of work as such, not just features of particular kinds of work. While some virtues—for example, the ability to think abstractly and apply concepts to cases or the capacity to feel compassion and yet maintain objectivity—are more important in some forms of work than others, none is entirely restricted to any particular form and the complex of professional virtues is not so relevant to a particular set of forms as to set them apart as "professional" in any strong sense. In a word, the professional virtues are relevant to all forms of work. We have good grounds for saying that professionalism should be universalized.

To be more specific, in an organic system of specialized social labor, each member of society would contribute to every other by diligent and expert work. Contributing one's fair share to society in this way would give meaning to work and raise it above the level of mere necessity and self-interest. And since work is a central part of life, the meaningfulness of work would go a long way toward giving meaning to life.

There is no reason in fact or justice to restrict meaningful work to one group of occupations. It should be available to everyone. But it will be objected that the demands of competition and productivity make it necessary for the majority of the labor force to work under conditions where the professional virtues are simply superfluous. The answer to this objection has two parts.

The first is that some degree of professionalism is possible on almost every job and any degree is better than none at all. Even workers on the assembly line can be concerned with quality and conscientious about carrying out their assignments, and they will respect themselves more if they are. This is certainly true of other relatively unskilled jobs that allow more initiative, such as farm labor.

The second part of the answer is that the very fact that many jobs do not provide much scope for the professional virtues is a reason to criticize the way those jobs are organized. It is a problem that needs to be addressed by the societies in which professions flourish. The challenge is to alter the conditions of other kinds of work so as to foster greater self-development and self-expression and to provide conditions in which workers will know and approve the products of their labor. Introducing variety into routine work, involving workers in its management, and other techniques should be tried not just to increase productivity, but because society is obligated to enable its members to find meaning in their work and lives. It is one more professional challenge to find the way.

Ideals and Moral Suasion

Universalization of professionalism requires action on two fronts. Professions need to be reformed so that they will populate themselves with more members who consistently put the ideal ahead of other considerations. And the prejudice must be broken that professionalism is only for professionals.

In addressing the first problem, a fundamental change in attitude must somehow be brought about. To do so, we must come to terms with an unfortunate psychological fact. Making some norms mandatory by formal sanctions or even peer pressure diverts attention from other norms put forward as ideals that are to be pursued primarily for the intrinsic value of living by them. Enforcement of even broad limits on conduct tends to transmute the moral into the prudential point of view.

This may be illogical but it does take place. It is reflected in the way professional associations sell morality to their members. Having codified rules and established enforcement mechanisms, they think it necessary to persuade practitioners that ethics pays in terms of professional success. Unfortunately, they leave the impression that ideals are not worth adherence when adherence does not pay.

We have observed that the limited sanctions available to professional institutions result in punishment of only the most egregious malefactors and individuals can cut ethical corners with impunity if they are discreet. Since the struggle for professional employment, business, and clients is a competitive affair, those who do not cut corners may come in second in the competition. For example, it is sometimes a handicap to observe agreements scrupulously, be honest about one's limitations, admit mistakes, avoid conflicts of interest, or blow the whistle on colleagues or superiors. This unhappy fact of life appears to frighten leaders of professions. They earnestly desire ethical behavior, at least in others. They are not convinced that practitioners will be sufficiently attracted by morality for its own sake to behave as they should. They are not able to make morality pay consistently. They, therefore, are forced to pretend that it does pay in order to persuade others to behave as they wish them to. Speakers for professional associations promulgate the myth.

To illustrate: John Carey maintains that ethics pays for accountants in a two step argument. First, he maintains that an association's ethical code (in his case, that of the American Institute of Certified Public Accountants) reflects an effort to protect the profession's reputation in the interest of all of its members.

> A code of ethics . . . is a set of rules or precepts designed to induce a type of behavior on the part of practitioners of the profession concerned that will maintain public confidence. This is a very practical purpose. The practicality of the rules of ethics in the accounting profession is shown partly by the manner in which the rules were developed. Nobody ever sat down and wrote what he thought would be an ideal code of behavior for certified public accountants. On the contrary, most of the rules were developed as a result of the incidents which came before the governing bodies of the accounting societies, and which they feared might impair the confidence in the profession if repetition were not prevented in the future.

This frankly states that the code is primarily a public relations document.

Carey recommends the code to individuals on the basis of self-interest. The accountant must follow it if he is to maintain his reputation and retain his clients.

> Relationships may shift very rapidly in the business world. A client for whom an accountant tried too assiduously to reduce a tax bill might, as a stockholder, wonder if the same accountant would display similar zeal in the interests of the management. Even the beneficiaries of practices bordering on the unethical would be likely to lose their respect for an accountant who forgets his professional responsibilities in the hope for financial rewards.[2]

Unfortunately the moral is not that one should be ethical, but that one should be discreet so that one's reputation for ethics is maintained.

The disastrous consequences of this approach have been noted by moralists since ancient times. Plato has Adeimantus observe that when parents and teachers praise justice for its rewards, children—no dummies they—see that the same rewards can be won by *seeming* just without the burden of *being* so. They resolve to practice injustice while cultivating the appearance of justice: "I will describe around me a picture and shadow of virtue to be the vestibule and exterior of my house; behind I will trail the subtle and craft fox . . ."[3] And Kant, while conceding to Aristotle that pleasure and pain must be used to habituate a person to right action and allow him to experience its satisfactions,[4] argues,

> as soon as this mechanical work, these leading-strings, have produced some effect, then we must bring before the mind the pure moral motive, which, not only because it is the only one that can be the foundation of a character (a practically consistent habit of mind with unchangeable maxims), but also because it teaches a man to feel his own dignity, gives the mind a power unexpected even by himself, to tear himself from all sensible attachments so far as they would fain have the rule, and to find a rich compensation for the sacrifice he offers, in the independence of his rational nature and the greatness of soul to which he sees he is destined.[5]

The attempt to derive morality from self-interest is not only mistaken, it is pernicious. It seduces us from respect for the moral law and its command to do what is right despite contrary inclinations, desires, and appetites.

True morality is taught, Kant instructs us, by the example of heroes who sacrifice all to duty, not people who happen to prosper by doing what it requires. In this way Kant hopes to teach people to "feel their own dignity" and find a "rich compensation" for doing their duty at whatever cost in "the independence of their rational nature and the greatness of soul to which they see they are destined."

Are there any reforms in professions and other institutions that shape people before or independently of whether they become professionals that might help instill the ideal of professionalism for its own sake?

My last remarks will be devoted to a review of what might be done to make the professions more effective in producing and supporting true professionals and to universalize the professional ideal for all work. Though the professions have created the ideal, they do not have exclusive proprietary rights to it. I will suggest how their hold on it might be loosened while at the same time trying to see that they adhere more closely to it.

What Can Be Done

Let me briefly review my proposals for reconstructing professions to promote the ideal of professionalism among their own members. In view of the danger of giving further power to groups that have not proved worthy of the power they have seized, I am not ready to advocate the Durkheimian constitution of professions as political estates without a fundamental reconstitution of society. Nor do I advocate any program that would impose the same form on all occupations. Trial and error no doubt would reveal that some elements of the functionalist model would work for some occupations but not others, both for those currently recognized as professions and those denied the title. Hence, I do not urge that all occupations professionalize and certainly not that current professions further distance themselves from other occupations. Nevertheless, a few across-the-board reforms are attractive.

1. Professional associations should continue to try to perfect their codes. We have discussed modifications in the content of codes in view of the professional ideal and measures to increase their clarity and logical form. We have argued that rules need to be derived from a defensible moral philosophy based on a sound understanding of the dynamics of the particular occupation. There is no reason to start from

scratch. Codes exist. They have valid content and at least lip service is paid them. Moreover, the professions contain people of good will and ordinary conscientiousness. If properly challenged, they would be willing to sacrifice some privileges for meaningful reforms. They would accept codes and ideals that authentically spoke to their conscience and represented more than an ideological facade.

2. The public, acting through political representatives and assisted by intelligentsia from outside particular occupations, should be involved more intimately in shaping and implementing occupational codes. No group's moral standards are its sole responsibility. Standards concern all of society because they affect everyone in it. Perhaps the idea of professional covenants designed for the common good, drawn up by the professions and the rest of society, and voluntarily accepted by both parties is utopian. The country is too large and complex for the public to inform itself and act very effectively. But steps in this direction could not help but improve the situation.

3. Time and again, we have observed how good intentions and high pretensions are subverted by the competitive economic environment. Anyone interested in effective reform must continue to seek arrangements that would ensure competent practitioners a decent but not excessive income. Temptations as well as pressures are the enemy of ideals. They must be limited to allow the intrinsic interest of competent work and its moral imperatives to come to the fore. In some cases, this might require public ownership of organizations that employ professionals as in education and social work. In others, the objective might be achieved incident to pursuit of distributive justice by requiring public services from privately employed professionals or heavily taxing their income.

4. Some social controls are legitimate though they limit freedoms because they clear a space for more important or legitimate ones. Some powers of professionals and those who make use of professionals must be limited to protect the opportunity of moral professionals to act conscientiously. Disciplinary mechanisms of quasipublic professional associations or agencies of the state are necessary to deter gross malfeasance. By chartering professions and perfecting their codes, a de jure basis would be provided for the task. Then more resources might safely be devoted to making enforcement work. But in view of the monopolistic tendencies of the professions, safeguards are necessary to prevent abuse and these limit the degree of control that is

possible. The most we can hope is to establish institutions strong enough to enable persons of limited good will and ordinary conscientiousness to follow their conscience without undue sacrifice or heroic virtue in a world in which unscrupulous competitors remain.

5. This leads to the crucial role of moral training. Morality must be taught for its own sake despite the existence of rewards and punishments to encourage proper behavior. The inculcation of work ethic must begin at the beginning of the cultivation of character, in the home, school, church, and workplace, well before people are exposed to the social-izing institutions connected with a lifelong career. For this it would be essential to universalize the professional ideal. People need to be taught to value professionalism long before they learn what their work will be.

I will not attempt to specify how this might be done, but I will make a few comments about the final stage, the kind of moral education that should occur in the professions on the basis of the already well formed character of the people entering it. While moral training in professional schools is a means to a further end, moral practice in professional life, it also may be viewed as an end for which prior training is designed. A consideration of the end will suggest things about the prior stages that lead up to it, though I shall leave the suggestions undeveloped.

Cultivation of Character

In the absence absolute control over another's physical and social environment, one cannot *make* the other into a particular sort of person. One can only provide conditions that will encourage his or her natural tendencies to realize themselves.

The control over individuals that institutions of the professions have and should have is limited. They are agencies of socialization, but those whom they socialize are already adults with ingrained habits, beliefs, and attitudes. The professions, therefore, can only invite and equip individuals to become true professionals, that is, not just certified as a professional engineer or whatever, but deeply committed to the professional ideal and incorporating its virtues in their character. This invitation is important. Entry into the profession is a voluntary act and most people who perform it are disposed to learn its ways and take its ideology seriously. They need only be told how.

Clearly, the professional school plays the critical role. Professional associations and peer groups continue the process of socialization, but these are not likely to be effective if the individual is not aimed in the proper direction at the outset. Unfortunately, professional elites, who exercise considerable control over the curricula of schools, think of moral training as indoctrination in group standards and appeal to prudence rather than genuinely moral intentions to persuade people to follow those standards.

It is easy to understand why those who profit from the social system cherish indoctrination and detest criticism. Indoctrination does not raise questions about the system behind it. Moreover, indoctrination is easier than critical education. It can be handled expeditiously without diverting time from technical training. As a ceremonial exercise, ritual recitation of professional codes and creeds provides an outlet for moral impulses without forcing difficult choices. Dogmatic ethics thus helps the system work without calling attention to its flaws, whereas searching criticism causes difficulties everywhere.

If the established elites of professions cannot be expected to take the lead in inculcating ideals that generate critical attitudes toward the status quo, the burden must fall on educators. They must break rank with the leadership if necessary.

The potential is there. Faculties of professional schools are not directly accountable to employers with a material interest in their philosophy. Their students have not yet identified with the profession, committed themselves to its special interests, or fully absorbed its ideology. The academic profession has won strong guarantees of freedom to think, speak, and criticize for both faculty and students.

Thus professional schools have the opportunity to pump practitioners into society with new ideas about the old ways of doing things, critical conceptions of the corporate responsibilities of occupations, and a healthy skepticism about the way institutions actually work.

Some progress has been made in the education of critical professionals. One thinks of new specialties such as public interest law, public health medicine, and environmental engineering, and activist groups such as Physicians, Lawyers, and Educators for Social Responsibility. But I have in mind particularly the socially conscious, critical, and innovative professionals in *all* specialities and *all* modes of employment, penetrating *all* institutions and working their way up to positions of influence in *every* hierarchy. Professional schools have an unrivaled opportunity to be a leaven for society by turning out this sort of graduate.

Traditional ways of teaching ethics and social responsibility are not adequate. Training in codes, etiquette, and business practices stultifies the critical spirit if not salted with the dialectical methods of philosophical thought turned upon fundamental questions of human existence. The philosophy of work has received this kind of attention only in recent times.

I have in mind an education in which students are exposed to no-holds-barred debates on the ethical dilemmas of professional practice and every position—radical, reformative, conservative, reactionary—regarding the socioeconomic system and the place of professions in it. Students should not only witness debates, but be required to enter into them. An informed, practiced, and critical grasp of alternative moral and social perspectives should become as integral an element of professionalism as technical skill.

I shall not propose a comprehensive plan for professional education. I shall only suggest that it needs be quite different than it typically is. Its aim must be breadth of vision as well as depth of expertise. It must cultivate judgment as well as impart theoretic knowledge. It must develop interpersonal skills and nurture growth of the individual as a person not just as a technician. It must bring to life the vision of a better society and a passion to contribute to it. It must arouse a deep and abiding resolution to become fit for membership in the ideal moral community. Professional education is not geared to attempt these things in any serious way.

The Fate of Profession

To end the proprietary claim of professions to professionalism, I recommend the systematic subversion of the generic distinction between professions and other kinds of occupations that, as we have seen, sets them apart in status and power. This recommendation may seem incompatible with the ideas just advanced about professional education and the possible reforms in the structure considered in Part III. How can we propose both the end of profession and the reform—that is, preservation and strengthening—of professional institutions?

The point is that an experimental approach should be taken to the organization of occupations. Components of the functionalist model may indeed be appropriate for different occupations, but this is no reason for this or any model to be taken as a single pattern for a limited number of occupations and used to measure their worthiness for superior status. It certainly is no reason for believing that the professional ideal can be realized only in "professions," by the members of occupations that are so labeled by society or social scientists.

My modest proposal, therefore, is that the social sciences abandon 'profession' as a descriptive term. Little would be lost for analytical purposes. Semantically, the term is more obscurant than illuminating. It has become encrusted with a family of different meanings as ever more occupational groups have claimed it for themselves. The family continues to grow as new occupations are created by technological advances. Common elements of meaning become ever more attenuated. "The" meaning for any given speaker becomes more and more nebulous.

Sociologists have tried to staunch the semantic hemorrhage by essentialist definitions of ideal types. Their failure to come up with useful generalizations, not to mention explanatory theories with predictive power, has demonstrated the bankruptcy of the approach. We have suggested that the reason is that the product, the functionalist model, is an ideological rather than a scientific tool.

The abandonment of 'profession' as a technical term would not mean that it would pass out of the vocabulary of social scientists. They would continue to *refer* to the term as long as it continues to be *used* by people in society. By investigating its ideological role, they would explain its use without legitimating it.

Social scientists, even of the conflict persuasion, are not ready to conclude that the category leads to conceptual dead ends. None seem ready to jettison it. Habenstein comes closest. After reviewing its vagaries of use, he remarks, "In my judgment, 'profession' does not have the stature of a sociological category, that is, of a concept with analytic power, describing a limited number of characteristics whose relations and order are demonstrable."[6] However, he does not conclude that it be dumped. Rather it might be salvaged to deal with "the way human associations function to handle emotional crisis, stress, and vulnerability of self in modern societies." Professions are occupations that perform this function in a distinctive way. "From this point of departure, which we might label offhand as the 'crisis-stress' approach, we may better be able to develop a body of propositions to serve as a theoretical flooring for those who seek to expand knowledge in the nebulous area of the sociology of the professions."[7]

This theoretical flooring is yet to be laid. If it is true that otherwise the concept of profession lacks analytic power, its drawbacks warrant discarding it. Alternative concepts tracing reality along different lines would permit the social scientist to escape not only the semantic confusion of ordinary usage, but the blandishments of ideology and cooptation by occupations on the make.

One reason *not* to drop the category is that a set of occupations do display similar characteristics because they have imitated the structure of the medical and legal professions in the hope of emulating their success in the professional project. The functionalist model might be viewed as a plan for social engineering rather than a representation of reality.

I have argued, however, that it is not a very good plan from the standpoint of the interests of society. Which "professional" institutions are best for helping ensure that an occupation will make its proper contribution to society must be decided on a case-by-case basis. Certainly it is not evident a priori that all occupations should be like the medical profession (or even that the medical profession should be exactly like it is). The functionalist model should not be used uncritically for normative purposes any more than for descriptive purposes, and social scientists should not legitimate either use by continuing to advance the model as if it somehow represents reality.

What about the utility of the word 'profession' in universalizing the professional ideal? Whatever we think, it cannot be banished from the popular lexicon. I therefore shall make another proposal. Instead of jealously guarding the term for a few select occupations and inventing denigrating border categories, such as semiprofession or marginal profession, why not encourage the use of the term for all occupations that want it? Call *all* occupations professions, careers, and vocations. This would dilute the prestige of the labels and discourage the unseemly struggle to monopolize them. Their use would become casual and dispensable. At the same time, the professional ideal could be promoted. After all, the honorific connotations of the professional terminology reflect a widespread popular response to true professionalism. The response reflects a preanalytic appreciation of a form of human excellence. There are good reasons to call that form of excellence by its established name.

To summarize, profession should be abandoned as an ideological category that sets some occupations apart from the rest in a social hierarchy, as an analytical concept for theoretical generalizations in social science, and as a normative pattern for select occupations to emulate. Professionalism should be rescued from the social structures in which it is embedded and recognized as a personal ideal available to all who work. What is needed is professionalism without professions.

Postscript

I shall end as I began, with a personal note. In attempting to put the professional ideal into words, I have been aware of coming to know myself. I have articulated what I sensed and admired when I faced the fundamental choice of an occupation to which I would devote my life. What I wanted but only vaguely understood was an opportunity to do my best at a job that would utilize my native talents, challenge me to a form of excellence, and indisputably contribute to the welfare of others.

From the outset, the ideal told me that whatever work I chose, I should do a professional job of it. I should become as skillful as I could and use my skills to the best of my ability. Upon reflection, the ideal now tells me that the most unprofessional thing is to forget what the skills are for. If I have done my job well for the right purpose, my life has substance and meaning. If I have done my job poorly or for the wrong purpose, I have squandered my life, however much I have prospered.

I recognize these values as a heritage. Both of my parents admired professionals without the opportunity of becoming such. Each displayed the virtues I describe, though the one lacked a higher education and devoted his life to business and the other, though enjoying an education, eschewed a profession to maintain a home. Both displayed the dignity of hard work done intelligently in the service of others. Both were more professional than most professionals.

There is no way to repay our parents except by passing on the gifts they have given us. The most important of these are values. I hope that I have had a part in conveying the professional ideal to my children. Whether or not this is so, they are without exception able, just, and compassionate people who devote their talent to honorable occupations. They may in turn inculcate similar values in *their* children. I may hope, therefore, that my heritage has become a legacy.

In this work I have expressed frustration at the structure of society, which seems incapable after all these centuries to put the abilities of human beings to the most beneficial use. But, to be fair, I must also express gratitude at the opportunity for professional life for myself and my family. More generally, I am obliged to give my society and its culture credit for making the sturdy spirit of professionalism widely available to fortify individuals with stoicism and compassion to face the fate of the human species whatever it may prove to be. Professionalism also provides a basis for human solidarity across class and national boundaries, which in some meager way may help human history turn out right.

The professions bitterly disappoint us for falling victim to the imperfections of human nature and human institutions. The professional spirit is a ray of hope in the lowering gloom.

Notes

1. *Nicomachean Ethics*, Book II, Chapters 7 and 9, pp. 66 and 73.
2. "The Realities of Professional Ethics," p. 120.
3. The Republic, 365c, in *The Dialogues of Plato*, Vol. I, p. 628.
4. *Nicomachean Ethics*, Book. II, Chapters 1–2, pp. 55–61.
5. *Kant's Critique of Practical Reason*, p. 250 (Rosenkrantz, p. 301).
6. "Critique of 'Profession' as a Sociological Category," p. 298.
7. *Ibid.*, p. 300.

APPENDIX

Ethical Codes of Professional Associations
Discussed in Text

American Association of University Professors: Statement on Professional Ethics (1969)

American Bar Association: Model Code of Professional Responsibility (1980)

American Dental Association: Principles of Ethics (1980)

American Football Coaches Association: Code of Ethics (1953)

American Institute of Certified Public Accountants: Rules of Conduct (1973)

American Medical Association: Principles of Medical Ethics (1980)

American Nursing Association: Code for Nurses (1976)

American Psychological Association: Ethical Principles of Psychologists (1981)

American Personnel and Guidance Association: Ethical Standards (1972)

American Society of Chartered Life Underwriters: Professional Attitude and Code of Ethics (1961)

American Veterinary Medical Association: Principles of Veterinary Medical Ethics (1970)

Engineers Council for Professional Development: Code of Ethics for Engineers (1977)

Institute of Electrical and Electronic Engineers: Code of Ethics (1979)

National Association of Realtors: Code of Ethics (1970)

National Association of Social Workers: Code of Ethics
(1980)
National Council of Engineering Examiners: Model
Rules of Professional Conduct (1979)
National Association of Life Underwriters: Code of
Ethics (1973)
National Society of Professional Engineers: Code of
Ethics (1981)
Sigma Delta Chi (Professional Journalists): Code of
Ethics (1973)

BIBLIOGRAPHY

Alexander-Smith, Robin. Commentary. *Business and Professional Ethics Journal* I, 3 (Spring 1982): 71–73

Anderson, Robert, *et al. Divided Loyalties.* West Lafayette IN: Purdue University Press, 1980.

Aristotle. *The Nicomachean Ethics.* Translated by J. A. K. Thompson. London: George Allen & Unwin, 1953.

Arneson, Richard J. "Mill versus Paternalism" *Ethics* XC, 4 (July 1980): 470–489.

Auerbach, Jerold S. *Unequal Justice.* New York: Oxford University Press, 1976.

Bachrach, Peter. *The Theory of Democratic Elitism.* Boston: Little, Brown, 1967.

Baier, Kurt. *The Moral Point of View.* (Abridged Edition) New York: Scott Foresman, 1970.

——."Responsibility and Action." In *The Nature of Human Action,* edited by Myles Brand. New York: Scott Foresman, 1970.

Barber, Bernard. "Some Problems in the Sociology of the Professions." In *The Professions in America,* edited by Kenneth Lynn. Boston: Houghton Mifflin, 1965.

Baum, Robert, and Albert Flores, eds. *Ethical Problems in Engineering.* Troy NY: Renssalaer Polytechnic Institute, 1978. Second edition, two volumes, 1980.

Bayles, Michael. *Professional Ethics.* Belmont CA: Wadsworth, 1981.

Beauchamp, Tom L., and James F. Childress. *Principles of Biomedical Ethics.* New York: Oxford University Press, 1979.

Benn, S. I. "Freedom, Autonomy and the Concept of a Person," *Proceedings of the Aristotelian Society* LXXXVI (1975–1976): 109–130.

Bentham, Jeremy. *An Introduction to the Principles of Morals and Legislation.* New York: Hafner Publishing Co., 1948.

Berger, Peter L., and Thomas Luckmann. *The Social Construction of Reality*. Garden City NY: Doubleday, 1967.

Bok, Sissila. *Lying: Moral Choice in Public and Private Life*. New York: Random House, 1979.

Bowen, H. R. "Business Management: A Profession?" *The Annals of the American Academy of Political and Social Science* CCXCVII (January 1955): 111–117.

Bradley, F. H. *Ethical Studies*. 2nd ed. London: Oxford University Press, 1962.

Brandt, Richard. "A Defense of Utilitarianism." *The Hastings Center Report* XIII, 2 (April 1983): 37–43.

———. "Some Merits of One Form of Rule-Utilitarianism." *University of Colorado Studies, Series in Philosophy*, No. 3. Boulder CO: University of Colorado Press, 1967.

———."Toward a Credible Form of Utilitarianism." In *Morality and the Language of Conduct*, edited by Hector-Neri Castenada and George Naknikian. Detroit: Wayne State University Press, 1963.

Brodbeck, May. "Explanation, Prediction, and 'Imperfect Knowledge.' " In *Minnesota Studies in the Philosophy of Science*, Vol. III. Minneapolis: University of Minnesota Press, 1962.

Buchanan, Allen. "Medical Paternalism." *Philosophy and Public Affairs* VII, 4(1978): 370–398.

Callicott, J. Baird. "Animal Liberation: A Triangular Affair," *Environmental Ethics* II, 4 (Winter 1980): 311–338.

Callis, Robert, Sharon K. Pope, and Mary E. DePauw. *APGA Ethical Standards Casebook*. Falls Church VA: American Personnel and Guidance Association, 1982.

Carey, John. "The Realities of Professional Ethics" *The Accounting Review* (April 1947): 119–123.

Caro, Robert A. *The Path to Power: The Years of Lyndon Johnson*. New York: Alfred A. Knopf, 1982.

Carr-Saunders, A. M., and P. A. Wilson. *The Professions*. Oxford: The Clarendon Press, 1933.

———."Professions" *Encyclopedia of the Social Sciences*. New York: The Macmillan Company, 1934.

Centers, Richard. "Toward an Articulation of Two Approaches to Social Class Phenomena." *International Journal of Opinion and Attitude Research* IV (1950): 499–514; and V (1951): 159–178.

Christie, A. G. "A Proposed Code of Ethics for All Engineers." *The Annals of the American Academy of Political and Social Science* CI (May 1922): 97–104.

Clapp, Jane. *Professional Ethics and Insignia*. Metuchen NJ: The Scarecrow Press, 1974.

Cogan, Morris L. "The Problem of Defining a Profession," *The Annals of the American Academy of Political and Social Science*, CCXCVII (January 1955): 105–111.

———."Toward a Definition of a Profession." *Harvard Educational Review* XXIII (1953): 33–50.

Collins, Randall. *The Credential Society.* New York: Academic Press, 1979.

Crew, A. *The Profession of Secretary.* Cambridge, 1942.

Dahl, Robert A. *A Preface to Democratic Theory.* Chicago: University of Chicago Press, 1956.

Drinker, H. S. *Legal Ethics.* New York: William Nelson Cromwell Foundation, 1953.

Durkheim, Emile. *Lecons de Sociologie Physique des Moeurs et du Droit.* Paris: Universitaires de France, 1950. *Professional Ethics and Civic Morals.* Translated by Cornelia Brookfield. London: Routledge and Kegan Paul, 1957.

Dworkin, Gerald. "Paternalism." *The Monist,* LVI, 1. Also, in *Morality and the Law,* edited by R. A. Wasserstrom. Belmont CA: Wadsworth Publishing Co., 1971.

Elliott, Philip. *The Sociology of the Professions.* New York: Herder and Herder, 1972.

Engineers Council for Professional Development. *47th Annual Report.* New York: The Council, 1979.

Ettling, John. *The Germ of Laziness.* Cambridge MA: Harvard University Press, 1981.

Etzioni, Amitai, ed. *The Semi-Professions and Their Organization.* New York: The Free Press, 1969.

Ewing, David. *Do It My Way or You Are Fired.* New York: John Wiley and Sons, 1982.

———. *Freedom Inside the Organization.* New York: McGraw-Hill, 1977.

Feinberg, Joel. "Legal Paternalism." *Canadian Journal of Philosophy* I, 1 (1971): 105–123.

Feuer, Lewis S. *Ideology and the Ideologists.* New York: Harper and Row, 1975.

Flexner, Abraham. "Is Social Work a Profession?" *School and Society* I, 26 (June 26, 1915): 901–911.

Fowler, H. W. *A Dictionary of Modern English Usage.* New York: Oxford University Press, 1950.

Frankena, William. *Ethics.* Englewood Cliffs NJ: Prentice-Hall, 1963.

Freidson, Eliot. "Client Control and Medical Practice." *American Journal of Sociology* LXI (1960): 374–382.

———. *Profession of Medicine.* New York: Dodd and Mead, 1970.

———, ed. *The Professions and Their Prospects.* Beverly Hills CA: Sage Publications, 1971.

Galtung, Johan. *The True Worlds.* New York: The Free Press, 1980.

Garceau, Oliver. *Political Life of the American Medical Association.* Cambridge MA: Harvard University Press, 1941.

Gert, Bernard. *The Moral Rules.* New York: Harper and Row, Torchbook Edition, 1973.

Goldman, Alan H. *The Moral Foundations of Professional Ethics.* Totowa NJ: Rowman and Littlefield, 1980.

Goode, William J. "Community within a Community," *American Sociological Review* XXII (1957): 194–200.

————."Encroachment, Charlatanism and the Emerging Professions." *American Sociological Review* XXV (December, 1960): 902–914.

————."The Theoretical Limits of Professionalization." In *The Semi-Professions and Their Organization*, edited by Amitai Etzioni. New York: The Free Press, 1969.

Goodpaster, Kenneth. "On Being Morally Considerable." *The Journal of Philosophy* LXXV, 6 (1978): 308–325.

Gramsci, Antonio. *Prison Notebooks*. New York: International Publishers, 1971.

Greenwood, Ernest. "Attributes of a Profession." *Social Work*, II (1957): 45–50.

Habenstein, R. A. "A Critique of 'Profession' as a Sociological Category." *Sociological Quarterly* IV (1963): 291–300.

Halevy, Elie. *The Growth of Philosophic Radicalism*. Boston: Beacon Press, 1966.

Halmos, Paul. *The Personal Service Society*. New York: Schocken Books, 1970.

————. *Professionalisation and Social Change*. Keele (UK): University of Keele, 1973.

Hanson, Norwood. *Patterns of Discovery*. Cambridge, England: The University Press, 1958.

Harvey, Van A. *A Handbook of Theological Terms*. New York: The Macmillan Company, 1964.

Hastings Center Monographs on the Teaching of Ethics. Hastings-on-Hudson, NY: Institute of Sociology, Ethics, and the Life Sciences, 1980.

Hazzard, Geoffrey C. *Ethics and the Practice of Law*. New Haven CN: Yale University Press, 1978.

Haug, Marie R., and Marvin B. Sussman. "Professional Autonomy and the Revolt of the Client." *Social Problems* XVII (1969): 153–161.

————."Professionalization and Unionism." *American Behavioral Scientist* XIV (1971): 525–540.

Heidegger, Martin. *Being and Time*. Translated by John Macquarrie and Edward Robinson. New York: Harper and Brothers, 1962.

Howitt, Sir Harold. "Training for the Professions: Accountancy." *Journal of the Royal Society of Arts* XCIX (1951): 741–748.

Hughes, Everett C. *Men and Their Work*. Glencoe IL: The Free Press, 1958.

————. *The Sociological Eye: Selected Papers*. Chicago: Aldine-Atherton, 1971.

Illich, Ivan, et al. *Disabling Professions*. London: Marion Boyars, 1977.

Inkeles, Alex, and Peter H. Rossi. "National Comparisons of Occupational Prestige." *American Journal of Sociology* LVI (1956): 329–339.

Jackson, J. A. ed. *Professions and Professionalization*. Cambridge: The University Press, 1970.

Jamous, J., and B. Peloille. "Professions or Self-Perpetuating Systems?" In *Professions and Professionalization*, edited by J. A. Jackson. Cambridge: The University Press, 1970.

Johnson, Terence J. *Professions and Power*. London: Macmillan, 1972.

Jones, James. *Bad Blood*. New York: Free Press, 1981.

Jury, Mark. *Gramp*. New York: Viking Pres, 1976.

Kant, Immanuel. *Kant's Critique of Practical Reason*. Translated by Thomas Abbott. New York: Longmans, Green, 1909.

Kaye, Barrington. *The Development of the Architectural Profession in Britain*. London: G. Allen & Unwin, 1960.

Kessel, Reuben A. "Price Discrimination in Medicine." *The Journal of Law and Economics* I, 1 (October 1958): 20–53.

Kinn, John M. *The IEEE Role in Engineering Ethics*. New York: Institute of Electrical and Electronics Engineers, 1980.

Kohlberg, Lawrence. "Stage and Sequence: The Cognitive-Developmental Approach to Socialization." In *Handbook of Socialization Theory and Research*, edited by David A. Goslin. Chicago: Rand McNally, 1969.

Kultgen, John. "Evaluating Codes of Professional Ethics." In *Profits and Professions*, edited by Wade Robinson, Michael Pritchard, and Joseph Ellin. Clifton NJ: Humana Press, 1983.

————."The Ideological Use of Professional Codes." *Business and Professional Ethics Journal* I, 3 (Spring 1982): 53–69.

————."Veatch's New Foundation for Medical Ethics," *The Journal of Medicine and Philosophy* X (1985): 369–386.

Kuznets, S., and M. Friedman, *Income from Independent Practice*. Washington, DC: National Bureau of Economic Research, 1945.

Ladenson, Robert F. "Adversary Criminal Procedure and Ethics: An Impossible Combination?" *Perspectives on the Professions* II, ¾(September/December 1982). Chicago: Center for the Study of Ethics in the Professions.

Larson, Magali Sarfatti. *The Rise of Professionalism*. Berkeley: University of California Press, 1977.

Layton, E. T. "Engineering Ethics and the Public Interest." In *Ethical Problems in Engineering*, edited by Robert Baum and Albert Flores. 2nd ed., vol. 2. Troy NY: Renssalaer Polytechnic Institute, 1980.

Lees, D. S. *The Economic Consequences of the Profession*. London: Institute of Economic Affairs, 1966.

Leigh, R. D. *The Public Library in the U. S.* New York: Columbia University Press, 1950.

Lewis, R., and A. Maude. *Professional People*. London 1952.

Liebermann, Jethro K. *The Tyranny of the Experts*. New York: Walker, 1970.

Lorber, Judith. "Women and Medical Sociology: Invisible Professionals and Ubiquitous Patients." In *Another Voice*, edited by Marcia Millman and Rosabeth Moss Kantor. Garden City NJ: Anchor Press/ Doubleday, 1975.

Lynn, Kenneth, ed. *The Professions in America*. Boston: Houghton Mifflin, 1965.

MacIntyre, Alasdair. *After Virtue*. 2nd ed. South Bend IN: University of Notre Dame Press, 1984.

McIver, R. M. "The Social Significance of Professional Ethics." *The Annals of the American Academy of Political and Social Science* CI (May 1922): 5–12.

McMinn, Jack. "Ethics Spun from Fairy Tales." In *Ethical Problems in Engineering*, edited by Robert Baum and Albert Flores, 2nd ed. vol. 1. Troy NY: Renssalaer Polytechnic Institute, 1980.

McPherson, C. B. *The Political Theory of Possessive Individualism.* New York: Oxford University Press, 1962.

Marshall, T. H. "The Recent History of Professionalism in Relation to Social Structure and Social Policy." *The Canadian Journal of Economics and Political Science* V (1939): 325–340.

Matthews, Robert E. *Problems Illustrative of the Responsibilities of Members of the Legal Profession.* Austin: University of Texas Law School Foundation, 1974.

Mead, Daniel W. *Manual of Engineering Practice. No. 21. Standards of Professional Relations and Conduct.* New York: American Society of Chemical Engineers, 1940.

Mill, John Stuart. *Utilitarianism. On Liberty. Essay on Bentham.* Edited by Mary Warnock. New York: New American Library, 1962.

Miller, Casey, and Kate Swift. *Words and Women.* New York: Anchor Press/Doubleday, 1977.

———.*Handbook of Nonsexist Writing.* New York: Lippincott and Crowell, 1980.

Millerson, Geoffrey, "Dilemmas of Professionalism." *New Society* (June 4, 1964): 15–16.

———.*The Qualifying Associations.* London: Routledge and Kegan Paul, 1964.

Millman, Marcia. *The Unkindest Cut.* New York: William Morrow, 1978.

Mills, C. Wright. *White Collar.* New York: Oxford University Press, 1953.

Milne, K. L. *The Accountant in Public Practice.* London: Butterworth, 1959.

Moore, Wilbert E. *The Professions: Roles and Rules.* New York: Russell Sage Foundation, 1970.

———. "Changes in Occupational Structure." In *Social Structure and Social Mobility in Economic Development*, edited by Neil Smelser and Seymour Lipset. Chicago: Aldine, 1966.

Morison, Robert S. "A Further Note on Visions." *Daedalus* CIX, 1 (Winter 1980): 55–64.

Munson, Ronald. *Intervention and Reflection.* Belmont CA: Wadsworth Publishing Co., 1979.

Noble, David. *America by Design.* New York: Alfred Knopf, 1977.

Parsons, Talcott. *Essays in Sociological Theory.* Rev. Ed. Glencoe IL: The Free Press, 1954.

———."Remarks on Education and the Professions." *International Journal of Ethics* XLVII, 3 (1937): 365–369.

———.*The Social System.* Glencoe IL: The Free Press, 1951.

Pavalko, Ronald M. *Sociology of Occupations and Professions.* Itasca IL: F. E. Peacock, 1971.

Perucci, Robert, and Joel E. Gerstl, eds. *The Engineers and the Social System.* New York: Wiley, 1969.

Petit, Philip. *Judging Justice.* London: Routledge and Kegan Paul. 1980.

Plamenatz, John. *Ideology.* New York: Praeger Publishers, 1970.

Plato. *The Dialogues of Plato,* 2 vols. Translated by Benjamin Jowett. New York: Random House, 1892.

Popper, Karl R. *The Poverty of Historicism,* 3rd ed. New York: Harper and Row, 1964.

Prandy, Kenneth. *Professional Employees.* London: Faber and Faber, 1965.

Quine, Willard Van Orman. *Word and Object.* Cambridge MA: Massachusetts Institute of Technology Press, 1960.

Rawls, John. *A Theory of Justice.* Cambridge MA: Harvard University Press, 1971.

Reader, W. J. *Professional Men.* London: Weidenfeld and Nicolson, 1966.

Ritzer, George. *Man and His Work: Conflict and Change.* New York: Appleton-Century-Crofts, 1972.

————."Professionalism and the Individual." In *The Professions and Their Prospects,* edited by Eliot Freidson. Beverly Hills CA: Sage Publications, 1971.

Ross, E. A. *Principles of Sociology.* 3rd ed. New York: D. Appleton-Century, 1938.

Rothman, David J. "Were Tuskegee and Willowbrook 'Studies in Nature'?" *Hastings Center Report* XII, 2 (April 1982): 5–7.

Rothstein, William J. "Engineers and the Functionalist Model of the Professions." In *The Engineers and the Social System,* edited by Robert Perucci and Joel Gerstt. New York: Wiley, 1969.

Rueschemeyer, Dietrich. "Doctors and Lawyers: A Comment on the Theory of the Professions." *Canadian Review of Sociology and Anthropology* I (1964): 17–30.

Sartre, Jean Paul. *Being and Nothingness.* Translated by Hazel Barnes. New York: The Philosophical Library, 1956.

Schutz, Alfred. *The Phenomenology of the Social World.* Translated by George Walsh and Frederick Lehnert. Evanston IL: Northwestern University Press, 1967.

Seliger, M. *Ideology and Politics.* New York: The Free Press, 1976.

Sennett, Richard, and Jonathan Cobb. *The Hidden Injuries of Class.* New York: Vintage, 1973.

Seymour, Whitney North, Jr. *Why Justice Fails.* New York: William Morrow, 1973.

Simon, Lord. *The Accountant.* Quoted by G. F. Saunders, "The Accountant in General Practice," *6th International Congress on Accountancy,* 1952.

Smelser, Neil, and Seymour Lipset, eds. *Social Structure and Social Mobility in Economic Development.* Chicago: Aldine, 1966.

Solomon, David. "Ethnic and Class Differences Among Hospitals as Contingencies in Medical Careers." In *Medical Men and Their Work,* edited by Eliot Freidson and Judith Lorbor. Chicago: Aldine, 1972.

Special Committee on Standards of Professional Conduct for Certified Public Accountants. *Restructuring Professional Standards to Achieve Professional Ethics in a Changing Environment.* New York: American Institute of Certified Public Accountants, 1986.

Taeusch, Carl. *Professional and Business Ethics.* New York: Henry Holt, 1926.

Tawney, R. H. *The Acquisitive Society.* New York: Harcourt-Brace, 1948.

Taylor, Charles. "Neutrality in Political Science." In *The Philosophy of Social Explanation,* edited by Alan Ryan. London: Oxford University Press, 1973.

Theodorson, George A., and Achilles G. Theodorson. *A Modern Dictionary of Sociology.* New York: Barnes and Noble, 1979.

Thomas, William I. "The Relation of the Medicine Man to the Origin of Professional Occupations." *University of Chicago Decennial Publications, Investigations Representing the Departments,* IV, pp. 239–256. First Series. Chicago: University of Chicago Press, 1903.

Thompson, Joyce Beebe, and Henry O. Thompson. *Ethics in Nursing.* New York: The Macmillan Company, 1981.

Toulmin, Stephen. *An Examination of the Place of Reason in Ethics.* Cambridge: The University Press, 1960.

————."The Limits of Allegiance in a Nuclear Age." In *Nuclear Weapons and the Future of Humanity,* edited by Avner Cohen and Steven Lee. Totowa NJ: Rowman and Littlefield, 1986.

Ulich, Robert. *Crisis and Hope in American Education.* Boston: Beacon Press, 1951.

Unger, Stephen H. *Controlling Technology: Ethics and the Responsible Engineer.* New York: Holt, Rinehart and Winston, 1982.

Veatch, Robert M. *Case Studies in Medical Ethics.* Cambridge MA: Harvard University Press, 1977.

————.*A Theory of Medical Ethics.* New York, Basic Books, 1981.

Veblen, Thorsten. *Engineers and the Price System.* New York: Harcourt, Brace and World, 1921.

Webb, Sidney, and Beatrice Webb. Special Supplement on Professional Associations, *The New Statesman* IX (April 21 and 28, 1917).

Weil, Vivian. *Report of the Workshops on Ethical Issues in Engineering.* Chicago: Center for the Study of Ethics in the Professions, 1980.

Weinreb, Lloyd L. *Denial of Justice.* New York: The Macmillan Company, 1977.

Westin, Alan. *Whistle Blowing!* New York: McGraw-Hill, 1981.

Whitehead, A. M. *Adventures of Ideas.* New York: The Macmillan Company, 1933.

Wickenden, W. E. *A Professional Guide for Junior Engineers.* New York NY: Engineers Council for Professional Development, 1949.

Wilensky, Harold L. "The Professionalization of Everyone?" *American Journal of Sociology* LXX (1964), 137–158.

————."Varieties of Work Experience." In *Man in a World of Work,* edited by Henry Borow. Boston: Houghton-Mifflin, 1964.

————."Work, Careers and Social Integration." *International Social Science Journal*, XII (1960), 543–460.

Wise, Raymond. *Legal Ethics*. 2nd ed. New York: M. Bender, 1970.

Wittgenstein, Ludwig. *Philosophical Investigations*. New York: The Macmillan Company, 1953.

Young, Michael D. *The Rise of Meritocracy*. London: Thames and Hudson, 1958.

INDEX OF NAMES

Habenstein, R. A., 370–371
Halevy, Elie, 119
Halmos, Paul, 62
Hanson, Norwood, 71
Harey, Van A., 152
Haug, Marie and Marvin B. Sussman, 119
Hazzard, Geoffrey C., 340–341
Hegel, G. W. F., 48
Heidegger, Martin, 284–285
Howitt, Sir Harold, 70
Hughes, Everett C., 9, 11, 14, 54, 68, 70, 82–83, 86–87, 96–97, 107, 118, 152, 193, 207

Ickes, Harold, 325
Illich, Ivan, 275–277, 323
Inkeles, Alex and Peter H. Rossi, 14

Jamous, J. and B. Peloille, 106
Jesus, 13
Johnson, Lyndon, 325–326
Johnson, Terence J., 7, 62–63, 70, 100, 103
Jones, James, 152
Jury, Mark, 229

Kant, Immanuel, 49, 259, 297, 329, 363–364
Kaye, Barrington, 70
Kessel, Reuben A., 126–127
King, W. J., 191–192
Kinn, John M., 251
Kline, Benn, 229
Kohlberg, Lawrence, 11
Kuball, Huseyn B. Nail, 54
Kuhn, Thomas, 106
Kultgen, John, 180, 251
Kuznets, S. and M. Friedman, 62

Ladenson, Robert E., 344
Lamb, Lawrence E., 319
Larson, Magali Sarfatti, 63, 67–68, 100–103, 110–118, 122–123, 129, 142–144, 148–153, 158–160, 202, 207
Layton, E. T., 214
Lees, D. S., 62
Leigh, R. D., 70
Lewis, R. and A. Maude, 70
Lieberman, Jethro K., 275–276, 323
Lorber, Judith, 190–191

Machiavelli, 172
MacIntyre, Alisdair, 260–262
Marshall, T. H., 62, 70, 90–91, 96, 98, 118, 158–159, 207
Matthews, Robert E., 208
McIver, R. M., 98
McMinn, Jack, 214
McPherson, C. B., 119
Mead, Daniel, 180
Mill, John Stuart, 21, 143–144, 196, 274, 279–280, 285–288
Miller, Casey and Kate Swift, 222–223
Millerson, Geoffrey, 59–60
Millman, Marcia, 140–142, 291
Mills, C. Wright, 63
Milne, K. L., 70
Moore, Wilbert E., 8–9, 54, 68, 73, 118, 152–153, 289–290
Morison, Robert S., 22
Munson, Ronald, 5, 204

Neustadt, Sara Jane, 192

Parsons, Talcott, 9, 67, 70, 73–74, 76–77, 87, 97, 105, 124, 150–153, 288
Pavalko, Ronald M., 70
Petit, Philip, 195
Piaget, Jean, 11
Plamenatz, John, 103–107, 117
Plato, 42, 189, 307–309, 363
Pope, Alexander, 192
Popper, Karl, 41–42

Quine, Willard Van Orman, 158

Rawls, John, 37, 169, 171
Reader, W. J., 118, 191, 193
Ritzer, George, 77–78, 145
Roosevelt, Franklin, 325–326
Ross, E. A., 70
Rothman, David, 152
Rothstein, William J., 142
Reuschemeyer, Dietrich, 97, 134, 291

Santayana, George, 238
Sartre, Jean-Paul, 172, 280
Schutz, Alfred, 71
Seliger, M., 104, 119
Seymour, Whitney North, 139–140, 197–198
Simon, Lord, 70
Socrates, 42, 351

INDEX OF SUBJECTS